LAW AS CHANGE

This book is available as a free fully-searchable ebook from
www.adelaide.edu.au/press

LAW AS CHANGE

ENGAGING WITH THE LIFE AND SCHOLARSHIP OF ADRIAN BRADBROOK

Edited by

Paul Babie and Paul Leadbeter

Adelaide Law School, The University of Adelaide

THE UNIVERSITY
of ADELAIDE

UNIVERSITY OF
ADELAIDE PRESS

EMERITUS PROFESSOR ADRIAN J BRADBROOK

Dr iur (hc) (Mannheim) LLD (Melbourne)
PhD (Cantab) LLM (York) MA BA (Cantab)

Emeritus Professor of Law in The University of Adelaide 2011-
Dean of the Faculty of Law in The University of Adelaide 1991-95,
Bonython Professor of Law in The University of Adelaide 1988-2011,
John Bray Professor of Law in The University of Adelaide 1987-88,
Reader in Law in The University of Melbourne 1980-87,
Senior Lecturer in Law in The University of Melbourne 1972-79,
Assistant Professor of Law in Dalhousie University 1970-72.

Sometime Visiting Professor of Law
in the University of Calgary,
à L'Université de Poitiers,
à L'Université Paris Descartes (Paris V),
in der Universität Mannheim,
in der Philipps-Universität Marburg.

Sometime Researcher in Law
in Queens' College in the University of Cambridge,
in McGill University,
in the University of Colorado,
in the University of Hong Kong,
in the International Academy of the Environment, Geneva.

Barrister and Solicitor of the Supreme Court of Nova Scotia,
Barrister and Solicitor of the Supreme Court of Victoria.

Fellow of the Center for Environmental Legal Studies in Pace University.
Fellow and Member of the Board of Directors of the International Energy Foundation.
Fellow of the Australian Institute of Energy.
Member of the International Bar Association's Academic Advisory Group to the Section on
Energy, Environment, Resources and Infrastructure.

Sometime Consultant to the United Nations (UN DESA, UNEP, UNDP).

Sometime Chair of the Energy and Environmental Section,
International Union for Conservation of Nature (IUCN).

Member of the Board of Editors of
the *Journal of Energy & Natural Resources Law,*
the *Australasian Journal of Natural Resources Law and Policy,*
the *Journal of Renewable Energy Law and Policy,*
the *Australian Property Law Journal.*

Life and Law

Emeritus Professors Adrian J Bradbrook and Judith G Gardam at the dinner to celebrate their lives in the law, 26 October 2011, Adelaide, Australia

Photograph © Matthew Stubbs, 2011

Published in Adelaide by

University of Adelaide Press
The University of Adelaide
Level 14, 115 Grenfell Street
South Australia 5005
press@adelaide.edu.au
www.adelaide.edu.au/press

The University of Adelaide Press publishes externally refereed scholarly books by staff of
the University of Adelaide. It aims to maximise access to the University's best research by
publishing works through the internet as free downloads and for sale as high quality printed
volumes.

For the full Cataloguing-in-Publication data please contact the National Library of Australia:
cip@nla.gov.au

ISBN (paperback) 978-1-922064-78-3
ISBN (ebook: pdf) 978-1-922064-80-6
ISBN (ebook: epub) 978-1-922064-79-0
ISBN (ebook: mobi) 978-1-922064-81-3

Editors: Patrick Allington and Rebecca Burton
Book design: Zoë Stokes
Cover design: Emma Spoehr
Cover image: *Fox Breaking Cover*. Reproduction after Francis Calcraft Turner (1782-1846).
Plate A290 in the Thomas Ross Collection. Reproduced with permission from the Thomas
Ross Collection, www.rosscollection.co.uk

Contents

LIST OF CONTRIBUTORS

Paul Babie is Associate Professor and Reader, Associate Dean of Law (Research), Adelaide Law School, and Associate Dean (Research), Faculty of the Professions, at the University of Adelaide. He holds a BA in sociology and political science from the University of Calgary, a BThSt from Flinders University, an LLB from the University of Alberta, an LLM from the University of Melbourne, and a DPhil in law from the University of Oxford. His primary research area is legal theory, especially the nature and concept of property; he has published widely in this field. He is a Barrister and Solicitor (inactive) of the Court of Queen's Bench of Alberta (Canada), and an Associate Member of the Law Society of South Australia, through which he serves as a Member of the Property Law Committee.

Barry Barton is Professor of Law and Director of the Centre for Environmental, Resources and Energy Law at the University of Waikato, Hamilton, New Zealand. His current research is in energy efficiency and other aspects of energy law and policy, the law concerning the use of geothermal resources, carbon capture and storage, and comparative mining law. He teaches in these fields, in property law and in other aspects of energy and natural resources law. He is part of the 'Energy Cultures' research programme based at the University of Otago. He is active in the International Bar Association Section on Energy, Environment, Resources and Infrastructure Law ('SEERIL').

Adrian J Bradbrook is Emeritus Professor of Law at the University of Adelaide. Until his retirement in 2011 he was the Bonython Professor of Law (since 1988) and served as Head of the School of Law (1989-91) as well as Dean of the Faculty of Law (1991-95). He held earlier academic appointments at the law schools of the University of Melbourne (1972-88) and Dalhousie University, Canada (1970-72). His major teaching and research specialties are sustainable energy law and real property law. He has written eighteen books, including *Australian Real Property Law, Easements and Restrictive Covenants, Commercial Tenancy Law, Energy Law and the*

Environment, and *Solar Energy and the Law*. He has worked on a range of sustainable energy legal projects as a United Nations consultant and served for 18 years as a part-time member of the South Australian Residential Tenancies Tribunal.

Judith Gardam is Emeritus Professor at the University of Adelaide Law School and a Fellow of both the Academy of Social Sciences in Australia and the Australian Academy of Law. She is an international lawyer and a feminist scholar. Her particular areas of expertise are international humanitarian law and the international law rules that regulate the use of force between states. She has researched and published widely on these topics.

Lee Godden is Professor at the University of Melbourne Law School. She has research qualifications in law and geography, which have fostered a long-standing interest (beginning with her PhD) in the intersections between property law, environmental law and Indigenous peoples' land rights. She has published extensively in that field. More recently, as the Director of the Centre for Resources, Energy and Environmental Law (Melbourne Law School) she broadened this scope to examine energy-related impacts, including climate change law. She is a colleague of Adrian Bradbrook in the SEERIL Academic Advisory Group, International Bar Association, and joined him and others from the group in co-authoring *Property and the Law in Energy and Natural Resources* in 2010.

Paul Leadbeter has an LLB and LLM from the University of Adelaide. He has been a Senior Lecturer at Adelaide Law School since 2010, where he teaches administrative law, environmental law, water resources law and international environmental law. His particular research interests are land use planning law, heritage law and pollution control. He is the South Australian State Editor of *Planning Law in Australia* and the *Local Government Law Journal*. In addition to his academic role he maintains an ongoing private legal practice providing specialist environmental and land use planning law advice and advice on local government matters. He also serves on a number of government committees relevant to his areas of research interest and is actively involved in the management of two environmental NGOs.

Rosemary Lyster is Professor of Climate and Environmental Law at the University of Sydney Law School, where she is also Director of the Australian Centre for Climate and Environmental Law. Rosemary specialises in the area of climate law including mitigation, adaptation, loss and damage, and climate justice. She has published widely in these areas including three books with Cambridge University Press — two of which are on energy law (and both of which are collaborations with Adrian Bradbrook) and another on 'Reducing Emissions from Deforestation and Degradation' ('REDD+'). She is currently writing *Climate Justice and Disaster Law* for Cambridge University Press. She is also lead author of *Environmental and Planning Law in New South Wales*, published by Federation Press. Rosemary has developed and teaches a range of climate law units — including water law and climate change — in the Master of Environmental Law at Sydney Law School. In 2013, she was a Herbert Smith Freehills Visiting Professor at Cambridge Law School. She has also held two Visiting Scholar appointments to Trinity College, Cambridge.

Anthony Moore is a retired academic who lives with his chihuahua dogs and holds the positions of Adjunct Associate Professor of Law at Adelaide and Flinders Universities. He taught at the two law schools between 1970 and 2004 and was Dean of the Flinders Law School between 2000 and 2003. He is a co-author with Adrian Bradbrook and Susan MacCallum of *Residential Tenancy Law and Practice — Victoria and South Australia* (1983), *Australian Real Property Law* (1st to 5th editions 1991-2011) and *Australian Property Law Cases and Materials* (1st to 4th editions, 1996-2011). He is also the co-author of *Debt Repair Kit for Dummies* (2010) and Title Editor of 'Title 28 (Real Property)' for *Laws of Australia*. He was editor of volumes 10-16 of the *Adelaide Law Review* and volumes 1-3 of the *Flinders Journal of Law Reform*. He has maintained a particular interest in tenancy law and consumer law generally. He was a South Australian Residential Tenancies Tribunal Member from 1988 to 2003, a Council Member of the Australian Federation of Consumer Organisations between 1992 and 1993, and is an Executive Member of the Consumers Association of South Australia and Member of the Energy Consumers Council of South Australia.

Richard L Ottinger came to Pace Law School, New York, when he retired from Congress in 1984. As a Professor he taught in the environmental law program. As Co-director of the Center for Environmental Legal Studies, he started the 'Energy Project', which raises $900 000 per year, advocating utility investment in conservation and renewable energy resources. In his sixteen years as a member of the United States House of Representatives, he authored a substantial body of energy and environmental laws. He was one of the earliest environmentalists in Congress in 1965. As chairman of the Energy Conservation and Power Subcommittee, Energy & Commerce Committee, he was instrumental in adopting key energy and environmental legislation. Dean Ottinger was a founding staff member of the Peace Corps, serving it during 1961-1964. He was appointed Dean in December 1994. He retired as Dean in July 1999 and currently serves as Dean Emeritus.

Ralph Wahnschafft is an Independent Senior Advisor on Sustainability Policies associated with the Division for Sustainable Development, United Nations Department of Economic and Social Affairs ('UN DESA'), and the Global Forum on Human Settlements ('GFHS'), New York. He has worked with the United Nations for more than twenty-five years in various duty stations, including in Africa (Lesotho, South Africa), the Middle East (Baghdad, Iraq), South-East Asia (Bangkok, Thailand), and at UN Headquarters in New York (2003-13). His priority professional interests relate to international affairs, political economy, development concerns and sustainable development, in particular with regard to (renewable) energy issues, analysis of market trends, urban (re)development, transport, tourism, and all aspects of environmental concerns, including air pollution and climate change. He has initiated a considerable number of technical co-operation and technical assistance projects in developing countries, in particular in Asia. He holds a Doctoral Degree from the University of Göttingen, Germany. He was a leading team member in servicing the Rio+20 UN Conference.

Alexandra Wawryk received First Class degrees in Economics and Law, and a PhD in Law, from the University of Adelaide. She is a Lecturer at the University of Adelaide in mining and energy law, international energy law and contract law. She is a Barrister and Solicitor of the Supreme Court of South Australia, and has been a member of the South Australian Law Society's Planning, Environment and Local Government Committee, and a Committee Member of the Environmental Defenders Office (SA). She is currently a member of the World Conservation Union's Specialist Group on Energy Law. She is a member of, and the Adelaide Law School representative to, the cross-disciplinary Institute for Mining, Energy and Resources at the University of Adelaide. She has published articles in a number of journals, including the *Oxford Journal of Environmental Law*, the *Journal of Energy & Natural Resources Law*, the *University of New South Wales Law Journal*, the *Melbourne University Law Review*, the *Australasian Journal of Natural Resources Law and Policy*, and the *Environmental and Planning Law Journal*. She is an Associate Editor for renewable energy for OGEL, a specialist online database for oil, gas and energy law.

Acknowledgements

A project such as this requires a great deal of support from many people. The Editors wish here to thank those who have been central to making this collection possible. Above all, of course, we are indebted to Professor Adrian Bradbrook for inspiring this volume. To the contributors, for their wonderful essays and patience along the way; to the anonymous reviewers for making the essays, and so the collection, much better; to our research assistants, Richard Sletvold (LLB, 2013), Seb Tonkin (LLB, 2014) and Zoe Irwin (LLB, 2014); and, to our publisher, the University of Adelaide Press, and its Director, Dr John Emerson, and its Editors, Dr Patrick Allington and Rebecca Burton.

Paul Babie and Paul Leadbeter
3 September 2014
Adelaide, Australia

1

THE WILY QUADRUPED MEETS A SAUCY INTRUDER: HOW LIFE AND LAW INTERSECT

Paul Babie[1]

I Setting the Scene: Pierson v Post, the Wily Quadruped, a Saucy Intruder, and Capture

Speaking at his retirement dinner on 26 October 2011, I suggested that I was perhaps not the right person to comment upon Adrian Bradbrook's long and distinguished career. My overriding concern then, as now, was simple: how to capture the essence of such a remarkable career; the work of someone who has contributed so much to scholarship, so much to the law, so much to an institution. Fittingly, I thought, it was a property case — Pierson v Post[2] ('Pierson') — that best summarised my feelings about the task.

A case about the legal concept of capture, decided by the New York State Supreme Court of Judicature in 1805, Pierson involved a fox hunt, and, more

---

[1] Richard Sletvold (LLB, 2013) provided outstanding comments and research assistance in the preparation of this chapter, for which I am extremely grateful. Any errors which remain are, of course, entirely my responsibility.

[2] 3 Cai R 175 (NY Sup Ct, 1805). For a recent essay summarising studies of this well-known first-year property law case, see Daniel R Ernst, 'Pierson v Post: The New Learning' (2009) 13 The Green Bag 31.

specifically, property in a fox. My analogy is certainly not to the activity of the hunt itself, which most today would agree is a barbaric one. It is to the facts, or more specifically, the way in which they were related in the dissenting judgment of Livingston J. Justice Livingston, having made this decision in 1805, wrote with a slightly greater flare for the dramatic than we find in judicial writing today. He wrote that the case

> reduces the controversy to a single question. Whether a person who, with his own hounds, starts and hunts a fox on waste and uninhabited ground, and is on the point of seizing his prey, acquires such an interest in the animal, as to have a right of action against another, who in view of the huntsman and his dogs in full pursuit, and with knowledge of the chase, shall kill and carry him away?[3]

> … By the pleadings it is admitted that a fox is a 'wild and noxious beast.' But who would keep a pack of hounds; or what gentleman, at the sound of the horn, and at peep of day, would mount his steed, and for hours together … pursue the windings of this wily quadruped, if, just as night came on, and his stratagems and strength were nearly exhausted, a saucy intruder, who had not shared in the honours or labours of the chase, were permitted to come in at the end, and bear away in triumph the object of pursuit?[4]

In dissent, Livingston J held that the hunt, as represented by Post, in which had pursed this 'wily quadruped', had possession, had captured the fox and so had property. But the Court held that Pierson, the 'saucy intruder', the one who stepped in at the last moment, had captured, and so possessed, and so had property in, the fox; as the majority wrote, 'however uncourteous or unkind the conduct of Pierson'.

In honouring the life and career of Adrian Bradbrook, *I* am the 'saucy intruder'. I have known him for only a portion of his life and his distinguished career, and have contributed nothing like what he has contributed to the academy, to scholarship and, above all, to the development of the law. And, clearly, there are many others who are far more qualified to 'capture' the essence of his career. But I am the 'saucy intruder', and though I was not part of the chase, I will nonetheless partake in the 'capture'.

Of course, on its facts, *Pierson* must be distinguished, for the essence of Bradbrook's contribution to law, which is the *object* to be captured in this collection

---

[3]   *Pierson v Post*, 3 Cai R 175, 180 (NY Sup Ct, 1805).

[4]   *Pierson v Post*, 3 Cai R 175, 180-1 (NY Sup Ct, 1805).

of essays, is certainly no 'wild and noxious beast'! As the Ancient Greek maxim says, πάσα μέταφορά σκάζει or 'all metaphors limp'. I've used *Pierson* only to describe my unworthiness for the task — though I hope not my lack of courtesy or kindness — for while the principle of capture in *Pierson* applies to me, I hope that Adrian Bradbrook, and all who read this, will indulge me, if only for a moment, in referring to him as that 'wily quadruped', in the sense of having 'stratagems and strengths' which were put to use in leading the pack — the rest of us — over new landscapes and geographies of law, to new insights and to new developments previously unknown. 'Wily', then, in that sense only: of having the stratagems and strengths to look at law and see its future as few of us are able to do. If one will indulge me, then, to complete the metaphor, imperfect as it is, this wily quadruped — Adrian Bradbrook — has led us on a remarkable, distinguished and great journey in life and in law.

Yet although I have not shared the honours or labours of that chase, along the windings of the pursuit of new learning, understandings and theories of law, I can nonetheless look back over the landscapes and geographies of Adrian's life in the law. And in this introductory essay, I attempt to do that. More importantly, with the benefit of time, Paul Leadbeter and I have been able to assemble in one volume the reflections of those who travelled that route with Bradbrook — the members of the 'hunt', as it were — to give him back to those who followed him so closely along those windings, rather than trying ourselves to reduce-into-possession a summary of the impact of his scholarship on the development of the law. The essays collected here have been written by the scholars who shared in the pursuit: scholars who are thus eminently qualified to bear away its object: the impact of Bradbrook's career on the life of the law.[5] And it is for that reason that the cover image of this volume, 'Fox Breaking Cover', the wily quadruped, bears meaning if we understand it as symbolising the life in the law, the windings of the pursuit, of Adrian Bradbrook.

This introduction, then, first takes a look back over Bradbrook's life in the law, before turning his career over to those who have been there along the way, who will explain his contribution — a unique and lasting contribution — to the life of the law.

---

[5] Thus satisfying the criteria set out for a successful *Festschrift* in law by Michael Taggart, 'Gardens or Graveyards of Scholarship?: *Festschriften* in the Literature of the Common Law' (2002) 22 *Oxford Journal of Legal Studies* 227.

II THE WINDINGS OF THE PURSUIT: A LIFE IN THE LAW[6]

Oliver Wendell Holmes, Jr, wrote that '[t]he life of the law has not been logic: it has been experience.'[7] While it is trite to resort to this oft-cited phrase, in my conversations with Bradbrook over the years, it strikes me just how much this phrase actually describes his life in the law. At his own retirement dinner, he described his career as a series of chance events which, at once, always seemed not only to point him in a new direction, but also to move him forward in an ongoing unfolding of the law; not only in its exposition, but also in its development — indeed, in its very creation.

Adrian John Bradbrook was born in Portsmouth, England, the only child of Arthur and Edna Bradbrook, on 21 April 1948. He received most of his early education at Portsmouth Grammar, before attending Cambridge University in 1966, where he won a Foundation Scholarship during his time studying for the LLB.

While fed on the usual fare of law subjects at Cambridge, one of his lasting memories, and one which clearly had an impact on the course of his later career, was Roman law, taken with the well-known South African scholar Colin Turpin. While he initially decided to take the subject because he had studied Classics (Latin and Greek) in A-levels, it made such an impact on him that he enrolled also for the Advanced Roman law subject, and still remembers using WW Buckland's classic text.[8] Moreover, it gave him a chance to use his Greek, forcing him to focus attention to detail, proving to be a very good training for legal scholarship. Some of the others at Cambridge who had an impact on the development of his legal studies were John Tiley (Senior Tutor in Law at Queen's) in contracts; JL Smith, a 'great lecturer' who taught criminal law; John Hall in family law, for which it was worth being there because 'every word that came out of his mouth was a gem'; Michael Pritchard of the renowned law college Gonville and Caius, who would comment, if sports were given as a reason for lateness, that it was 'nice of you to row in'.

Bradbrook's girlfriend during his time at Cambridge lived in London, so he would often make the commute there by train on the weekends. This did not present

---

6   This section is based on two interviews with Adrian Bradbrook (Adelaide, 21-22 February 2012).

7   Oliver Wendell Holmes, Jr, *The Common Law* (Dover Publications, first published 1881, 1991 ed) 1.

8   WW Buckland, *A Textbook of Roman Law: From Augustus to Justinian* (Cambridge University Press, 1921).

the problem it might for today's student — extracurricular employment was not allowed during one's studies; other than studying, there was little else with which to occupy oneself, so a weekend trip to London was always welcome. In fact, this was a golden era of English post-secondary education, one that would scarcely be recognised not only by English students today, but also in any of the places in which Bradbrook has since taught: the entire cost of one's education was covered by the government, including a living allowance.

During holidays, Bradbrook worked at the Post Office and spent some summers in Greece working as a travel guide for tourists in Rhodes and Athens. It was here that he added Modern Greek — at school he had only learned Koine, the ancient form — to his growing repertoire of languages.

During his time at Cambridge a minor dispute broke out between Bradbrook and his father. While the elder Bradbrook had wanted the younger to study law in order to obtain a good professional job, Adrian really had no interest in such a career. Still, as his father had contacts with the Town Clerk of Ipswich City Council, he dutifully took the train out to Ipswich, where his worst fears were confirmed: it was something out of a Dickens novel. The elder Bradbrook had a back-up plan. A similar contact was arranged at the bar in London, but the prospect of meals in the Inns was enough to turn Adrian's stomach. A stand-off ensued.

But a First in the LLB (the MA would follow in 1972) changed everything — the first of this wily quadruped's windings, setting his life, and his career, on an entirely unexpected path. While he had never thought about the academy, and certainly his father would have been perplexed by it, nonetheless the thought of staying on at Cambridge for the LLM began to occupy Bradbrook's mind. Yet, having learned from a tutor that a scholarship at Columbia University in New York was available, he set his sights westward, and duly obtained it in 1969. Remember that year, because here the first obstacle in the geography of life, one of those events beyond one's control, caused the first switchback in his windings.

Opposition to the Vietnam War had already been raging for years, but it further erupted in the late 1960s in the form of massive protests in major US cities. In New York, Columbia University's students not only protested, as others did on college campuses elsewhere across the United States, they also brashly occupied the President's Office for a week, from Tuesday 23 April to Tuesday 30 April 1968. The very day that Bradbrook received his scholarship letter from Columbia, there appeared on the front page of the London *Times* graphic photos of the University in flames. His parents, troubled enough by the choice of the academy as a career choice, blanched at the sight of these photos. Columbia was decidedly off.

The wily quadruped reversed field. Ever resourceful, Bradbrook sought the advice of his Cambridge contracts tutor, John Tiley, who advised that a visitor from Osgoode Hall Law School, in Toronto, Canada, might be able to get him something on short notice. Canada's then Prime Minister, Pierre Trudeau, himself a citizen of the world as Adrian was becoming, had kept Canada out of Vietnam. This raised the ire of Richard Nixon, who called him 'an asshole',[9] but earned him the eternal gratitude of draft dodgers, who fled across the border in droves, establishing themselves permanently in Canada and deciding not to return even years later when Bill Clinton offered an unconditional pardon. In any case, in the fall of 1969, Bradbrook set out for a comparatively peaceful — one might say 'boring' in comparison to New York — Toronto, and the LLM program at Osgoode.

Bradbrook was to make criminology his field of study at Osgoode, although few would associate him with that socio-legal area today. He found it interesting. Yet a hedgerow obstructed our fox. Upon arrival at Osgoode, the Dean, Harry Arthurs, took him for dinner to discuss which area of *family law* Bradbrook would cover in his thesis. There was no one available to supervise a criminology thesis. Without missing a beat, Bradbrook turned to family law, an area he would come to master.

Osgoode's LLM rules had been changed shortly before Bradbook's arrival, requiring a candidate to complete three subjects in addition to a thesis. Bradbrook chose legal education, family law, and law and psychology. This last subject was an eye-opener, as it was taught as a true seminar, something with which few of the students who enrolled in the class had prior experience. Bradbrook initially thought that none of the 12 people who turned up would ever have enough to say about law and psychology. In the end, though, the experience was an enriching one, as was the entire Osgoode LLM, which he obtained in 1970, completing a 60 000-word LLM thesis on child custody law in just nine months.

Bradbrook's LLM thesis offers the first glimpse of the intellectual power that would be brought to bear on whatever area of the law presented itself: exploring the

---

9   Martin O'Malley and Justin Thompson, 'Prime Ministers and Presidents', *CBC News* (online), 22 November 2003 <http://www.cbc.ca/canadaus/pms_presidents1.html>.

traditional way of resolving child custody cases, he argued that rather than showing any objective rules, the guiding principles were in fact very subjective. The keystone chapter of the thesis surveyed judges of the Ontario High Court of Justice on their attitudes towards child protection law. Using an early form of qualitative empirical legal research, Bradbrook concluded that the outcome of such disputes depended not on any identifiable legal criteria but, as the American legal realists might argue, on nothing more significant than the judge assigned to the case. Ultimately published in the *Canadian Bar Review*,[10] this realist conclusion is founded upon one of the earliest examples in Canadian or Australian legal literature of qualitative empirical legal research. It continues to be influential.[11]

Near the end of Bradbrook's time at Osgoode, a professor from Warwick University in England visited and offered him a job. Once again, though, the course of our quarry was forced to act quickly; through a mix-up, the Warwick post never materialised and, in 1970, Bradbrook ended up at Dalhousie University in Halifax, Canada, for his first academic post. At the height of its powers as one of Canada's premier law schools, Dalhousie provided an environment studded by Canada's legal luminaries in which to nurture an early career, although the legendary John Willis had retired by the time Bradbrook arrived.[12]

While in Halifax, Bradbrook began to reconsider the earlier decision about the practice of law, thinking he had perhaps dismissed that option too hastily. While the Nova Scotia Law Society would have required nine months of articles, the interim Dean at Dalhousie, Bob Donald, suggested that he write and ask for an exemption. In another of the twists that set his career on a new path, the Law Society reduced

---

[10] Adrian Bradbrook, 'An Empirical Study of the Attitudes of the Judges of the Supreme Court of Ontario Regarding the Workings of the Child Custody Adjudication Laws' (1971) 49(4) *Canadian Bar Review* 557, which was an abridged version of Adrian Bradbrook, *The Inter-Parental Conflict Over Ownership of Children: Judicial Discretion versus Behavioral Science* (LLM Thesis, Osgoode Hall, York University, 1970).

[11] See, eg, Suzanne Williams, 'Through the Eyes of Young People: Meaningful Child Participation in BC Court Processes' (Report, International Institute for Child Rights and Development, 2006) 184 <http://iicrd.org/system/files/Meaningful%20Child%20Participation.pdf>; Christine D Davies, 'Access to Justice for Children: The Voice of the Child in Custody and Access Disputes' (Paper Presented at the Australasian Law Reform Agencies Conference, Wellington, 15 April 2004) 21 n 41 <http://www.lawcom.govt.nz/sites/default/files/speeches/2004/04/Session%205B%20-%20Children%20-%20Davies.pdf>.

[12] RCB Risk, 'John Willis — A Tribute' (1985) 9 *Dalhousie Law Journal* 521, 521.

the requirement to six months of articled clerkship, which he completed with Stewart MacKeen & Covert, the largest law firm in Atlantic Canada. Still, it was not long until he realised this was not for him, although he did complete the articles, as well as an exam in Nova Scotia Statutes (for which Dean Donald had given him the questions with which to prepare).

A second interim Dean, Murray Fraser, chose one subject that Bradbrook would teach, while Bradbrook could choose the second. Bradbrook chose family law, which he co-taught with Fraser, while Fraser chose property law. While not entirely pleased with the Dean's choice, in time Bradbrook took to liking it and it came to be one if his many areas of expertise. From that one choice foisted upon him, his career path was set. As with so many of the other twists in his career, fate played a large role in how it turned out.

Bradbrook spent two years at Dalhousie before deciding it was time to move on, still anxious to see more of the world. This time his sights were set south, to Australia. He wrote a letter attaching his *curriculum vitae* to all nine Australian law Deans at that time. Eight replied with information about jobs for which he could apply, and Bradbrook wrote to each of those to be considered as an applicant. He subsequently obtained an offer from each. Harold Ford, Dean at the University of Melbourne, offered him a Senior Lectureship, which he accepted, holding that rank from 1972 until 1978, when he was promoted to Reader. Interestingly, he might have come to the University of Adelaide in 1972 had Horst Lücke and Alex Castles, who wrote to him, offered more than a Lectureship!

Property law remained his focus at Melbourne, and in 1980 he completed a book on easements and restrictive covenants which he had been working on for two years.[13] In fact, he had written a book on easements, and Marcia Neave had written on restrictive covenants, and the publisher, Butterworths in Sydney, suggested that it would be best to put the two together, which is how this ground-breaking text came into existence. In writing his part on easements, Bradbrook came across an article on solar access easement cases in the United States. After the book was finished, he

---

[13] Published the following year as Adrian J Bradbrook and Marcia A Neave, *Easements and Restrictive Covenants in Australia* (Butterworths, 1st ed, 1981). It is now in its third edition and, such is the influence of the title, it is now named in honour of Adrian Bradbrook and Marcia Neave: Adrian J Bradbrook and Susan V MacCallum, *Bradbrook and Neave's Easements and Restrictive Covenants in Australia* (Butterworths, 3rd ed, 2010).

followed up the solar access easement, considering the law's relevance to solar energy. That project occupied much of his time, before he went on to take the same approach to wind energy and, finally, to geothermal energy. This opened his interest in energy efficiency across an entire economy and in international law. All of this led to project work with the United Nations, allowing him to continue to see new parts of the world, places which he would otherwise never have been able to see.

Having entered the academy, still, he did not cease his studies. Bradbrook embarked on a PhD while at Melbourne, the thesis for which was a modified and expanded version of the research report that he wrote for the Commonwealth Commission of Inquiry into Poverty, chaired by Ronald Sackville.[14] He worked on it full-time under the supervision of Ted Sykes and later Frank Meagher, completing the thesis in 1975.

Two years later, in 1977, Bradbrook met Judith Gardam, whom he went on to marry in 1980, the year Judith completed her LLM at The University of Melbourne. Together, they spent the next 33 years (and counting) with their four daughters from previous marriages — Fiona, Frances, Georgia and Selena — and became proud grandparents to Nessa, Freyja, Levi, Bleue and Phoenix. Each of them also, first at the Melbourne Law School and later at the Adelaide Law School, became internationally recognised experts in their respective fields. More recently, they have combined their formidable talents and expertise to consider the human rights implications of access to energy.[15]

During the 1980s, Bradbrook's career took another turn when he began teaching tax, largely as a result of Sanford 'Sandy' Clark's appointment to the Melbourne Law School and his taking over the property law subject. Subsequently, though, following the creation of Property Law II, Bradbrook went back to teaching property: Property Law I consisted of tenure and estates, and the Torrens system, while Property Law II

---

[14]   Adrian J Bradbrook, *Poverty and the Residential Landlord-Tenant Relationship* (Australian Government Publishing Service, 1975), which was the published result of his doctoral research: Adrian Bradbrook, *The Law Relating to the Rights and Duties of Landlords and Tenants Concerning Residential Premises: A Re-Assessment* (PhD Thesis, University of Melbourne, 1975).

[15]   See, eg, Adrian Bradbrook and Judith Gardam, 'Energy and Poverty: A Proposal to Harness International Law to Advance Universal Access to Modern Energy Services' (2010) 57(1) *Netherlands International Law Review* 1. From 2007-11, Adrian and Judith jointly held a $361 000 Australian Research Council Discovery Project grant for a research project entitled 'Creating a Comprehensive International Law of Sustainable Energy: The Contribution of Law to Sustainable Development and Climate Change'. See also Judith Gardam, Chapter 3, this book.

comprised 'all the rest'. He used the change to his advantage, editing a casebook on tax law with Yuri Grbich and Kevin Pose, published by Butterworths in 1990.[16]

Bradbrook served under five Deans during his time at Melbourne, each a leader in his own field and among the pantheon of the Australian legal academy: Harold Ford (corporations law), followed by Sandy Clark (natural resources, especially water law), Peter Brett (jurisprudence and criminal law), Colin Howard (also criminal law), and finally Harold Luntz (torts). In fact, Bradbrook himself got his first taste of decanal administration when he served as Deputy Dean under Colin Howard from 1978-81 and again later under Harold Luntz from 1984-87. But it was Colin Howard who nominated Bradbrook as Head of the Australian Law Teachers Association ('ALTA'), and he soon became the first non-decanal holder of that post. For Bradbrook, Colin Howard was and remains someone from whom he learned a lot about style and approach in decanal office.

In 1987, though, Bradbroook was on the move again, this time — having missed the opportunity to get there 15 years earlier — to Adelaide, where he took up a Professorship in 1988. Here his career crossed paths with the great historian of Australian law, Alex Castles,[17] who was Dean and Bonython Professor of Law at the time of his arrival. In fact, one year after his arrival, the John Bray Chair was created, which Marcia Neave would have held if not for her departure, upon which Bradbrook became the first holder. And on Castles's retirement in 1988, the University Council — having first determined that, because it was the oldest and most prestigious Chair of Law in the University, it should go to the most senior Professor in the Law School — conferred the Bonython Chair of Law on Bradbrook, then only 40.

At Adelaide, Bradbrook again taught tax in the LLB program, and energy law in the LLM, until he was appointed Head of the Law School in 1990, and 23rd Dean of the Adelaide Law School from 1991-95. Of the 28 Deans of the Adelaide Law School, only six have served longer than Bradbrook, and of those, five did so prior to 1971. The success story of Bradbrook's Deanship was two-fold: taking a more sustained approach to research, and internationalising both the focus and the status of the Law School. Both processes took a great deal of time, and every Dean who has followed has continued Bradbrook's pioneering work.

---

[16] Yuri Grbich, Adrian Bradbrook and Kevin Pose, *Revenue Law: Cases and Materials* (Butterworths, 1990); owing to demand, it was reprinted by Butterworths in 1994 with a supplement.

[17] See, eg, his seminal work: Alex C Castles, *An Australian Legal History* (Law Book, 1982).

In the case of internationalisation, Bradbrook led by example, holding at various times during his career visiting professorships at the Universities of Calgary, Poitiers, Paris Descartes (Paris V), Mannheim and Marburg; research positions at Queens' College, Cambridge, the International Academy of the Environment, and the Universities of McGill, Colorado and Hong Kong; and fellowships or memberships of various bodies around the world, including the United Nations. At the time of writing he continues to be a Member of the Board of Editors of the *Journal of Energy & Natural Resources Law*, the *Australasian Journal of Natural Resources Law and Policy*, the *Journal of Renewable Energy Law and Policy*, and the *Australian Property Law Journal*. In the case of institutional internationalisation, the connections forged by Bradbrook included the University of Poitiers in France, the University of Mannheim in Germany and the College of William and Mary in the United States.

As with every other challenge Bradbrook faced, administrative service failed to slow scholarly pursuits. When he decided to write a book about solar energy law, and no publisher was prescient enough to publish it, he submitted the manuscript — at the encouragement of Professor Harold Luntz — as an original thesis for the rare LLD degree, which was duly conferred by the University of Melbourne in 1987. In 1994, Bradbrook obtained a third doctorate through publication from Cambridge University, on the strength of the property law books he had published throughout his career. A doctorate (*honoris causa*) from Mannheim University followed in 2001. In amongst these academic honours — and the service to scholarship which they represent — his other services to the legal profession continued apace. In 1992, he was elected a Fellow of the Institute of Arbitrators Australia, serving as a Grade 2 Arbitrator. In typical style, he took the opportunity to further serve the community by spreading his knowledge of arbitration law by offering suggestions on how best to teach arbitration to non-lawyers,[18] by providing a clear overview of the commercial arbitration legislation[19] and by offering suggestions for further reforms in the area.[20]

It was around this time, in 1999, that I came to the Adelaide Law School. I had long been a fan from afar. My teaching in property law, both at the Melbourne

---

[18]   See Adrian J Bradbrook, 'Teaching Arbitration to Non-Lawyers' (1998) 17 *The Arbitrator* 173.

[19]   See Adrian J Bradbrook, 'The Commercial Arbitration Legislation' in Vicki Waye (ed), *A Guide to Arbitration Practice in Australia* (Institute of Arbitrators and Mediators Australia, 2001) 55.

[20]   See Adrian J Bradbrook, 'Section 27 of the Uniform Commercial Arbitration Acts: A New Proposal for Reform' (1990) 18 *Australian Business Law Review* 214; republished as Adrian J Bradbrook, 'Section 27 of the Uniform Commercial Arbitration Acts: A New Proposal for Reform' (1990) 9 *The Arbitrator* 107.

Law School and at the University of Oxford, and my LLM (Melbourne) and DPhil (Oxford) theses drew heavily on Bradbrook's property law scholarship. I therefore felt a mixture of excitement and trepidation when the Dean of the Adelaide Law School, Michael Detmold, told me upon my appointment that I would be teaching property law with Bradbrook. When we met he soon put me at ease. I found him to be not only genuinely interested in what I was doing, but truly supportive. It is some measure of the respect which I had for him, and the esteem with which I regarded him, that upon being asked by my mother in 1998 why I wanted to go to the Adelaide Law School, my first response was heartfelt and simple: 'to work with Adrian Bradbrook'. And my mother still remembers only one person at the Adelaide Law School, and often asks after him, referring to him as 'that person who is very important in property law': that person, Adrian Bradbrook, is the reason I came to Adelaide. His reputation truly is widespread.

A final word about Adrian, the person, before turning to Adrian Bradbrook, the scholar. One might be forgiven for thinking that the pace and quality of his scholarship and service left little time for personal pursuits. But while establishing a reputation as a leader in more than one field of law and in running the Adelaide Law School, he also pursued musical interests. His grandmother, herself a concert pianist, nurtured his interest in the piano, an instrument he continued to play until he was 15. While he might have gone to London and the Musical Academy, musical pursuits were placed on hold for 30 years, until, in his early forties, he took them up again, this time concentrating on the flute and then the saxophone, before coming full circle to the piano.

What is perhaps most amazing about Bradbrook's career is that following his retirement, almost none of the activities he began during his career have ceased, or even slowed. He continues to write, speak, teach and pursue his international relationships and his personal interests with the same vigour displayed through the 45 years spanning the time he entered Cambridge in 1966 to his retirement in 2011. What remains, though, is to assess the impact of that time on the life of the law. Suffice to say, it is an understatement in the extreme to say that his impact has been substantial.

III THE OBJECT OF THE PURSUIT: IMPACT ON THE LIFE OF THE LAW

Even the most cursory review of Adrian Bradbrook's publications reveals a scholar of great breadth and depth, of international stature, with a prodigious output. In fact, at the time of writing, Bradbrook has published 24 books, including several new editions of his most significant works in property law, and well over 100 articles and book chapters, not to mention talks, papers, public lectures, and countless other forms of scholarly work and service. And of those published works, they are with prestigious publishers and journals — Oxford and Cambridge University Presses, Butterworths, Thomson Lawbook, *Melbourne University* and *Sydney Law Reviews*, *McGill*, *Toronto* and *Dalhousie Law Journals*, the *Hong Kong Law Journal* and the *Human Rights Quarterly*, to name only a few of the most prestigious.

While Bradbrook has published extensively in many fields, including tax and revenue law, arbitration, family law, the study of law, and legal history, his research truly coalesces around two main themes: property law and sustainable energy law. Nonetheless, in every field in which he has worked, he has not only published but also made a major contribution, in some cases defining the very field itself. Bradbrook has published at least one book in every area in which he has worked, not only property law and sustainable energy law but also including revenue law, arbitration, family law and legal history. How did he do it?

A *Methodology*

In the interviews Bradbrook gave for this volume, he describes his own approach to law as one that looks for an area where the law is inadequate, in need of reform, typified by poor decisions or burdened by anachronisms, and then attempts to determine what it would take to undertake its reform. In many cases, he argues with characteristic modesty, it would not take much to do that work, if only one would do it, starting from a unifying theme, from which reform might grow. This approach is summarised in the initial question that always haunted his coming to a new area of law: why did governments fail to reform the area, whatever it might be?

The answer always seemed simple, at least to Bradbrook: there are no votes in reforming highly technical and complex areas of the law. Having asked the question, he would commit himself to the task, while striving always to ensure that the line between the academy and activism was never crossed. This approach to scholarship would serve any early career researcher well, and Bradbrook first applied it to property law, where he demonstrated that legal scholarship can drive law reform.

B   *The First Major Theme: Property Law*

Bradbrook's book *Poverty and the Residential Landlord-Tenant Relationship*,[21] published in 1975 as part of the Commonwealth Commission of Inquiry into Poverty, led gradually to the enactment of residential tenancies legislation, and the establishment of Residential Tenancies Tribunals, in Australia.[22] It was a long process, but Bradbrook saw early on that what might make sense in the case of commercial leases did not make sense in the case of residential tenancies; in fact, it might do precisely the opposite, causing injustice. Some of these problems first appeared in his work in Canada, and when he arrived in Australia, he saw the same problems. The reform he initiated in the residential context became a 'creeping' reform, extending ultimately to caravans and retail tenancies, but always retaining the principles of justice which lay behind the original residential reforms.

The attempt to do justice did not come without its risks, although Bradbrook was willing to take them. Not a few people criticised him as being anti-landlord. But, for him, it was simply a matter of doing justice and ensuring a level playing field. And it revealed his passion for working in areas that contained a substantial 'human factor', as he put it, which is what he found in child custody, in residential tenancies, and in the second major theme of his work, solar energy.

---

[21]   Adrian J Bradbrook, *Poverty and the Residential Landlord-Tenant Relationship* (Australian Government Publishing Service, 1975), which was the published result of his doctoral research: Adrian Bradbrook, *The Law Relating to the Rights and Duties of Landlords and Tenants Concerning Residential Premises: A Re-Assessment* (PhD Thesis, University of Melbourne, 1975).

[22]   See, eg, Ronald Sackville, 'Law Reform Agencies and Royal Commissions: Toiling in the Same Field?' in Brian R Opeskin and David Weisbrot (eds), *The Promise of Law Reform* (Federation Press, 2005) 274, 278; Adrian J Bradbrook, 'Residential Tenancies Law — The Second Stage of Reforms' (1998) 20 *Sydney Law Review* 402, 402-5. It seems fitting that it was the Dunstan Labor Government in South Australia, where Adrian would ultimately find his home, that led the way in adopting the majority of the Commission's recommendations and enacting them in the *Residential Tenancies Act 1978* (SA) (later repealed and replaced by the *Residential Tenancies Act 1995* (SA)): at 404. The Hon DHL Banfield, in his second reading speech for the Residential Tenancies Bill 1978 (SA) noted that '[i]n particular, the Bill relies upon the recommendations of the report of A J Bradbrook, MA, LLM, entitled "Poverty and the Residential Landlord-Tenant Relationship" prepared for the Australian Commission of Inquiry into Poverty, and the Law Reform Committee of South Australia in its thirty-fifth report relating to standard terms in tenancy agreements': South Australia, *Parliamentary Debates*, Legislative Council, 22 February 1978, 1706 (DHL Banfield).

C   The Second Major Theme: Solar Energy Law

As with residential tenancies legislation, in energy law, and especially solar energy law, Bradbrook's work again drove the development of both scholarship *and* law in that area; not only in Australia, but globally. While his early approach was to analogise generally to the common law of easements as a means of determining how best to protect solar access for the purposes of generating energy, Bradbrook ultimately concluded that the most effective way to achieve this objective was through legislation: to simply legislatively declare such access a property interest.

In an effort to show the way for legislative reform in the protection of solar access, Bradbrook explored the common law easement and the equitable restrictive covenant as possible vehicles for this reform. And regulatory reforms have followed his lead.[23] Again, in this area, as with property law and residential tenancies, Bradbrook saw the human factor, teaming up in recent years with Judith Gardam to work on the human rights dimensions to energy access. Together, they saw this as an issue of justice in the developing world: if in 11 countries in Africa more than 90 per cent of people have no access to electricity at all, that is a reality which affects development, and which must be addressed in a sustainable way.[24] In many ways, then, just as residential tenancies law in Australia owes much to the work of Adrian Bradbrook, so, too, does that of solar energy law globally.

D   Measuring the Impact

There is no question, then, that Bradbrook's scholarship has made an impact; in every area to which he has contributed, he is recognised as a leader in the field. In one of the latest of what has become in recent years a steady stream of Australian property law books, *Australian Land Law in Context*, the authors write in their preface that '[a]nyone writing and teaching on Australian land law owes an enormous debt to the

---

[23]   See, eg, *Adelaide (City) Development Plan* (Consolidated 25 October 2012) principle 29 (requiring that solar panels have access to sunlight between certain hours); *Burnside (City) Development Plan* (Consolidated 19 April 2012) objective 15, principle 167(e) (both restricting overshadowing), objective 56, principles 14, 15(c) (both promoting solar energy). There are many other examples where regulatory reforms have followed Adrian's lead. For a survey of such progress, see generally Adrian J Bradbrook, 'Solar Access Law: 30 Years On' (2010) 27 *Environmental and Planning Law Journal* 5.

[24]   See, eg, Nathanial Gronewold, 'One-Quarter of World's Population Lacks Electricity', *Scientific American* (online), 24 November 2009 <http://www.scientificamerican.com/article.electricity-gap-developing-countries-energy-wood-charcoal>.

pioneering works of Helmore (*The Law of Real Property in New South Wales*), Butt (*Land Law*), Bradbrook, Grattan, MacCallum and Moore (*Australian Real Property Law*) and Sackville and Neave (*Property Law, Cases and Materials*)'.[25] Those seven authors, Bradbrook being one of them, represent the vanguard of Australian property law scholarship. And, as already noted, he has contributed not only the development of scholarship but the development of law itself. It is perhaps prescient, then, that an early book he co-edited was entitled *The Emergence of Australian Law*,[26] for Bradbrook himself has become a part of that emergence.

Still, measuring the true impact of a legal scholar's work can be a difficult task. Citation counts, impact factors and other such devices are woefully inadequate proxies for the true impact of a scholar's lifetime of research in the law. But it would be remiss not to try — however poorly — to make a few remarks on the influence of Bradbrook's research.

It is natural to divide a legal scholar's impact into three overlapping spheres: that on the profession, that on the judiciary and that on the academy. Bradbrook's impact on the profession, and those students of law who will soon join the profession, is considerable. He has co-authored several leading textbooks across his fields of expertise. His classic text, *Australian Real Property Law*,[27] now in its fifth edition, and its trusty companion, *Australia Property Law: Cases and Materials*,[28] now in its fourth edition, are to be found on lawyers' and law-students' bookshelves around the country. Similarly, his *Commercial Tenancy Law*,[29] now in its third edition, and *Bradbrook and Neave's Easements and Restrictive Covenants in Australia*,[30] also in its third edition, have both become standard references for practitioners. Add to this his

---

[25] Ken Mackie, Elise Bennett Histed and John Page, *Australian Land Law in Context* (Oxford University Press, 2012) liv.

[26] MP Ellinghaus, AJ Bradbrook and AJ Duggan (eds), *The Emergence of Australian Law* (Butterworths, 1989).

[27] Adrian Bradbrook, Scott Grattan, Susan MacCallum and Anthony Moore, *Australian Real Property Law* (Thomson Reuters, 5th ed, 2011).

[28] Adrian Bradbrook, Susan MacCallum, Anthony Moore, Scott Grattan and Lynden Griggs, *Australian Property Law: Cases and Materials* (Thomson Reuters, 4th ed, 2011).

[29] Adrian J Bradbrook, Clyde E Croft and Robert S Hay, *Commercial Tenancy Law* (LexisNexis, 3rd ed, 2008).

[30] Bradbrook and MacCallum, above n 13.

more recent textbook with Rosemary Lyster, *Energy Law and the Environment*,[31] and Bradbrook's service to the profession is clear.[32]

The profession — and its students — are not the only ones who have benefited from Bradbrook's scholarship. Bench and Bar alike read his work. Take, for example, his leading property textbook, *Australian Real Property Law*. It is not difficult, with even the most rudimentary electronic search of recent cases, to find that it has been cited in the High Court of Australia,[33] in the Federal Court[34] and in its Full Court,[35] in the Supreme Court of Victoria[36] and in its Court of Appeal,[37] in the Supreme Court of Queensland[38] and in its Court of Appeal,[39] in the Supreme Court of Western Australia[40] and in its Court of Appeal,[41] and in the Supreme Courts of New South Wales,[42] South Australia,[43] Tasmania[44] and the Northern Territory.[45] And these are only examples of those times when the judiciary has *acknowledged* their reference to Bradbrook's text.[46]

---

[31] Rosemary Lyster and Adrian Bradbrook, *Energy Law and the Environment* (Cambridge University Press, 2007).

[32] For a full list of Bradbrook's books, see page 283.

[33] See, eg, *Braidotti v Queensland City Properties Ltd* (1991) 172 CLR 293, 305 (Deane J).

[34] See, eg, *Haslam v Money for Living (Aust) Pty Ltd* (2008) 172 FCR 301, 317 [23] (Middleton J).

[35] See, eg, *Perpetual Trustee Company Limited (ACN 000 001 007) v Smith* (2010) 186 FCR 566, 581 [48] (Moore and Stone JJ).

[36] See, eg, *Obeid v Victorian Urban Development Authority* (2012) 188 LGERA 56, 78 n 55 (Cavanough J).

[37] See, eg, *Horvath v Commonwealth Bank of Australia* [1999] 1 VR 643, 661-2 [46], 678 [86] (Phillips JA).

[38] See, eg, *Eckford v Stanbroke Pastoral Co Pty Ltd* [2012] QSC 48 (15 March 2012) n 34 (Dalton J).

[39] See, eg, *Elroa Nominees Pty Ltd v Registrar of Titles* [2003] QCA 165 (24 April 2003) n 3 (Jerrard JA).

[40] See, eg, *Carroll v Investments (WA) Pty Ltd* [2012] WASC 93 (22 March 2012) [145] (Simmonds J).

[41] See, eg, *Westpac Banking Corporation v The Bell Group Ltd (in liq) [No 3]* (2012) 89 ASCR 1, 57 [349] (Lee AJA), 638 [3453] (Carr AJA).

[42] See, eg, *Cram Foundation v Corbett-Jones* [2006] NSWSC 495 (26 May 2006) [56] (Brereton J).

[43] See, eg, *Stone v Leonardis* (2011) 110 SASR 503, 511 n 19 (White J).

[44] See, eg, *Quarmby v Keating & Qasair Investments Pty Ltd* [2007] TASSC 65 (23 August 2007) [54] (Tennent J).

[45] See, eg, *CEO (Housing) v Brown* (2000) 156 FLR 158, 164 [27] (Thomas J).

[46] These examples are each selected as the most recent mention in a judgment of the relevant court which is available by an electronic search. It is easy to find many more examples.

Now we come to the academy. Bradbrook's enormous scholarly impact can be seen through only the most cursory glance at his voluminous contributions on the subjects that most fascinated him: energy law, environmental law, and property law. There is no easy way to pick a single contribution. Instead, take as examples two articles published in 1988, the year he took up the Bonython Chair of Law at the University of Adelaide. The first, published in his new home review, the *Adelaide Law Review*, was entitled 'The Relevance of the *Cujus Est Solum* Doctrine to the Surface Landowner's Claims to Natural Resources Located Above and Beneath the Land'.[47] Again, using only a simple electronic search,[48] it is easy to find 20 citations to this article alone.[49] The impact is felt across the globe — in articles, in textbooks, in cases, in theses, in reports and in enclyopædias — with citations from publications in Australia,[50] New

---

[47] Adrian J Bradbrook, 'The Relevance of the *Cujus Est Solum* Doctrine to the Surface Landowner's Claims to Natural Resources Located Above and Beneath the Land' (1988) 11 *Adelaide Law Review* 462.

[48] That is, including only a sample of the sources that are available electronically.

[49] I exclude here Bradbrook's citations (as author or co-author) to his own prior work.

[50] Michael Weir and Tina Hunter, 'Property Rights and Coal Seam Gas Extraction: The Modern Property Law Conundrum' (2012) 2 *Property Law Review* 71, 76 n 43; Jason G Allen, '*Salus Populi Supreme Lex*: Justifying Compulsory Mineral Leases in the *Mineral Resources Development Act 1995* (Tas)' (2011) 30(1) *University of Tasmania Law Review* 1, 10 n 27; Lynden Griggs, '*Cujus Est Solum* — An Unfortunate Scrap of Latin, Doctrine in Disarray or a Brocard of Relevance? Its Applicability to the Subterranean and the United Kingdom Supreme Court Decision in *Star Energy v Bocardo* (2011) 19 *Australian Property Law Journal* 155, 160 n 33; *Finlay Stonemasonry Pty Ltd v JD & Sons Nominees Pty Ltd* (2011) 249 FLR 462, 473 n 45; Michael O'Donnell, 'Indigenous Rights in Water in Northern Australia' (Report, NAILSMA-TRaCK Project 6.2, March 2011) 34 n 26, 38 nn 42-3; George Cho, *Geographic Information Science: Mastering the Legal Issues* (John Wiley & Sons, 2005) 268 n 136; Thomson Reuters, *The Laws of Australia* (at 1 April 1999) 28 Real Property, '15 Physical Limits to Land' [28.15.11] n 1; Bradley Selway, *The Constitution of South Australia* (Federation Press, 1997) 220 n 188; Mako John Kuwimb, *An Examination of Papua New Guinea's Petroleum Law and Policy* (LLM(Hons) Thesis, University of Wollongong, 1997) 34 n 56; Poh-Ling Tan, 'Finders Keepers? Heritage Protection of Found Objects in Queensland' (1994) 11 *Environmental and Planning Law Journal* 507, 515 n 13; John Nonggorr, 'Resolving Conflicts in Customary Law and Western Law in Natural Resource Developments in Papua New Guinea' (1993) 16(2) *UNSW Law Journal* 433, 442 n 27; Kibuta Ongwamuhana and Anthony Regan, 'Ownership of Minerals and Petroleum in Papua New Guinea: The Genesis and Nature of the Legal Controversy' (1991) 7 *Queensland University of Technology Law Journal* 109, 118 n 18; LD Griggs and R Snell, 'Property Boundaries and Incidental Rights Attached to the Ownership of Land in Tasmania' (1991) 10 *University of Tasmania Law Review* 256, 258 nn 11-12, 264 n 44, 268 n 55.

Zealand,[51] Papua New Guinea,[52] England,[53] Canada[54] and Nigeria.[55] Bradbrook's scholarly reach even extends to a citation in a German textbook, *Das Umweltrecht des Auslandes*.[56] From this selection — and it *is* only a selection — we can see that nearly 25 years on Bradbrook's thoughts on Accursius's brocard, and on its impact on natural resources, still continue to shape legal discussion.

The second article, titled 'Future Directions in Solar Access Protection',[57] appeared in 1988 in volume 19 of *Environmental Law*, the oldest environmental law journal published in the United States, and the only one to have ever been commended by a US President for simply existing.[58] A similar elementary electronic database search likewise easily yields 20 citations for this article. Writers of articles, notes, books, working papers, theses, looseleaf commentaries and submissions to government inquiries all draw upon his expertise. Again, the appeal spans the globe. In this small sample, the authors engaging with Bradbrook's ideas come from Australia,[59]

---

[51] Barry Barton, 'Carbon Capture and Storage Law for New Zealand: A Comparative Study' (2009) 13 *New Zealand Journal of Environmental Law* 1, 18 n 54.

[52] John T Mugambwa and Harrison A Amankwah, *Land Law and Policy in Papua New Guinea* (Cavendish Publishing, 2nd ed, 2002) 107 n 7; and see the articles on Papua New Guinean law published in Australia: above n 50.

[53] These are both international journals: Robert Pritchard, 'The Ownership of Petroleum in Papua New Guinea — A Lesson for Resources Lawyers' (2012) 5 *International Energy Law Review* 166, 175 nn 5, 11; Helen Cooper, 'Bibliography' (1990) 8(2) *Journal of Energy & Natural Resources Law* 152, 154 n 195.

[54] Brian Ballantyne (ed), *Surveys, Parcels and Tenure on Canada Lands* (Natural Resources Canada/ Ressources Naturelles Canada, 2010) 63 n 243.

[55] Eme N Ekekwe, *Nigeria, Leadership and Development: Essays in Honour of Chibuike Rotimi Amaechi* (Author House, 2011) 98.

[56] Michael Kloepfer and Ekkehart Mast, *Das Umweltrecht des Auslandes* (Duncker & Humblot, 1995) 294 n 26.

[57] Adrian J Bradbrook, 'Future Directions in Solar Access Protection' (1988) 19 *Environmental Law* 167.

[58] See Richard Nixon, 'Letter' (1970) 1 *Environmental Law* 1 (a reproduction of the letter sent by President Nixon to the journal's editors).

[59] Anna Kapnoullas, 'The Idea Model for Solar Access Rights' (2011) 28 *Environmental and Planning Law Journal* 416, 438 n 227; James Prest, Submission to Senate Standing Committee on Environment, Communications and the Arts, Parliament of Australia, *Inquiry into the Renewable Energy (Electricity) Amendment (Feed-in Tariff) Bill 2008*, 29 August 2008, 48 n 133 <http://law.anu.edu.au/sites/all/files/lrsj/prest_renewable_energy_submission_29_aug_08.pdf>.

the US,[60] England[61] and other international publications.[62] Again, nearly 25 years after it first appeared in print it continues to be cited in articles.

These two examples make my point: Adrian Bradbrook's scholarship has begun many conversations in the academy, decades ago, that continue today, with new conversants and new issues, but tracing their origins to Bradbrook's pioneering work. This should be the test for true scholarly impact.

IV CAPTURE

As I noted at the outset, *I* am the saucy intruder: I have not shared in the honours and certainly not in the labours of the chase. Rather, I have 'come in at the end', in Livingston J's words, to attempt to 'bear away in triumph the object of pursuit'. I can only summarise what I have read and what I have heard. However, there are those who have followed, to continue with the *Pierson v Post* metaphor, this wily

---

[60] Thomson Reuters, *Miller & Star California Real Estate* (3rd ed), vol 6 (at 2 January 2013) § 15:11 (Solar Easements) n 2; Anna Fedman, 'Protecting Solar Rights in California Through an Exploration of the California Water Doctrine' (Working Paper No LA 222, Water Resources Collections and Archive, University of California, 15 May 2011) 14 <http://escholarship.org/uc/item/5915z1xc>; Jamie E France, 'Note: A Proposed Solar Access Law for the State of Texas' (2010) 89 *Texas Law Review* 187, 203 n 88; Troy A Rule, 'Shadows on the Cathedral: Solar Access Laws in a Different Light' (2010) 2010(3) *University of Illinois Law Review* 851, 869 n 109; Uma Outka, 'Siting Renewable Energy: Land Use and Regulatory Context' (2010) 37(4) *Ecology Law Quarterly* 1041, 1081 n 233; Sara C Bronin, 'Solar Rights' (2009) 89(4) *Boston University Law Review* 1217, 1223 n 18; Sara C Bronin, 'Modern Lights' (2009) 80(4) *University of Colorado Law Review* 881, 888 n 21; KK Duvivier, 'Animal, Vegetable, Mineral — Wind? The Severed Wind Power Rights Conundrum' (2009) 49(1) *Washburn Law Journal* 69, 97 n 206; Carol M Rose, 'Seeing Property' in Carol M Rose (ed), *Property and Persuasion: Essays on the History, Theory and Rhetoric of Ownership* (Westview Press, 1994) 267, 298 n 11; Aimée L Lesieutre, 'Residential Solar Energy Use: Barriers and Incentives in a Historical Perspective' (MSc Thesis, Oregon State University, July 1992) 26; Editors, 'Index and Twenty-Second Selected Bibliography on Computers, Technology and the Law' (1990) 16 *Rutgers Computer and Technology Law Journal* 667, 704; Carol M Rose, 'Property Rights, Regulatory Regimes and the New Takings Jurisprudence — An Evolutionary Approach' (1990) 57 *Tennessee Law Review* 577, 587 n 46; C Martin Wilson III, 'Recent Publications' (1989) 20 *State Bar of Texas Environmental Law Journal* 57, 58; Theron R Nelson, 'Ancient Lights: Will Real Estate Finds its Place in the Sun?' (Working Paper, Department of Finance, University of North Dakota) 11 n 3 <http://citeseerx.ist.psu.edu/viewdoc/summary?doi=10.1.1.202.3957>.

[61] Igor V Novkov, 'State of Solar Rights Across the United States' (Working Paper, Suffolk University Law School, 20 July 2009) 7 n 47, 8 n 52 <http://ssrn.com/abstract=1490349>.

[62] Dan van der Horst and Saskia Vermeylen, 'Wind Theft, Spatial Planning and International Relations' (2010) 1 *Renewable Energy Law and Policy Review* 67, 68 n 4; Saskia Vermeylen, 'Resource Rights and the Evolution of Renewable Energy Technologies' (2010) 35 *Renewable Energy* 2399, 2404 n 6.

quadruped, the one who held the stratagems and strengths to look at law and see its future in ways unavailable to many of us. And so, I am happy to stop short of fully reducing into possession this career, and to return it to those to whom it rightfully belongs, according to Livingston J's analysis: to those who have been with him along the way of his life in the law, and who have contributed in their own ways to the development of the life of the law.

I turn the capture of this life in the law to those who have shared in the life of the law with Adrian Bradbrook. I turn it over to Richard L Ottinger, who provides a very personal tribute to Bradbrook's contribution to the laws governing energy, climate change and poverty alleviation; to Paul Leadbeter, who outlines Bradbrook's contribution to sustainable energy in the case of urban environments; to Judith Gardam, who examines the human factor in so much of Bradbook's work (specifically in the case of access to energy); to Barry Barton, to demonstrate the need for energy efficiency; to Rosemary Lyster, who shows how renewable energy is inextricably linked to climate change; to Lee Godden, to show how property law develops over time (through inputs such as Bradbrook's); to Anthony Moore, to explain Bradbrook's contribution to tenancy law more fully; to Ralph Wahnschafft, who considers sustainable transport after Rio+20 and shows Bradbrook's practical engagement with the world beyond the academy; and to Alexandra Wawryk, who reveals the vista of international energy law.

Most importantly, I ultimately give Bradbrook's contributions back to him. In the final essay of this volume, Bradbrook himself reveals the physical and temporal human landscape that lies before us, which we must follow using his contributions as a guide, and to which the law must respond in an effort to do justice, wherever it is needed and whatever is required.

2

CONTROLS ON URBAN TREE REMOVAL IN SOUTH AUSTRALIA: AN EXAMPLE OF RESTRICTING PROPERTY RIGHTS FOR THE GREATER COMMUNITY BENEFIT

PAUL LEADBETER

I INTRODUCTION

For over 30 years, Adrian Bradbrook has been a leading figure both within Australia and internationally on the law and its application to the area of solar energy in Australia. His seminal work on the subject, *Solar Energy in Australia*, was published in 1984[1] and in 2010 he reviewed the contemporary situation in Australia regarding solar access law in a major article for the *Environmental and Planning Law Journal*.[2] His writing in this area was influenced by his work in property law and particularly (from the solar access point of view) his work on easements and restrictive covenants, which was the basis for an earlier publication in 1981 with Marcia Neave.[3] The work on solar energy led Bradbrook to look more broadly at the topic of energy law and

---

[1] Adrian Bradbrook, *Solar Energy and the Law* (Law Book, 1984).

[2] Adrian J Bradbrook, *Solar Access Law: 30 Years On* (2010) 27 *Environmental and Planning Law Journal* 5.

[3] Adrian Bradbrook and Marcia Neave, *Easements and Restrictive Covenants in Australia* (Butterworths, 1st ed, 1981 2nd ed, 2000).

that has been his particular focus for the past 20 years or so. His work in the energy law area has focused particularly on the concept of sustainable energy, both from the concept of more sustainable use of energy and more sustainable energy production.[4]

This chapter addresses the issue of land use planning controls applying in South Australia at the time of writing which regulate the removal and damaging of urban trees. The topic is not as remote from the fields of Bradbrook's work as it might, initially, appear. First, the regulatory mechanisms which control and restrict urban tree removal relate to the use of land. They impose, as do all land use planning controls, restrictions on what a person can do with their land. In that sense they demonstrate a theme that has emerged generally from Bradbrook's work in the property law area, namely that the use of land does change over time to address a range of social exigencies and shifts in our societal value and that property law evolves to reflect and account for those changes. Second, when contemplating sustainable approaches to energy there is the need to both reduce overall energy consumption and use more sustainable methods of generating energy, such as solar power.

The South Australian urban tree controls, as this chapter will show, can indirectly work towards reducing the overall consumption of energy within buildings and reduce the generation of energy through what is known as the 'urban heat island effect'. Although those controls were not introduced with any direct intention to address the urban heat island effect they nevertheless do assist in that process. They are also unique, particularly in the Australian context, because they are the only statutory controls in any Australian state designed to protect urban trees of a certain size and scale for those reasons alone and not because of the tree's heritage significance or botanical importance.

II URBAN HEAT ISLAND EFFECT

The city of Adelaide, home to Adrian Bradbrook for the past 24 years, has a population of 1.26 million.[5] Its core city area was planned by Colonel William Light[6] and the

---

[4] Rosemary Lyster and Adrian Bradbrook, *Energy Law and the Environment* (Cambridge University Press, 2006).

[5] Simone — Myth Buster, apos;Adelaide's Population 2011 — Growth and Change Since 2006apos; on .idblog, *.id the population experts* (4 September 2012) <http://blog.id.com.au/2012/australian-population/adelaides-population-2011-growth-and-change-since-2006/>.

[6] For a description of the original plans, see Alan WJ Hutchings (ed), *With Conscious Purpose —*

state's citizens and local and state governments have long prided themselves on being a place at the forefront of land use planning trends. It is also the capital city of the driest state on the driest inhabited continent on earth. It has long, hot summers with little or no rain and relatively dry, mild winters. There is a significant degree of insolation throughout the year across all of the state of South Australia.[7] The state and the city of Adelaide face significant adverse impacts from climate change, including less rainfall, more extreme weather events (such as sudden violent storms and flash flooding) and many more hot days each year:

> Based on a trajectory of mid-range greenhouse gas emissions in 2030, the average number of days a year over 35°C is projected to increase to 21-26 and the average number of days a year over 40°C is projected to increase to 3-5.[8]

Given these predictions (which are similar for the entire southern part of Australia), urban trees will play an increasingly important role in our cities and towns. They provide shade and aesthetic improvements to our streetscapes, privacy, shelter for fauna and humans during inclement weather and contribute to biodiversity and the overall maintenance of a healthy ecosystem.

Urban areas dominated by buildings and hard impermeable surfaces generate considerable energy and thus heat. This urban heat island effect has been well documented.[9] Studies have shown that urban areas are hotter than the surrounding unbuilt and undeveloped areas. The reasons such studies cite for this are many. There is a significant heat release from human activities within those urban areas from building heating and cooling systems, public transportation systems, vehicular traffic and energy use within commercial and residential buildings.[10] There is less of an albedo effect,[11] which results in shortwave radiation being absorbed within the dark

---

a History of Town Planning in South Australia (Planning Institute of Australia, South Australian Division, 2nd ed, 2007).

[7] 'Insolation' is a term used to describe incident or incoming solar radiation. It describes the solar radiation that actually reaches the earth's surface. The longer the daylight time the greater the level of insolation received, hence Australia has significant amounts of insolation.

[8] Government of South Australia, Department of Planning and Local Government, *The 30 Year Plan for Greater Adelaide — A Volume of the South Australian Planning Strategy* (2010) 44.

[9] See, eg, Cynthia Rosenweig et al (eds) 'Climate Change and Cities-First Assessment Report of the Urban Climate Change Research Network' (Cambridge University Press, 2011); Brian Stone, Jr, *The City and the Coming Climate: Climate Change in the Places We Live* (Cambridge University Press, 2012).

[10] Rosenweig et al, above n 9, 47.

[11] *Albedo* is a term derived from the Latin 'albedo' meaning 'whiteness'. It is used by climatologists

surfaces of roads and buildings rather than being reflected back into the atmosphere resulting in a build-up of heat within the urban area. The greater preponderance of impervious surfaces results in less natural soil and vegetation, thereby reducing evapotranspiration and latent heat cooling.[12] The urban heat island ('UHI') effect was recognised in the 30 Year Plan for Greater Adelaide:

> Open space, greenways, parklands and dense green spaces such as green roofs and walls can reduce the UHI effect. The development of these green spaces will also help to reduce water consumption during hot weather and energy consumption by the built environment.[13]

Adelaide is not a large, densely built city like many others in the world and even elsewhere in Australia and therefore its urban heat island effect is likely to be less severe. It also has the Adelaide parklands, which provide over 7.6km² of open space and vegetation surrounding the city centre. There are presently extensive plantings of indigenous vegetation being undertaken in various parts of the Adelaide parklands, which will provide significant benefits for the city in terms of addressing some of the urban heating effects. Nevertheless, the issue of suburban trees — the planting, maintenance and replacement of them — is an important one which will continue to remain so as climate change impacts grow. It might therefore be seen as a little surprising that on 17 November 2011 the State government introduced changes to the provisions in the *Development Act 1993* (SA) ('Development Act') dealing with controls over trees in the metropolitan area — which changes actually allow a greater number of urban trees to be removed than was previously allowed under the former controls over significant trees.

III   Background to Controls on Significant Trees

The original provisions providing protection for urban trees, described at the time as 'significant trees', were introduced by way of amendments to the Development Act in the year 2000.[14] That legislation had provided for the creation of the concept of a 'significant tree' and made 'tree damaging activity' in relation to a significant tree

---

to describe the reflecting power of a surface. Thus a dark surface will absorb much more incident solar radiation than a white surface, which will reflect a lot more of the solar radiation back into space.

[12]   Rosenweig et al, above n 9, 45.

[13]   Government of South Australia, Department of Planning and Local Government, above n 8, 45.

[14]   *Development (Significant Trees) Amendment Act 2000* (SA).

something for which development approval had to be obtained. The controls only applied in the metropolitan Adelaide area (not an insubstantial area in any event) and controls over native vegetation pruning and clearance elsewhere in the state were within the province of the *Native Vegetation Act 1991* (SA) ('Native Vegetation Act'). With the exception of the controls over 'pest plants', there were (and continue to be) no controls over the pruning and removal of non-indigenous vegetation. Substantial exotic trees outside the metropolitan Adelaide area are not protected unless given designation as a State or local heritage place under either the *Heritage Places Act 1993* (SA) or by a development plan. In 2002, a review of the significant tree controls was undertaken by Alan Hutchings, then a Commissioner of the Environment Resources and Development Court ('ERD Court'). There was no immediate follow-up by the State government of any of the recommendations made by Hutchings after he delivered his report, although some of the recent changes can be seen to have their genesis in Hutchings's recommendations.

In the background statement to the Regulated Trees Development Plan Amendment ('Regulated Trees DPA'),[15] it is stated that there was general community support for the significant trees provisions. It is noted that in 2008 the District Council of Mount Barker, an area in the Adelaide Hills, requested that the controls be extended to apply within that council area. There were some issues with the provisions or more particularly how those provisions were applied. On a number of occasions in the suburban residential context, either the planning authority at first instance, or the ERD Court on appeal, did not allow removal of a tree which was seen as being healthy and not posing any unacceptable risk to public or private safety despite the fact that the tree was clearly an inappropriate one in a domestic dwelling setting. Often the authorities or the court found that there had not been sufficient consideration of alternative remedial treatments or exploration of all reasonable alternative development options and design solutions.

In taking this approach the court and authorities were seeking to apply the policy criteria specified in the development plans for significant trees. But this is not an entirely satisfactory approach when a person's domestic property is dominated by a massive tree planted many years ago by an unwitting gardener when the tree is one most suitable in a large park-like setting and certainly not a residential property.

---

15   Released for public consultation on 17 November 2011, see South Australia, *The South Australian Government Gazette*, No 79, 17 November 2011, 4535.

However, if the tree was a healthy specimen and posing no unreasonable risk to persons or property it was often very difficult to obtain clearance approval, particularly when the tree made an important contribution to the character or amenity of the local area. Furthermore, councils were increasingly requesting that applicants seeking development approval for tree removal and pruning provide expensive reports from arborists and landscape specialists in support of their application.

The background statement in the Regulated Trees DPA also refers to a number of other matters that had precipitated an intention on the part of the state government to refine the significant tree provisions. They included in summary:

1. Evolution of significant tree controls enforcement by local government

2. Experiences of the Courts in interpreting the legislation

3. Differing expectations from the community and industry

4. Changing development pressures in metropolitan Adelaide associated with:

    a. Existence of the urban boundary

    b. Market conditions

    c. Increasing population

    d. Higher building densities

    e. Smaller residential allotments combined with larger footprints of houses.[16]

The matters that were arguably the real catalyst for the changes are listed in points 3 and 4 above. In particular, the existence of trees that were classified as significant trees on existing residential allotments under the previous controls would often be seen to hamper the redevelopment of those allotments for more intensive forms of development, or create significant costs for developers as they sought alternative design solutions to accommodate those trees. Increasing the density of residential development in the Metropolitan Adelaide area is part of the state government's overall strategy for development in South Australia and there was an obvious inconsistency between the two policy positions. It is also this writer's perception that the state Labor government led by Premier Mike Rann[17] had been

---

[16]   Minister for Planning (SA), *Regulated Trees Development Plan Amendment, 1* <www.sa.gov.au/planning/dpas>.

[17]   Premier of South Australia between 2002 and 2011.

particularly beholden to the development industry, which can be seen to have had particularly favourable treatment in a number of areas of state planning policy and legislative enactments.[18]

There is a cautionary note to be made in relation to the more relaxed controls over urban trees — and that comes back to the earlier point made about the benefits of urban trees in reducing energy use within the urban setting. Increasing the density of urban built form is commendable in terms of trying to reduce the overall carbon footprint, but if it comes at the expense of less vegetative cover within the urban area, then there may well be a price to pay for that in terms of the city's urban heat effect. At the time of writing, planning policy does not, as yet, adequately address this problem.

The South Australian Minister for Planning, the Hon John Rau, at the time of announcing the new controls, said:

> The changes are designed to balance protection of trees with the need to remove inappropriately located trees and inappropriate tree species for reasons such as public safety. The intention is to provide greater clarity for people wanting to undertake reasonable and expected development or to remove inappropriate trees for legitimate reasons, while also providing appropriate protection for trees that give Adelaide much of its character.[19]

IV   How does the New System of Controls Work?

The Development Act provides that no development may be undertaken unless it is an approved development.[20] In s 4 of the Act 'development' is defined to include any tree-damaging activity in relation to a regulated tree. In the same section 'tree-damaging activity' is defined as:

(a)   the killing or destruction of a tree; or

(b)   the removal of a tree; or

(c)   the severing of branches, limbs, stems or trunk of a tree; or

---

[18]   This favourable treatment is exemplified by the state government's use of the major project provisions in s 46 of the Development Act to approve controversial developments such as the Buckland Park subdivision, the LeCornu site redevelopment in North Adelaide and the shopping centre at Encounter Bay.

[19]   John Rau, 'Revised Controls to Protect Trees' (News Release, 17 November 2011).

[20]   Development Act s 32.

(d)   the ringbarking, topping or lopping of a tree; or

(e)   any other substantial damage to a tree,

and includes any other act or activity that causes any of the foregoing to occur but does not include maintenance pruning that is not likely to affect adversely the general health and appearance of a tree or that is excluded by regulation from the ambit of the definition.

Thus, at times excavation work associated with building construction, such as for a pool or dwelling, may sever significant roots of trees and therefore come within that definition on the basis it comprises 'other substantial damage to a tree'. The type of pruning of regulated trees which is excluded from the definition is set out in regulation 6A(8) and involves pruning

(a)   that does not remove more than 30% of the crown of the tree; and

(b)   that is required to remove —

(i)   dead or diseased wood; or

(ii)   branches that pose a material risk to a building; or

(iii)   branches to a tree that is located in an area frequently used by people and the branches pose a material risk to such people.

If it is necessary to remove more than 30 per cent of the tree's crown, then development approval will be required even if the pruning is necessitated to remove dead or diseased branches or branches posing a risk to people or property.

What, then, is a regulated tree? This requires consideration of provisions in both the Development Act and the *Development Regulations 2008* (SA) ('Development Regulations'). Section 4 of the Act provides that 'regulated tree' means:

(a)   a tree, or a tree within a class of trees, declared to be regulated by the regulations (whether or not the tree also constitutes a significant tree under the regulations); or

(b)   a tree declared to be a significant tree, or a tree within a stand of trees declared to be significant trees, by a Development Plan (whether or not the tree is also declared to be a regulated tree, or also falls within a class of trees declared to be regulated trees, by the regulations).

A 'significant tree', in turn, is:

(a)   a tree declared to be a significant tree, or a tree within a stand of trees declared to be significant trees, by a Development Plan (whether or not the tree is also declared to be a regulated tree, or also falls within a class of trees declared to be regulated trees, by the regulations); or

(b)   a tree declared to be a regulated tree by the regulations, or a tree within a class of trees declared to be regulated trees by the regulations that, by virtue of the application of prescribed criteria, is to be taken to be a significant tree for the purposes of this Act.

Regulation 6A of the Development Regulations provides details of the possible declarations referred to in the above definitions. In essence, the details can be summarised as follows:

1.   The provisions regarding regulated trees only apply in the designated area.[21] The designated area includes the whole of Metropolitan Adelaide,[22] with some exceptions in parts of the areas of the Adelaide Hills Council[23] and the City of Playford,[24] and the whole of the area of the District Council of Mount Barker with certain designated exceptions.[25]

2.   Regulated trees are any trees within the designated area that have a trunk with a circumference of 2 metres or more or, in the case of trees with multiple trunks, that have trunks with a total circumference of 2 metres or more and an average circumference of 625 millimetres or more, measured at a point 1 metre above natural ground level.[26]

3.   However, even if trees meet these measures they will not be regulated trees if they are located within 10 metres of an existing dwelling or an existing in-ground swimming pool unless they are a tree of the *Agonis Flexuosa* (Willow Myrtle) or Eucalyptus species,[27] or if they are trees within a list of a range of exotic tree species.[28] Trees falling into any of these categories

---

[21]   Development Regulations regs 6A(1), (3).

[22]   Defined in s 4 of the Development Act.

[23]   Applies within the Country Township Zone but not within the Extractive Industry Zone, the Public Purpose Zone or the Watershed (Primary Production) Zone.

[24]   Not within the Watershed Zone or the Mount Lofty Ranges Rural Zone on the eastern side of the Hills face Zone.

[25]   Not within the Industry (Kanmantoo) Zone, the Rural Watershed Protection Zone, the Rural (Mount Barker) Zone, the Rural (Kanmantoo) Zone or the Rural (Kondoparinga) Zone.

[26]   Development Regulations reg 6A(1).

[27]   Ibid reg 6A(5)(a).

[28]   Ibid reg 6A(5)(b): The list is replicated in the Appendix to this chapter.

can be removed or pruned heavily without having to go through the requirements of obtaining development approval.

4.   If the tree or trees within the designated area belong to a class of plants that have been subject to a Ministerial declaration under ch 8, pt 1 of the *Natural Resources Management Act 2004* (SA), the tree or trees will not be regulated or significant trees by virtue of their measurements alone[29] and can therefore also be removed or heavily pruned.[30] Basically, trees in this category would be pest plants for the purposes of the *Natural Resources Management Act 2004* (SA) which promotes the removal and destruction of such species.

5.   Trees within the designated area which meet the definition of 'native vegetation', and which require clearance approval under the Native Vegetation Act, will not be regulated or significant trees as a result of their measurements, although they will still not be able to be pruned or removed without the consent of the Native Vegetation Council.[31] There are unlikely to be many trees in this category as most of the designated area (with the exception of the City of Onkaparinga) is outside the area governed by the Native Vegetation Act.[32]

6.   Trees which meet the prescribed measurements for regulated or significant trees but are trees planted as part of a woodlot, orchard or other form of plantation created for the purpose of growing and then harvesting trees or any produce will not be regulated or significant trees by virtue of their measurements alone.[33] They could possibly be declared significant trees within a development plan, although the occasions when that action is likely to occur would seem to be fairly limited.

7.   While many significant trees will also meet the criteria required to be regulated trees, not all significant trees must be regulated trees.

---

[29]   Although they could well be significant trees if designated as such by the provisions of a Development Plan.

[30]   Development Regulations reg 6A(5)(c).

[31]   Ibid reg 6A(5)(d).

[32]   Native Vegetation Act s 4.

[33]   Development Regulations reg 6A(5)(e).

8. Significant trees are trees declared to be significant trees by a development plan[34] or regulated trees with a trunk with a circumference of 3 metres or more or, in the case of a tree with multiple trunks, with trunks with a total circumference of 3 metres or more and an average circumference of 625 millimetres or more, measured at a point that is 1 metre above natural ground level. It is therefore possible for a tree to be declared a significant tree within a development plan even though that tree does not meet the measurement criteria specified within reg 6A of the regulations.

A Development Plan may declare a tree to be a significant tree if:

(i)   it makes a significant contribution to the character or visual amenity of the local area; or

(ii)   it is indigenous to the local area, it is a rare or endangered species taking into account any criteria prescribed by the regulations, or it forms part of a remnant area of native vegetation; or

(iii) it is an important habitat for native fauna taking into account any criteria prescribed by the regulations; or

(iv)   it satisfies any criteria prescribed by the regulations.[35]

There are similar requirements in relation to the listing of a stand of trees as significant trees.[36]

At the time of writing there are no relevant criteria prescribed by the Regulations. The owners of land where a proposed significant tree or stand of trees is situated must be given notice of the proposal to list the tree or stand of trees and the opportunity to make submissions on the amendment to the council within the period provided for public consultation under the regulations.[37] Obviously there is scope for such submissions to be prepared on the owner's behalf by their legal advisers and to incorporate expert advice in support of their submission.

9. Where a tree was declared to be a significant tree by virtue of a declaration in a Development Plan prior to the regulated trees provisions coming into force on 17 November 2011 that declaration continues under the

---

34   Development Act s 4.

35   Ibid s 23(4a)a.

36   Ibid s 23(4a)b.

37   Ibid s 25(12a).

new provisions until amended or revoked so that it no longer has effect in relation to that tree.[38] However, if a tree has measurements which are less than the minimum specified for a significant tree under the new provisions (that is, a circumference of 3 metres) and it has not been listed as significant in a development plan then from 17 November 2011, it will no longer be significant although it may be a regulated tree provided it meets the relevant criteria.

Listing trees as regulated or significant is only one element of the process. There also need to be criteria in place to enable planning authorities to determine when it is and is not appropriate to consent to development applications for tree-damaging activity to significant and regulated trees. There have been policies within development plans for the assessment of proposals for tree-damaging activities to significant trees since the provisions on significant trees were originally inserted into the Development Act in the year 2000. To support the legislative controls regarding regulated and significant trees, a ministerial Development Plan Amendment was prepared and released for public consultation on 17 November 2011.[39] At the same time in exercise of his powers under s 28(1) of the Development Act, the Minister declared that the Regulated Trees DPA would come into operation from 17 November 2011 on an interim basis. During the period of interim operation, public consultation on the amendment took place. The Regulated Trees DPA was finally authorised on 15 November 2012 without any apparent changes following the consultation process.[40]

The Regulated Trees DPA provides that the current planning policies applying to significant trees will remain in place. There will be additional policies that address the issue of tree removal and pruning in relation to regulated trees. With respect to significant trees, the current policies provide that significant trees should be preserved and tree-damaging activity should not be undertaken except in circumstances where:

(1) (i)   the tree is diseased and its life expectancy is short; or

(ii) the tree represents an unacceptable risk to public or private safety; or

(iii) the tree is within 20 metres of a residential, tourist accommodation or otherwise habitable building and is a bushfire hazard within the

---

[38] *Development (Regulated Trees) Amendment Act 2009* (SA) sch 1, -Transitional Provisions, cl 2.

[39] Minister for Planning (SA), above n 16.

[40] South Australia, *The South Australian Government Gazette*, No 75, 15 November 2012, 4971.

Bushfire Protection Area as shown in the relevant development plan or

(iv) the tree is shown to be causing or threatening to cause, substantial damage to a substantial building or structure of value; and all other reasonable remedial treatments and measures have been determined to be ineffective, and

(2) it is demonstrated that all reasonable alternative development options and design solutions have been considered to prevent substantial tree-damaging activity occurring.[41]

In addition, where the issue is not with tree removal itself but rather pruning or other similar tree-damaging activity, it is a requirement that 'the aesthetic appearance and structural integrity of the tree is maintained'.[42]

The Regulated Trees DPA contains criteria that in many respects mirror the planning criteria that had originally applied to significant trees. There is an emphasis on the balancing of development (presumably of the built form) and preservation of regulated trees. As would be expected, given the exclusion of many exotic trees from the controls, the focus is on preservation of regulated trees that are indigenous to the local area, of a rare or endangered species or provide an important habitat for native fauna. They are also important and warrant preservation if they significantly contribute to the character or visual amenity of the local area.[43]

As with the significant tree provisions, there is an expectation that a regulated tree should not be removed or damaged except in situations where one or more of the following circumstances apply:

1. If the tree is diseased or has a short life expectancy;

2. If the tree poses a material risk to public or private safety;

3. If the tree is causing damage to a building;

4. If the work is required for the removal of dead wood, treatment of disease, or is in the general interests of the health of the tree.[44]

---

[41] City of Burnside Development Plan Consolidation, 10 April 2012, Principle of Development Control ('PDC') 53 <http://www.sa.gov.au/upload/franchise/Housing,%20property%20and%20land/PLG/Online%20DPs/Greater%20metropolitan/Burnside_Council_Development_Plan.pdf>.

[42] City of Burnside Development Plan, above n 41, PDC 53(b)(v).

[43] Minister for Planning (SA), above n 16, Attachment A, Objective 2.

[44] Ibid app A, PDC 2.

However, there is a significant variation from the significant trees criteria in terms of when regulated trees can be removed or damaged in Principle of Development Control 2(d) in the new policy. It provides that removal or damage may be appropriate when 'development that is reasonable and expected would not otherwise be possible'. It is not clear what this means. There appear to be no objective criteria for determining what is 'reasonable' development. Nor does the policy explain by whom or what the development is expected. Perhaps it means development that the development plan expects within a particular zone or policy area. These would be extremely broad criteria. The policy as expressed gives planning authorities a very broad discretion as to when they authorise the removal or damage to a regulated tree. As such, the protection ultimately afforded to trees classified as regulated trees but not significant trees is arguably minimal.

V Expert/Technical Reports

In an attempt to reduce the costs for people making development applications in relation to trees, s 39 of the Development Act has been amended. Section 39(3a) provides that unless special circumstances apply, planning authorities should seek to make an assessment as to whether a tree is a significant tree without requesting an expert or technical report from the applicant in relation to the issue.[45] Further, s 39(3b) provides that unless special circumstances apply, a planning authority should assess an application that relates to a regulated tree that is not a significant tree without requesting the applicant to provide an expert or technical report. For significant trees expert reports may still be presumably sought by the planning authority where it considers it necessary.

VI Conditions of Consent

The recent amendments also incorporate provisions requiring that if the planning authority issues an authorisation providing for the killing, destruction or removal of a regulated tree or a significant tree it must attach conditions to the authorisation requiring the applicant to plant and maintain a prescribed number of trees in

---

[45] The qualifications of a person providing an expert or technical report within the contemplation of either s 39(3a) or (3b) is Certificate V in Horticulture (Arbour culture), or a comparable or higher qualification. See Development Regulations reg 117.

replacement. The cost of the trees and the planting is to be at the expense of the applicant or anyone who acquires the benefit of the consent, and the maintenance is the responsibility of the landowner.[46] An alternative is that the applicant pays a prescribed amount of money into a relevant fund in lieu of planting the trees.[47] At the time of writing, the relevant amount is $77.50 for each replacement tree that is not planted.[48] There are certain prescribed criteria which any replacement trees must meet, namely that they cannot be a tree within the species excluded from the regulated tree category by reg 6A(5)(b)[49] and they cannot be planted within 10 metres of an existing dwelling or existing in-ground swimming pool.[50] In terms of the number of replacement trees required for every tree removed, killed or destroyed there must be two replacement trees for every regulated tree and three replacement trees for every significant tree.[51]

There is also provision for an exemption from the requirements to plant a replacement tree or pay money in lieu of planting if the relevant tree is of a class excluded from the operation of those provisions or where the relevant authority has granted an exemption having taken into account any prescribed criteria and having obtained the Minister's concurrence.[52] At the time of writing there have been no criteria prescribed and it is in fact difficult to imagine when this exemption provision might be deemed appropriate.

However, quite clearly the requirement for a developer to replace regulated or significant trees with replacement trees will potentially restrict the way that land might be developed in the future. A person's right to do what they wish with their property is through these mechanisms being curtailed, arguably for the greater community benefit.

---

[46]   Development Act s 42(4).

[47]   Ibid s 42(6).

[48]   Development Regulations reg 117(4).

[49]   See the Appendix to this chapter.

[50]   Development Regulations reg 117(3).

[51]   Ibid reg 117(2).

[52]   Development Act s 42(8).

VII The Urban Trees Fund

As noted above, if an applicant elects to make a monetary contribution rather than plant replacement trees those funds have to be paid into the relevant fund. This fund will be either an urban trees fund set up by the relevant council for a designated area under s 50B of the Development Act, or the Planning and Development Fund,[53] in cases where a council does not have an urban trees fund or the planning authority is the Development Assessment Commission.[54] The funds are to be used to maintain or plant trees in the designated area which are or will when fully grown constitute significant trees under the Development Act or to purchase land within the designated area in order to maintain or plant trees which are or will (when fully grown) constitute significant trees.[55] Interestingly, unless the Council immediately declares via a Development Plan Amendment that the planted trees are significant trees they will not become regulated or significant until they reach the statutory size requirements. There does not seem to be any protection for those trees from tree-damaging activity until then, which is perhaps a deficiency in the overall scheme.

VIII Make Good Orders

The final point to make about the new provisions on regulated trees is that in relation to any finding by a court that a person has breached the Development Act by undertaking tree-damaging activity the court is empowered to order the person to make good their breach. Obviously they cannot literally make good their breach in the circumstances of tree removal, destruction or even pruning but they can be ordered to plant replacement trees in a place specified by the court, remove any buildings, works or vegetation that have been erected, undertaken or planted at or near the place where the regulated tree was situated since the breach occurred and to nurture, protect and maintain any replacement trees through to maturity.[56]

The Court can make such an order directed at a person who is not the owner or occupier of land and may authorise that person to enter the land to carry out the

---

53   Development Act pt 10.

54   Ibid s 42(7).

55   Ibid s 50B(6).

56   Ibid s 106A(1).

make good works.[57] However, the Court must endeavour to take reasonable steps to give notice of the relevant make good proceedings to the owner or occupier of the land, although the Development Act is silent on whether that person has the right to make any submissions in relation to the matter.[58]

Further, s 106A(6) clearly contemplates that the order may be registered against the title to the land but there is no indication of how that is to occur nor who can make that application. This is in contrast to the situation with land management agreements when the Act specifically provides that the application to the Registrar General can be made by a party to the agreement.[59] Whether it was thought that the charge provisions in s 107 of the Act would suffice is not clear but the make good orders are clearly not charges for the purpose of that provision. This is unsatisfactory, particularly given the provision in s 106A(5), which provides that an order under the section will cease to apply with respect to land if or when the land is sold to a genuine arms-length purchaser for value.

It is also worth noting that the Court has the power to vary or revoke the make good order[60] and that failure to comply with an order is an offence for which there is a maximum penalty of $60 000.[61] A failure to comply with the order is also contempt of the court.

IX Conclusion

As part of the South Australian Government's 30 Year Plan for Greater Adelaide there are a number of climate change policies, including Policy No 13:

> Create a more liveable urban environment through the establishment of a network of greenways, tree-lined streets and open spaces, which will have a cooling effect on nearby new neighbourhoods and new buildings.[62]

When reviewing the Regulated Trees DPA while it was still in the consultation phase the drafters of the development policy had to give consideration to how the Regulated Trees DPA dealt with this requirement. They said:

---

57 Ibid s 106A(4).

58 Ibid s 106A(3).

59 Ibid s 57(5).

60 Ibid s 106A(7).

61 Ibid s 106A(8).

62 Government of South Australia, Department of Planning and Local Government, above n 8, 140.

The DPA supports this policy by protecting trees that would be likely to have a tall height or large canopy. This in turn could result in an increased cooling effect in areas prone to the urban heat island effect. The legislation's allowance for the establishment of urban tree funds also facilitates the creation of designated areas (potentially greenways and open spaces) for the planting of replacement trees that will be legally protected.[63]

All the comments are correct; however, the Regulated Trees DPA also enables a greater number of urban trees to be removed, which cannot help to minimise the urban heat island effect. It contemplates replacement trees and while, in the longer term, those replacement trees once established will also help with mitigating the urban heat island effect, nevertheless there is a period of time after removal of the original trees during which the effect is likely to be more pronounced.

The changes to the significant trees controls have increased the complexity of the rules and requirements in this area of land use planning law. Somewhat ironically, despite that increased complexity, they afford less protection to trees in the urban landscape. In particular, many of the exotic trees commonly planted on the Adelaide plains and in the foothills are no longer protected by law. Upon perusing that list which is an appendix to this chapter it is readily apparent that some of the listed trees would be considered pests yet others, such as the London Plane tree, are a popular street tree planted by many metropolitan local government authorities. Many have been planted in the metropolitan area since the very early days of the founding of the South Australian colony. These trees currently make a significant contribution to the character and amenity of the Metropolitan Adelaide area as well as contributing to a reduction in the city's urban heat bank.

While in the longer-term, climate change adaptation requirements will require the planting of more climate- and water-sensitive indigenous trees and vegetation rather than exotic foreign species, there should still be protection mechanisms in place for such species for the time being. Under the new regulated trees provisions it will be easier to obtain development approval for the removal of many trees in that category. Without careful long-term management, the removal of a greater number of urban trees when accompanied by increased urban densities will result in a future metropolitan area that is warmer and less attractive. Perhaps the monies from the

---

63   Minister for Planning (SA), above n 16, 4.

urban trees funds will be used to try and redress some of these issues. It remains to be seen how successful they will be with that approach.

Preventing landowners from removing or even pruning trees on urban properties would be seen by many as a fairly significant curtailment of the traditional rights of a property owner. However. there are examples of other statutory mechanisms placing restrictions on how private property owners can deal with their land, such as zoning controls under land use planning laws and restrictions on demolition and alteration of buildings under heritage laws. Australian property owners nevertheless appear to accept such curtailment of their private property rights as restrictions that must arguably be borne for the overall benefit of the greater community, although in some circumstances the restrictions are accepted rather begrudgingly.

In terms of reducing energy use for artificial cooling of buildings and reducing the overall output of urban generated heat trees have a role to play. As such the regulatory controls and associated planning policies are a modest measure in the overall scheme of measures for mitigating and adapting to the effects of climate change.

Urban tree protection controls in South Australia were originally driven by a desire to protect habitat and for character and amenity reasons and not with the reduction of the urban heat island effect foremost in the minds of the legislators. However, with the increased awareness and knowledge of climate change and its predicted impacts, the role that urban trees play in moderating temperatures within urban areas and buildings has become increasingly apparent and accepted. When the South Australian government has put in place a unique set of regulatory controls to protect urban trees it seems a retrograde and unfortunate step for that government to now make major amendments to those controls, thereby facilitating a greater level of urban tree removal.

APPENDIX

List of Exotic Species which will not be treated as regulated trees even though they may meet the prescribed measurement criteria:[64]

- *Acer negundo* (Box Elder)
- *Acer saccharinum* (Silver Maple)
- *Ailanthus altissima* (Tree of heaven)
- *Alnus acuminate* subsp. *Glabrata* (Evergreen Alder)
- *Celtis australis* (European Nettle Tree)
- *Celtis sinensis* (Chinese Nettle Tree)
- *Cinnamomum camphora* (Camphor Laurel)
- *Cupressus macrocarpa* (Monterey Cypress)
- *Ficus* spp. (Figs), other than *Ficus macrophylla* (Moreton bay fig) located more than 15 metres from a dwelling
- *Fraxinus angustifolia* (Narrow-leaved Ash)
- *Fraxinus angustifolia* ssp. *Oxycarpa* (desert ash)
- *Pinus Radiata* (Radiata Pine/Monterey Pine)
- *Platanus x acerifolia* (London Plane)
- *Populus alba* (White poplar)
- *Populus nigra* var. *italica* (Lombardy Poplar)
- *Robinia pseudoacacia* (Black Locust)
- *Salix babylonica* (Weeping Willow)
- *Salix chilensis 'Fastigiata'* (Chilean Willow, Evergreen Willow, Pencil Willow)
- *Salix fragilis* (Crack Willow)
- *Salix x rubens* (White Crack Willow, Basket Willow)
- *Salix x sepulcralis* var. *chrysocoma* (Golden Weeping Willow)
- *Schinus areira* (Peppercorn Tree)

---

[64] Development Regulations reg 6A(5)(b).

3

A ROLE FOR INTERNATIONAL LAW IN ACHIEVING A GENDER AWARE ENERGY POLICY

JUDITH GARDAM

I INTRODUCTION

It is one of the most significant insights of Adrian Bradbrook's work that he was the first legal expert to recognise the connection between access to modern energy services for domestic and personal use and poverty and to incorporate it in his research and writing. In doing so he has been instrumental in highlighting the fact that law, both national and international, has something to offer to the process of achieving progress on this issue. In this chapter I focus on one aspect of Bradbrook's wide-ranging work on access to modern energy services — namely, establishing a role for international law, in particular international human rights law, in the energy poverty debate. I choose this focus, representing as it does only a small part of his considerable published work in the field of energy, because we worked together on this topic and it is one I am familiar with. Moreover, it was whilst working in this area that it became apparent to me that the topic of women, gender and energy is neglected in mainstream accounts. I therefore build on Bradbrook's advocacy role for law and energy and the legal strategies that he has so creatively identified over the years and consider what international law can offer as a strategy for creating and implementing a gender aware energy policy.

II   Energy and Poverty

Although the connection between development and energy has long been accepted, the link between access to modern energy services and poverty was slow to be recognised.[1] There is nowadays worldwide recognition, albeit belated, that energy belongs at the forefront of the debate on the eradication of poverty.[2] The Millennium Development Goals ('MDG's), declared by the United Nations General Assembly in the *United Nations Millennium Declaration* in 2000,[3] make no mention of energy. However, as the UN Secretary General recognised in 2011, the reality is that the universal access to modern energy services is fundamental to the realisation of all the stated goals: eradicating extreme poverty and hunger; achieving universal primary education; promoting gender equality and empowering women; reducing child mortality; improving maternal health; combating HIV/AIDS, malaria and other diseases; ensuring environmental sustainability; and developing a global partnership for development.[4] The Rio+20 2012 Conference outcome document also recognises the connection between access to affordable energy and the eradication of poverty.[5]

---

[1]   See Joy Clancy et al, *Gender Equity in Access to and Benefits from Modern Energy and Improved Energy Technologies: World Development Report Background Paper* (ETC Nederland BV, 2011) 3.

[2]   See, eg, José Goldemberg and Thomas B Johansson (eds) *World Energy Assessment Overview: 2004 Update* (United Nations Development Programme, 2004) 18; Gail V Karlsson (ed), *Generating Opportunities: Case Studies on Energy and Women* (United Nations Development Programme, 2001) 7; Adrian J Bradbrook and Judith G Gardam, 'Placing Access to Energy Services within a Human Rights Framework' (2006) 28 *Human Rights Quarterly* 389; Adrian J Bradbrook, Judith G Gardam and Monique Cormier, 'A Human Dimension to the Energy Debate: Access to Modern Energy Services' (2008) 26 *Journal of Energy & Natural Resources Law* 526. For a discussion of the various measures of poverty, see Goldemberg and Johansson, above n 2, 43-4.

[3]   GA Res 55/2, UN GAOR, 55th sess, 8th plen mtg, Agenda Item 60(b), Supp No 49, UN Doc A/RES/55/2 (18 September 2000).

[4]   *Sustainable Energy for All: A Vision Statement by Ban-ki Moon Secretary General of the United Nations* (United Nations, 2011) and see International Energy Agency ('IEA'), *Energy Poverty: How to Make Modern Energy Access Universal? Special Early Excerpt of the World Energy Outlook 2010 for the UN General Assembly on the Millennium Development Goals* (International Energy Agency, 2010) 8, 16 ('*How to Make Modern Energy Access Universal?*').

[5]   See United Nations Conference on Sustainable Development Rio+20, *The Future We Want*, UN Doc A/CONF.216/L.1 (19 June 2012) [125]-[129] ('*The Future We Want*').

What are the facts in relation to access to modern energy services for domestic use? One out of every five people on earth lives without access to electricity, some 85 per cent of them in rural areas.[6] The problem is almost exclusively one of developing countries primarily in South Asia and Sub-Saharan Africa — the latter posing the greatest challenge, with only 13 per cent of the population having access to electricity.[7] Indeed the whole of Sub-Saharan Africa excluding South Africa uses approximately the same annual amount of electricity for residential purposes as New York State.[8] Consequently the majority of the population of most developing countries do not have available to them electric lighting, clean cooking facilities, modern, efficient and non-polluting fuel supplies or adequate clean water and sanitation systems, and must rely on traditional energy sources for their basic needs such as cooking.[9] Nearly 3 billion people worldwide rely on biomass fuels such as wood, coal, charcoal or animal waste to cook their meals and heat their homes, exposing themselves and their families to smoke and fumes which damage their health and lead to the premature death of some 1.45 million people a year, primarily women and children.[10] Unless there is fundamental change, this situation will deteriorate rather than improve over the next 20 years.[11]

III   THE PLACE OF LAW IN THE DEBATE

Here was a fertile field and a new challenge for a legal academic who had already distinguished himself in the field of renewable energy — namely, to consider the possible contribution of law to addressing the human dimensions of the energy debate. But it was a slow and difficult process and Bradbrook was frequently discouraged by the lack of interest shown by his colleagues working in the energy field, particularly in

---

[6]   Ibid [125].

[7]   Gunnar Köhlin et al (eds), *Energy, Gender and Development: What are the Linkages? Where is the Evidence? Policy Research Working paper 5800: Background Paper to the 2012 World Development Report* (World Bank, 2011) 2.

[8]   *Sustainable Energy for All*, above n 4; *How to Make Modern Energy Access Universal?*, above n 4.

[9]   *How to Make Modern Energy Access Universal?*, above n 4, 11. Note that a further 2 billion people are severely under-supplied in energy: WEHAB Working Group, *A Framework for Action on Energy* (Working Group report prepared for the World Summit on Sustainable Development) (WEHAB Working Group, 2002) 7.

[10]   *How to Make Modern Energy Access Universal?*, above n 4, 13.

[11]   Ibid 8-9.

Australia, as to the possibility that law had an integral role to play in the achievement of their goals. This is despite the fact that there is a clearly identified lack of regulatory and legal frameworks for the energy industry generally, especially in relation to access issues, in many less developed states.[12]

It is a common perception amongst non-lawyers and indeed amongst lawyers themselves that law performs a narrow range of functions in society, primarily regulatory. In fact, as Bradbrook has ably demonstrated in many aspects of his work, law can serve also as an educational and stimulatory tool.[13] Legislation mandating the display of the efficiency rating in terms of water and power of domestic appliances is an apt example of the former and the use of taxes to encourage certain types of behaviour in the marketplace is an example of the latter. Indeed, the World Bank has stressed the importance of public awareness campaigns and education to achieving successful household energy programs in the developing world.[14] Legislation could be a part of such a program.

Even more of a barrier to realising law's potential as an agent of change is the lack of understanding as to what can be achieved by international law. At one extreme there are those who doubt whether international law is law at all. Even amongst those who recognise such a system as law, many do not see its relevance to energy issues. For them the solution to access to modern energy services lies in the purely domestic or national sphere — international law has nothing to offer. A little reflection demonstrates that this is not the case and to make the point a parallel can be drawn between access to modern energy services and climate change. The latter is a phenomenon that arises from the activities that states pursue within their own national boundaries, and consequently requires national action to confront its causes. States nevertheless have recognised that international law is part of the

---

[12] See, eg, Vijay Modi et al, *Energy Services for the Millennium Development Goals*, (The International Bank for Reconstruction and Development/The World Bank and the United Nations Development Programme, 2005) 66.

[13] See, eg, Adrian J Bradbrook, *Solar Energy and the Law* (Law Book, 1984); Adrian J Bradbrook, 'Energy Law as an Academic Discipline' (1996) 14 *Journal of Energy & Natural Resources Law* 193; 'Solar Access Law: 30 Years On' 27 *Environmental and Planning Law Journal* 5 (2010) and Adrian Bradbrook 'Drafting a New International Convention on Energy Efficiency and Renewable Energy', in Peter Catania, Brian Golchert and Chenn Q Zhou (eds), *Energy 2000: The Beginning of a New Millennium* (Technomic Publishing; Balaban International Science Publishers, 2000) 1105.

[14] See World Bank, 'Household Energy Access for Cooking and Heating: Lessons Learned and the Way Forward' (Energy and Mining Sector Board Discussion Paper, Paper No 23, 2011) x-xi.

solution to addressing climate change and, what is more, have been prepared to adopt mandatory legal constraints on their freedom of action in order to achieve progress.[15] Admittedly, the consequences of climate change are global and affect developed states as well as those less developed states. No doubt, self-interest is a major factor in the international legal strategies that have been adopted by states. Unfortunately, although access to modern energy services and poverty are properly seen as global issues, there is not the same motivation for developed states to be proactive in finding solutions. In such circumstances international action becomes even more important. An international legal instrument can be specifically designed, for example, to advance the goal of universal access to modern energy services by encouraging less developed states not only to adopt domestic law and policies to achieve such an end but also to encourage developed states to assist in this process through such initiatives as technology transfer.[16] Obviously, progress on issues such as access to modern energy services requires a concerted, sustained and co-ordinated campaign from a wide range of actors, both national and international, to have any prospect of success. Law, however, should take its place as an integral partner in this process.

Some years ago, Bradbrook and I were discussing whether there might be another way of approaching this challenge of demonstrating to his colleagues in what way law might be an effective agent of change in the energy field. We agreed that perhaps international human rights law might have some potential to frame the debate in a somewhat different way. The reasoning behind this approach was not that this was in any way a comprehensive solution to all the difficulties but that conceptualising the debate as one of human rights might capture the imagination in the way that other areas of law both national and international do not. Not to put too fine a point on it, human rights not only enjoy a high profile but also their basic precepts are familiar to all. Since the adoption of the UN Charter in 1945, the protection and realisation of human rights has slowly and inexorably moved to the centre stage of the aspirations of the UN and the international community

---

[15] See *Kyoto Protocol to the United Nations Framework Convention on Climate Change*, opened for signature 11 December 1997, 2303 UNTS 148 (entered into force 16 February 2005).

[16] See, eg, art 4.5 of the 1992 *United Nations Framework Convention on Climate Change*, which requires developed countries to 'take all practicable steps to promote, facilitate and finance, as appropriate, the transfer of, or access to environmentally sound technologies and know-how to other Parties, particularly developing country parties to enable them to implement the provisions of the Convention'; see also *The Future We Want*, above n 5, [73].

generally. Many disparate areas of human enterprise are now being seen as allied with the need to promote human rights, and the interrelationship between sustainable development, the environment and human rights is already well established in the international arena.[17] It seemed worth considering the potential of such a strategy as a way to circumvent existing obstacles to achieving more equitable access to energy services on a worldwide scale. In particular, by adopting the language of human rights, pressure could be brought to bear at the national and international level for recognition of access to energy services as integral to the realisation of the vast bulk of socio-economic rights contained in the 1966 *International Covenant on Economic, Social and Cultural Rights*.[18]

Bradbrook's work over the years has always demonstrated his ability to think innovatively, so he was more than willing to look at a new approach. We subsequently wrote in some detail about the possibility that access to modern energy services could be viewed as part of the human rights regime. Our most recent paper was basically a law reform project in which we stepped outside a specifically human rights context and drafted a general international instrument entitled *Governing Principles on Ensuring Access to Modern Energy Services*.[19] The idea behind this document was to develop a prototype of the steps that could be taken by a range of international actors to achieve progress in this issue. I return to this idea later in the context of gender and access to modern energy services.

It is somewhat premature to determine to what extent the linking of access to modern energy services with human rights will bear fruit, but what is clear is that the climate change debate has led to a greater focus on access to modern energy services and poverty in the context of sustainable energy.[20] It is increasingly recognised that existing fuel used in less developed states, such as fuel woods for cooking and heating, significantly contributes to climate change.[21] In addition, less developed states are

---

[17] See, eg, *Human Rights and the Environment: Rio+20: Joint Report OHCHR and UNEP* (2012).

[18] Opened for signature 16 December 1966, 993 UNTS 3 (entered into force 3 January 1976). For an in-depth examination of the link between access to modern energy services and the realisation of socio-economic rights see Bradbrook and Gardam, above n 2, 405-7.

[19] See Adrian J Bradbrook and Judith G Gardam 'Energy and Poverty: Harnessing International Law to Advance Universal Access to Modern Energy Services' (2010) 57 *Netherlands International Law Review* 1.

[20] *The Future We Want*, above n 5, [128].

[21] World Bank, 'Household Energy Access for Cooking and Heating: Lessons Learned and the Way

understandably not too choosy when it comes to the sources of energy they rely on for development. Indeed, renewable energy for domestic use, such as solar power, is sometimes perceived as somehow second-best to energy delivered in more traditional ways.[22] It is nevertheless crucial that the international community takes steps to achieve a sustainable energy future, and addressing poverty and access to energy services is part of the picture. In response to these pressing concerns, the UN General Assembly declared 2012 the year of Sustainable Energy for All.[23] This initiative aims to encourage states to achieve three main objectives by 2030: ensuring universal access to modern energy services, doubling the global rate of improvement in energy efficiency and doubling the share of renewable energy in the global energy mix.[24]

One area of access to modern energy services and poverty which has been particularly slow in gaining recognition is the issue of women, gender and access to modern energy services. The 1995 Beijing Conference on Women and its Platform for Action surprisingly made no mention of women and energy.[25] There were those, however, who were well aware of the link between gender, energy and poverty and the topic slowly became an aspect of the campaign to achieve gender equality, women's empowerment and progress in eradicating poverty. Nowadays, there is an impressive range of initiatives, both at the national and international level, which focus on this question.[26] There is also recognition of the integral role of access to modern energy services in achieving the MDGs of promoting gender equality and

---

Forward' (Energy and Mining Sector Board Discussion Paper, Paper No 23, 2011) ix.

[22] Comments by Yinka Omorogbe at Symposium on Energy and Climate Change Law, Faculty of Law, University of Copenhagen, Denmark, 28 April 2008. For further discussion of behavioural issues associated with energy, see, eg, Willett Kempton and Max Neiman (eds), *Energy Efficiency: Perspectives on Individual Behaviour* (American Council for an Energy-Efficient Economy, 1987).

[23] *International Year of Sustainable Development for All*, GA Res 65/151, UN GAOR, 2nd Comm, 65th sess, 69th plen mtg, Agenda Item 20, Supp No 49, UN Doc A/RES/65/151 (16 February 2011).

[24] See The Secretary-General's High-level Group on Sustainable Energy for All, *Sustainable Energy for All: A Framework for Action* (The Secretary-General's High-level Group on Sustainable Energy for All, 2012).

[25] *Report of the Fourth World Conference on Women, Action for Equality, Development and Peace, Beijing Declaration and Platform for Action*, Beijing, 4-15 December 1995, UN Doc A/CONF.177/20 (27 October 1995).

[26] See, eg, ENERGIA, an international network on gender and sustainable energy, founded in 1996 shortly after the Beijing Conference, whose focus is the empowerment of women and engendering energy to achieve sustainable development: <http://www.energia.org/nl/home>.

empowering women.[27] In fact, there is a close connection between gender, energy and the realisation of all the MDGs.[28] Law, however, remains on the sidelines.

IV THE GENDERED FACE OF ENERGY POVERTY

What do we mean when we speak of gender? According to a World Bank definition, 'Gender refers to the social, behavioral, and cultural attributes, expectations, and norms associated with being a woman or a man'.[29] The term 'gender' is distinct from sex, which is based on the biological differences between men and women.[30] Gender roles are by no means universal or immutable and may differ widely amongst societies. To further complicate this picture, gender also intersects with a number of other categories such as age, class, race or ethnicity. Consequently, analyses that focus on gender require careful, contextualised and nuanced methodology if they are to provide useful information.

With respect to gender and energy, Clancy et al encapsulate it well when they write that '[t]he gendered dimensions of energy are embedded in the gender division of labour, and energy needs reflect gender roles'.[31] Consequently, men and women experience the lack of access to modern energy services differently and this experience is determined by their gendered societal roles.[32] For a start, it is estimated that 70 per cent of the approximately 1.3 billion people living in poverty are women, many

---

[27] See, eg, Soma Dutta et al, 'Empirical Evidence for Linkages: Energy, Gender and the MDGs' (2005) 8 *ENERGIA News* 6; Caroline Sweetman (ed), *Gender And The Millennium Development Goals* (Oxfam, 2005); ECLAC (UN Economic Commission for Latin America), *Contribution of Energy Services to the Millennium Development Goals and to Poverty Alleviation in Latin America and the Caribbean* (January 2010). See also *The Future We Want*, above n 5, 15.

[28] Ines Havet, 'Linking Women and Energy at the Local Level to Global Goals and Targets' (2003) 7 *Energy for Sustainable Development* 75, 76-8.

[29] World Bank, *World Development Report* (World Bank, 2012) 4.

[30] Feminist scholars are far from unanimous on the 'naturalness' of the category of sex, see, eg, Margaret Davies, 'Taking the Inside Out: Sex and Gender in the Legal Subject' in Ngaire Naffine and Rosemary J Owens (eds), *Sexing the Subject of Law* (LBC Information Services, 1997) 25, 27.

[31] See Joy Clancy et al, 'Appropriate Gender-analysis Tools for Unpacking the Gender-energy-poverty nexus' (2007) 15(2) *Gender & Development* 241, 242.

[32] See, eg, Elizabeth Cecelski, *Gender Perspectives on Energy for CSD 9: Draft Position Paper Including Recommendations Proposed by the ENERGIA Support Group And The CSD NGO Women's Caucus* (2000) 3; Clancy et al, above n 1.

of whom live in female-headed households in rural areas.[33] Since women generally have less access to resources and decision-making than men, many of these households are characterised by extreme energy poverty. Part of the challenge to obtaining a clear picture of how gender intersects with energy is the lack of available data. According to one recent study, drawing generalised conclusions from what information there is on hand is a risky process.[34] Not only are there considerable relevant differences in gender roles within the various energy-poor societies, but also very little of the available data focuses on such differences. In other words, gender disaggregated information is the exception rather than the rule. Within these limitations the following general trends have been observed.

Because of their gender roles, women and girls assume a higher proportion of the burden of unavailable energy services and inefficient energy use.[35] In energy-poor societies, women and girls are primarily responsible for the provision of fuel for cooking and heating.[36] Consequently, without such energy services they are forced to spend a significant amount of time searching for and collecting fuel.[37] This is back-breaking and exhausting work that can lead to long-term physical problems. Women and girls are at increased risk of sexual assault during these times and are exposed to other hazards such as snake-bites.[38] These risks increase the further women are forced to walk. They are also the primary users of traditional fuels for cooking purposes and thus along with children experience a higher level of respiratory disease from indoor pollution than men.[39] The same situation applies to water, with women traditionally being responsible for ensuring the water supply for the household needs.[40] The absence of energy for water pumps substantially increases the time spent on such activities.[41]

---

[33]   Beatrice Khamati-Njenga and Joy Clancy, *Concepts and Issues in Gender and Energy* (2002) 35.

[34]   Ibid 6. See also Clancy et al, above n 1; Clancy et al, above n 31, 243-4.

[35]   Jyoti Parikh and Saudamini Sharma, *Mainstreaming Gender in Energy Policy*, Integrated Research and Action for Development.

[36]   But not exclusively, see World Bank, 'Energy, Gender and Development: What are the Linkages? Where is the Evidence?' (Background Paper to the 2012 World Development Report, Policy Research Working Paper 5800, September 2011) 5.

[37]   See *How to Make Modern Energy Access Universal?*, above n 4, 14.

[38]   See United Nations Development Programme ('UNDP'), *Gender & Energy for Sustainable Development: A Toolkit and Resource Guide* (United Nations Development Programme, 2004) 9.

[39]   World Bank, above n 36, 1, 3.

[40]   Ibid 5.

[41]   UNDP, above n 38, 14.

A significant consequence of the time spent in the acquisition of fuel and water is that it prevents women from engaging in income-producing and community activities and from improving their levels of education.[42] It is these opportunities that hold the real promise of empowering women and altering existing unequal gender relations.

Women also experience discrimination in national policy decisions as to allocation of scarce energy resources.[43] The supply of energy is assumed to be gender neutral and to equally benefit both men and women, but this is far from the reality.[44] ENERGIA describes energy policy as in fact 'gender blind', in that many issues that are relevant to women are overlooked, with the ensuing policy frequently discriminating against women.[45] For example, electrification projects have been directed to activities that are of more benefit to men, and in some cases children, rather than the provision of modern cooking fuels and appliances.[46]

In light of these distinctive gender patterns of energy poverty, what has been the response at the international level? One may have expected more in the way of the recognition of the link between modern energy services, women and poverty from international initiatives such as the Beijing Platform for Action from the Fourth UN World Conference on Women in Beijing in 1995.[47] As I mentioned earlier, the Platform makes no mention of gender and energy despite the central role it plays in the realisation of the vast majority of economic and social rights which are of such significance for advancing the position of women worldwide.[48] The MDGs continue this pattern of by-passing the issues of gender and energy. In 2012, however, the

---

[42] Karlsson, above n 2, 9.

[43] See ibid 10; Daniel Theuri, 'Access to Modern Energy Services: The Gender Face of Energy Technologies' (2007) 10(1) *Energia* 16.

[44] See Clancy et al, above n 31, 242-3.

[45] Joy Clancy and Mariëlle Feenstra, *How to Engender Energy Policy* (ENERGIA Technical Briefing Paper, December 2006) 7; see Goldemberg and Johansson, above n 2, 47-8.

[46] See UNDP, above n 38, 10 (pointing out that projects involving the supply of solar home systems tend to improve the quality of life primarily for men and in some cases children by providing illumination and entertainment but are not sufficient for energy for cooking). See also Clancy and Feenstra, above n 45.

[47] See *Report of the Fourth World Conference on Women, Action for Equality Development and Peace, Beijing Declaration and Platform for Action*, Beijing 4-15 December 1995, UN Doc. A/CONF.177/20 (27 October 1995).

[48] See Clancy et al, above n 31, 241.

Rio+20 Outcome document finally links the issues of energy, gender equality and the eradication of poverty.[49]

Despite the silence of the Beijing Platform on gender and energy, one of the major international strategies adopted for achieving equality and the empowerment of women within the Critical Areas of Concern identified in the Platform has considerable potential for women and energy, particularly in the context of energy allocation. I refer here to the process of gender mainstreaming:[50]

> Mainstreaming a gender perspective is the process of assessing the implications for women and men of any planned action, including legislation, policies or programmes, in any area and at all levels. It is a strategy for making women's as well as men's concerns and experiences an integral dimension in the design, implementation, monitoring and evaluation of policies and programmes in all political, economic and societal spheres so that women and men benefit equally and inequality is not perpetuated. The ultimate goal is to achieve gender equality.[51]

Gender mainstreaming is thus focused on the actual impact of policies and so on — on men and women — rather than ensuring formal equality and non-discrimination.

Charlesworth distinguishes between the practice of 'gender mainstreaming' and what she describes as 'gender sidestreaming', thus capturing a perennial dilemma for feminist international lawyers.[52] Are women's concerns better addressed by general laws that may sacrifice their perspectives in favour of what are perceived as more pressing global issues or by special laws, thereby running the risk of marginalisation as women's issues? Neither approach is a panacea but gender mainstreaming has come to dominate within international institutions. For example, the landmark Security Council Resolution 1325 on Women, Peace and Security relies on mainstreaming policies to implement its reforms.[53] What exactly has been achieved by this strategy

---

[49] *The Future We Want*, above n 5, 125-6.

[50] For an explanation and history of the concept of gender mainstreaming, see Hilary Charlesworth, 'Not Waving but Drowning: Gender Mainstreaming and Human Rights in the United Nations' (2005) 18 *Harvard Human Rights Journal* 1.

[51] *Report of the Economic and Social Council for 1997*, UN GAOR, 52nd sess, UN Doc A/52/3/Rev.1 (18 September 1997) 24.

[52] See Charlesworth, above n 50.

[53] SC Res 1325, UN SCOR, 4213th mtg, UN Doc S/RES/1325 (31 October 2000).

is another matter and there appears to be more form than substance to many gender mainstreaming initiatives.[54]

Some argue that gender mainstreaming has had some success in areas such as health and education; however, there is widespread agreement that it has had little impact in the energy sector.[55] The energy industry is one which is particularly male-dominated and it has proved difficult to persuade economists and engineers, who dominate the industry, that gender is a factor that needs consideration when assessing what policies and processes should be adopted.[56] If one adds to this the endemic inability of women in society generally to make their voice heard in the public sphere, the failure of gender to influence the energy sector is not surprising.[57]

To summarise, gender and energy are now a recognised though somewhat peripheral aspect of the international focus on poverty, energy, climate change and sustainable development. But how do we advance beyond aspirations and achieve concrete outcomes in terms of gender equality and empowerment of women in the energy field? Access to modern energy services is not a remedy in itself for achieving development for women. As long as access to such services remains gender neutral and fails to reflect the different energy needs of men and women, it will not lead directly to the empowerment of women. For example, providing clean cooking facilities certainly benefits women, in that they no longer suffer the health ill-effects of dirty fuel and long hours spent in its collection. But studies have shown that the free time thereby made available is spent on further domestic duties rather than pursuing education or economic activities that could fundamentally transform their lives. Similarly, electricity supplies are primarily used in many instances for television viewing and social activities for men, and the provision of lighting results in women once again undertaking further domestic tasks in the evening. There is agreement amongst commentators that the emphasis should be placed on supplying energy in

---

[54] See Charlesworth, above n 50 (discussing the impact of gender mainstreaming in the human rights system) and see A Barrow, '"[It's] like a rubber band". Assessing UNSCR 1325 as a gender mainstreaming process' (2009) 5(1) *International Journal of Law in Context* 51.

[55] See Joy Clancy, *Late Developers: Gender Mainstreaming in the Energy Sector* (UKDSA Annual Conference, Colerain, 2-4 September 2009) 2-4.

[56] Ibid 2; See also ENERGIA/DfID Collaborative Research Group on Gender and Energy (CRGGE), *From the Millennium Development Goals towards a Gender-Sensitive Energy Policy Research and Practice: Empirical Evidence and Case Studies: Synthesis Report* (ENERGIA/DfID Collaborative Research Group on Gender and Energy, 2006) ix.

[57] See, eg, Clancy et al, above n 31, 243-4.

ways that allows women to use the increased energy resources for education and for freeing them up from work within the home rather than increasing the time they may have available in the evening for home duties.[58]

There are some who have taken up the challenge of identifying how energy can contribute to achieving the MDGs of the empowerment of women and lead to fundamental change in their gendered roles in society. Anneke, for example, has identified what she regards as the components of a gender sensitive energy policy as follows: access, affordability, availability, security/safety and sustainability. All of these seemingly neutral factors need to be assessed from a gender perspective. Clancy et al go further and analyse which energy interventions will merely decrease the time burden and adverse health effects on women from lack of energy and which have the potential to alter gender relations. For example, the provision of better stoves and lighting in work areas, as we have seen, will improve women's health and alleviate the drudgery of their everyday tasks, but it will not serve to empower them or lead to fundamental change in their social position. However, including women in the decision-making as to how energy is to be introduced into the community could lead, for example, to the provision of street lighting. Such an initiative can facilitate women's evening meetings and has the promise of changing gender roles.[59]

V A ROLE FOR LAW

The ideas outlined above are all in their own way promising initiatives, but my final step is to reflect a little on how law, in this case international law, might usefully be incorporated into the gender and energy project. Among the few international law instruments that specifically refer to energy in the context of overcoming poverty is in fact the specialist Women's Convention, the 1979 *Convention on the Elimination of All Forms of Discrimination against Women* ('CEDAW').[60] Article 14(2)(h) of this Convention obliges state parties to eliminate discrimination against women, particularly in rural areas, and to ensure that they 'enjoy adequate living conditions, particularly in relation to housing, sanitation, electricity and water supply, transport

---

[58] See, eg, Commission on the Status of Women, *Report on the 54th session* (13 March and 14 October 2009 and 1-12 March 2010) UN ESCOR Supp No. 7, UN Doc E/2010/27 (6 May 2010) Resolution 54/4: Women's economic empowerment.

[59] See Clancy et al, above n 31, 247.

[60] Opened for signature 18 December 1979, 1249 UNTS 13 (entered into force 3 September 1981).

and communication'. The express recognition of electricity as a requirement for adequate living conditions is an acknowledgment of the unfair burden traditionally placed on women in developing countries by the lack of access to modern energy services.[61]

Governments are required to submit reports on measures taken to implement the provisions of CEDAW to the Committee on the Elimination of Discrimination against Women.[62] In the past, the Committee has commended Nigeria 'for improving rural women's access to drinking water and electricity'[63] and praised such countries as Bosnia and Herzegovina,[64] and Trinidad and Tobago,[65] for implementing training programmes in electrical installation and maintenance specifically targeted at women.

Apart from this instrument, there is a deafening silence in the increasing international initiatives on gender and energy as to law being part of the equation. There is acceptance that women's empowerment generally can be facilitated by law as, for example, through the enactment of equal rights and non-discrimination legislation — but equality legislation, although important, will not change gender relations.[66] To take just one example in the present context, legislating that women should have equal access to available energy sources takes no account of the fact that what energy is available may not be useful for their purposes, as their energy needs are distinct from those of men. In addition, female-headed households traditionally have less economic resources than male-headed households, so it achieves little to make available to them resources that they cannot afford.

The failure to consider the broader potential of law in the context of women and energy mirrors that identified by Adrian Bradbrook in relation to energy generally. Why is it that the numerous energy policy research projects and initiatives

---

[61]   John Scanlon, Angela Cassar and Noémi Nemes, 'Water as a Human Right' (IUCN Environmental Policy and Law Paper No 51, IUCN, Gland, 2004) 6.

[62]   See art 19 of CEDAW.

[63]   Committee on the Elimination of Discrimination Against Women, *Report of the Eighteenth & Nineteenth Sessions*, UN GAOR, 53rd sess, Supp No 38, UN Doc A/53/38/Rev.1 (14 May 1998) 62 [152].

[64]   Committee on the Elimination of Discrimination Against Women, *Report of the Thirteenth Session*, UN GAOR, 49th sess, Supp No 38, UN Doc A/49/38 (12 April 1994) 128 [743].

[65]   Committee on the Elimination of Discrimination Against Women, *Report of the Committee on Elimination of Discrimination Against Women*, UN GAOR 57th sess, Supp No 38, UN Doc A/57/38 (2 May 2002) pt 1, 20 [128].

[66]   See, eg, Clancy et al, above n 1, 8; Clancy and Feenstra, above n 45, 3.

on gender never envisage law as a component of implementing their policies? There are no ready answers to this question, but in my view a useful contribution to the debate would be through the vehicle of an international law instrument. Nowadays there is a wide and diverse range of international law-making instruments that could be adopted for such a purpose.[67] All have their strengths and weaknesses. They range from binding instruments such as treaties and Security Council resolutions to so-called soft law instruments, a term used to describe 'a variety of non-legally binding instruments used in contemporary international relations'.[68] Such instruments include General Assembly resolutions, resolutions of international conferences of states and intergovernmental organisations, statements of principles, codes of conduct and guidelines of international organisations. Soft law instruments are particularly useful when the subject in question is one about which there may be considerable difficulty in reaching consensus amongst states. Such a topic as gender and access to modern energy services is a case in point. Issues of gender inevitably provoke considerable tensions amongst various actors, as illustrated by the debate over the definition of gender in the 1998 Statute of the International Criminal Court.[69]

The provisions of such an instrument could take those components of a gender sensitive energy policy identified by writers such as Anneke and Clancy and develop their detailed application in a legal framework. Stakeholders at both the international and national level would then have available to them a roadmap for moving towards gender aware laws and policies in the energy field.

VI Conclusion

On reflection, it appears that the major challenge in relation to gender and energy is to convince those in charge of energy policy and decision-making that there is in fact a problem and that the energy needs of women and men differ and need to be

---

[67]   See generally Alan Boyle and Christine Chinkin, *The Making of International Law* (Oxford University Press, 2007), 104-8, 210-60 (for a comprehensive discussion of international legal instruments and how they evolve into international law).

[68]   Ibid 212-13 (for a description of the wide range of instruments and bodies which contribute towards the category of soft law), 216-29 (explaining how soft law instruments facilitate the evolution of international law).

[69]   See, eg, Valerie Oosterveldt, 'The Definition of "Gender" in the Rome Statute of the International Criminal Court: A Step Forward or Back for International Criminal Justice' (2005) 18 *Harvard Human Rights Journal* 55.

acknowledged in the implementation of programmes and policies. Women's voices can all too readily be lost in the push for progress in achieving access to modern energy services. All too frequently, the response to calls to consider gender is that this is an issue that can be sorted out at a later date. Accordingly, many will argue that the priority in this context must be to establish the energy services in the first place. But in fact once decisions are made as to the means and methods of supply of energy, and once the infrastructure and so on is put in place, it is too late in many cases to make the fundamental changes that might be needed to better reflect the respective needs of men and women in terms of energy access. A legal template could be one way to draw attention at the planning stage to the factors that have a gender component — and could make it more likely that access to modern energy services is achieved on an equitable gender basis.

4

ENERGY EFFICIENCY AND RENTAL ACCOMODATION: DEALING WITH SPLIT INCENTIVES

BARRY BARTON

Energy law and energy policy, to which Adrian Bradbrook has contributed so much, are significant for several reasons. The first reason, very relevant to the concern of this chapter, is to meet human needs. In New Zealand dwelling-houses are often colder than international standards stipulate,[1] and that causes health problems, especially for the young, the old and other vulnerable members of the population. The second main reason is the significant adverse effect on the environment of the production of energy and its use. The third reason is climate change; energy production is the main source of greenhouse gas emissions.[2]

---

[1] Nigel Isaacs et al, 'Energy in New Zealand Houses: Comfort, Physics and Consumption' (2010) 38 *Building Research & Information* 470.

[2] The drivers of government energy efficiency policies have recently been summarised under the headings of: energy security, economic development and competitiveness, climate change, and public health. Sara Pasquier and Aurelien Saussay, *Progress Implementing the IEA 25 Energy Efficiency Policy Recommendations: 2011 Evaluation* (OECD/IEA Insights Series, 2012) 13. Another good recent explanation of the various rationales of energy efficiency action generally is Lisa Ryan and Nina Campbell, *Spreading the Net: The Multiple Benefits of Energy Efficiency Improvements*, 2nd ed (OECD/IEA Insights Series, 2012) 14.

While energy law and policy can focus on change in the way that energy is supplied, such as by increasing renewable energy supplies, the demand side requires much more attention; in fact, the demand side, including energy efficiency, is where the big gains are to be made. In climate change terms, this important truth has been demonstrated by comprehensive studies by the International Energy Agency in its annual *World Energy Outlook*.[3] It estimates that if governments worldwide put in place policies to stabilise atmospheric concentrations of carbon dioxide at 450 parts per million, then 57 per cent of the change would come from energy efficiency measures. Another study shows that the most cost-effective technologies to reduce greenhouse gas emissions are efficiency measures; in fact, many efficiency measures have a negative cost.[4] The key message is that energy efficiency is more important, and more possible, than technologies and policy measures on the supply side.

Energy efficiency is a ratio of function, service or value provided to the energy converted to provide it.[5] One would think that people would invest to increase the energy efficiency of their houses, cars and industries, but the record is that people often fail to make such investments that appear to be rationally justified. This phenomenon, which is spread widely through society and economy, is the 'energy efficiency gap' — a series of barriers that inhibit investment.[6] A number of barriers can be identified: information gaps, averseness to risk and the presence of multiple gatekeepers whose approval or disapproval will influence an investment in energy-efficient technology. One of the most apparent barriers is the 'principal-agent' gap

---

[3] International Energy Agency ('IEA'), *World Energy Outlook 2009*. Similar data is presented in subsequent annual versions.

[4] Per-Anders Enkvist, Jens Dinkel and Charles Lin, *Impact of the Financial Crisis on Carbon Economics: Version 2.1 of the Global Greenhouse Gas Abatement Cost Curve* (McKinsey & Co, 2010) available at <http://solutions.mckinsey.com/climatedesk/>. The original version was Per-Anders Enkvist, Tomas Nauclér and Jerker Rosander, 'A Cost Curve for Greenhouse Gas Reduction' (2007) 1 *McKinsey Quarterly* 35.

[5] *Encyclopedia of Energy* (2004) vol 2 Energy Efficiency, Taxonomic Overview (Author: Amory B Lovins) [383]; IEA, *Implementing Energy Efficiency Policies: Are IEA Member Countries on Track?* (2009) 19. Generally, see Marcel Eusterfeldhaus and Barry Barton, 'Energy Efficiency: A Comparative Analysis of the New Zealand Legal Framework' (2011) 29 *Journal of Energy & Natural Resources Law* 431.

[6] Marilyn A Brown, 'Market Failures and Barriers as a Basis for Clean Energy Policies' (2001) 29 *Energy Policy* 1197; Alan H Sanstad, W Michael Hanemann and Maximillian Auffhammer, 'End-Use Energy Efficiency in a "Post-Carbon" California Economy: Policy Issues and Research Frontiers' in W Michael Hanemann et al, *Managing Greenhouse Gas Emissions in California* (Berkeley: California Climate Change Center at UC Berkeley, 2006) 6-9, 6-17; IEA, *Mind the Gap: Quantifying Principal-Agent Problems in Energy Efficiency* (2007) 20.

which exists where incentives, costs and benefits are not divided evenly — where the incentives are split.

The 'landlord-tenant problem' is a classic example of the principal-agent gap, and therefore one of the market failures affecting efficiency in markets for energy and energy products.[7] The landlord is responsible for the fabric of the building and the main appliances, but it is usually the tenant who is responsible for paying the energy bills and who is affected by the building's heating and ventilation performance. A landlord has no interest in investing in extra insulation or better appliances, because the benefits will be reaped by the tenant, without a direct influence on the rent the landlord can charge. The energy use affected by the principal-agent problem in the United States residential sector for refrigerators, space heating, water heating and lighting has been estimated as 31.4 per cent of the total sectoral energy use,[8] so the issue is a substantial one. The landlord-tenant problem is therefore the subject of this chapter, with particular reference to the way that it manifests itself in New Zealand.

Conventional policy instruments to improve residential energy efficiency, such as subsidies, rebates or certificates, are less effective because of the different interests of landlords and tenants. It can be complicated to get the benefits of such schemes. Alterations to a dwelling require the landlord's consent, and a tenant can be reluctant to ask for improvements, or indeed to have any more dealings with the landlord than are absolutely necessary.[9] Similarly, policy action to improve the quality of new housing, such as in a building code, does not benefit tenants except those who happen to move into new housing. Because buildings last many years, action in building codes, while vital, is slow to have an effect.

---

[7] IEA, above n 6. In spite of the substantial international understanding of the issue, during the 1990s, the New Zealand Treasury disputed the existence of market failures in relation to insulation, saying that there was no reason to suggest that rental streams and property values did not adequately reflect energy-efficiency investment decisions. Parliamentary Commissioner for the Environment, *Getting More from Less: A Review of Progress on Energy Efficiency and Renewable Energy Initiatives in New Zealand* (Wellington, 2000) 60-5.

[8] IEA, above n 6, 191. Analysis suggesting that the issue is smaller can be found in Kenneth Gillingham, Matthew Harding and David Rapson, 'Split Incentives in Residential Energy Consumption' (2012) 33 *Energy Journal* 37.

[9] See Centre for Social Research and Evaluation, 'Household Energy Affordability: Qualitative Research Report' (Ministry of Social Development and Energy Efficiency and Conservation Authority, 2010) 42.

Adrian Bradbrook analysed the landlord-tenant problem over twenty years ago in his article 'The Development of Energy Conservation Legislation for Private Rental Housing'.[10] He considered several law reform measures from the US, arguing that the landlord should have a legal duty to make rental housing energy efficient, just as the landlord had a legal duty to carry out repairs. His evaluation led him to conclude that a carrot-and-stick approach was desirable: inducements in the form of new tax credits or rebates, and new requirements under the law of landlord and tenant. The same issues were part of his analysis in a chapter entitled 'The Role of the Common Law in Promoting Sustainable Energy Development in the Property Sector' in 2010.[11] He held that action, whether legislative or judicial, was required to impose an energy efficiency duty on landlords, to set minimum energy performance standards and to make disclosure requirements.

I Rental Dwellings

Several characteristics of rental housing are significant to this matter. First, the percentage of households living in rental accommodation is increasing in New Zealand. (Bradbrook had noted the same thing in his research in Australia in 1991.) Twenty years or so ago, 26 per cent of households were in rentals; in 2011 it was 33 per cent.[12] If the rental part of the residential sector is difficult to reach in energy efficiency, then the performance of the sector as a whole is affected.

Secondly, poor people tend to live in rental housing. At the time of writing, around half (49 per cent) of all those aged under 65 who are in poverty live in private rental accommodation; the figure rises to two-thirds (65 per cent) when Housing New Zealand ('Housing NZ') and private rentals are counted together.[13] Poverty rates are higher in rental housing for those under 65 and those who are elderly. The

---

[10] (1991) 8 *Environment & Planning Law Journal* 91.

[11] Adrian Bradbrook, 'The Role of the Common Law in Promoting Sustainable Energy Development in the Property Sector' in Aileen McHarg et al (eds), *Property and the Law in Energy and Natural Resources* (Oxford University Press, 2010) 391.

[12] Department of Building and Housing, *Briefing for the Minister of Housing* (December 2011) 11.

[13] All the figures in this paragraph are from Bryan Perry, *Household Incomes in New Zealand: Trends in Indicators of Inequality and Hardship 1982 to 2011* (Wellington: Ministry of Social Development, August 2012) 119, 125. Also see Expert Advisory Group on Solutions to Child Poverty, *Solutions to Child Poverty in New Zealand: Issues and Options Paper for Consultation* (Office of the Children's Commissioner, August 2012).

concentration is even higher for children; over 70 per cent of all children in poverty live in rental accommodation (20 per cent in Housing NZ dwellings, 50 per cent in private rentals). To put it another way, the child poverty rate is 50 per cent in Housing NZ houses and 30 per cent in private rentals, while it is 10 per cent in privately owned homes with a mortgage and 6 per cent where there is no mortgage. The significance of these figures is that a low-income household has fewer options available to invest in energy efficiency improvements. It is also more likely to have weak market power to bargain with a landlord about the state of the dwelling on offer.

The feature of low income is disclosed in a survey of New Zealand households in the Energy Cultures research programme. It showed four distinct clusters or segments of energy culture: Energy Economic, Energy Extravagant, Energy Efficient and Energy Easy.[14] Rental housing, youth and low income were associated in the Energy Economic cluster; but so were environmental awareness and good energy-saving practices. Significantly, this group had the lowest levels of house insulation and energy-efficient heating. From a policy point of view, the Energy Economic group (within the meaning of the Energy Cultures research) must be reached by addressing their material needs rather than their opinions or knowledge base, and the landlord-tenant problem must be tackled in any policy measures.

Thirdly, rental properties are more likely to be cold than other dwellings, and that is bad for human health. One of the leading reviews of the energy characteristics of New Zealand households found that dwellings rated with indoor temperatures below 16°C are more likely to be accommodating tenant households than owner-occupiers.[15] To put this in context it should be noted that New Zealand houses as a whole have low indoor temperatures owing to persistent under-heating; commonly, only in living rooms on winter evenings does the temperature even come close to the World Health Organisation's healthy indoor temperature range of 18-24°C.[16] An Expert Advisory Group on poverty believes that many poor families are by necessity

---

[14] Janet Stephenson et al, 'Energy Cultures: A Framework for Understanding Energy Behaviours' (2010) 38 *Energy Policy* 6120; Rob Lawson and John Williams, 'Understanding Energy Cultures' (Paper presented at Australian and New Zealand Marketing Academy 2012 Conference, University of South Australia, 3-5 December 2012).

[15] Nigel Isaacs et al, 'Energy Use in New Zealand Households: Report on the Year 10 Analysis for the Household Energy End-Use Project (HEEP)' *BRANZ Study Report* SR 155 (2006) 28.

[16] Ibid.

endangering the health of their children by living in poor-quality housing.[17] The health dimension is perhaps the most important dimension of residential energy efficiency. Low indoor temperatures are associated with poor health and excess winter mortality.[18] A recent cost-benefit analysis of New Zealand's main subsidy programme for residential insulation and clean heating showed that the benefits of the programme were five times its resources costs, and that virtually all the benefits (99 per cent) were in the health of the occupants, not energy savings or employment.[19]

One therefore sees several substantial reasons for action on residential energy efficiency: climate change, environment, energy policy and human health. But it is also possible to state a rationale in human rights terms. Adrian Bradbrook, Judith Gardam and Monique Cormier have argued in persuasive terms that access to modern energy services should be incorporated within the human rights framework.[20] Energy services are already implicit in a range of existing human rights obligations, in particular obligations in the field of socio-economic rights, and deserve greater clarity and prominence. Access to modern energy services can be identified as an independent human right, but other lines of reasoning, such as consumer rights, are also possible.[21] Another line of argument is the right to habitable rental housing. Most nations have ratified the *International Covenant on Economic, Social and Cultural Rights*.[22] Article 11(1) of the Covenant addresses housing as part of the standard of living:

> The States Parties to the present Covenant recognize the right of everyone to an adequate standard of living for himself and his family, including adequate food, clothing and housing and to the continuous improvement of living conditions. The States Parties will take appropriate steps to ensure the realization of this right, recognizing to this effect the essential importance of co-operation based on free consent.

---

[17]   Expert Advisory Group on Solutions to Child Poverty, above n 13, p 29.

[18]   Philippa Howden-Chapman et al, 'Effect of Insulating Existing Houses on Health Inequality: Cluster Randomised Study in the Community' (2007) 334 *British Medical Journal* 460 <http://www.bmj.com.proxy.library.adelaide.edu.au/content/334/7591/460.pdf%2Bhtml>.

[19]   A Grimes et al, *Cost Benefit Analysis of the Warm Up New Zealand: Heat Smart Programme* (prepared for Ministry of Econmic Development, 2011 revised 2012).

[20]   Adrian J Bradbrook, Judith G Gardam and Monique Cormier, 'A Human Dimension to the Energy Debate: Access to Modern Energy Services' (2008) 26 *Journal of Energy & Natural Resources Law* 526.

[21]   Gretchen Larsen and Rob Lawson, 'Consumer Rights: An Assessment of Justice' (2012) 112 *Journal of Business Ethics* 515.

[22]   Opened for signature 16 December 1966, 9936 UNTS 3 (entered into force 3 January 1976).

The right to housing concerns unhealthy and demeaning living conditions as much as forced evictions or homelessness.[23] Rights to health and the rights of children are related. Parties to the Covenant must report periodically on progress.[24] Ratifying the Covenant binds New Zealand, Australia and other countries to give effect to the rights guaranteed, and a commitment like Article 11 cannot be ignored in administrative and legal decision-making; it is a proper rationale for the development of policy in relation to the quality of housing.[25] However, the obligation is a general one; it is to be realised progressively and in view of the availability of resources. Moreover, it is not enforceable as part of New Zealand law; it does not create a legal right of action against a landlord or against the government. The Human Rights Commission's role in relation to such rights is one of inquiry, education and encouragement. *Lawson v Housing New Zealand* held that it was for international forums and not the High Court to judge whether New Zealand had fulfilled its international obligations.[26] In any event, the housing obligation in Article 11 was phrased in general terms, and the complained-of state housing policy (i.e. market-level rentals accompanied by a targeted accommodation benefit) did not appear to have run counter to it. Nor could the right under the *New Zealand Bill of Rights Act 1990* (NZ) not to be deprived of life be read to apply.

II Existing New Zealand Law

With these rationales for action in mind, we can turn to consider the existing legal situation, primarily in New Zealand law but also in terms that share much with other

---

[23] Scott Leckie (ed), *National Perspectives on Housing Rights* (Kluwer Law International, 2003).

[24] United Nations Committee on Economic, Social and Cultural Rights, Implementation of the International Covenant on Economic, Social and Cultural Rights, *Third Periodic Reports Submitted by States Parties under Articles 16 and 17 of the Covenant: New Zealand*, UN Doc E/C.12/NZL/3 (17 January 2011). The report describes government policies in relation to insulation, clean heating and energy efficiency in housing.

[25] Karen Meikle, 'Economic, Social and Cultural Rights: Protection in Aotearoa New Zealand — An Overview' in Margaret Bedggood and Kris Gledhill (eds), *Law Into Action: Economic, Social and Cultural Rights in Aotearoa New Zealand* (Human Rights Foundation / Thomson Reuters, 2011) 39, 58; also, using the right to housing as an example, Peter Hosking, 'Freedom from Poverty: The Right to an Adequate Standard of Living' in Margaret Bedggood and Kris Gledhill (eds), *Law Into Action: Economic, Social and Cultural Rights in Aotearoa New Zealand* (Human Rights Foundation / Thomson Reuters, 2011) 112.

[26] [1997] 2 NZLR 474.

common law countries. The underlying common law is reasonably clear although not altogether satisfying. In the absence of any express covenant, and in the absence of any statutory requirement, the landlord has no duty to ensure that premises are in repair, kept in repair, or fit for any particular purpose. There is no implied condition that the land shall be fit for the purpose for which it is taken. 'The general rule must therefore be, that where a man undertakes to pay a specific rent for a piece of land, he is obliged to pay that rent, whether it answer the purpose for which he took it or not.'[27] The rule applies to the letting of an unfurnished dwelling-house: 'It appears, therefore, to us to be clear upon the old authorities, that there is no implied warranty on a lease of a house, or of land, that it is, or shall be, reasonably fit for habitation or cultivation.'[28] While the letting of a readily-furnished house could be distinguished, the Court decided, 'We are all of the opinion, for these reasons, that there is no contract, still less a condition, implied by law on the demise of real property only, that it is fit for the purpose for which it is let.'[29] *Chappell v Gregory* held that in the absence of a promise to put a house in repair, a person who takes the lease of a house from a lessor takes it as it stands.[30] This is the position in New Zealand as much as in the United Kingdom. Even where the only use of the property which the lease allows is as a boarding house, and upgrading is required before it can be so used, the rule is caveat lessee; the lessee must take the property as he or she finds it.[31] 'Apart from express stipulations there is no obligation on a lessor during the term of the lease to repair or maintain improvements.'[32] A warranty as to the quality of land sold or leased is not generally to be implied, but a court may decide to imply one where the totality of the circumstances requires it.[33]

---

[27]   *Sutton v Temple* (1843) 12 M & W 52, at 64, 152 ER 1108.

[28]   *Hart v Windsor* (1843) 12 M & W 68, 86, 152 ER 1114. See also Lewison (ed), Sweet & Maxwell, *Woodfall on Landlord and Tenant* [13.001].

[29]   *Hart v Windsor*, 87. Also, *Edler v Auerbach* [1950] 1 KB 359.

[30]   (1864) 34 Beav 250, 253; 55 ER 631.

[31]   *Balcairn Guest House Ltd v Weir* [1963] NZLR 301.

[32]   *Felton v Brightwell* [1967] NZLR 276, 277 (Wild CJ).

[33]   *Gabolinscy v Hamilton City Corp* [1975] 1 NZLR 150, 163. There may be a growing willingness to imply such obligations, especially as contract law is more generally applied to leasing disputes: D Grinlinton, 'Fitness for Purpose of Leased Premises' [2000] *New Zealand Law Journal* 105. However, as a rule, obligations will be implied to give business efficacy to a lease only under stringent conditions; *BP Refinery (Westernport) Pty Ltd v Shire of Hastings* (1977) 180 CLR 266, 283 (PC).

In *Southwark London Borough Council v Mills*,[34] Lord Millett explains that this doctrine is based not on fictions such as the ability of the tenant to inspect the property before taking the lease, but solely on the general rule of English law, which accords autonomy to contracting parties. In the absence of statutory intervention, the parties are free to let and take a lease of poorly constructed premises and to allocate the cost of putting them in order between themselves as they see fit. Indeed, the case is a clear — if unhappy — modern illustration of the limits of the common law in reshaping the landlord-tenant relationship for modern housing needs. Council tenants sued because of the lack of sound insulation between one flat and the next. Even the normal noise of the neighbouring household was plainly audible and the lack of privacy caused tension and distress. There was no warranty in the tenancy agreements that the flats had sound insulation or were in any other way fit to live in. 'Nor does the law imply any such warranty. This is a fundamental principle of the English law of landlord and tenant.'[35] There was a covenant to repair but no such obligation requires a landlord to make it a better house than it originally was. 'The law has long been settled that there is no implied covenant on the part of the landlord of a dwelling house that the premises are fit for human habitation, let alone that they are soundproof.'[36] The covenant for quiet enjoyment, which the law does imply, did not help because it is prospective in its nature and does not apply to things done before the grant of the tenancy.[37]

Lord Hoffman observed that in England, Parliament has intervened in the rental housing market in different ways; but so far it has declined to impose an obligation to install soundproofing in existing dwellings. The development of the common law should not get out of step with legislative policy. Similarly, Lord Millett recognised that the case illuminated a problem of considerable social importance. No one would wish anyone to live in these conditions. But there was a huge stock of pre-war housing, much of which admitted damp and was scarcely fit for human habitation. Southwark Borough alone estimated the cost of upgrades as £1.271 billion. 'These cases raise issues of priority in the allocation of resources. Such issues must be resolved by the democratic process, national and local. The judges are not equipped to resolve

---

[34]   [2001] 1 AC 1, 17 ('*Southwark v Mills*').

[35]   Ibid 7 (Lord Slynn).

[36]   Ibid 17 (Lord Millett).

[37]   Ibid 11 (Lord Hoffman). It should be added that the covenant for quiet enjoyment is not for acoustical peace but for undisturbed title.

them.'[38] It is likely that judges in most parts of the common law world would speak similarly of the limitations on judicial creativity in efforts to solve a social problem.

III   RESIDENTIAL TENANCIES ACT 1986

The *Residential Tenancies Act 1986* (NZ) ('Residential Tenancies Act') is the main New Zealand statutory intervention of this kind. It provides a general code for the residential landlord-tenant relationship, modifying rules of common law, and (with few exceptions) preventing parties from contracting out of its provisions. Historically, New Zealand has had various kinds of tenant protection legislation. In the context of this volume, it is pleasing to observe that the 1986 Act is modelled on that of the state of South Australia, and is similar to Acts in other Australian jurisdictions.[39]

Section 45(1) imposes responsibilities on landlords that are as close as one gets to obligations as to fitness:

The landlord shall —

(a)   Provide the premises in a reasonable state of cleanliness; and

(b)   Provide and maintain the premises in a reasonable state of repair having regard to the age and character of the premises and the period during which the premises are likely to remain habitable and available for residential purposes; and

(c)   Comply with all requirements in respect of buildings, health, and safety under any enactment so far as they apply to the premises ...

The landlord therefore need not undertake that the dwelling is habitable, or that it provides a healthy indoor living environment. (There is no equivalent of the American warranty of habitability.)[40] There is no undertaking that the dwelling will be warm or capable of being kept warm. (A landlord may agree to such undertakings, and will be bound by them, but there is no reason to think that many landlords offer them.) What is compulsory is, firstly, a warranty as to cleanliness. Then there is a warranty as to repair, but it is restricted by the reference to the age and character of the premises. Even without that restriction, an obligation to repair cannot justify a claim

---

[38]   Ibid 26.

[39]   David Grinlinton, *Residential Tenancies: The Law and Practice* (LexisNexis, 4th ed, 2012) 2.

[40]   In the United States, nearly all courts have held that a residential lease includes a non-disclaimable implied warranty that the premises are habitable: *Javins v First National Realty Corp*, 428 F.2d 1071 (DC Cir 1970). See Joseph William Singer, *Introduction to Property* (Aspen, 2nd ed, 2005) 480.

for energy efficiency improvements; the warranty to repair will not be interpreted to turn the building into something different in character from what it was.[41]

The third warranty is for compliance with requirements under other enactments. It takes our inquiry primarily to the *Housing Improvement Regulations 1947* (NZ) ('Housing Improvement Regulations'). In passing, however, one may note requirements under the *Building Act 2004* (NZ) ('Building Act') and the *Education Act 1989* (NZ) for minimum temperatures of 16°C in old people's homes and early childhood centres.[42] Leaving to one side our opinion whether that is warm enough, we should note that the Building Act is otherwise almost entirely focused on the way that buildings are designed and constructed. It will therefore help the tenants of newly constructed dwellings, but not residents in old ones.

IV HOUSING IMPROVEMENT REGULATIONS 1947

The Housing Improvement Regulations occupy an important position in the law on the quality of residential accommodation, but they do so in an anomalous and unsatisfactory manner. They are dated; they were originally made under the *Housing Improvement Act*. Their historical origins reflect the perceptions of the 1930s and 1940s about health in housing.[43] They are now in force under the *Health Act 1956* (NZ) ('Health Act') s 120C,[44] which authorises the making of regulations for purposes including '(e) The protection of dwellinghouses from damp, excessive noise, and heat loss'. Our particular concern, 'heat loss', has not been specifically addressed,

---

[41] The law on this point has been worked out in relation to obligations to repair incurred by a tenant, in cases such as *Lister v Lane* [1893] 2 QB 212. Repair does not go as far as replacement or making a new and different building. See generally GW Hinde, Neil Campbell and Peter Twist, *Principles of Real Property Law* (LexisNexis, 2007) [11.092].

[42] The Building Code, being sch 1 of the *Building Regulations 1992* (NZ), cl G5.3.1 provides, for old people's homes and early childhood centres only, that habitable spaces, bathrooms and recreation rooms shall have provision for maintaining the internal temperature at no less than 16°C measured at 750 mm above floor level, while the space is adequately ventilated. The *Education Early Childhood Centres Regulations 1998* (NZ) under the *Education Act 1989* (NZ), cl 22 require a temperature of 16°C measured between 0.5 metres and 1.0 metre above the floor.

[43] Sarah Bierre et al, 'Institutional Challenges in Addressing Healthy Low-Cost Housing for All: Learning from Past Policy' (2007) 30, *Social Policy Journal of New Zealand* 42, 48.

[44] The Act of 1945 was renamed the *Urban Renewal and Housing Improvement Act* in 1969 by the *Urban Renewal and Housing Improvement Amendment Act 1969* (NZ), and was repealed by the *Local Government Amendment Act 1979* (NZ) s 9.

but Regulation 15 declares in simple terms that '[e]very house shall be free from dampness'. Regulation 6 requires that every living-room of a house be fitted with a fireplace and chimney or other approved form of heating. Regulation 11 requires that habitable rooms be fitted with windows for the admission of air. The Regulations prescribe requirements for minimum room sizes for houses, requirements for toilets, requirements to apply to boarding houses, and occupancy ratios to prevent overcrowding. Non-compliance with the Regulations or general unfitness for human habitation are grounds for the local body to issue a repair notice or a closure notice.[45] These requirements are imposed on houses and habitable rooms without distinguishing between owner-occupied dwellings and tenanted dwellings.

Housing NZ Corp v Ladbrook shows the potential of the Regulations to be useful to tenants.[46] The tenant of a state house had long complained of dampness and mould, and applied to the Tenancy Tribunal for work to be done and for compensation. The landlord installed extractor fans and heat pumps, and made repairs where wood had rotted. The Tribunal did not accept that the problems were caused solely by lifestyle factors and by the tenant's failure to do more to prevent condensation, so that the landlord had breached its responsibility to provide premises free from dampness. That responsibility must be the duty in the Housing Improvement Regulations, because it is not in the Residential Tenancies Act. The Court agreed that a small compensation payment was due to the tenant.

However, the Regulations would have been difficult to enforce when they were made, and they have not adjusted to changes in expectations. Regulation 18(1), for example, declares that '[e]very house and all the appurtenances and appliances of every house shall at all times be kept in a state of good repair'. What happens if I am an owner-occupier and am behind with my house maintenance? Enforcing the provisions about the number of people who may sleep in a room would be, so to speak, nightmarish. There is reported uncertainty about the application of the Regulations to apartment sizes, and to boarding-houses, and there can be no surprise that there is considerable inconsistency reported in the administration of

---

45 The procedures for issuing a repair notice or a closure notice are in s 42 of the Health Act. At least under the former Act, there was no requirement for a repair notice that it be practicable to bring a house into compliance: *Hiatt v Christchurch City Council* (Unreported, HC Christchurch, A179/77, 7 October 1980). Failure to comply with a notice is an offence: *Garden City Developments Ltd v Christchurch City Council* (Unreported, HC Christchurch, AP168/92, 29 July 1992).

46 [2010] DCR 102.

these provisions by local authorities.[47] The Regulations are prescriptive, in contrast to modern legislation that focuses on outcomes rather than solutions, and they are not often enforced because they are thought to be dated.[48] Quite likely, the dominance of the Building Act puts the 1947 Regulations into the shade; as well as being less well-known, less comprehensive and less modern, they are subject to that Act, so in case of conflict they give way.[49] Yet they occupy different terrain: while the Building Act ensures that houses and other structures are well-built, the Regulations ensure that they are, and remain, fit for human habitation.

Overall, the Housing Improvement Regulations are dated; they are prescriptive in an old-fashioned way; they deal with damp but not with heat loss; they are little understood and often overlooked. But they are the only protection against substandard housing which the law, at the time of writing, offers to tenants.

V   CONSUMER LEGISLATION

It may be asked whether other consumer protection legislation can come to the tenant's aid. The answer is not very clear. The *Consumer Guarantees Act 1993* (NZ) ('Consumer Guarantees Act') provides guarantees to consumers where goods and services are supplied in trade. Goods must be of acceptable quality and must be reasonably fit for purpose. Services must be carried out with reasonable care and skill, and must be fit for purpose. 'Goods' are defined not to include a whole building attached to land unless the building is a structure that is easily removable and is not designed for residential accommodation. A 'whole' building has been held to mean an entire building, not a complete one, but how the term applies to multi-unit buildings is unclear; it would be odd if different rules applied.[50] Nor is it clear whether 'services' include the provision of rental housing; the term is defined to include rights under a contract for the provision in trade of 'facilities for accommodation, amusement,

---

[47]   Department of Building and Housing, *Getting the Balance Right: Review of the Residential Tenancies Act 1986*, (2004) 15.

[48]   Bierre et al, above n 43, 47.

[49]   The *Health Act 1956* s 120C(1) says that the power to make regulations is subject to the Building Act. On its history, see Bierre et al, above n 43, 52. The *Building Act 2004* s 18 may also be relevant in restricting requirements made under that Act.

[50]   *Jackson v McClintock* (1998) 8 TCLR 161 (HC); noted, D McMorland, (1998) 8 *Butterworths Conveyancing Bulletin* 64; David Grinlinton, 'Fitness for Purpose of Leased Premises' [2000] *New Zealand Law Journal* 105.

the care of persons or animals or things, entertainment, instruction, parking, or recreation'. As for the requirement that the goods or services be supplied 'in trade', a commercial provider or Housing New Zealand would be caught, but the case of a residence that is the investment property of an individual, a couple or a family trust is less sure. In none of these respects is the law clear. It remains for an enterprising and a receptive court to explore whether the Consumer Guarantees Act's guarantees of acceptable quality, reasonable care and reasonable fitness for purpose apply to residential accommodation in a way that requires housing that is protected against dampness and heat loss.

The *Fair Trading Act 1986* (NZ) also provides consumer protection, requiring, in trade, the accuracy of representations and the avoidance of misleading and deceptive conduct. The Act applies to representations made by any person in trade concerning the nature of any interest in land or the characteristics of land. Grinlinton shows that these requirements must apply to leases just as much as to sales of fee simple estates in land, even if there are few such cases, and that they must apply to real estate agents.[51] *Small v Lawry* suggests that a tenant can obtain compensation under general contract law if a landlord makes a misrepresentation that a house is insulated, although the tenant there was unsuccessful.[52]

Under the *Real Estate Agents Act 2008* (NZ), consumer protection does not appear to extend to direct regulation of the residential tenancy or letting agency operations which are part of many real estate agencies. Section 4(1) of the Act defines 'transaction' (which is an element of 'real estate agency work' for which one needs a licence under the Act) as not including any tenancy to which the Residential Tenancies Act applies. This is a pity, because it would be desirable to have the *Real Estate Agents Act (Professional Conduct and Client Care) Rules 2009* (NZ) spelling out required standards of conduct, such as not withholding information from a customer, and not failing to disclose known or likely defects.

---

[51] Grinlinton, above n 50, 107.

[52] [2011] NZTT Hamilton 11/01447/HN (26 September 2011).

VI State of New Zealand Law at the Present

The state of the law in New Zealand, then, is that in a lease or tenancy there is no implied warranty of habitability or fitness for purpose. It is unlikely that the courts will take the initiative to fashion one out of the general law of landlord and tenant, especially in the face of the policy enunciated by senior judges in *Southwark v Mills*. It is unknown whether some such protection can be found as part of the guarantee of services fit for purpose under the Consumer Guarantees Act; the breadth and purpose of the guarantee does seem to give some space for judicial activism. There is a duty on residential landlords, under the Residential Tenancies Act and the Housing Improvement Regulations, to ensure that dwellings are free from dampness, but the duty seems little known and little enforced. There is no legal duty for the Housing NZ Corporation to do any better than other landlords. It is therefore desirable to consider what two other relevant jurisdictions have done.

VII Australia

Australia has opted for information disclosure mechanisms as a key part of its action on the landlord-tenant problem, but so far in the commercial sector only. The *Building Energy Efficiency Disclosure Act 2010* (Cth) applies to a corporation that owns a 'disclosure affected' building or disclosure affected area of a building.[53] The owner must provide a building energy efficiency certificate to any prospective purchaser, lessee or sublessee. This certificate must at a minimum state the energy efficiency rating for the building, an assessment of the energy efficiency of the lighting for the building or area, and guidance on how energy efficiency may be improved. The energy efficiency rating in the certificate must also be stated in any advertisement of the building or space for sale or lease. Certificates and ratings are supplied by accredited assessors, and are registered. The requirements are backed up by civil penalties and infringement notices. These obligations under the Act are restricted to buildings and areas in buildings that are used or capable of being used as an office, and where at least 75 per cent of the space in the building by net lettable area is for administrative, clerical, professional or similar information-based activities, including

---

[53] *Building Energy Efficiency Disclosure Act 2010* (Cth) ss 11-13. For constitutional reasons, it targets 'constitutional corporations' which include foreign corporations and trading and financial corporations formed within the limits of the Commonwealth; that is, virtually all corporations.

any support facilities for those activities, where the area of the building for such activities is at least 2000 m².[54]

Australian national policy is to go further and make similar disclosure requirements for the sale and rental of residential properties. At the time of writing, disclosure requirements are not consistent between states and territories,[55] and the Australian Capital Territory is the only jurisdiction where purchasers can expect independent energy efficiency assessments of properties. In the ACT, energy efficiency ratings will gradually apply to the housing stock. From 1999, on the sale of a house, the vendor is required to obtain an energy efficiency rating and make it available to purchasers.[56] More recently, the *Residential Tenancies Act 1997* (ACT) has required a landlord who is advertising premises for lease to state any existing energy efficiency rating for them.[57] The rating to be supplied is the most recent energy efficiency rating, prepared for the premises for the purpose of a sale of the premises. These statements are prepared by licensed building assessors.[58] Thus a rating is required to sell a house, and once it is rated the rating must be disclosed to prospective tenants, so many rental properties will remain unrated for some time.

In July 2009, presumably stimulated by the ACT's example, the Council of Australian Governments agreed to a National Strategy on Energy Efficiency which includes requirements for the disclosure of energy efficiency for residential rentals, along with disclosure of greenhouse gas and water performance.[59] As part of this effort, a Residential Building Disclosure Programme is being developed.[60]

---

[54] *Building Energy Efficiency Disclosure (Disclosure Affected Buildings) Act 2010* s 3 and the *Building Energy Efficiency Disclosure (Disclosure Affected Buildings) Determination 2011* ss 5-6.

[55] Nicola Durrant, *Legal Responses to Climate Change* (Federation Press, 2010) 142; Alexander Zahar, Lee Godden and Jacqueline Peel, *Australian Climate Law in Global Context* (Cambridge University Press, 2012) ch 9.

[56] *Civil Law (Sale of Residential Property) Act 2003* (ACT) s 23. See generally Australian Capital Territory Government Environment and Sustainable Development Directorate, *AP2: A New Climate Change Strategy and Action Plan for the Australian Capital Territory* (2012) 34.

[57] *Residential Tenancies Act 1997* (ACT) s 11A.

[58] *Construction Occupations (Licensing) Act 2004* (ACT) s 123AC.

[59] *National Strategy on Energy Efficiency*, July 2009, s 3.3.2, annexed to Council of Australian Governments, *National Partnership on Energy Efficiency*, 2 July 2009.

[60] Department of Resources, Energy and Tourism, *Draft White Paper, Strengthening the Foundations for Australia's Energy Future* (Canberra: December 2011) 189. This may require state legislation, unless the Commonwealth can find another constitutional head; the corporation's power is unlikely to be adequate.

Australia therefore points to information measures as a path ahead. In the ACT there is growing experience of their use in the rental market.

VIII United Kingdom

In the United Kingdom, energy performance certificates are a compulsory form of information disclosure, pursuant to a European Union Directive. The *Energy Performance of Buildings (Certificates and Inspections) (England and Wales) Regulations 2007* apply to dwellings and certain other buildings.[61] When a building owner is selling or renting out a building, he or she must supply a current energy performance certificate, without charge. The certificate, valid for ten years, is produced by a qualified assessor who inspects the dwelling as to construction, insulation, heating and ventilation. (Multiple-unit buildings may be reviewed together.) The builder of a new or refurbished house must obtain a certificate for it. The certificate rates the building on a scale from A to G, so that the prospective tenant or buyer can compare it with other properties. It estimates the costs of lighting and heating the property. It recommends specific measures to improve the rating of the building, with indicative costs and likely savings. It is limited in accuracy, in being derived from modelling the performance of a building of a given size, shape, orientation and materials; and it does not use invasive inspection techniques. A different requirement, for certain publicly-owned buildings, is a display certificate, which discloses actual energy operation ratings, including use of fuel.

Going beyond energy performance certificates, the United Kingdom has had a variety of incentive schemes to improve the quality of its housing stock generally.[62] From October 2012, the key scheme is the Green Deal. The Green Deal was an important component of the United Kingdom government coalition agreement of 2010, and was the chief subject of the *Energy Act 2011* (UK) ('Energy Act'). The Green

---

[61] (UK) SI 2007/991, made to implement European Union Directive 2002/91/EC on the energy performance of buildings. It required minimum energy performance standards for new buildings, certificates for existing buildings (as implemented in the UK Regulations discussed here) and regular inspection of boilers, heating systems and air-conditioning systems. The European Commission has proposed more vigorous activity: 'Proposal for a Directive of the European Parliament and of the Council on Energy Efficiency and Repealing Directives 2004/8/EC and 2006/32/EC' COM/2011/370. It is unclear at the time of writing whether this proposal will proceed.

[62] Mark Dowson et al, 'Domestic UK Retrofit Challenge: Barriers, Incentives and Current Performance' (2012) 50 *Energy Policy* 294.

Deal is a financing framework, using private funds to pay for fixed improvements for the energy efficiency of households and non-domestic properties. The financing, from a Green Deal provider, can be obtained for energy efficiency purposes after evaluation by an accredited Green Deal assessor. The funds are repayable only from the energy bills for the property, under an arrangement with the energy suppliers. The householder is not liable otherwise, so that the obligation to make repayments runs with the land rather than the individual. If all goes well, the repayments are outweighed by the energy savings; indeed the 'golden rule' is that the expected financial savings must be greater than the costs attached to the energy bill.[63]

The landlord-tenant problem has plainly been a major driver in the design of the Green Deal. Landlords will face no capital costs, and the repayments will come out of the tenants' energy bills. However the Energy Act goes further, and requires regulations to be made — to come into effect by 1 April 2016 — that a landlord of a domestic private rental property may not unreasonably refuse the tenant's request to make energy efficiency improvements funded by a Green Deal plan or a like mechanism.[64] The Act goes even further on 1 April 2018, by when regulations must be in place to prohibit the landlord of a domestic private rental property that falls below a prescribed standard of energy efficiency (as demonstrated by the energy performance certificate) from letting the property out until energy efficiency improvements have been made.[65] The intention is for the minimum standard to be set at E on the A-to-G scale. However, this requirement is limited to improvements that can be funded by a Green Deal plan or equivalent, so that there are no capital costs to the landlord; if all possible Green Deal improvements are made but still do not bring the property up to the E standard, then it may be let out anyway.

The Green Deal has been criticised as regressive, complex, unattractive to consumers and likely to reduce the amount spent on insulation.[66] It may not be

---

[63] Department of Energy and Climate Change, *The Green Deal: A Summary of the Government's Proposals* (2010).

[64] *Energy Act 2011* (UK) s 46.

[65] *Energy Act 2011* (UK) s 43.

[66] Dowson et al, above n 62; Miguel A Tovar, 'The Structure of Energy Efficiency Investment in the UK Households and its Average Monetary and Environmental Savings' (2012) 50 *Energy Policy* 723; Rowena Mason, 'Coalition's Green Deal Plans to Insulate 14 million Homes "Spiralling out of Control"', *The Telegraph*, 8 June 2012; Damian Carrington, 'Green Deal would See Home Insulation Rate Plummet', *The Guardian*, 11 June 2012.

well-targeted at the needs of the poor. It contains no element of subsidy for retrofit works. It may not be effective in reaching low-adoption households such as private renters. The rate of interest to be paid on the improvements may turn out to be higher than mortgage rates, which will be unattractive to house owners, and, if to run long into the future, may depress the value of a house. The finance companies may lend selectively, only on the most inefficient houses, in order to obtain adequate returns. The scheme requires elaborate administration and regulation of the work of the financial providers, assessors and energy companies; it is legally complicated. It is technically complex in estimating the annual energy savings from different retrofit packages.

As part of EU requirements, the United Kingdom experience therefore shows the way ahead for Australia in energy information disclosure. Once the Green Deal is fully under way, it will also provide insights into a determined effort to bring energy efficiency improvements into rental accommodation.

IX   Policy Options

With a clear picture of the present state of New Zealand law, and with the benefit of comparisons with two other countries, it is now possible to evaluate some options for policy change and law reform.

A   *Ordinary Energy Efficiency Schemes*

Initially, an important general point should be made: that ordinary energy efficiency schemes that are aimed primarily at owner-occupiers must also, as far as possible, be made accessible to landlords and tenants. Some schemes may be better than others; it is said that the South Australia Residential Energy Efficiency Scheme is just as likely to be taken up by tenants as by owner-occupiers.[67] This accessibility of general measures to landlords and tenants should be high on any New Zealand policy agenda. In addition, modifications to the ordinary rules of tenancies seem necessary. Tenants may need the right to remove energy efficiency installations that become fixtures, or compensation where that is impossible.[68]

---

[67]   Australian Capital Territory, above n 56, 34.

[68]   Bradbrook, above n 10, 92.

B   Public Housing

If we proceed on the assumption that we wish to improve energy efficiency in rental accommodation with the minimum of complexity in law reform, then the simplest option of all is to improve public housing. No law reform is required: only funding. Four per cent of New Zealand housing is social housing provided by the Housing New Zealand Corporation.[69] Its legislation requires it to exhibit a sense of social and environmental responsibility, but only in giving effect to the Crown's social objectives in a businesslike manner.[70] (Otherwise, it is subject to the general law of residential tenancies, just as are private landlords.) The present Crown social objectives are silent on habitability, but the Corporation states that its role is to provide safe, warm and dry homes for people in the greatest need. It identifies an urgent need to reconfigure the state housing portfolio, in part because of houses that are in poor condition.[71] It intends to insulate every state rental property where practicable,[72] and in recent months the Energy Efficiency Retrofit programme has effectively reached this target.

C   Housing Improvement Regulations

The next simple option, needing no change in the law, is to use the *Housing Improvement Regulations 1947* (NZ) more vigorously. Non-governmental organisations concerned with poverty, health and tenants' rights need not wait for the government. Publicity and training would increase the willingness of local authorities and Tenancy Tribunal adjudicators to enforce the duty to provide housing free from dampness. A higher profile for the Regulations may bring on scrutiny and criticism along with better outcomes for tenants, but a policy review would probably be no bad thing.

D   New General Requirement for Protection from Heat Loss

A policy review of the Housing Improvement Regulations could produce a requirement that houses be free from undue heat loss, as the parent Act allows for. Such a simple

---

[69]   Department of Building and Housing, *Briefing for the Minister of Housing* (December 2011) 12 (4.3 per cent). Another 1.2 per cent is social housing provided by local authorities and not-for-profits.

[70]   *Housing Corporation Act 1974* (NZ) ss 3B and 3C.

[71]   Housing New Zealand, *Briefing for the Minister of Housing* (December 2011) 3, 5, 8. The closest the Crown social objectives come to this is that 'New Zealanders have access to housing that meets their needs and is affordable'.

[72]   Housing New Zealand, *Statement of Intent 2012-2015*, 22, 38.

non-quantified requirement could provide a minimum standard, capable of being applied in the most serious cases. Courts and tribunals are accustomed to applying general standards, such as reasonable fitness for purpose, in a common-sense manner even if an engineer might ask for something more exact.[73] The prescriptive and old-fashioned character of the Regulations would be a problem in any effort to amend them; it is very likely that a policy consensus would be for something better, and that could mean delay. It would be a pity if the quest for perfect regulations becomes the enemy of the good.

Alternatively, a new modern requirement could be devised that residential rental accommodation be free from heat loss and dampness. While this rubric from the Health Act seems workable, the obligation could be expressed as an obligation to provide the premises in a state reasonably capable of being maintained warm and free of damp at a reasonable expense. It could be incorporated in section 45 of the *Residential Tenancies Act 1986* (NZ); that specific Act would be a better fit than the broad *Consumer Guarantees Act 1993* (NZ) or the construction-oriented *Building Act 2004* (NZ).[74] Another option is for a 'minimum energy performance standard' ('MEPS') under the *Energy Efficiency and Conservation Act 2000* (NZ). MEPS lend themselves to technically-specific requirements, and are in effect in New Zealand for various appliances. The Act authorises the government to make MEPS for 'energy-using products and services, including all vehicles', which is probably too narrow to include dwellings, so that an amendment is needed.[75] A MEPS for rental housing would require technical work but seems to deserve active examination.

Perhaps the most active or most restrictive law reform would be to impose a new general requirement but then to require periodic inspection to verify compliance. It could be a building warrant of fitness.[76] As noted, energy performance certification

---

[73] A very different approach is minimum heat rules made by many municipalities in the United States and Canada, where the provision of heat is more essential, but also where many rental dwellings are in multi-unit buildings. For example, City of London, Ontario, Vital Services By-law, PH-6, s 3.4: between 15 September and 15 June the landlord must maintain a continuous supply of heat to a rented unit so that a minimum temperature of 20°C shall be maintained, 6 am to 11 pm, 18°C at night.

[74] The possibility of specifying fire standards and insulation was mentioned in the Department of Building and Housing, *Getting the Balance Right: Review of the Residential Tenancies Act 1986* (2004) 16.

[75] Such a proposal is the Energy Efficiency and Conservation (Warm Healthy Rentals) Amendment Bill, Consultation Draft, H Walker MP, 20 June 2012. The relevant section is s 36, *Energy Efficiency and Conservation Act 2000*.

[76] Expert Advisory Group on Solutions to Child Poverty, above n 13, 30.

with prescribed performance minima is to be introduced in the UK from 2018. It will be a considerable challenge, and it is not surprising that a considerable lead-time is planned; but it shows what a determined effort to improve building performance would look like. It would not be unduly intrusive but it would put pressure on the owners of poor-quality housing.

E *Information Disclosure*

Less intrusive are information disclosure mechanisms. The British energy performance certificate, and the Australian building energy efficiency certificate, only require that performance be measured and disclosed. They increase the amount of information available to a prospective purchaser, or (in the future) a prospective tenant. Better information reduces transaction costs and enables purchasers more accurately to price the energy efficiency aspects of a dwelling; so information disclosure is arguably compatible with the free play of market forces.[77] An information disclosure regime should be pursued. It does require a complex technical framework for assessors to make accurate and meaningful ratings. It also requires attention for the tenants at the bottom of the market who may not have the luxury of turning down rentals with poor ratings.

Nonetheless, we should be open to the power of information to bring about change. One promising information measure is a website for information about the quality of rental accommodation, for the benefit of prospective tenants. It needs no formal regulation or law reform at all.[78] The information on a website could be the result of a detailed assessment, or it could be a quicker and cheaper walk-through assessment checking for basics such as insulation in the ceiling, insulation in the crawl space, double glazing, lack of visible mould and so on. Cheaper still would be reports of consumer satisfaction: the entries by tenants about how they found the place, in the same way as tourists report their experiences in travel adviser websites.[79] This would be less reliable information, perhaps, but better than no information at all.

---

[77] There is of course a great deal of evidence that conventional market explanations of conduct are inadequate in relation to energy efficiency: Brown, above n 6.

[78] A website of this kind is a form of 'decentred regulation' which can be understood as regulation, but not state regulation. See Julia Black, 'Decentring Regulation: Understanding the Role of Regulation and Self-Regulation in a "Post-Regulatory" World' (2001) 54 *Current Legal Problems* 102.

[79] In the travel industry, for example, a useful website for condominiums or units is <https://www.condoadvisory.com>.

One website with basic information is the Student Tenancy Accommodation Rating Scheme ('STARS'), sponsored by Dunedin City Council, the University of Otago and Otago Polytechnic.[80] Ratings are made from landlord answers to a questionnaire about fire safety, security, insulation, heating and ventilation, and general amenities. There is no complaints system for objections to ratings, but there is an audit process. Such rating systems allow the landlords of good-quality premises to differentiate them from poor-quality housing and segment the market. There could be benefits for landlords in higher rentals and higher occupancy rates, and benefits for communities and institutions in a good profile for their city and in health benefits for its residents. Such information systems pose consequential legal issues, such as the rights of tenants to bring in building assessors and publish the assessment on the web, and to report their own opinions without suffering eviction or legal action. Once again, we must note that such systems may do little for the most vulnerable tenants. Nonetheless, they provide a path for concerned landlords, tenants and citizens to take action themselves.

X   CONCLUSION

Thus, a range of policy options exists to deal with the unsatisfactory aspects of the law of residential tenancies in respect to energy efficiency: some options for more vigorous use of the existing law and of information-sharing possibilities, some for changes of the law with varying degrees of complexity and departure from the status quo. The present law in New Zealand, as in a number of other jurisdictions, needs reform in order to meet energy policy and climate change objectives, and, no less importantly, to improve human health and well-being.

---

[80]   See <http://www.housingstars.co.nz/the-scheme>.

5

RENEWABLE ENERGY IN THE CONTEXT OF CLIMATE CHANGE AND GLOBAL ENERGY RESOURCES

ROSEMARY LYSTER[1]

Renewable energy is regarded as one of the primary technology solutions to combat climate change, caused undoubtedly by continued heavy reliance on fossil fuels since the Industrial Revolution. Yet the development and commercialisation of renewable energy technologies have faced a number of significant barriers in recent times. These may be regarded as: regulatory and policy risk; uncertainty about whether governments should support renewable energy technologies as a complementary measure where they have imposed a carbon price mechanism; concerns about energy security and the ability of renewable energy to provide baseload power and barriers to entry on conventional electricity grids; and ongoing subsidies, both direct and indirect, to the fossil fuel industry.

I   THE CURRENT STATUS OF INTERNATIONAL CLIMATE CHANGE NEGOTIATIONS

The most recent international negotiations under the *United Nations Framework Convention on Climate Change* ('UNFCCC'), the second commitment period of the

---

[1]   Rosemary Lyster wishes to acknowledge and thank her research assistant Christiane Cain for her invaluable work in collecting the materials relied upon in this chapter.

Kyoto Protocol and a new agreement post 2020, concluded in Warsaw in December 2013. The negotiations reinforced a number of key decisions reached at Doha in 2012, which were in themselves a last-ditch attempt to finalise arrangements for the post-2012 world, with the first commitment period (2008-12) under the *Kyoto Protocol* ending in December 2012. All recent negotiations have taken place amidst warnings about the urgent need to close the gap between current commitments, of both developed and developing countries, to reduce greenhouse gases ('GHG's) and the parties' stated goal of keeping the rise in average global temperatures, compared with pre-industrial times, at below 2°C or even 1.5°C.

Immediately before the Doha negotiations, the International Energy Agency ('IEA') warned that current emissions reduction commitments correspond to an increase of long-term average global temperatures of 3.6°C.[2] The World Bank also concluded that present emission trends put the world plausibly on a path toward 4°C within the century and that without further commitments and action to reduce GHGs global temperatures are likely to rise above 3°C,[3] which is consistent with IEA projections. However, even if all current commitments are implemented there is a 20 per cent likelihood of exceeding 4°C by 2100 — and if they are not met this warming could occur as soon as 2060. This level of warming and associated sea-level rise of 0.5 to 1 metre, or more, by 2100 is not the end point, as further warming over 6°C with several metres of sea-level rise are likely to occur over the following centuries. The World Bank acknowledged that uncertainties remain in projecting both the extent of climate change and its impacts but warned that no country will escape the impacts of climate change. Indeed, the world's poorest regions, which have the least economic, institutional, scientific and technical capacity to adapt, will suffer most.[4] Meanwhile, scientists are warning that carbon dioxide and methane emissions from thawing permafrost could amplify the global warming caused by anthropogenic GHG emissions.[5] Overall, their current observations indicate that large-scale thawing

---

[2] *World Energy Outlook 2012* (International Energy Agency, November 2012) 1 <http://www.worldenergyoutlook.org/publications/weo-2012/#d.en.26099>.

[3] *Turn Down the Heat: Why a 4°C Warmer World Must be Avoided* (World Bank, November 2012) <http://climatechange.worldbank.org/sites/default/files/Turn_Down_the_heat_Why_a_4_degree_centrigrade_warmer_world_must_be_avoided.pdf>.

[4] Ibid xiii.

[5] See *Policy Implications of Warming Permafrost* (United Nations Environment Program, November 2012) <http://www.unep.org/pdf/permafrost.pdf>.

of permafrost may have already started. Permafrost contains 1700 gigatonnes of carbon dioxide (CO_2), almost twice as much currently in the atmosphere. If permafrost thaws, the organic matter, which was buried and frozen thousands of years ago, could emit amounts of CO_2 and methane which are irreversible on human time scales.

A Outcomes of the Doha Negotiations

Despite this, international climate change negotiations have, over the past five years, delivered outcomes that are entirely inadequate to save the planet from the effects of climate change, many of which are already locked in. The Eighteenth Conference of the Parties ('COP 18') to the *United Nations Framework Convention on Climate Change* and the Eighth Meeting of the Parties ('MOP') to the *Kyoto Protocol* proceeded at Doha across three tracks:

- the Advance Working Group on Long-term Cooperative Action ('AWG-LCA')
- the Advance Working Group on Further Commitments for Annex I Parties (developed countries) under the Kyoto Protocol ('AWG-KP')
- the Ad Hoc Working Group on the Durban Platform for Enhanced Action ('ADP').

The first two working groups were established in 2007 at the Bali climate change negotiations to delay a decision on whether future legally binding GHG reduction commitments would be made under the *Kyoto Protocol*. Only developed countries accepted legally binding reduction targets under this Protocol to reduce their emissions by 5 per cent below 1990 levels by 2012. The AWG-LCA was consequently established to keep discussions alive on mitigation, adaptation, finance, technology transfer and capacity building until a decision was taken on the future of the *Kyoto Protocol*, or some other mechanism post-2012, when the first commitment period of the *Kyoto Protocol* expires. A key achievement of this working group is that developed and developing countries made voluntary, albeit inadequate, emissions reduction commitments at the Copenhagen negotiations in December 2009, which were confirmed at Cancun in December 2010.[6] A key achievement of the AWG-KP, meanwhile, was the decision taken at the Seventeenth Conference of the

---

[6] Commitments made by developed and developing countries are available here: UNFCC, *Mitigation: Reducing and Limiting Greenhouse Gas Emissions* UNFCC The Cancun Agreements <http://cancun.unfccc.int/mitigation/>.

Parties ('COP 17') in December 2011 to commence a second commitment period for the *Kyoto Protocol*. COP 17 also saw the establishment of the ADP to work on 'a protocol, or other legal instrument or an agreed outcome with legal force under the UNFCCC', intended to include both developed and developing countries. At COP 18 the work of both the AWG-LCA and the AWG-KP concluded, so all future international negotiations will now occur under the auspices of the ADP.

A number of decisions were made at Doha,[7] one of which was that the second commitment period of the *Kyoto Protocol* would commence on 1 January 2013 and end on 31 December 2020.[8] Also, developed countries should achieve aggregate emissions reductions of 25-40 per cent below 1990 levels by 2020.[9] It is important to note, however, that Canada withdrew from the *Kyoto Protocol* in November 2012, the United States has never ratified it and Russia and Japan have not signed up to the second commitment period. This compromises the overall reductions expected of developed economies. Essentially, it will be the task of the ADP to work with developed and developing countries to achieve the level of reductions needed to achieve all of the Parties' stated goal of holding the increase in global average temperatures to below 2°C above pre-industrial levels in accordance with the principle of common but differentiated responsibility,[10] as well as to attain a global peaking of emissions as soon as possible.[11] The key terms of this agreement will be concluded by 2015 and come into effect in 2020. Australia's emissions reduction commitment under the second commitment period of the *Kyoto Protocol* is 5 per cent below 2000 levels of emissions by 2020. However, Australia retains the option to move up within its 2020 target of 5 to 15 or 25 per cent below 2000 levels at a later stage should all countries agree to significant emissions reduction targets.[12]

---

[7] FCCC/KP/CMP/2012/L.9 available at: *Full Library Record* (2013) United Nations Framework Convention on Climate Change <http://unfccc.int/documentation/documents/advanced_search/items/6911.php?priref=600007290>.

[8] Ibid Art 4.

[9] Ibid Art 7.

[10] Draft decision -/CP.18 available at *Bonn Climate Change Conference — June 2013* (2013) United Nations Framework Convention on Climate <http://unfccc.int/2860.php#decisions>.

[11] Ibid Art 1.

[12] See *Doha Amendment to the Kyoto Protocol* available at <http://unfccc.int/files/kyoto_protocol/application/pdf/kp_doha_amendment_english.pdf>.

II International Energy Agency World Energy Outlook 2012

When discussing renewable energy in the context of climate change it is important to understand the global context of energy resources as contained in the IEA's *World Energy Outlook 2012* report released on 12 November 2012.[13] This chapter discusses some of the report's key points.

A A New Global Energy Landscape is Emerging

The IEA reports that a new global energy landscape is emerging with potentially far-reaching consequences for energy markets and trade evidenced by a resurgence of oil and gas production in the US, while international oil markets hinge on Iraq's ability to revitalise its oil sector; a retreat from nuclear energy in some countries; rapid growth in wind and solar technologies; and the global spread of unconventional gas production. The IEA also noted that a concerted effort to improve global energy efficiency could be a 'game-changer'.

The IEA identifies three critical issues facing the energy sector: meeting ever-growing energy needs driven by rising incomes in emerging economies; providing the world's poorest with access to energy; and meeting the world's climate change objectives.[14] Yet the world is failing to put the global energy system onto a more sustainable path, in spite of all current developments and policies. To this end the IEA has developed a New Policies Scenario, which is its central scenario. Key features include that over the period to 2035, global energy demand grows by one-third, with China, India and the Middle East accounting for 60 per cent of this growth. There is a pronounced shift away from oil, coal and, in some countries, nuclear energy towards natural gas and renewable sources of energy. That said, fossil fuels remain dominant in the global energy mix, supported by subsidies amounting to $523 billion in 2011, up almost 30 per cent since 2010 and six times more than that for renewable sources of energy. Subsidies are most prevalent in the Middle East and North Africa. Given this, the IEA states that emissions correspond to an increase of long-term average global temperatures of 3.6°C.

---

[13] IEA, *World Energy Outlook* (2013) <http://www.worldenergyoutlook.org/publications/weo-2012/#d.en.26099>.

[14] Ibid 1.

B   *Limiting Temperature Rise to 2°C*

One of the most salient warnings from the IEA is that no more than one-third of proven reserves of fossil fuels can be consumed prior to 2050 if the world is to limit the rise in temperature to 2°C, absent a wide deployment of Carbon Capture and Storage ('CCS').[15]

C   *Different Shades of Gold for Natural Gas*

The IEA predicts that natural gas is the only fossil fuel for which global demand will grow; and it is also the only fossil fuel which, in the author's view, presents a substantial threat to the deployment of renewable energy resources. Demand for growth in China, India and the Middle East is strong while domestic reforms in China increase consumption from 130 billion cubic metres (bcm) in 2011 to 545 bcm in 2035. In the US, gas is likely to overtake oil in 2030 while by 2020 the EU will revert to demand levels in 2010. Consumption in Japan is limited by high prices and a shift to renewable energy sources and energy efficiency. However, public concerns about the environmental impact of producing unconventional gas could impact seriously on its production unless robust regulatory frameworks are developed and exemplary industry performance demonstrated.[16] The IEA previously expressed similar views in two previous special reports on unconventional gas entitled *Golden Age of Gas*,[17] released in 2011, and *Golden Rules for a Golden Age of Gas*,[18] released on 29 May 2012.

D   *Will Coal Remain a Fuel of Choice?*

The IEA expects that the most important low emissions policy choices to impact on coal will emerge in India and China, given that these countries will account for three-quarters of non-OECD growth in demand. China's demand is expected to peak in 2020 and remain steady to 2035, and by 2025 India is expected overtake the US as the world's second-largest user of coal. Coal trade will continue to grow to 2020 when India will become the largest net importer, but will then level off as China's

---

[15]   Ibid.

[16]   Ibid 5.

[17]   IEA, *World Energy Outlook 2011 — Special Report* (2013) World Energy Outlook <http://www.worldenergyoutlook.org/goldenageofgas/>.

[18]   *Golden Rules for a Golden Age of Gas (Released 29 May 2012)* (2013) World Energy Outlook <http://www.worldenergyoutlook.org/goldenrules/>.

imports decline.[19] Note, however, that in February 2013 China's State Council set a total primary energy consumption (including renewable energy and transport fuel) of 4 billion tonnes of standard coal equivalent in the five years to 2015.[20]

E   Renewables Take their Place in the Sun

The IEA is optimistic about the future of renewable energy, stating that increases in hydro-electric, wind and solar power make renewable energy sources an indispensable part of the energy mix, accounting for almost one-third of the energy mix, with solar power growing most rapidly. By 2015, renewable energy will be the second-largest source of generation (half that of coal) and by 2035, it will approach coal as the primary source of energy. Subsidies for renewable energy are expected to grow from US$88 billion globally in 2011 to US$240 billion in 2035.[21]

III   ENERGY IN AUSTRALIA 2012

The IEA's prognosis of world energy resources provides a useful background against which to view Australia's current and future energy resources and consumption scenarios as discussed in *Energy in Australia 2012*.[22]

A   Resources

With regard to the share of global energy resources, Australia has:

- 33 per cent of the world's uranium resources, which has more than doubled over the past two decades and increased 62 per cent from 2006-10, and which is located in South Australia (SA), Northern Territory (NT) and Western Australia (WA)

- 10 per cent of the world's black coal resources (high quality bituminous coal, characterised by low sulphur and low ash resources)

---

[19]   Ibid.

[20]   See John Garnaut, 'Time for Change: China Flags Peak in Coal Usage', *Sydney Morning Herald* (online), 6 February 2013 <http://www.smh.com.au/business/carbon-economy/time-for-change-china-flags-peak-in-coal-usage-20130206-2dxrv.html>.

[21]   Above n 10, 5.

[22]   Australian Government: Department of Resources, Energy and Tourism, *Energy in Australia Publication* (14 September 2012) <http://bree.slicedlabs.com.au/sites/default/files/files/publications/energy-in-aust/energy-in-australia-2012.pdf>.

- 2 per cent of the world's conventional gas resources, with increasing utilisation of coal seam gas ('CSG'), which is located in Queensland (Qld) and New South Wales (NSW) and which stands at about one-third of conventional gas identified resources

- a small proportion of world crude oil, mostly located off the coasts of WA, NT and Victoria (Vic)

- extensive renewable energy resources, currently underdeveloped except for hydro-electricity and wind energy, which are growing rapidly.[23]

The ratio of current production to demonstrated reserves means that Australia has resources to last 517 years for brown coal, 128 years for black coal, 66 years for conventional gas, 175 years for CSG and 134 years for uranium.[24]

B *Consumption*

Australia is the eighteenth-largest energy consumer in the world and ranks fourteenth on a per person basis. It is composed of 95 per cent fossil fuels and 5 per cent renewable energy (mainly wood and woodwaste, biomass and biogas).[25] The energy intensity of the Australian economy has declined due to energy efficiency gains and growth of the commercial and services sectors.[26]

Energy consumption by type is 37 per cent black and brown coal, 35 per cent petroleum, 23 per cent gas and 5 per cent renewable energy (which has remained stable for the last decade).[27] With regard to renewable energy, 67 per cent is biomass (wood and bagasse, largely from sugarcane in Qld), 16 per cent is hydro-electric power and 17 per cent is biofuels, wind and solar power.[28]

Energy consumption by sector shows that 75 per cent of energy consumption is by electricity generation, transport and manufacturing, with the next largest energy-consuming sectors being mining, residential and commercial and services sectors.[29]

---

[23] Ibid 10.

[24] Ibid 14.

[25] Ibid 19.

[26] Ibid 20.

[27] Ibid 21.

[28] Ibid 22.

[29] Ibid 25.

C   Electricity

Resources used for electricity generation include 52 per cent black coal, 23 per cent brown coal, 15 per cent gas, 5 per cent hydro-electricity; 2 per cent wind and 3 per cent other.[30] With regard to capacity, in 2009-10, Australia's principal electricity generation was around 54 gigawatts ('GW') with capacity utilisation between 49-56 per cent over the past 5 years. As at October 2011, there were 19 major electricity generation projects at an advanced stage of development representing combined capacity of 2668 megawatts ('MW') at a cost of $4.8 billion. Of these, 7 are wind-powered, representing 41 per cent of advanced electricity projects with gas-fired 37 per cent, black coal-fired 17 per cent and hydro- and solar-powered 5 per cent respectively of planned capacity.[31]

With regard to pricing, Australia's electricity prices are relatively low and below the OECD average in 2010. Energy represents about 2.2 per cent of household expenditure with the major driver of rising retail prices being investment in infrastructure. This is estimated to be 44-53 per cent of prices in 2009-10, with wholesale prices comprising 35-40 per cent.[32]

D   Clean Energy

With regard to future prospects for renewable energy, the capacity of planned wind farms is increasing, concentrated in Vic, NSW and SA, with an average size of 190 MW with some at 1000 MW. There are a number of large-scale solar power projects under consideration around the country which will be supported by the Solar Flagships program. Australia has considerable geothermal capacity, which can produce baseload power, with one 80 kW facility in Qld and several at the approval stage in Vic and SA.[33]

---

[30]   Ibid 33.

[31]   Ibid 36.

[32]   Ibid 40. (Note: the Report released in September 2012 does not include the impact of any carbon price mechanism on prices. At time of writing, other sources place this at around 6 per cent of the price increases.)

[33]   Ibid 57.

E   Coal Production and Trade

Coal is Australia's largest commodity export, earning $44 billion in 2010-11, although in 2013 Indonesia overtook Australia as the world's largest coal exporter. With regard to production, Australia accounts for 6 per cent of world black coal production with 97 per cent sourced from NSW and Qld. Production increased 3.6 per cent between 2005-06 and 2009-10, supported by the commissioning of new mines, rail networks and ports in Qld and NSW. In 2010-11, production declined 10 per cent because of Qld floods and heavy rainfall in NSW, but production rebounded in 2011-12. Production is likely to increase with, as at October 2011, 20 committed coal mining projects and 76 proposed.[34]

F   Gas Production and Trade

Australia is a significant exporter of liquefied natural gas ('LNG') given that half of all gas produced is exported at a value in 2010-11 of $10.4 billion. Since 1999-2000 domestic consumption increased at an average annual rate of 4 per cent. Gas accounted for 23 per cent of domestic energy consumption and 15 per cent of electricity generation in 2009-10.[35]

With regard to production, Carnarvon (WA), Cooper/Eromanga (central Australia) and Gippsland (Vic) basins account for 98 per cent of production in 2010-11. WA produces more than two-thirds of national production in 2010-11 with production growing 6 per cent over five years. The domestic gas market is uniquely exposed to international energy market conditions because of high level of production in WA far from the Eastern seaboard gas market. CSG increased its share of total gas production in the eastern market from 2 per cent in 2002-03 to 11 per cent in 2010-11, with 98 per cent of production occurring in Qld in 2010-11.[36]

With regard to trade, as of 2010-11 Australia's LNG exports were 20 million tonnes, an increase of 12 per cent on the previous year. Exports had a value of $10.4 billion in 2010-11 representing a 30 per cent increase on prices in the previous year as a result of higher oil prices to which a number of LNG contracts are indexed. The Asia Pacific is the major trading region, including Japan, China and Korea.[37]

---

[34]   Ibid 60.

[35]   Ibid 67.

[36]   Ibid 69.

[37]   Ibid 71.

G   *Petroleum Production and Trade*

Australia's petroleum production is not a significant part of its energy resources profile. A great deal — 73 per cent — of Australia's petroleum production occurs in the Carnavon Basin and most of it is exported given its proximity to Asian refineries, with only 17 per cent produced in the Gippsland Basin. In 2010-11 Australia imported 31.8 gigalitres ('GL') of crude oil and other refinery feedstock, with Malaysia being the largest source of crude oil (19 per cent) and Indonesia providing 15 per cent. In 2010-11 Australia exported 19.6 GL largely to Singapore, Korea, China and Japan, with Japan accounting for 61 per cent of Australia's liquefied petroleum gas ('LPG') exports in 2010-11. Australia exported 0.8 GL of refined petroleum in 2010-11 with 54 per cent going to Singapore and 29 per cent to New Zealand. Australia's earning from crude oil and other refinery feedstock exports was AU$11.8 billion in 2010-11.[38]

H   *Prospects of Energy in Australia*

Over the medium- to longer-term, a major change in the Australian energy landscape is expected to be driven by the Renewable Energy Target ('RET'), discussed in depth below, and was also expected under the former Labor government's Clean Energy Future package. The Abbott government has introduced legislation to repeal various aspects of the Clean Energy Future package, including the carbon price mechanism[39] and the abolition of the Clean Energy Finance Corporation.[40] The fate of the repealing legislation remains undecided until the Senate has had the opportunity, especially when it is reconstituted on 1 July 2014 following the 2013 elections, to vote on it. Furthermore, the full implications of the Abbott government's Direct Action Plan are not fully understood at the time of writing given the very recent release of the Emissions Reduction Fund Green Paper.[41] The Green Paper is directed specifically to emissions reduction programs such as gas capture and energy efficiency but also reiterates that an element of the Direct Action Plan is funding for the One Million

---

[38]   Ibid 83.

[39]   See Clean Energy Legislation (Carbon Tax Repeal) Bill 2013 (Cth).

[40]   See Clean Energy Finance Corporation (Abolition) Bill 2013 (Cth). Note that on 10 December the Senate rejected this Bill. At the time of writing, the government needed to wait three months before reintroducing the Bill.

[41]   The Emissions Reduction Fund Green Paper was released on 20 December 2013. See <http://www.environment.gov.au/topics/cleaner-environment/clean-air/emissions-reduction-fund/green-paper>.

Solar Roofs and the Solar Towns and Solar Schools initiatives.[42] At the time of writing the RET remains unchanged, although a review of the Act is due in 2014. According to then Department of Resources, Energy and Tourism, the largest renewable energy expansion is likely to be in wind energy followed by solar power and geothermal energy. In the non-renewable energy sector a large increase in the use of gas, especially in electricity generation, is expected. CCS will be critical in maintaining coal in Australia's electricity production. A lower carbon economy, necessitated by Australia's international commitment under the second commitment period of the *Kyoto Protocol* and any future international agreements, will inevitably involve long-term structural adjustment of the energy sector while considerable investment is required in energy supply chains to meet demand and integrate low emission technologies. Trade and investment opportunities in new industries and technologies will arise.[43]

IV   RENEWABLE POWER GENERATION COSTS IN 2012

The author turns now to consider renewable power generation costs in 2012 which are relevant to Australia, especially should the domestic legal, policy and incentive regimes match those in countries where prices are reaching parity with that of fossil fuel energy. At the start of 2013, the International Renewable Energy Agency ('IRENA') published an important report, *Renewable Power Generation Costs in 2012: An Overview.*[44] IRENA is an intergovernmental organisation dedicated to renewable energy and was founded on 26 January 2009 in Bonn, Germany, by seventy-five states that signed its Statute. As of September 2012, one hundred states and the EU have ratified the Statute and are IRENA Members. Australia is a member.

IRENA's objective is to promote the widespread and increased adoption and the sustainable use of all forms of renewable energy. These include energy produced from renewable sources in a sustainable manner such as bioenergy, geothermal energy, hydro-electric power, ocean, solar and wind energy. The report has been published out of concern that the absence of accurate and reliable information on the cost and performance of renewable technologies presents a significant barrier to the

---

[42]   Ibid 2.

[43]   Ibid 110, n 22.

[44]   IRENA, *Renewable Power Generation Costs in 2012: An Overview* (2013) <http://www.irena.org/ menu/index.aspx?mnu=Subcat&PriMenuID=36&CatID=141&SubcatID=277>.

uptake of these technologies.[45] A key point of the report is that the rapid uptake of renewable sources of energy means that the cost for wind, solar photovoltaic energy ('solar PV'), concentrating solar power ('CSP', that is, parabolic troughs and solar towers) and some biomass technologies is declining. Meanwhile hydro-electric power and geothermal energy produced at good sites is often the cheapest way to generate power.[46]

A   A Solar PV

In September 2012, solar PV module prices were selling for US$0.75 per watt. Installed costs in Germany for under 100 kilowatts ('kW') rooftop systems fell by 65 per cent between 2006-12 to US$2.2 per watt, making solar PV competitive with current residential electricity prices.[47] The weighted average levellised cost of electricity ('LCOE') of grid connected solar PV varies per kilowatt hour ('/kWh') from US$0.15/kWh to US$0.31/kWh.[48] This analysis does not include, however, the impact of government incentives or subsidies, CO_2 pricing, reduction by renewable energy of non-CO_2 externalities such as air quality, and insulation from volatile fossil fuel prices. If these were quantified the economics of renewable energy would be improved.[49]

B   Concentrated Solar Power ('CSP') Systems

CSP systems include parabolic trough systems and solar towers. Parabolic trough systems have LCOEs of US$0.20-0.36/kWh while that of solar towers is between US$0.17-0.36/kWh. LCOEs of CSPs in areas with excellent solar resources drop to US$0.14-0.18/kWh with solar towers having greater capacity for cost reductions into the future.[50]

---

[45]   Ibid 13.

[46]   Ibid 14.

[47]   Ibid 14. Note that at the time of writing, current residential prices in NSW, not including time of use pricing, is approximately AU$0.27/kWh or AU$0.00027W, which indicates different renewable energy economics for Australia.

[48]   This makes the cost of grid connected solar power in the US competitive with cheap fossil fuel prices in Australia.

[49]   IRENA, above n 44, 14.

[50]   Ibid 17.

C   Onshore Wind Farms

The LCOE of new onshore wind farms in 2011 was between US$0.06 to US$0.14/kWh, assuming a cost of capital of 10 per cent. At the best sites in the US, wind delivers electricity at US$0.04-0.05/kWh making wind competitive with, or cheaper than, gas-fired generation — even in the 'golden age of gas'.[51]

D   Biomass

Biomass can be very cost competitive where low-cost feedstocks from industry, forestry or agriculture are available. In the OECD prices are typically US$0.06/kWh and US$0.02/kWh in developing countries.[52]

E   Geothermal Energy

Geothermal energy is a mature, baseload technology with the LCOE varying from US$ 0.09-0.14/kWh assuming a 10 per cent cost of capital.[53]

F   Off-grid Electrification

IRENA concludes that renewable technologies provide the best priced solution for off-grid supply as well as for centralised grid supply in locations with good supply. So, they can assist countries to improve energy security, promote economic development, reduce GHG emissions and reduce energy price volatility given the global volatility in fossil fuels.[54]

G   Total Installed Costs per Technology

Installed onshore wind costs in major OECD markets in 2011 were between US$1750-2200/kW but in the US some were as low as US$1500/kW with costs in 2012 trending lower to an average US$1750 in the US in the first half of 2012. Costs in China and India are lower due to lower turbine prices (US$630/kW for Chinese

---

[51]   Ibid 16.

[52]   Ibid 17. Note that the report does not mention some of the already identified conflicts between biofuels and food security, especially in developing countries.

[53]   Ibid 17.

[54]   Ibid 15.

turbines in 2012) with installed costs ranging between US$925 and US$1470/kW.[55] Offshore wind farms are more capital intensive and expensive at US$4000-4500/kW due to installation and grid connection costs as well as equipment needed to operate in harsh environments.

The installed costs of solar PV depend on the subsector such as residential or commercial rooftop and on the regions where installation occurs. Ground-mounted utility scale systems in India, Germany and China have the lowest cost at US$1720, US$2008 and US$2160/kW respectively. Germany has the lowest cost for residential PV at US$2200/kW in 2012. In China, California and Italy the costs were US$3100, US$3300 and US$3400/kW respectively.

CSP plants are only recently being installed at a scale and cost of US$4600/kW in OECD countries and US$3500/kW in developing countries. However, when 6 hours of energy storage is added, costs increase to US$7100-9800/kW but capacity factors double. With 6-15 hours of energy storage, solar towers cost US$6300-10 500/kW.[56]

Biomass with low-cost feedstock costs between US$660-1860/kW with plants in OECD countries costing more.[57]

Hydro-electric power installation costs vary, depending on remoteness from existing infrastructure and so on, between US$1050-4215/kW. Small hydro-electric power costs between US$1300-5000/kW while in developing countries it can be as low as US$500-600/kW at good sites.[58]

Geothermal (flash power plants) costs US$2000-4000/kW and (binary cycle plants) US$2400-5900/kW.[59]

The report does caution that it has assumed a cost of capital of 10 per cent for projects but that this may well differ country by country depending on its risk profile.[60]

---

[55]   Ibid 18.

[56]   Ibid 19.

[57]   Ibid.

[58]   Ibid.

[59]   Ibid.

[60]   Ibid.

V   COMPLEMENTARY MEASURES AND REGULATORY RISK

Despite the IEA's prognosis, as stated in its *World Energy Outlook 2012*,[61] that renewable energy will, as the saying goes, 'take its place in the sun', there are many challenges that still need to be resolved. Fossil fuel resources are plentiful and cheap, especially when the externalities, both CO_2 and non-CO_2, of their use are not priced. High direct and indirect subsidies for fossil fuels are also masked, while subsidies and support schemes for renewable energy have recently been criticised in jurisdictions like Australia, particularly where a carbon price mechanism is in place. As the ensuing case study demonstrates, government support for renewable energy through the adoption of a renewable energy target, coupled with other measures such as 'feed-in' tariffs, is controversial.

When an Australian emissions trading scheme ('ETS') was first proposed, economists expressed the view that an RET was unnecessary. The Productivity Commission, for example, stated that additional measures could significantly increase abatement costs yet would provide no additional emissions reductions unless they were carefully conceived.[62] In its view, an ETS could shoulder much of the abatement effort, meaning that other policies would only be needed to fill the gap.[63] This is because the market is likely to achieve an efficient outcome through the decentralised price-responsive actions of everyone in the economy. Furthermore, an RET would result in electricity prices that are higher than without an RET, and market co-ordination about the appropriate time to introduce low emissions technologies would be overridden.[64] Similarly, the Garnaut Review stated that the Carbon Pollution Reduction Scheme would deliver the required emissions reductions and that other policies to reduce emissions can have no useful role once the ETS is in place.[65]

In spite of this advice, the Rudd government increased Australia's existing RET under the *Renewable Energy (Electricity) Act 2000* (Cth) from 2 per cent to 20 per cent by 2020 before being phased down from 2025 and terminated at the

---

[61]   *World Energy Outlook 2012*, above n 2.

[62]   See 'What Role for Policies to Supplement an Emissions Trading Scheme' (Productivity Commission, 2008) xiii <http://www.pc.gov.au/__data/assets/pdf_file/0003/79716/garnaut.pdf>.

[63]   Ibid.

[64]   Ibid xvii.

[65]   Garnaut Climate Change Review, *Draft Report: June 2008* (4 July 2008) See <http://www.garnautreview.org.au/CA25734E0016A131/pages/all-reports--resources-draft-report.html>.

end of 2030.[66] The legislation establishes a renewable energy trading scheme whereby eligible generators create renewable energy certificates ('REC's) which are tradeable. Meanwhile, electricity retailers are 'liable entities' and must surrender RECs to satisfy a legal obligation to purchase renewable energy. In order to stimulate investment in small-scale solar power, the Australian Government provided a Renewable Energy Bonus Scheme — Solar Hot Water Rebate ('REBS'). REBS provided householders a rebate of $1000 to install a solar hot water system or $600 to install a heat pump hot water system from 19 February 2010 through to 30 June 2012. In addition, if a small-scale PV system was installed between 9 June 2009 and 30 June 2012, the homeowner would receive five times as many RECs as under the standard deeming arrangements. On 16 November 2012, the Australian Government announced that this Solar Credits multiplier would be phased out for small-scale systems installed from 1 January 2013.[67]

The unintended consequence of these government support schemes is that between 2001-10 the market experienced an oversupply of RECs from small-scale generators such as solar water heaters and solar panels. This resulted in the deflation of the price for RECs and lessened the financial incentives to establish large-scale renewable energy projects.[68] In 2011, the scheme was converted into a Large-scale Renewable Energy Target ('LRET') and a Small-scale Renewable Energy Scheme ('SRES'). Two types of certificates may now be created: large-scale generation certificates ('LGC's), which are created in relation to generation by accredited power stations, and small-scale technology certificates ('STCs'), which are created in relation to the installation of solar hot water systems and small generation units. The LRET is currently fixed at 41 000 gigawatt hours ('GWh') per annum between 2020-30. The SRES is uncapped.[69]

---

[66] For an extensive discussion of the RET see Rosemary Lyster and Adrian Bradbrook, *Energy Law and the Environment* (Cambridge University Press, 2006); see also Rosemary Lyster et al, *Environmental and Planning Law in New South Wales* (Federation Press, 3rd ed, 2012) ch 7.

[67] See <http://ret.cleanenergyregulator.gov.au/Latest-Updates/2012/November/3>.

[68] See <http://www.google.com.au/search?q=OFFICE+OF+RENEWABLE+ENERGY+BOOKLET &hl=en-AU&gbv=2&prmd=ivns&ei=lDYyU_LVH8fEkQXN14HgBg&start=10&sa=N> for a good summary of the changes to the Renewable Energy Target since 2011.

[69] Note that on 19 December 2012, the Climate Change Authority ('CCA') released its final report on its review of the Renewable Energy Target ('RET') and the government has six months in which to respond to the recommendations. The report is available at: CCA, *Renewable Energy Target Review* (2012) <http://climatechangeauthority.gov.au/ret>.

One of the concerns about the RET is that its costs are borne by consumers, as costs are passed on as increased electricity prices. Low-income households spend a larger proportion of their income on electricity. Fossil fuel generators are also affected through lower wholesale prices and reduced market share.[70] Recent analysis suggests that under the RET, the estimated cost of abatement is around $87-115 per tonne of carbon dioxide equivalent (CO_2e) at 2020, compared with a carbon price in the range of $45-50 per tonne CO_2e at 2020.[71] The Independent Pricing and Regulatory Tribunal ('IPART') estimated that the impact of the RET on an average customer bill in NSW in 2012-13 would be be $100 per annum or 5 per cent of the total electricity bill.[72] While there is an assistance package to reduce the impact of the carbon price, nothing similar exists for the RET.[73] As discussed below, substantial investments in transmission infrastructure, smart load control systems and closely located peak generation capacity are likely to be required to facilitate the penetration of the large quantities of intermittent generation (especially wind) encouraged by the RET. This will also add to overall electricity costs for users. This is of concern given that electricity prices in Australia for both industrial and residential customers have risen in real terms: prices have increased by around 30 per cent since 2006, with electricity prices for households rising more than for businesses.[74]

Concern about the costs of RETs has also arisen with regard to 'feed-in' legislation such as that introduced in NSW and other states.[75] In 2009, the NSW government introduced a 'gross' Feed-in Tariff ('FIT') payable to generators of electricity from solar PV systems and wind turbines of no more than 10kW capacity.[76] The FIT requires an electricity retailer to pay 60 cents/kWh for all electricity generated from

---

[70] Ibid 5.

[71] *Assessing the Impact of Key Climate Change Policies on Energy Users* (Deloitte Access Economics, June 2011) <http://www.euaa.com.au/wp-content/uploads/2011/02/EUAA-report-Final-20-June-2011-2.pdf>.

[72] Climate Change Authority RET Review, above n 69, 20.

[73] Ibid 23.

[74] *Assessing the Impact of Key Climate Change Policies on Energy Users*, above n 71.

[75] The South Australian, Victorian and Queensland governments have also introduced 'feed-in' legislation; see div 5A pt 2 of the *Energy Legislation Act 2000* (Vic) and *Electricity (Feed-In Scheme — Solar Systems) Amendment Act 2008* (SA) and *Clean Energy Act 2008* (Qld). Note that these schemes are 'net' feed-in schemes where the householder is only paid for excess electricity not consumed by the household.

[76] The FIT was established by an amendment to the *Electricity Supply Act 1995* (NSW) s 34A.

a household PV system installed on or before 27 October 2010.[77] It was intended to operate from 1 January 2010 to 31 December 2016. Given costs blowouts and a rise in electricity prices, in October 2010 the then NSW Government announced that it would reduce tariff payments from 60 cents to 20 cents for all customers joining the scheme after 18 November 2010, and the scheme capacity was limited to 300 MW. Subsequently, systems connected from 1 July 2012 are not eligible to receive Scheme tariff payments. Given concerns about the cost of the Feed-in Tariff, IPART was appointed to investigate and report on a 'fair and reasonable' value for small-scale solar PV.[78] IPART's determination of 'a fair and reasonable solar feed-in tariff' is 7.7-12.9 cents/kWh, which is a far cry from the 60 cents/kWh originally paid by the government.[79]

VI   SUBSIDIES TO, AND SUPPORT FOR, THE FOSSIL FUEL INDUSTRY

There has been quite a significant backlash against government subsidies to, and support for, renewable energy technologies in Australia because of their effect on price. Yet this ignores the various fossil fuel subsidies which have a significant impact on the ability of renewable energy sources to compete on a 'level playing field' in terms of price. Subsidies to fossil fuels may include:

- direct support in the form of prices, taxes and support mechanisms, production support and consumption support

- indirect support in the form of the existing electricity infrastructure and rules catering exclusively for fossil fuel electricity

- indirect support in the form of infrastructure facilitated by government for the production, transport and export of fossil fuels

- indirect support by failing to cost the externalities, both climate and non-climate, of fossil fuels.

---

[77]   *Electricity Supply General Regulation 2001* (NSW) cl 104L.

[78]   See <http://www.ipart.nsw.gov.au/Home/Industries/Electricity/Reviews/Retail_Pricing/Solar_feed-in_tariffs/04_Aug_2011_-_Terms_of_Reference/Terms_of_Reference_-_Solar_feed-in_tariffs_-_August_2011>.

[79]   IPART, *Determination — Solar Feed-in Tariffs — Retailer Contribution and Benchmark Range for 1 July 2012 to 30 June 2013* <http://www.ipart.nsw.gov.au/Home/Industries/Electricity/Reviews/Retail_Pricing/Solar_feed-in-tariffs_-_2012-2013/27_Jun_2012_-_Determination_-_Solar_feed-in_tariff_-_Retail_contribution_and_benchmark_range_for_1_July_2012/Determination_-_Solar_feed-in-tariffs_-_Retailer_contribution_and_benchmark_range_for_1_July_2012_to_30_June_2013>.

A Direct Support

The International Institute for Sustainable Development ('IISD') released a report in May 2012 on fossil fuel subsidies and government support in the OECD.[80] The report notes the irony that while developing countries are struggling to mobilise US$100 billion a year by 2020 to support climate mitigation and adaptation, fossil fuel subsidies of up to US$750 billion are being committed from public funds.[81] The report refers to the first ever OECD *Inventory of Support to Fossil Fuel Production or Use* which places Wealthy Country subsidies at US$45-75 billion per year. It places Developing Country Subsidies at US$409 billion in 2010, expected to reach US$630 billion in 2012.[82] The report claims that reforming these subsidies would lead to significant GHG reductions and aggregate increases of GDP in both OECD and non-OECD countries of up to 0.7 per cent per year until 2050.[83] The report notes that at the Rio+20 Conference on Sustainable Development the UN Secretary-General's High Level Panel on Global Sustainability produced a consensus report, *Resilient People Resilient Plant: A Future Worth Choosing*, which recommended that the nations of the world phase out fossil fuel and reduce other perverse or trade-distorting subsidies by 2020.[84] Meanwhile, a separate study places subsidies to China's fossil fuel energy at US$50 billion in 2007.[85]

B Barriers to Entry to Incumbent Electricity Grids

A 2002 report entitled *Towards a Truly National and Efficient Energy Market*[86] found that there are barriers to embedded generation,[87] and recommended that a mandatory

---

[80] See *Fossil Fuel Subsidies and Government Support in 24 OECD Countries* (IISD, 31 May 2012) <http://www.iisd.org/gsi/sites/default/files/ffs_report_sustain_energy.pdf>.

[81] Ibid 4.

[82] Ibid.

[83] Ibid 5.

[84] Ibid 7.

[85] See Wei Liu and Hong Li, 'Improving Energy Consumption Structure: A Comprehensive Assessment of Fossil Energy Subsidies Reform in China' (2011) 39 *Energy Policy* 4134, 4137.

[86] *Towards a Truly National and Efficient Energy Market* (Council of Australian Governments' Independent Review of Energy Markets Directions, 2002) <http://www.efa.com.au/Library/ParerFinRpt.pdf>.

[87] Ibid 74.

code of practice governing arrangements between distribution companies and prospective embedded generators be introduced into the *National Electricity Law*.[88]

Further, in 2006 the Ministerial Council on Energy Standing Committee of Officials released a Discussion Paper entitled *Impediments to the Uptake of Renewable and Distributed Energy*.[89] Although there are different impediments to Renewable and Distributed Generation ('R&DG') depending on the size of a given generator, there are a number of impediments commonly faced by all renewable generators. These are:

- Approvals processes for R&DG projects can be complex and inconsistent across jurisdictions.

- Per-unit generation costs are generally higher than conventional technologies.

- There is no strategic regional focus on planning for R&DG technologies and current network planning tends to be incremental.

- It is often difficult for new technologies to obtain planning approval, financing and skilled labour while access to support infrastructure can be difficult.

- Economic signals for distributed and close-to-load generation is often muted or lost because of a lack of locational and cost reflective pricing (and associated metering).

- Incremental connection costs can be potentially prohibitive for new R&DG projects, particularly where projects require network augmentations or provision of a major new line. Although the National Electricity Rules require connection agreements to be fair and reasonable, it may be necessary to develop further guidance on what this amounts to. Network connection regulations can also be complex.

- Network Service Provider concerns about the reliability of R&DG may be a barrier to active uptake.

The Paper states that these problems can only be overcome if emerging technology issues are adequately addressed, R&DG proponents and consumers are able to

---

[88] Ibid 96.

[89] *Impediments to the Uptake of Renewable and Distributed Energy* (Discussion Paper, Ministerial Council on Energy Standing Committee of Officials, 2006).

participate effectively in the market, and the network is capable of managing increased levels of R&DG in a cost-effective manner.

Progress on addressing these issues has been slow. However, the Australian Energy Market Commission is currently considering a rule change request in relation to the process for connecting embedded generators to the distribution network under ch 5 of the National Electricity Rules ('NER'). The process is regarded as creating uncertainty for connection applicants while the lack of a technical standard under the rules for embedded generators means that technical requirements vary greatly between distributors. Further, the current provisions under the NER for determining connection costs and charges are not sufficiently clear and transparent. On 14 June 2012, the Australian Energy Market Commission ('AEMC') initiated the rule change process[90] and it subsequently published the draft *National Electricity Amendment (Connecting Embedded Generators) Rule 2013* on 27 June 2013.[91]

The AEMC also released the *National Electricity Amendment (Small Generation Aggregator Framework) Rule 2012* on 29 November 2012.[92] The rule creates a new category of Market Participant that will be able to sell the output of geographically dispersed multiple small generating units without the expense of individually registering every generating unit. This change should facilitate a more direct exposure to market prices for small generating units, so creating a more efficient wholesale market. Consumers should also benefit through lower prices paid for electricity, especially in peak times.

One of the more difficult aspects of renewable energy sources is its intermittent nature, which in itself creates problems with regard to reliability, energy security and grid integration. In 2012 the Clean Energy Council released a report, *Energy Storage in Australia*, (the 'Report')[93] which points to the commercial opportunities, barriers and policy opportunities to energy storage in Australia as a means to support existing electricity networks. Energy storage is also regarded as facilitating the efficiency of

---

[90]   See AEMC, *Rule Changes: Open* (14 June 2012) <http://www.aemc.gov.au/Electricity/Rule-changes/Open/connecting-embedded-generators.html>.

[91]   See <http://www.aemc.gov.au/Media/docs/Draft-rule-determination-20877d82-a966-471e-a71a-9e6dac7545b6-0.pdf>.

[92]   Available at <http://www.aemc.gov.au/media/docs/Final-determination-25d1102a-fd76-4dde-a0e5-470d92b30387-0.pdf>.

[93]   See *Energy Storage in Australia: Commercial Opportunities, Barriers and Policy Options* (Marchment Hill Consulting, November 2012). See <http://energystoragereport.info/tag/marchment-hill/>.

electricity markets, providing stability to the grid and the National Electricity Market as intermittent renewable energy sources are integrated, servicing remote communities by allowing greater independence from the grid and providing storage to residential and commercial customers.[94] Storage systems could charge during off-peak times and discharge electricity at peak times so minimising supply interruption. This also avoids the need for new capital investment in transmission and generation capacity and can smooth out the fluctuating frequency associated with solar and wind energy.[95] The Report finds that by 2030 the commercial market for storage could reach 3000 MW, which is a significant proportion of current generation capacity.[96]

The Report identifies a number of technical, economic and regulatory barriers to energy storage. From a regulatory perspective it suggests that the barriers might be adequately addressed by the proposed *Connecting Embedded Generators and Small Generators Aggregator framework* electricity rule changes,[97] especially if the AEMC were to explicitly recognise energy storage as a qualifying form of embedded generation.[98] As well, the Report recommends that the *Small Generation Aggregator Factor* electricity rule change should be supported and energy storage recognised as a qualifying form of small generation.[99]

This situation is not unique to Australia. In China, for example, structural problems exist for renewable energy in spite of China accounting for a quarter of total global investment in clean energy, amounting to US$269 billion in 2012. China invested US$68 billion compared with the US's US$44 billion.[100] Despite the enactment of China's *Renewable Energy Law 2005*, and amendments in 2009, wind farms performed below expectation due to long delays in connecting wind farms to the grid, the lower conversion efficiency of domestic turbines compared with international manufacturers and grid company curtailment of wind energy out of concern that it might destabilise the grid. Curtailments have resulted in 17 per cent

---

[94]   Ibid 5.

[95]   Ibid 20.

[96]   Ibid.

[97]   Ibid 52.

[98]   Ibid 56.

[99]   Ibid 57.

[100]   Bloomberg New Energy Finance, 'China Steps on the Clean Energy Pedal', *Climate Spectator* (online), 16 January 2013 <http://www.climatespectator.com.au/commentary/china-steps-clean-energy-pedal>.

of wind power being unused,[101] and this occurs in spite of the 2007 *Measures on Grid Company Full Purchase of Electricity from Renewable Energy* requiring prompt connection. To overcome such problems, the government issued draft *Regulations for Management of Renewable Power Quotas* in May 2012 for grid companies, power generators and provincial-level governments.[102] Other problems include inconsistency in planning laws,[103] development of resources in provinces far away from areas of need and international technology standards,[104] such as system frequency modulation, not being consistent with Chinese conditions.[105]

What these case studies demonstrate is that it is not sufficient for a government to simply set renewable energy portfolio standards and feed in tariffs and expect renewable energy to establish a presence in an energy market where fossil fuel electricity is the incumbent type of energy. Far more needs to be done at the legal and policy level to ensure that renewable energy technologies are given their best chance to succeed in spite of the inherent biases towards fossil fuel energy.

What is also clear is that the cost of renewable energy technologies needs to be set in the context of the many uncosted externalities of fossil fuel electricity, to which the discussion now turns.

C   The Hidden Externalities of Fossil Fuel Energy: a Disconnect between Energy Law and Environmental Law

While direct support for the fossil fuel industry and the barriers to entry for renewable energy have already been discussed, there is yet another way in which governments have protected the fossil fuel industry — by failing to constrain and price the air pollution associated with electricity generation. There are three ways in which environmental law has reified the 'cost-effectiveness' of fossil fuel energy, and consequently allowed renewable energy sources to be regarded as too expensive: structural support for the continued dominance of fossil fuel energy through a pollution law 'constrain-but-

---

[101]   See Sara Schuman and Alvin Lin 'China's Renewable Energy Law and Its Impact on Renewable Power in China: Progress, Challenges and Recommendations for Improving Implementation' (2012) 51 *Energy Policy* 89, 94.

[102]   Ibid 92.

[103]   See Ming Zeng, Chen Li and Lsha Zhou 'Progress and Prospective on The Police System of Renewable Energy In China' (2013) 20 *Renewable and Sustainable Energy Reviews* 36, 39.

[104]   Ibid 40.

[105]   Ibid 41.

permit' model, specific exclusions and exemptions for coal, oil and gas from various legal controls, and fossil-favouring implementation choices under existing statutory authority.[106] Here, this chapter focuses only on the failure by government in the US to adequately internalise the health and climate externalities of fossil fuel electricity. This case study could be, and indeed should be, replicated in all jurisdictions around the world.

In 2009 the US National Research Council ('NRC') responded to a request by Congress to examine the externalities of energy production in the United States and produced a report entitled *Hidden Costs of Energy: Unpriced Consequences of Energy Production and Use*.[107] The NRC's report provides a sophisticated and detailed economic analysis of the climate and non-climate related damages from coal-fired power stations and all other sources of energy.

Regarding non-climate externalities the NRC found that, in 2005, monetised damages from coal burning were greater than any other form of energy production, considering impacts on health, crop yields, building materials and other areas. These damages amounted to US$62 billion in 2005, or $156 million on average per plant.[108] If plants are weighted by the amount of electricity they generate, the mean damage is 3.2 cents/kWh with variations between plants explained by differences in emissions intensity.[109] These damages are 20 times higher than from electricity generated by natural gas. More than 90 per cent of the damages are associated with premature human mortality, with 85 per cent of those damages emanating from sulphur dioxide emissions.[110] If the figure of US$62 billion for damages is due to the US burning 940 million metric tonnes of coal in 2005, then the damages amount to $66/tonne of coal burnt.

In response, on 6 July 2011 the US Environmental Protection Agency ('EPA') finalised the making of the *Cross-State Air Pollution Rule* ('CSAPR ') under the *Clean Air Act* 42 USC § 7401 (1963) ('CAA'). The rule requires 23 states to reduce sulphur

---

[106] See Uma Outka 'Environmental Law and Fossil Fuels: Barriers to Renewable Energy' (2012) 65 *Vanderbilt Law Review* 1680.

[107] *Hidden Costs of Energy: Unpriced Consequences of Energy Production and Use* (The National Academies Press, 2010) <https://download.nap.edu/catalog.php?record_id=12794> '*Hidden Costs of Energy*'.

[108] Ibid 6.

[109] Ibid.

[110] Ibid 340.

dioxide and nitrogen oxide emissions from power plants starting in 2012.[111] This would help downwind areas attain the 24-Hour and/or Annual PM2.5 National Ambient Air Quality Standards.[112] The EPA predicted this would prevent 14 000 to 26 000 premature deaths, 21 000 cases of acute bronchitis, 23 000 non-fatal heart attacks, 26 000 hospital and emergency room visits, 1.9 million days of missed work or school, 240 000 cases of aggravated asthma and 440 000 cases of upper and lower respiratory symptoms. Reduced pollution would also lead to environmental improvements such as improvements in visibility in national and state parks, and increased protection for sensitive ecosystems including Adirondack lakes and Appalachian streams, coastal waters and estuaries, and forests. The Rule was expected to result in total annual monetary benefits of $120 to $290 billion.

In spite of the EPA's factual findings justifying its regulatory action, the US DC Circuit Court of Appeals struck down the CSAPR on the grounds that:

> EPA's authority derives from the statute and is limited by the statutory text.
> EPA's reading of Section 110(a)(2)(D)(i)(I) — a narrow and limited provision — reaches far beyond what the text will bear.[113]

The Court has also denied the EPA's request for an *en banc* rehearing of this matter,[114] meaning that the EPA will have to remake its Rule to ensure that it is consistent with the limitations, as identified by the Court, with the CAA.

The NRC also considered plausible scenarios of US$10, US$30, and US$100 per tonne of climate related damages per carbon dioxide equivalent ('CO_2e') from coal fired power stations (combined with up to 20 per cent biomass), with the ranges factoring in various uncertainties inherent in climate change modelling. It concluded that climate change damages of 1, 3 and 10 cents/kWh from these facilities were feasible.[115] On 13 May 2010, the EPA issued the 'Tailoring Rule' to address GHG

---

[111] Note that the sulphur content of coal in the US ranges according to the US Department of Energy from 0.6 pounds of sulphur dioxide per million British thermal units (lb/mm Btu) emissions limit (low sulphur), 0.61-1.67 lb/mm Btu emissions limit (medium sulphur) and 1.68 lb/mm Btu emissions limit (high sulphur); see *U S Coal Reserves. An Update by Heat and Sulfur Content* (Energy Information Administration:1993). See <http://large.stanford.edu/publications/coal/references/docs/052992.pdf>.

[112] Environmental Protection Agency, *PM2.5 NAAQS Implementation* (11 June 2013) <http://www.epa.gov/ttn/naaqs/pm/pm25_index.html>.

[113] *EME Homer City Generation LP v EPA*, 696 F 3d 7, 27-8 (DC Cir, 2012). The author was alerted to this case by Outka, above n 106, 1718.

[114] *EME Homer City Generation LP v EPA*, 696 F 3d 7 (DC Cir, 2012).

[115] *Hidden Costs of Energy*, above n 107, 307.

emissions from stationary sources under the CAA permitting programs. This requires all new facilities with GHG emissions of at least 100 000 tons per year ('tpy') CO_2e and existing facilities with at least 100 000 tpy CO_2e, which are changing their production processes and so increasing GHG emissions by at least 75 000 tpy CO_2e, to obtain Prevention of Significant Deterioration ('PSD') air pollution permits. Those facilities already required to obtain a PSD permit anyway, to cover other regulated pollutants, must also address GHG emissions increases of 75 000 tpy CO_2e or more. New and existing facilities with GHG emissions above 100 000 tpy CO_2e must obtain operating permits in addition to their PSD permits. This rule was challenged but upheld by the DC Circuit in *Coalition for Responsible Regulation v EPA*.[116]

VII   REAFFIRMING THE NEED FOR SUBSIDIES TO, AND SUPPORT FOR, RENEWABLE ENERGY

What the evidence establishes is that global fossil fuel resources are plentiful and that, absent the need to curtail their use in the context of climate and non-climate externalities, the world would continue to use them as the primary energy source. The only type of energy which has the lowest climate and non-climate externalities is renewable energy, as confirmed in the National Research Council's 2009 report *Hidden Costs of Energy*. Yet a case is constantly being made against reliance on renewable energy both on the grounds of reliability, energy security and price. Seldom considered, certainly by the public reacting to the price of renewable energy, are the inbuilt direct and indirect subsidies to fossil fuels and the failure to fully internalise the climate and non-climate externalities of this type of energy. It is very well known that the fossil fuel industry continues to actively lobby governments around the world to prevent them from internalising these costs. This chapter has shown the many reasons why, while this type of lobbying for fossil fuel energy and against renewable energy continues, renewable energy will struggle to take 'its place in the sun'.

---

[116]   684 F 3d 102, 117 (DC Cir, 2012). Note the author was alerted to this case by Outka, above n 106, 1718.

6

A BIOGRAPHY OF LAND, LAW AND PLACE

LEE GODDEN

I INTRODUCTION: LAND AS LAW

Land, as it is captured by the technicalities of law, is defined as a planar surface save for the imprint of title, registered legal interests and the overlay of planning regulations. These legal forms codify the human use and occupation of a given place. By contrast, this chapter seeks to unpack the layering of land which makes a place and which gives it both spatial and temporal dimension and a sense of history, including conflicts over land use and appropriation.[1] In short, it seeks to create a biography of land which is realised through the genealogical tracings of law. This biography is necessarily truncated; like photographs in a family album it provides snapshots through time mediated through the constructs and practices of law. The land in question is located in the South Gippsland coastal region of Victoria. Most recently it came to legal attention as the subject of a dispute around the location of a wind farm. Looking back from this conflict in 2006, this chapter describes three more slices of time. The first retrospective snapshot relates to the middle of the twentieth century, a time when Torrens Title registration systems predominated as a legal configuration for making ownership transparent, working in concert with emerging town and country

---

[1] Fred Bosselman, 'Four Land Ethics: Order, Reform, Responsibility, Opportunity' (1994) 24 *Environmental Law* 1439, 1447.

planning laws. The second step backward is to the early part of the nineteenth century, a time when colonial land law was asserted in what was to become the newly settled colony of Victoria. The final stage is both retrospective and prospective. It explores the occupation and governance of the land by Aboriginal peoples at the point of colonisation. Yet it looks forward to the time when parts of the land again might be governed under Aboriginal law as a consequence of a native title claim or as part of a settlement under the *Traditional Owners Settlement Act 2010* (Vic).

While it might be enough simply to describe these layers — to seek no other ontological meaning for land than its mere existence — law always demands more. Law needs to map the interface between a land and people so that it can decide the human questions of access, use, possession and ownership: both at the discrete level of property and land law but also more widely to satisfy the modern techniques and demands of land-use planning and resource management. Moreover, an acknowledgment that Australian land law differed in fundamental ways from its common law origins in deciding specific questions of access, use, possession and ownership was an important means of grounding that law in its 'place'. Distinctive Australian legal scholarship, including the major land law texts of Adrian Bradbrook and fellow authors, were an aspect of developing that *in situ* understanding. Accordingly, this chapter charts the interface between a land and its people by providing an understanding of the variety of forms of land law and legal regimes that have sought to regularise the conflicts over land and place in this region of South Gippsland.[2]

II   MAP, LAND AND LAW

The land to which this biography applies can be made known, located according to the transfixing of place that is achieved by Cartesian techniques of representing space.[3] Land law depends on this prior positioning of land through the techniques of survey and mapping. Control of land in this manner is premised upon standardisation of forms of representation. Survey and map are socio-technical systems with the character of immutable mobiles. Latour describes the development of 'immutable mobiles' being those inscription procedures and technologies which allow objects

---

[2]   Richard T Ford, 'Law's Territory (A History of Jurisdiction)' in Nicholas Blomley, David Delaney and Richard T Ford (eds), *The Legal Geographies Reader* (Blackwell, 2001) 205.

[3]   Roger JP Kain and Elizabeth Baigent, *The Cadastral Map in the Service of the State* (University of Chicago Press, 2009) 329.

to be at once represented consistently but yet made transferrable. Perhaps the most decisive development was printing. Later immutable mobiles built on print forms, and included mapping and legal instruments such as title deeds. In these forms, parts of the natural world including land could be symbolically represented by abstract signs such as legends on maps or survey coding on title documents. When inscripted into surveys, maps, diagrams and files they can be collected together. Once collected together, they can be manipulated by science; and beyond science by institutional bureaucracies and the administrative systems which characterise land law.[4]

These artefacts of land and associated institutional practices can be rapidly transmitted and disseminated as the technical form becomes readily reproducible over time and space. Thus the map that depicts land; that makes it knowable to law, and through law, has taken on a form that is at once standardised but 'transferable'. In turn, the map functions as a socio-technical device that allows the knowledge of land to transcend the local, intimate, visceral sense of occupation. So, too, property and land law no longer cling so closely to 'occupatio', the theory which grounds legal right in physical possession. Land law, though, has never quite been able to shed its origins in the practices of occupying, marking and bounding land.[5] The patterns on a map continue that cultural practice of marking land — simply at one remove from the visceral. Nor is the map ever entirely neutral in its depiction of space.[6] So we turn our gaze to the land for which law,[7] like the map, will be the interface; the mediation between external thing and person; and between *meum* and *tuum* as the property relationship has been characterised.[8]

But if we set aside our postmodern sensibilities for a moment and simply trust to the implacable reliability of geographic co-ordinates we can understand the relative

[4]   Bruno Latour, 'Drawing Things Together' in Michael Lynch and Steve Woolgar (eds), *Representations in Scientific Practice* (MIT Press, 1990) 21, 27-35.

[5]   Alain Pottage, 'The Measure of Land' (1994) 57(3) *Modern Law Review* 361, 384.

[6]   David Delaney, Richard T Ford and Nicholas Blomley, 'Preface: Where is Law?' in Nicholas Blomley, David Delaney and Richard T Ford (eds), *The Legal Geographies Reader* (Blackwell, 2001) xix.

[7]   For a discussion of the construct of the gaze of colonial law see Annelise Riles, 'The View from the International Plane: Perspective and Scale in the Architecture of Colonial International Law' in Nicholas Blomley, David Delaney and Richard T Ford (eds) *The Legal Geographies Reader* (Blackwell, 2001) 276.

[8]   Robert Gray, 'A Good Speed to Virginia' (1609) in John Payne Collier (ed), *Illustrations of Early English Popular Literature* (Benjamin Blom, 1966) vol 2, 23; Kevin Gray and Susan Francis Gray, *Land Law* (Oxford University Press), 2009) 2.

positioning of the place.[9] Bald Hills is situated some 10 kilometres or so from the small town of Tarwin Lower in South Gippsland, Victoria.[10]

The land is situated within rural zonings,[11] specifically the farming zone,[12] under the South Gippsland Planning Scheme. Gippsland is a region east of the metropolitan capital of Melbourne, named in honour of an early British Governor. So much of the Australian continent was made known to European civilisation through a nomenclature that was integral to the appropriation of the land under a colonial Empire.[13] The naming of the wider region after Governor Gipps resonates with the sense of the legal authority of a Governor as the British sovereign's representative in a new colony. In its very naming as 'Gipps land' — the land that belongs to Gipps, albeit as the legal representative of the British Crown — it points to the origins of land law and property within a colonial Empire. As *Mabo v State of Queensland (No 2)* confirmed some 200 years after the acquisition of British sovereignty over *terra australis*, that question of sovereignty was non-justiciable.[14] Further, upon acquisition of sovereignty, the common law of England settled like a proverbial cloak upon the land, bringing the rules and practices of the doctrine of estates and tenures drawn from a distant England.[15] As Justice Brennan noted, '[i]t has however long been incontrovertible that the provisions of the common law which became applicable upon the establishment by settlement of the Colony of New South Wales included the general system of land law'.[16]

---

[9] By contrast Ryan points out that, 'space is understood as objectively being "out there", a natural state, alternatives to which are difficult to imagine' in Simon Ryan, *The Cartographic Eye: How Explorers Saw Australia* (Cambridge University Press, 1996) 4.

[10] The site is situated in Cape Liptrap, South Gippsland Shire: *Bald Hills Wind Farm (EES)* [2004] PPV 73 (24 June 2004) [3.1] (Chair Smith, Member Banon, Member Finn); The site is 8-12 kilometres south west of Tarwin Lower: Wind Power Pty Ltd, *Environmental Effects Statement for the Bald Hills Wind Farm Project — Main Document 2003*, 14.

[11] *Bald Hills Wind Farm (EES)* [2004] PPV 73 (24 June 2004) [6.1] (Chair Smith, Member Banon and Member Finn).

[12] At the time of the Panel Hearing for the Bald Hills Wind Farm, the site for the proposed wind farm was zoned Rural Zone. See, though, Planning Scheme Amendments VC 24 (11 June 2004) and C36 (12 July 2007).

[13] George Seddon, 'Words and Weeds', *Landprints: Reflections on Place and Landscape* (Cambridge University Press, 1997) 23.

[14] *Mabo v Queensland [No 2]* (1992) 175 CLR 1, 31 (Brennan J).

[15] Ibid 25 (Brennan J).

[16] Ibid 60 (Brennan J). Note Gippsland originally formed part of the wider colony of New South Wales until the colony of Victoria gained independent status.

Those doctrines remain the key tenets of land law within Australia. Gippsland is a place crystallised by that legal inheritance. Moreover, the cloak of English common law settled over 'country' that had been occupied for millennia by Aboriginal peoples.[17] Until 1992, the common law legal inheritance obscured the conflict and violence brought by settlement to the land in South Gippsland. Thus, land is 'known' or 'recognised' by law through prisms of conflict and order.

III   FIRST SNAPSHOT: THE BALD HILLS WIND FARM

Shifting the gaze from the Gippsland region to the wind farm site and surrounds focuses attention on other conflicts over land. Here, too, law was an essential forum for mediating a conflict that referenced the competing power dimensions of the global and the local. The tensions played out around how the land and its use was to be positioned between the global concerns of reducing greenhouse gas emissions and the visual and amenity impacts on local communities. There is a map available from the website of the company that is developing a wind farm at Bald Hills.[18] The company gained development approval to build the wind turbines only after a major dispute. The history of dispute informs and carefully filters the construct of place that appears in this map through a 'cartographic eye'.[19] That lens illuminates the resource dimensions of the land. Accompanying the map is the description:

> [t]he northern section is approximately 10 kms from the coast with hilly terrain
> running north to south at the rear of the site at an appropriate angle to the
> prevailing wind … The southern section is located on gently sloping farmland,
> with turbines located more than 2kms from the coast.[20]

The map serves an instrumental purpose in its depiction of place; categorising land according to human values, while seeming neutral in its content.

---

[17]   Thomas Richards et al, 'Box Gully: New Evidence for Aboriginal Occupation of Australia South of the Murray River Prior to the Last Glacial Maximum' (2007) 42(1) *Archaeology in Oceania* 1, 9.

[18]   Bald Hills Wind Farm Pty Ltd, *Bald Hill Wind Farm — Where is Bald Hills Wind Farm?* (February 2014) <http://www.baldhillswindfarm.com.au/project/location.php>.

[19]   Simon Ryan argues in *The Cartographic Eye* that early explorers and settlers in Australia adopted a vantage point from which to describe the interior of southern Australia in terms of its potential economic value through utilisation.

[20]   Bald Hills Wind Farm, above n 18. Note that more recently, laws require wind farm developments to be located away from high value amenity areas such as the coast: Amendment VC78 to the Victorian Planning Provisions.

Law also participates in the interpretation of land as 'site' — it is no longer land per se, but the nominated locus of human activity. A similar instrumental perception is to be found in the assessment documentation for the wind farm site prepared pursuant to the *Environmental Protection and Biodiversity Conservation Act 1999* (Cth) ('EPBC Act'). It, too, downplays the aesthetic and environmental values. That documentation indicates that the proposed site is 'largely cleared for cattle and sheep grazing but with some remnant native vegetation'.[21] Land is perceived as already given over to the utilitarian ends of human use. The wind farm then on one level might simply represent the substitution of one use for another. That proposition, however, is belied by the vociferous local opposition to wind farm development which erupted in many parts of south-eastern Australia.

The global imperatives of mitigating climate change resulted in Australian government policies developing to support renewable technologies, such as wind farms and solar panels for electricity production.[22] The *Renewable Energy (Electricity) Act 2000* (Cth), for example, encourages 'the additional generation of electricity from renewable sources'.[23] Later laws have been more prescriptive with a Renewable Energy target coming into effect in later legislation.[24] Wind farms emerged as a major source of renewable energy in southern Australia, particularly in South Australia and Victoria.[25] Projects have been developed in suitable areas where there are significant

---

[21] *Bald Hills Wind Farm (EES)* [2004] PPV 73 (24 June 2004) [3.1] (Chair Smith, Member Banon and Member Finn); Gardner Group Pty Ltd, *Environment Protection and Biodiversity Conservation Act 1999 — Referral Form* (17 July 2002) [3.1] <http://www.environment.gov.au/cgi-bin/epbc/epbc_ap.pl?name=current_referral_detail&proposal_id=730>.

[22] See, eg, Department of Resources, Energy and Tourism, *Draft Energy White Paper: Strengthening the Foundations for Australia's Energy Future* (2011); Department of Climate Change and Energy Efficiency, *Securing a Clean Energy Future* (2011).

[23] *Renewable Energy (Electricity) Act 2000* (Cth) s 3.

[24] For more information on the Renewable Energy Target see Australian Government, Department of Climate Change and Energy Efficiency, *Renewable Energy Target* <http://www.climatechange.gov.au/government/initiatives/renewable-target.aspx>.

[25] There have been numerous referrals of wind farm projects under the *Environment Protection and Biodiversity Conservation Act 1999* (Cth) in recent years (for example, approximately 18 referrals during the period April 2011-April 2013): Department of Sustainability, Environment, Water and Communities, *Referrals List Page* (24 November 2008) EPBC Act — Public Notices <http://www.environment.gov.au/cgi-bin/epbc>.

wind resources.[26] Wind farms comprise turbines mounted on high towers to harness the wind energy; any single 'farm' can comprise many turbines. The invocation of the word 'farm' to describe these largely industrial technologies is interesting; it's suggestive of the older style bucolic windmills of the past which have featured in many agricultural settings.

Despite some allusion to the bucolic by advocates, opposition to wind farms has been voiced by local communities who object to such facilities, particularly in areas of high landscape value.[27] Objectors within communities typically regard the vital issues associated with wind farm development to be environmental impact and amenity concerns (turbine noise and shadow flicker, landscape degradation and biodiversity impacts). Alternatively, some community groups have supported wind farm development,[28] but all groups involved have asserted their rights of civic participation in planning law and development control processes.[29] The scale and policy significance of wind farm projects initially saw most assessment and approval processes managed by state and federal government authorities.[30] The Bald Hills project was assessed through a planning process in accordance with the *Planning and Environment Act 1987* (Vic) and an environmental assessment process in accordance with the EPBC Act.[31] The Victorian Minister for Planning appointed Planning Panels Victoria to investigate the required planning approvals and the environmental effects

---

[26]   Details of Australian wind farm installations are available from: Clean Energy Council <http://www.cleanenergycouncil.org.au/technologies/wind-energy.html>.

[27]   The Tarwin Valley Coastal Guardians made submissions to the Panel for the Bald Hills Wind Farm: see *Bald Hills Wind Farm (EES)* [2004] PPV 73 (24 June 2004) [2.3] (Chair Smith, Member Banon and Member Finn); see also *Taralga Landscape Guardians Inc v Minister for Planning and RES Southern Cross Pty Ltd* [2007] 161 LGERA 1.

[28]   See, eg, the Hepburn community group in Central Victoria that sought to develop their own wind farm in *Perry v Hepburn Shire Council* (2007) 154 LGERA 182.

[29]   See, eg, Misha Ketchell and Melissa Fyfe, 'A Blow or a Boon? Might Turbines Split Communities?', *The Age*, 26 August 2007, 7.

[30]   The Bald Hills project required planning approval by the Minister for Planning for the use and development of a wind energy facility over 30 MW in capacity (see clauses 35.01-1 and 52.32 of the South Gippsland Planning Scheme) and for the removal of native vegetation (the Minister for Planning called in the permit application from the Gippsland Shire Council). See *Bald Hills Wind Farm (EES)* [2004] PPV 73 (24 June 2004) [2.1.1] (Chair Smith, Member Banon and Member Finn).

[31]   The Commonwealth Minister for Environment accredited the assessment process under the *Environmental Effects Act 1978* (Vic).

of the proposal. State government in Victoria was strongly supportive of wind farm development at first, with the Victorian government designating the Bald Hills wind farm project as 'of great benefit for the environment across Victoria'.[32]

Within Victoria, the *Planning and Environment Act 1987* gives effect to the statutory planning framework. For wind farm developments, this system requires proponents of wind farm projects to apply and be granted a planning permit before proceeding with construction.[33] The application process also requires the project proponent to conduct related impact assessments,[34] and to consult with affected communities.[35] After the planning panel cleared the project, the State Government approved a 52-turbine wind farm on the Bald Hills site. The Bald Hills project also required approval from the Commonwealth Minister for Environment as a controlled action. The federal Minister of the time, Senator Ian Campbell, initially refused approval[36] on the basis of the cumulative risk presented by wind turbines to populations of the endangered orange-bellied parrot.[37] Under the EPBC Act, the federal government considers environmental impacts upon designated matters of national environmental significance.[38] The existence of endangered species, like the

---

[32] Victoria, *Parliamentary Debates*, Legislative Assembly, 25 August 2004, 110 (Stephen Bracks, Premier).

[33] Department of Planning and Community Development, Victoria Planning Provisions, Wind Energy Facility (29 August 2011) [52.32-2] accessible at The State of Victoria, *Victorian Planning Provisions* (2010) Victorian Planning Provisions <http://planningschemes.dpcd.vic.gov.au/vpps/>.

[34] As set out, for example, in the *Environment Effects Act 1978* (Vic); *Aboriginal Heritage Act 2006* (Vic); *Flora and Fauna Guarantee Act 1988* (Vic); *Environment Protection and Biodiversity Conservation Act 1999* (Cth); *Native Title Act 1993* (Cth).

[35] A study has found that transparency and proper consultation is determinative as to whether or not the community will ultimately support the development: Nina Hall, Peta Ashworth and Hylton Shaw, *Exploring Community Acceptance of Rural Wind Farms in Australia: A Snapshot* (Report) (CSIRO, 2012) 45-9.

[36] Wind Power Pty Ltd/Energy Generation and Supply/Bald Hills, Tarwin Lower to Cape Liptrap Rd/VIC/Bald Hills Wind Farm 80 Turbines, Date of Notice on Approval Decision 03 Apr 2006, Not Approved, Department of Environment and Heritage, EPBC Act Date Received: 23 Jul 2002 Reference Number: 2002/730 at 31 July 2006.

[37] See Minister for the Environment and Heritage, Senator Ian Campbell, 'Bald Hills Wind Farm and Cumulative Impact Study' Press Conference, Perth, 5 April 2006.

[38] Nevertheless, the federal government has received a high number of EPBC Act referrals concerning wind farms: see the public register maintained at <http://www.environment.gov.au/cgi-p://www.environment.gov.au/cgi-bin/epbc>.

orange-bellied parrot, are one such matter relevant to granting approvals for wind farms under the EPBC Act.[39] The company behind the Bald Hills proposal, Wind Power, said the federal decision was 'completely unreasonable'.[40] On the other hand, a spokesman for the Tarwin Valley Coastal Guardians lauded the federal decision, noting, 'There were over 1500 objections to the proposal'. Another local greeted the decision as a win for locals, commenting, 'If people want to put wind farms in

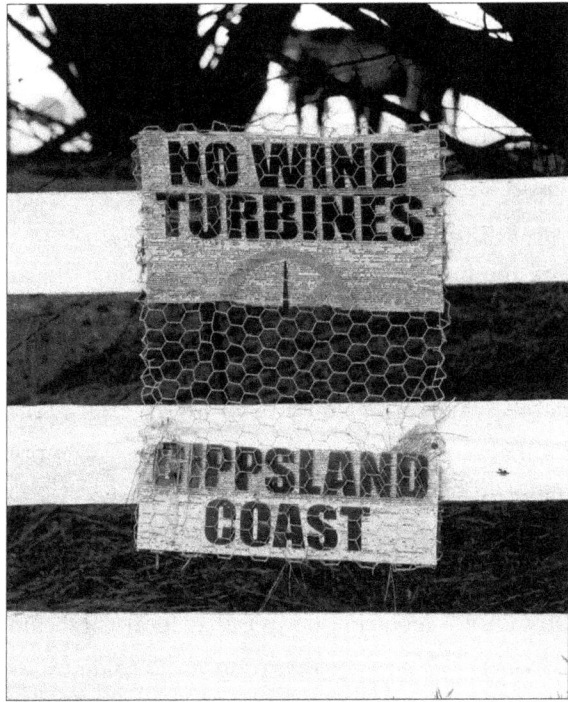

Figure 6.1: Farm gate protest, Gippsland Coast (Photograph, Lee Godden, 2011)

sensitive areas, they need to take a close look at how the local community is going to respond'.[41] The farm gate protest noted in Figure 6.1 demonstrates this response.

The Victorian government initiated a review of Senator Campbell's decision in the Federal Court, declaring the Minister's apparent concern with the health of parrots a 'political sham'[42] and suggesting instead that Senator Campbell was responding to concerns raised by landholders in order to bolster political support

---

[39] *Environment Protection and Biodiversity Conservation Act 1999* (Cth) s 16.

[40] See, eg, Ewin Hannan, 'Wind Farm Ban a Marginal Call', *The Weekend Australian*, 29 July 2006, 1; Jordan Chong, 'Minister Defends Wind Farm Veto' *The Age*, 6 April 2006 <http://www.theage.com.au/news/national/minister-defends-wind-farm-veto/2006/04/06/1143916631236.html>.

[41] Liz Minchin, Nassim Khadem and Peter Ker, 'Feathers Fly Over Wind Farm Ban', *The Age*, 6 April 2006 <http://www.theage.com.au/news/national/feathers-fly-over-wind-farm-ban/2006/04/05/1143916593234.html>.

[42] Minister for Planning, Rob Hulls, 'State to Launch Legal Challenge over Federal Wind Farm Stand' (Press Release, 27 April 2006).

for local candidates. The Federal Minister later reversed his decision, deciding to permit the Bald Hills wind farm to proceed.[43] In the disputes over wind farm developments, sometimes local communities' concerns triumph over nation-state or global interests.[44] Alternatively, global interests may be seen as paramount. Chief Justice Preston in the *Taralga* case described his task as that of resolving 'the conflict between the geographically narrower concerns of [the local community applicants] and the broader public good of increasing the supply of renewable energy'.[45] On balance, he found that the broader 'public good must prevail'.[46]

In the see-saw of opinion around wind farms, more recent legal and policy developments in Victoria have seen the locus of decision making change toward local government as the decision-making authority.[47] Typically, more local concerns about 'place' play an influential role where decision-making powers remain with local governments.[48] In March 2011 planning approval decisions for all wind farm projects were devolved to local government authorities.[49] This supported a government election promise to augment the role that local communities play in wind farm approval decisions.[50] A new consideration was introduced — the need to minimise the effects of wind farms on the local community.[51]

---

[43]   *Bald Hills Wind Farm Gets Green Light* (21 December 2006) ABC News Online <http://www.abc. net.au/news/2006-12-21/bald-hills-wind-farm-gets-green-light>.

[44]   See, eg, *Hislop & Ors v Glenelg SC*, Unreported, Victorian Civil and Administrative Tribunal, Tribunal Application No. 1997/88762; cf *Thackeray v Shire of South Gippsland* [2001] VCAT 739. See Alexandra Wawryk, 'Planning for Wind Energy: Controversy over Wind Farms in Coastal Victoria' (2004) 9(1) *Australasian Journal of Natural Resources Law and Policy* 103.

[45]   *Taralga Landscape Guardians Inc v Minister for Planning and RES Southern Cross Pty Ltd* (2007) 161 LGERA 1, 3.

[46]   Ibid.

[47]   Lisa Caripis and Anne Kallies, '"Planning Away" Victoria's Renewable Energy Future? Resolving the Tension Between the Local and Global in Windfarm Developments' (2012) 29 *Environmental and Planning Law Journal* 415.

[48]   Ibid 417.

[49]   Planning Scheme Amendment VC78 amended clause 61.01 of the Victorian Planning Provisions to reverse the previous automatic referral to the Minister for Planning as the decision-maker for wind farms with capacities of greater than 30 MW: Department of Planning and Community Development, *Amendment VC078 — List of changes to the Victorian Planning Provisions and Specified Planning Schemes* <http://planningschemes.dpcd.vic.gov.au/Shared/ats.nsf>.

[50]   See *The Victorian Liberal Nationals Coalition Plan for Planning* (2010) <http://vic.liberal.org.au/ webData/policies_others/Planning.pdf>.

[51]   New State Planning Policy Framework, cl 19.01; Victorian Planning Provisions Amendment VC 78 Explanatory Report.

Later amendments in 2011 adopted a more prescriptive planning approach based on the spatial exclusion of wind farms from defined zones. Planning controls now prohibit the building of wind farms in urban growth zones of regional centres in Victoria,[52] and in areas considered to have high amenity or to be significant tourist destinations.[53] This amendment has in effect zoned out wind farms from the land held to be most sensitive.[54] Prior to the amendments, wind farms were already excluded from national and state parks, coastal parks and Ramsar wetlands (comprising 43 per cent of the Victorian coastline and 32 per cent of all the land).[55] At the immediate site level, the proponent of a wind farm project now must obtain the written consent of the owner of any dwelling within two kilometres of the nearest turbine.[56] The legislative and planning scheme changes do not affect wind farms already granted approvals.[57] Thus, the Bald Hills Wind Farm will be able to be constructed. Whether a similar application in the area would be successful under current laws is more doubtful. The mix of competing values is clearly displayed on another farm gate (Figure 6.2).

The disputes over wind farms reveal how law mediates the interface between land and people, by seeking to regularise conflict — in this instance, conflict over competing land use and the values that are entailed. The vexed dispute around the Bald Hills wind farm also reveals much about how land is situated within a nested layering of global, national, state and local laws. Each layer of law may have its own objectives and orientations; and not all of these will be in alignment. Any place therefore exists within a reflecting prism of interacting laws, which in themselves may generate conflict. Maps, too, remain important. The designation of wind farm exclusion zones

---

52 Victoria Planning Provisions cl 37.07-01.

53 Victoria Planning Provisions cl 52.32-2 and Government of Victoria, Department of Planning and Community Development, Advisory Note 36: changes to wind energy facility provisions (August 2011).

54 A map depicting wind ban zones and the potential wind no go zones depending on owners' consent is available on the *Yes 2 Renewable* website managed by the Friends of the Earth Melbourne <http://yes2renewables.org/2011/09/19/maps-show-where-you-cant-build-a-wind-farm-in-victoria/>.

55 Department of Planning and Community Development, *Policy and Planning Guidelines for Development of Wind Energy Facilities in Victoria* (2009) 13. A 2012 version of the guidelines is available at <http://www.dpcd.vic.gov.au/planning/planningapplications/moreinformation/windenergy>.

56 Victoria Planning Provisions, cl 52.32-3; Environment Defenders Office (Vic) Ltd, *EDO Briefing Paper: Wind Farms or Coal Mines — Which One Will Be Subject to Stricter Planning Controls?* (13 December 2012) Wind Farms in Victoria (April 2011) <http://www.edovic.org.au/downloads/files/law_reform/edo_vic_wind_farm_comparison_paper.pdf>.

57 Victorian Planning Provisions, cl 52.32-7. The planning scheme amendments do not operate retrospectively for applications for permit extensions made by 15 March 2012 for wind farms approved by 15 March 2011.

under recent plan-
ning law amendments
again brings the map
into play as the pre-
requisite for legal de-
cision-making. The
Bald Hills project es-
caped the spatial net
of restrictions that
now surround wind
farm developments
in Victoria. Yet as the
wind power compa-
ny website reflects,
there remains an acute

**Figure 6.2: Competing values, farm gate protest
(Photograph, Lee Godden, 2011)**

awareness of how the wind farm exists, not as an excised space, but as place within a
'sensitive' local community and a web of laws.

IV   SNAPSHOT TWO: TOWN AND COUNTRY PLANNING: LAND AS
ORDERLY DEVELOPMENT

Planning controls and environmental impact assessment are central to the web of
laws constructing the legal understanding of the land on which the Bald Hills wind
farm is to be built. Balance and amenity are key concepts in these frameworks. Recent
interpretation of those principles in South Gippsland has tended to favour local
amenity values over broader environmental objectives.[58] These concepts of amenity
and balance are a legal link back to the next slice of time in the biography of this land.
Amenity, balance and social order were overarching objectives for the introduction
of the *Town and Country Planning Act 1944* (Vic),[59] the forerunner to the current
Planning and Environment Act 1987 in Victoria.

---

[58]   Judith Jones, 'Global or Local Interests? The Significance of the Taralga Wind Farm case' in Tim
Bonyhady and Peter Christoff (eds), *Climate Law in Australia* (The Federation Press, 2007) 262.

[59]   Victoria, *Parliamentary Debates*, Legislative Assembly, 12 September 1944, 839, 840 (Trevor Donald
Oldham).

Planning and development controls are significant for environmental protection at local and strategic levels. At their widest, they encompass environmental outcomes, including considerations of land use and degradation, biodiversity, pollution control, and retention of native vegetation.[60] Planning law systems, therefore, are fundamental to the legal regulation of human activities upon land. As the Bald Hills wind farm example demonstrates, the zoning controls operate in conjunction with the more discrete, site-based development control laws. Initially, planning law focused on the orderly development of urban buildings and infrastructure.[61] The spatial parameters and techniques of zoning land express this function of social 'ordering' of land most directly. The scope of planning laws was later extended to incorporate broadly-based land use management in rural areas. Most recently there has been an emphasis upon the attainment of ecologically sustainable development outcomes.[62] Nonetheless, the construct of amenity, together with the planning 'test' that requires the balancing of a range of considerations, remain core animating principles for planning law systems.

Planning law intersects in fundamental ways with property law and the land title system in determining questions of amenity and balance. A process of ordering and categorising land also exists within the property law and titling system. Most pertinently, this initial categorisation of land occurs in the division of land into public land under the Crown land system, and the private forms of landholding and title. Thus in returning to the Bald Hills land, we find another means of legal framing — a coding of the land through the planning law/property law interface. Thus the land becomes known to law in this instance as: 'some 1763 ha of private land in seven ownerships and nineteen separate titles, in the Rural Zone (RUZ) in the South Gippsland Planning Scheme'.[63]

The designation within the rural zone of the South Gippsland Planning Scheme reflects a more recent situating of the land within planning frameworks,[64] but it

---

[60]   Gerry Bates, *Environmental Law in Australia* (LexisNexis, 7th ed, 2010) 276.

[61]   Denzel Millichap, 'Law Myth and Community: A Reinterpretation of Planning's Justification and Rationale' (1995) 10 *Planning Perspectives* 279-80.

[62]   See, eg, *Planning and Environment Act 1987* (Vic) s 4; *Sustainable Planning Act 2009* (Qld) s 3.

[63]   *Bald Hills Wind Farm (EES)* [2004] PPV 73 (24 June 2004) [3.1] (Chair Smith, Member Banon, Member Finn).

[64]   Currently the relevant zone with respect to the Bald Hills wind farm is a Farming Zone under the South Gippsland Planning Scheme.

carries forward from the basic idea of ordering land for distinct rural purposes, which began with the *Town and Country Planning Act 1944*. The idea that some uses of land are quintessentially rural in character and afford rural amenity was embedded within that statute. The rural zoning of land therefore necessarily entails a value judgment about what human activities are characteristically rural. In turn, this value system draws on long historical associations between agricultural and pastoral settlement and 'land' in the common law. A pastoral vision of nature and rural lifestyles has long been regarded as an antidote to the excesses of progress.[65] The resistance of the South Gippsland Landscape Guardians to the 'progress' of wind farm development invokes a much longer legal history.[66] Historically, the need to 'use' rural land in a manner that fitted agricultural notions was a powerful impetus in shaping the settlement policy in south-eastern Australia.[67] The preference for rural landscapes to preserve a sense of historical continuity with Britain was an important means of defining land within rural Victoria. Constructs embodying idealised rural existence were important influences in developing ideas around sublime landscapes and associated aesthetic values. Lowenthal identifies trends to preserve sublime landscapes as a phenomenon apparent in many countries which came to the fore over the twentieth century.[68] In turn, these concepts became aligned to rational philosophies for 'ordering' land.

In introducing the Town and Country Planning Bill 1944 (Vic), The Minister noted that:

> the definition arrived at by experts is that town and country planning is the science of guiding and shaping the growth of our cities, towns and rural areas in association with the prevailing social and economic conditions of life, the physical characteristics of the land and its climatic conditions. The health and happiness of every member of the community is fundamental to all our endeavours to shape the physical growth of the town and country.[69]

---

[65]   Christopher Lasch, *The True and Only Heaven: Progress and its Critics* (WW Norton & Sons, 1991) 83.

[66]   Bruce Kercher, *An Unruly Child: A History of Law in Australia* (Allen & Unwin, 1995) 94.

[67]   Michael Williams, 'More and Smaller is Better: Australian Rural Settlement: 1788-1914' in JM Powell and Michael Williams (eds), *Australian Space, Australian Time: Geographical Perspectives* (Oxford University Press, 1975) 61-71.

[68]   David Lowenthal, *The Past is a Foreign Country* (Cambridge University Press, 1985) 385.

[69]   Victoria, *Parliamentary Debates*, Legislative Assembly, 12 September 1944, 839-40 (Trevor Donald Oldham).

Underpinning these sentiments is the idea that land exists as a malleable substratum upon which to achieve good social outcomes through the application of science to guide the physical processes of development. The second reading speech also queries whether these 'scientific' principles of planning are to apply across all of Victoria —a query which the Minister answers in the affirmative. Moreover, in an echo of present-day concerns, there is a view that the proposed legislation can assist in fostering regional development and in addressing metropolitan sprawl. There is an explicit recognition that country areas, like cities, must be planned — mindful of the soil, the natural resources and other place-specific factors.[70] In 1944, Victoria was on the cusp of introducing significant land use planning laws that would begin to impact upon the capacity of regional municipalities and local communities to foster growth in accordance with localised values and perceptions of amenity. Those laws were to grow in extent and complexity over the years as the possible uses for land such as that in Bald Hills proliferated under the pressures of population growth, rural structural change and increasingly as a result of the need to 'order' local land in alignment with state and national policy imperatives.

As Figure 6.3 depicts, principles of amenity and landscape value still mix with more utilitarian and instrumental uses of land in the zoning and 'orderly development' of land in South Gippsland. Under the Gippsland Planning Scheme, local planning policies provide the framework for rural land use and development in the region.[71] The 'protection of the character and significance of sensitive coastal landscapes'[72] is identified as a key influence, alongside the 'need to demarcate settlement boundaries and provide improved design guidance and control over development in coastal settlements, in order to protect settlement and coastal character as the pressure for development in these areas continues to increase'.[73] The need to balance rural amenity with industrial and farming land usage is captured in

> the need to raise the awareness of people who choose to live in rural areas
> that they must expect rural land uses and infrastructure levels, as well as a

---

[70] Ibid 844.

[71] The key land use issues that are expected to challenge South Gippsland Shire's future growth are identified in clause 21.02 of the South Gippsland Planning Scheme.

[72] South Gippsland Planning Scheme cl 21.02-1.

[73] Ibid cl 21.02-3.

Figure 6.3: Principles of amenity and landscape value still mix with more utilitarian and instrumental uses of land (Photograph, Lee Godden, 2011)

rural amenity and lifestyle, while supporting living opportunities in rural areas throughout the Shire.[74]

Encouragement of the development of alternative energy sources is also recognised as a key focus of future development under local planning policies.[75]

Amongst the objectives and strategies are specific approaches around minimising the impact of development on coastal values and the visual landscape. Specifically, policies direct that planning for the region ought to 'discourage development on prominent ridgelines, particularly those close to the coast' and 'protect locally significant views and vistas that contribute to the character of coastal and coastal hinterland areas'.[76] Thus the questions are clearly raised about how balance is to be achieved between amenity, aesthetic values, development and use of land in this part

---

[74] Ibid.

[75] Ibid cl 21.02-4.

[76] Ibid cl 21.04-1.

of Gippsland. This potential for conflicting values around land is magnified once the underlying land tenure, property law and land title regimes are taken into account.

V   LAND LAW AND THE TORRENS TITLE SYSTEM IN THE MID-TWENTIETH CENTURY

Gippsland, like many parts of Victoria and indeed Australia, is a patchwork of different tenures, Crown land and reserves and private land titles. Under the prevailing land law system, the State of Victoria is divided into Counties, Parishes, Townships, Sections and Crown allotments. This division is enduring. While some governing statutes have changed name, and there have been slight adjustments to their function, essentially this legal framework was in place in South Gippsland in the 1940s. It was a platform upon which the town and country planning system relied in important ways. Such dividing and categorising of land exemplified the processes of cadastral survey and mapping that constitute the foundation for the interface between law and place. Beyond these broader divisions sit the intricacies of private land division — distinguished by the markers of lots and title under the Torrens Title land registration system.[77]

The construct of title as a legal interface between land and people has ancient origins. Australian real property law has its origins in the English feudal system. The feudal system vested radical title to all land in the Crown. Parcels of rights in relation to the land, known as estates, were then granted to subjects of the Crown for their use.[78] Historically, in delineating land for use, land law systems relied not only on physical markers signified by prominent natural features but also upon being recorded in 'memory'. As Pottage notes in regard to medieval European titling and conveyancing practices: '[t]he factum of a conveyance was symbolised by a sword or parchment, [it] presupposed the existence of a resource of memory'.[79] In this sense, 'memory was a resource of trust. A title to land was a fragile commodity, which depended for its stability upon the vicissitudes of recollection'.[80] The introduction of the technology of writing and recording of land title was an attempt to overcome such vicissitudes. Practices around titling of land progressively took shape as an 'immutable

---

[77]   Adrian J Bradbrook et al, *Australian Property Law Cases and Materials* (Lawbook Co, 3rd ed, 2007) 352.

[78]   Adrian J Bradbrook et al, *Australian Real Property Law* (Lawbook Co, 5th ed, 2011) 4.

[79]   Pottage, above n 5, 361.

[80]   Ibid.

mobile' that came to depend less integrally on localised aide-mémoires, such as the clod of earth taken from the land.

Australia was colonised at a time when systems for remembering title to land had been removed from the realm of purely visceral recordings of land in local memory to a system of title deeds anchored in the private law of contract and equity.[81] There was a further step in the technologies of remembering title which has its specific origins in Australia. This was the development of the public registry and the construct of indefeasibility of title in the Torrens Title system. The public registration of land, though, has been described as an 'evolutionary response rather than a revolutionary reform'.[82] This concept was present, at least in inchoate form, in the creation of the Domesday Book in 1086.[83] The purpose of the public register was to create a system for the transfer of land which was 'reliable, simple, cheap, speedy and suited to the needs of the community'.[84] Early attempts at the creation of a public register permitted landholders to opt into the scheme which, according to Sir Robert R Torrens, made the system 'worse than useless'.[85] He, along with others, proposed a scheme whereby registered instruments should have priority over all unregistered interests, thus creating a powerful incentive for landholders to opt in to the scheme. This system, after some initial problems,[86] was implemented within South Australia and eventually spread across the world.

Public registration of land title 'remove[d] titles from networks of organic or practical memory, and deposit[ed] them in an administrative archive, accessible and decipherable by reference only to the index of the archive'.[87] Torrens Title systems established not only an administrative archive but a self-referential system of deciphering 'land' by reference to that system. Following inscription into surveys, maps, diagrams and files and registration folios, these representations of land can

---

[81] Bradbrook et al, above n 77, 474.

[82] Douglas J Whalan, *The Torrens System in Australia* (Law Book Co, 1982) 3.

[83] Ibid.

[84] Theodore BF Ruoff, *An Englishman Looks at the Torrens System* (Law Book Co, 1957) 6.

[85] Robert Torrens, *An Essay on the Transfer of Land by Registration* (Cassell & Co, 1882) 10.

[86] Whalan, above n 80, 6.

[87] For a discussion of the centrality of technological developments to bureaucratic property forms see Alain Pottage, 'Evidencing Ownership' in Susan Bright and John Dewar (eds), *Land Law: Themes and Perspectives* (Oxford University Press, 1998) 129, 133, 144.

be collected together, making a diversity of places readily accessible.[88] As a process for managing the interface between people and land, they facilitated efficient land administration by institutional bureaucracies over the nineteenth and twentieth centuries.

Torrens Title land registration systems emerged as one of the most significant legal means for ordering land within Australia. These statutory registration systems were successively adopted in all Australian jurisdictions from the 1860s and continue as the prevailing form for administering landownership across virtually all of Australia. In 1944, the Torrens title lots that now comprise the site where the wind farm is to be constructed were already recorded in that archive of title memory. The basic configuration of the lots has been retained in the Torrens title register (now available, through yet another technological evolution, as a searchable database on the internet).[89] The legal architecture of title records still makes decipherable, and publically accessible, the South Gippsland 'land' in the latest form of technology, via an online database.

The wind farm site, while it comprises private or freehold land, is in close proximity to several areas of Crown land. Private interests in land primarily represented through the Torrens Title system must also interface with 'public' designations and uses of land — pointing to a time a century earlier when this part of Gippsland was made known to law primarily through the Crown land model.

VI THIRD SNAPSHOT: CROWN, LAW AND LAND

In the development of land law in Australia, the ability of the Imperial bureaucratic state to make the newly acquired 'land' susceptible to accurate reproduction and to control its disposition and use was fundamental to establishing control over the continent.[90] As Campbell declares, 'One of the first and most important tasks of government in a newly settled colony — a colony to within which title to land originally vests in the government is to develop a scheme for the allocation of land'.[91] In New South Wales,

---

[88] Ibid.

[89] Department of Environment and Primary Industries, *Land Channel: Property, Titles and Maps* (26 August 2013) <http://www.dse.vic.gov.au/property-titles-and-maps/land-titles-home>.

[90] Pottage, above n 87, 133, 144.

[91] Enid Campbell, 'Conditional Land Grants by the Crown', [2008] 44 *University of Tasmania Law Review* 44.

the main legal measures to accomplish these purposes were a mixture of common law rules and equity, Imperial land law statutes and colony-specific measures developed around public policy objectives for the colonies. Decisions about the nature of those rules shaped 'so fundamental a relationship as that between individuals and land'.[92] Following the immediate establishment of the penal colony in New South Wales, significant decisions had to be made about whether land was to be freely granted, subject to purchase, whether settlements should be restricted to specific locations, 'and also whether the government should retain any power of controlling the use of the land it has made available for private settlement'.[93] This later question not only had particular bearing on the legal character of the proprietary rights to be granted but also on the manner in which the government (both the incumbent local governor of the time and the Colonial Office in London) was able to 'order' the relationship between individual and land.

After the initial penal period, a system of Crown grants of land developed. Small freehold grants were made in free and common socage, with no charges but quit rents.[94] Later, a process of Conditional Crown grants was instituted to deal with malpractices such as 'dummying' or fraud. The conditions placed on the Crown grants, such as bona fide residency and cultivation requirements, reflected the government's attempt to control how land was used in order to advance the economic 'improvement' of the colony. There were particular problems around enforcing breaches of the conditions, and practical difficulties in identifying when these breaches occurred.[95] Eventually the system of Conditional Crown grants was displaced as the public policy turned to favour private purchase of land at public auction. As Campbell notes, '[o]nce the free grants system was abandoned, the government gave up any pretence of seeking to control land use by annexation of conditions to freehold grants'.[96] In parts of South Gippsland, land was taken up by settlers during this period of transition from Conditional Crown grants to purchase of freehold land. A legal framework for systematic control of freehold land use by government was not to reappear in robust form in this area (which was to become part of Victoria) until the *Town and Country Planning Act 1944*.

---

[92] Ibid.

[93] Ibid.

[94] Bradbrook, above n 78, 245.

[95] Campbell, above n 91, 47.

[96] Campbell, above n 91, 48. This policy was consolidated in the *Waste Lands Act 1842* (Imp).

Further, while the system of Conditional Crown grants in the colonial era was no longer pursued in respect of freehold land after the 1840s, the concept of governments controlling the use of public lands by way of improvement-related conditions was to find expression in a system of Crown licences and leases. The extent to which the statutory regime of Australian land law diverged from common law precepts was examined at length in *Wik Peoples v Queensland* (1996) 187 CLR 1 (*'Wik'*).[97] The central issue was whether a pastoral lease conferred exclusive possession on the grantee and thus extinguished native title. As Justice Gummow stated:

> [l]and law is but one area in which statute may appear to have adopted general
> law principles and institutions as elements in a new regime, in truth the
> legislature has done so only on particular terms.[98]

Another very significant departure was the extent of land held by the state as public or Crown lands:

> A system of Crown leasehold tenures was introduced which led to the whole
> of Australia being transformed in subsequent decades into a patchwork quilt of
> freeholdings, Crown leaseholdings, and Crown 'reserves'.[99]

Land law instruments such as statutory leases were creatures of Australian law.[100] Accordingly, the law of real property as it developed in Australia from the mid-nineteenth century onward exhibited a very different character from that imposed by the received English law.

The *Land Act 1958* (Vic) is the successor of statutes that date back to the 1860s. The current day legislation deals principally with unreserved Crown land, and, inter alia, enables the grant of Crown leases and licences. It works in conjunction with the *Crown Land (Reserves) Act 1978* (Vic), which provides for the reservation of land for public purposes. These distinctive instruments of Crown land leases and licences have many local variants in other Australian jurisdictions.[101] Such Crown tenures facilitated the pastoral and agricultural occupation of South Gippsland, with these statutory instruments being part of the complex of circumstances which delivered economic and, later, political power to rural landholders, such as the squatters. Initially, debates

---

[97] *Wik Peoples v Queensland* (1996) 187 CLR 1, 246-8 (Gummow J).

[98] Ibid 242 (Gummow J).

[99] Ibid 265-9 (Kirby J).

[100] Ibid 266 (Kirby J).

[101] Bradbrook et al, above n 77, 919-20.

about 'land' were tied to questions of colonial self-government. With the advent of colonial legislatures around the mid-century, the push for land then intensified as it was fed by colonial aspirations of land for the small settler.

The selection Acts passed in various Australian jurisdictions, including Victoria, from the mid-nineteenth century onward, allowed 'selectors' to make a form of conditional purchase.[102] The right to qualify for, and retain, a Crown lease or other conditional purchase of Crown lands meant that a 'selector' or other Crown lessee had to make improvements to the land during the currency of the lease. Typical nineteenth-century 'improvement' conditions included the building of a dwelling and fencing, along with the requirement to clear native vegetation and to cultivate the land.[103] In many statutes, leases were forfeited if such improvements were not made. Thus, the conditions placed on Crown leases and licences were an impetus for the clearance of forested land in the colonial period. While it is impossible to determine this point accurately, perhaps the Bald Hills that now so conveniently allow the wind to turn turbines were naturally 'bald' land.[104] Alternatively, perhaps this baldness derives from the need to clear land as a condition placed upon the holders of Crown leases as colonisation proceeded through this southern region of Gipps' land.

VII   Fourth Snapshot: Settling 'Australia Felix'

Gippsland was colonised from both sea and land. Early colonial points of contact with this region occurred between whalers and sealers and the coastal Aboriginal peoples. Some ambiguity exists as to exactly which Aboriginal peoples occupied the land around the Tarwin River in the vicinity of what is now Tarwin Lower and the Bald Hills wind farm. Tarwin is a word of local Aboriginal derivation, thought to mean 'thirsty'.[105] It is generally accepted, though, that these people were the Bunuwurrung or Bunurong (various spellings)[106] and that '[t]he Bunuwurrung were

---

[102]   Selection usually entailed a form of conditional purchase, or Crown lease or licence. See, eg, the *Agricultural Reserves Act 1859* (Qld).

[103]   John Bradsen, 'Alternatives for Achieving Sustainable Development' in Laurie Cosgrove, David Evans and David Yencken, *Restoring The Land, Environmental Values, Knowledge and Action* (Melbourne University Press, 1994) 172.

[104]   A third explanation may be that Aboriginal fire practices left this area as grassland rather than forest.

[105]   Peter Dean Gardner, *Names of South Gippsland; Their Origins, Meanings and History* (Ngarak Press, 1992) 29.

[106]   William R Hayes, *The Golden Coast: History of the Bunurong* (South Gippsland Conservation

among the first Victorian Aboriginal people to be affected by the whalers and sealers from 1798 through the first decades of the 19th century'.[107] They were dispossessed of land and had inflicted upon them the debilitating ills of western disease, which affected their capacity to defend themselves against rival Aboriginal groups, although this is not regarded as the major reason for their decline. There were several massacres of Aboriginal groups in Gippsland, including the infamous Warrigal massacres in reprisal for the killing of a settler.[108] It remains unclear but it is likely that the groups most directly affected were Gunai/Kurnai peoples rather than Aboriginal people from the Tarwin area. By the early 1840s, it appears that the Tarwin area sat in something of a border-land or no man's land between the various Traditional Owners' lands, as can be seen from a variety of maps reproduced in various studies seeking to recreate the traditional territories of the Aboriginal groups.[109]

George Robinson provided a report of his journey through eastern Australia in 1844. He describes arriving in the Tarwin area on 29 April and makes a fulsome description of the land, animals and vegetation. He notes in passing that '[t]he forest animals have vastly increased since the destruction of the local inhabitants'.[110] Robinson also notes the depredations inflicted on Gippsland Aborigines by European settlers prior to his journey, and the appointment of Tyers as Commissioner for Aboriginals.[111]

Despite some incursions from Van Diemen's Land by sea, the main thrust of white 'settlement' into Gippsland followed the 'Major's line'. This line refers to the line of survey on the cadastral map followed by Major Mitchell as he explored this land in 1835 from established points of settlements in New South Wales. The ease of settlement of this part of eastern Australia was noted by Governor Gipps in 1840:

Society, 1998).

[107]   Isabel Ellender, 'The Yowenjerrre of South Gippsland: Traditional Groups, Social Boundaries and Land Succession' (2002) 25 *The Artefact* 9, 12.

[108]   George Mackaness, 'George Augustus Robinson's Journey into South-Eastern Australia, 1844' (1941) 27 *Journal and Proceedings of the Royal Australian Historical Society* 318, 323.

[109]   'There is consensus among the early writers, as well as in the current thinking of Indigenous peoples that Bunwurrung people lived west of the Tarwin River and Gunai/Kurnai people lived east of Yarram, but the location of the boundary and the precise identity of the people who lived in the middle remain enigmatic.' Ellender, above n 107, 10 and Gardner above n 105, 41.

[110]   Mackaness, above n 108, 321.

[111]   Ibid 323.

It is well known that Australia presents a surface to the settler very different from that of any other country into which Colonisation by Europeans has been introduced: that in consequence of the absence of dense forests or extensive swamps it is pervious to the settler in almost every direction, whilst the traffic over it is facilitated by the dryness of its soil.[112]

Major Thomas Mitchell identified similar advantages, calling the south-eastern parts of the continent '*Australia felix* — happy south land'.[113] Broome argues that this early explorer 'saw [the land] as a prize left for Englishmen by God. Mitchell's claim was wrong, in that Victoria was not a prize left by God, but one wrestled from Aboriginal people — the original owners and occupiers — in a fierce and determined colonial struggle'.[114] Land law played an integral role in that colonial struggle. The unique Crown land tenures that developed in colonial land law were an important means by which to impose British legal order on the land, and to appropriate the land for British settlement.[115]

VIII   ABORIGINAL LAW ON COUNTRY

The consequences of that imposition of legal order on a country occupied by Aboriginal peoples have been more openly acknowledged since *Mabo v Queensland [No 2]* (1992) 175 CLR 1. Native title is the recognition under common law and the *Native Title Act 1993* (Cth) of Indigenous Australians' rights and interests in land and waters in accordance with their traditional laws and customs. The *Native Title Act 1993* established the native title tribunal and the system of registration of native title claims. Native title can be determined by the Federal Court through either litigation or a consent-based process. The origin and content of native title rights are to be found in the continued acknowledgment of traditional laws and observance of the customs of an Indigenous group in a territory. In this sense, it is *sui generis* and therefore not derived from the imported legal system.[116] In order to claim native

---

[112] The quote is taken from Historical Records of Aust [1, 20 838] Library Committee of Commonwealth Parliament, 1918 and is cited in Martin Auster, 'The Regulation of Human Settlement: Public Ideas and Public Policy in New South Wales, 1788-1986' (1986) 3 *Environmental and Planning Law Journal* 40.

[113] Richard Broome, *Aboriginal Victorians: A History Since 1800* (Allen & Unwin, 2005) 1.

[114] Ibid.

[115] Bradbrook, above n 78, 4.

[116] *Mabo v Queensland (No 2)* (1992) 175 CLR 1, 13 (Brennan J).

title, a group of Indigenous peoples must show a connection with the relevant land which has been maintained through continued acknowledgment of the traditional laws and the customs of the group.[117] In accordance with the Act, and subsequent judicial decisions, native title can exist on unallocated Crown land, state forests, public reserves and certain land reserved for particular purposes, limited Crown-to-Crown grants, land allocated for Indigenous peoples, waters not privately owned and on some leases depending on State or Territory legislation.

The customs and laws governing Aboriginal relationships with land (or, as more coherently described, country) are holistic. Western settler legal systems, though, still refer to these relationships as normative or customary. The designation of the category of 'normative' or 'customary' subtly reinforces the dominant power relationships between settler law and Aboriginal law.[118] As Getzler notes, 'law is a complex reflection of economic interests and social ideology'.[119] Thus, law replicated economic interests such as the pastoral expansion in Gippsland, while simultaneously reflecting the social ideology of the virtues of rural life and 'improving' land through labour.[120] Moreover, in Western land law, the emphasis upon rationality and systems of categorisation effectively provide law with a capacity to govern relationships and resolve (or repress) conflict. Legal ordering processes around land produce categories of exclusion and inclusion.

This patterning is evident in the treatment of native title claims through the litigation process in Victoria. *Members of the Yorta-Yorta Aboriginal Community v Victoria* (2002) 214 CLR 422 affirmed that the 'normative systems' that characterise Indigenous relationships to land may be 'recognised'. Yet without the specific evidence of customs and traditions which satisfies Western concepts of rational 'proof', specific claims of occupation of land and waters cannot be sustained. Moreover, while in broad terms native title can co-exist with other land interests, extinguishment of native title — either in whole or in part — occurs where the exercise of native title rights would be inconsistent with these interests.[121] Native title remains an evolving doctrine, and

---

[117] Ibid 59-60 (Brennan J).

[118] Lee Godden, 'Grounding Law as Cultural Memory: A "Proper" Account of Property and Native Title in Australian Law and Land' (2003) 19 *Australian Feminist Law Journal* 61, 68.

[119] Joshua Getzler, *A History of Water Rights at Common Law* (Oxford University Press, 2004) 5.

[120] See, eg, Kevin Gray, 'Property in Thin Air' (1991) 50 *Cambridge Law Journal* 252.

[121] *Fejo v Northern Territory* (1998) 195 CLR 96; *Western Australia v Ward* (2002) 191 ALR 1.

the Courts continue to clarify the extent to which native title rights and interests can be recognised and protected. Notably, though, the impact of key decisions has been to narrow the test for recognition of native title interests[122] and thereby the scope of native title rights.[123] This has led commentators to reassess the promise of native title for Indigenous Australians.[124] Ironically, under native title law Aboriginal groups dispossessed by the violence of the colonisation may find it difficult to meet the standards of evidence required to establish a continuing connection to land.[125] Currently, there is no native title claim registered for the immediate area around the Bald Hills wind farm,[126] highlighting how laws around 'land' both structure and limit how Aboriginal relationships to country are expressed.

The *Traditional Owner Settlement Act 2010* (Vic) ('TOS Act') provides a state-based statutory regime as an alternative to the resolution of native title claims under the *Native Title Act 1993* (Cth). It establishes a framework for agreements between the state and Traditional Owner groups. Significantly, the TOS Act regime relaxes the threshold requirements for recognition of native title under Australian case law of an unbroken connection to country since settlement.[127] Rather, recognition of claims occurs where the state determines the groups that it will engage in negotiations.

A suite of agreements is provided for, through which the state acknowledges and confers rights upon Traditional Owner groups.[128] Traditional Owner rights are tempered by requirements to remain consistent with existing state laws. The agreements form a 'settlement package' governing relations between state entities and Traditional Owners. Similar to native title processes, the Recognition and Settlement Agreement ('RSA') demands that TOS Act rights attach to land. Such land is defined as the agreement area, and the boundaries are mapped and defined in the RSA. The

---

[122]   *Members of the Yorta Yorta Aboriginal Community v Victoria* (2002) 214 CLR 422.

[123]   *Wik v Western Australia* (2002) 191 ALR 1; *Western Australia v Ward* (2002) 191 ALR 1.

[124]   See Maureen Tehan, 'A Hope Disillusioned, An Opportunity Lost? Reflections on Common Law Native Title and Ten Years of the Native Title Act' (2003) 27 *Melbourne University Law Review* 523.

[125]   Lisa Strelein, *Compromised Jurisprudence: Native Title Cases Since* Mabo (Aboriginal Studies Press, 2006) 84-91.

[126]   National Native Title Tribunal, *National Native Title Register* (2008-11) <http://www.nntt.gov.au/Applications-And-Determinations/Registers/Pages/default.aspx>. The Bunurong peoples are pursuing a claim and have provided connection evidence.

[127]   *Members of the Yorta Yorta Aboriginal Community v Victoria* (2002) 214 CLR 422, 456-7.

[128]   This includes the Recognition and Settlement Agreement ('RSA'), Land Agreement ('LA'), Land Use Activity Agreement ('LUAA'), Natural Resource Agreement ('NRA'), and a Funding Agreement.

settlement process and accompanying map of the agreement area itself take on the character of immutable mobiles — ensuring that Aboriginal interests can be brought into the state's system for managing the uses of Crown land.

Negotiation between neighbouring Traditional Owner groups and internal decision-making parties plays a key role in defining the traditional country that forms the basis for a settlement. Prior uses of land held to be inconsistent with Indigenous-held interests cannot extinguish these rights. Nevertheless, the actual exercise of rights may be limited by the reservation status of the Crown land parcel itself. Traditional Owner group rights to land are contained in the Land Agreement. They take effect as either an estate in fee simple where the land is unreserved public land; an estate in fee simple over any public land,[129] with conditions including the entering into a land management co-operative agreement; an estate in fee simple where the land is public land with conditions (known as Aboriginal Title); or management of public land by a Traditional Owner Land Management Board ('TOLMB').[130] The third and fourth arrangements are conditional upon the making of a Joint Management Agreement.[131]

Co-operative management principles apply to Aboriginal title and public land managed by a TOLMB, meaning that Traditional Owner control over land arises in respect of relational, policy-making and operational spaces, rather than the ability to exclude and possess the land. The TOS Act requires that the various uses and management of Crown land and natural resources be unified for the purposes of the provisions negotiated under the TOS Act Agreements. In effect, these still form a complex tapestry of entitlement that sits across the defined area of land. This system for the Crown to engage with Aboriginal people with respect to their country provides a potential foundation for yet another 'layering of law over land' in this legal biography of land. The TOS Act, though, still requires Aboriginal groups to negotiate across the Crown land law structures and divisions in order to allow them to participate in the management of land that once was solely theirs to possess, occupy and use. This latest ordering of land through law, while an acknowledgment in part of past conflicts, is limited in terms of reproducing the more holistic Aboriginal relationships with country which once defined this part of the Gippsland coast.

---

[129]   Public Land is defined to refer to land, inter alia, under the *Crown Land (Reserves) Act 1978* (Vic), reserved forest within the meaning of the *Forests Act 1958* (Vic); and unreserved Crown land under the *Land Act 1958* (Vic).

[130]   *Traditional Owner Settlement Act 2010* (Vic) s 12(2)-(5).

[131]   *Conservation, Forests and Lands Act 1987* (Vic) s 8A.

IX Conclusion

Relationships between people and their surrounds in legal terms are first reduced to 'land' and then to 'property' by means of administrative and legal forms. In turn, these forms, such as title and Crown grant, are progressively dislodged from a nexus with a distinctive or intrinsically valuable place; they take effect as immutable mobiles. Legal and bureaucratic forms such as planning systems that validate rights of access, use and management, as they have developed within Australia, emphasise the standardisation of place. The rise of successive socio-technical forms for organising land suggests that land is no longer predominantly embedded in a culturally specific, local context. The recognition of native title, though, has been a major source of challenge to those trends. Further, as the snapshots through time in this legal biography of land have revealed, land may still remain acutely anchored in local place and value, while still being captured by more abstract processes. A strong sense of place resonates through the wind farm dispute, even though the land at the same time is required to accord with regional and global imperatives. As the later snapshots have demonstrated, the impetus to order land through law remains strong, and those divisions endure as markers for determining in critical ways the interface between law and land.

7

ADRIAN BRADBROOK AND RESIDENTIAL TENANCY REFORM

Anthony Moore

I The Residential Tenancy Law Legacy

In 1983 a text on residential tenancies law in Victoria and South Australia was published;[1] Adrian Bradbrook was a co-author of that text. Publication followed the enactment in the two states of the first comprehensive legislation in Australia for residential tenancy rights and obligations.[2] The text is an exhaustive examination of the legislation and considers the detail of the statute despite the lack of any existing judicial interpretation of its words. It thus analyses the extent to which previous common law principles can be applied. It is also concerned with the provisions for the administration of the legislation, the process of law reform and relevant economic theories. The text further examines the role of the Victorian and South Australian governments in the provision of welfare housing, the enforcement of housing standards and access to housing assistance. At that time the governments of both states had housing authorities which constructed and leased buildings to a broad

---

[1] Adrian J Bradbrook et al, *Residential Tenancy Law and Practice: Victoria and South Australia* (Law Book, 1983).

[2] *Residential Tenancies Act 1980* (Vic); *Residential Tenancies Act 1978* (SA).

social group and enforced housing standards for owner-occupied and privately rented premises.

From the particular area of residential tenancy law, Bradbrook and his co-authors progressed in 1991 to a detailed examination of real property law throughout Australia through a textbook and casebook, which have now been in publication for thirty years.[3] The original aim was to establish an authoritative text on the topic at a time when even the existence of a distinct Australian law was disputed. The books identified an individual Australian system where title flows from public records and rights in land only exist to the extent that they are recognised by statute. Distinctive features of the system include rural leases, Indigenous title, suburban relationships based on unit title, and processes for boundary definition and dispute resolution. Continuing publication and acceptance of the work indicate that Bradbrook has more than fulfilled the original aim.

The 1983 text on residential tenancy law is a commentary on legislation largely inspired by Bradbrook's reform work. Indeed Bradbrook's outstanding contribution in practice and theory has been towards the introduction of an Australian residential tenancy law. The reform is properly described as an introduction of an area of law, as prior to his work the area was simply a part of the law of leases. In a country where bickering amongst the states and territories is commonplace, the impact of his work can be seen in the fact that all jurisdictions have adopted and maintained a legislative code governing the relationship of residential landlord and tenant. Whereas Australia's earlier property reforms, including the Torrens system and strata titles, were the work of practitioners, this is an academic-inspired reform.

Bradbrook's reform proposals are set out in a report on poverty and residential tenancies ('*Poverty Report*');[4] this report was part of an inquiry into the Law and Poverty, chaired by Ronald Sackville.[5] That inquiry was established by the Whitlam federal government of 1972-75 and reflects an optimism of the time, with faith in law reform and the role of government to better the lives of ordinary citizens. The

---

[3] Now Adrian J Bradbrook et al, *Australian Real Property Law* (Thomson Reuters, 5th ed, 2011) and Adrian J Bradbrook et al, *Australian Property Law: Cases and Materials* (Thomson Reuters, 4th ed, 2011).

[4] Adrian J Bradbrook, *Poverty and the Residential Landlord-Tenant Relationship* (Australian Government Publishing Service, 1975).

[5] Ronald Sackville, *Law and Poverty in Australia: Second Main Report, October 1975* (Australian Government Publishing Service, 1975) ch 3.

residential tenancy recommendations could better be described as protecting the less well-off, as little attention is given to the plight of the homeless. The report did envision support through community groups, but only in Victoria has there been a community law reform centre.[6] However, this centre can be linked to the subsequent Victorian Consumer Law Centre and that state's clear leadership in consumer law reform and consumer advocacy.

The most far-reaching significance of the *Poverty Report* was its recognition of the fact that a fundamental distinction must be drawn in future between the laws relating to commercial and residential tenancies. The reason for the historical similarity between the laws was that at common law a lease is regarded as an estate in land, and the use to which the land is to be put and the bargaining capacity of the parties are regarded as largely irrelevant. However, the *Poverty Report* concluded that whereas the principle of freedom of contract may be reasonable in the case of commercial premises, where it may sensibly be argued that each party has a roughly equal bargaining strength, it is inappropriate in the case of residential premises where a tenant seldom seeks legal advice and where standard forms of lease are invariably used. Subsequently, regulation of retail tenancies, where landlords of large suburban centres have acquired considerable power, has been introduced.[7] Once this rejection of freedom of contract for residential tenancies is accepted, it follows that remedial legislation, which benefits tenants of only residential premises, is required, and that in future, the body of landlord-tenant law concerning commercial premises must diverge from that concerning residential premises.

The *Poverty Report* made many specific recommendations for reforms to the laws relating to residential tenancies in each Australian state. These reforms included the need for a new decision-making body to be styled the Residential Tenancies Tribunal, the need for a state government advice and information service, the application of contractual principles, the revision of the laws relating to repairs and cleaning, new and speedier procedures relating to the recovery of possession from defaulting or

---

[6] See Community Committee on Tenancy Law Reform, *Reforming Victoria's Tenancy Laws* (Victorian Council of Social Service, 1978). For a discussion of the Committee's work, see Ronald Sackville, 'Residential Tenancies Reform in Victoria: A Study of a Consultation' in Ronald F Henderson (ed), *Consultation and Government* (Victorian Council of Social Service, 1981).

[7] Legislation for retail tenancies now exists in all jurisdictions except Tasmania, see Adrian J Bradbrook et al, *Australian Real Property Law* (Thomson Reuters, 5th ed, 2011) 733-41.

over-holding tenants, special controls over security deposits, a new system of excessive rent control, the need to create miscellaneous tenant rights (for example, a right to privacy), a right to the continued maintenance of services and controls over rent increases.

Reform of landlord and tenant law as it applies to residential premises has been accepted as necessary by the legislatures in every Australian jurisdiction (the 'Common Legislation').[8] All jurisdictions ultimately passed legislation governing residential tenancies. Comprehensive legislation regulating residential tenancies was initially introduced[9] in South Australia in 1978[10] and Victoria in 1980.[11] Subsequently, similar legislation was enacted in New South Wales and Western Australia in 1987[12] and in Queensland in 1994.[13] The two pioneering states then decided upon a total rewriting of their legislation, and new legislation was enacted in South Australia in 1995[14] and Victoria in 1997.[15] These reforms significantly broadened the scope of the legislation by extending the coverage so that the legislation applies to caravan parks and rooming houses. New South Wales[16] and Queensland[17] then updated their laws incorporating later ideas than those of Victoria and South Australia. At the same time, the remaining jurisdictions have all enacted reasonably comprehensive legislation. The Australian Capital Territory and Tasmania passed Acts in 1997,[18] and the Northern Territory passed an Act in 1999[19] replacing what had been a limited Act of 1979.[20] The Northern Territory, Tasmanian and Western Australian residential

---

[8]   *Residential Tenancies Act 1997* (ACT); *Residential Tenancies Act 2010* (NSW); *Residential Tenancies Act 1999* (NT); *Residential Tenancies Act 1994* (Qld); *Residential Tenancies Act 1995* (SA); *Residential Tenancy Act 1997* (Tas); *Residential Tenancies Act 1997* (Vic); *Residential Tenancies Act 1987* (WA).

[9]   Detailed analysis of this initial stage of reform is set out in Adrian J Bradbrook, Susan V MacCallum and Anthony P Moore, *Residential Tenancy Law and Practice: Victoria and South Australia* (Law Book, 1983).

[10]   *Residential Tenancies Act 1978* (SA).

[11]   *Residential Tenancies Act 1980* (Vic).

[12]   *Residential Tenancies Act 1987* (NSW); *Residential Tenancies Act 1987* (WA).

[13]   *Residential Tenancies Act 1994* (Qld).

[14]   *Residential Tenancies Act 1995* (SA).

[15]   *Residential Tenancies Act 1997* (Vic).

[16]   *Residential Tenancies Act 2010* (NSW).

[17]   *Residential Tenancies Act 1994* (Qld).

[18]   *Residential Tenancies Act 1997* (ACT); *Residential Tenancy Act 1997* (Tas).

[19]   *Residential Tenancies Act 1999* (NT).

[20]   *Tenancy Act 1979* (NT).

tenancies legislation today is somewhat less comprehensive than that of the other five jurisdictions.

Although residential tenancy legislation has been enacted in different forms and at different times, the legislation can be grouped into three phases. The first phase can be described as a statement of new tenant rights with a new forum for the resolution of landlord-tenant disputes. The second stage was primarily concerned with the extension of tenant protection to other residential occupants.[21] During the second phase of residential tenancy reform there were administrative changes, particularly with respect to the specialist tribunals. In some jurisdictions a residential tenancy tribunal was replaced by a tribunal with broader concerns of a consumer nature. By contrast, in some jurisdictions dispute resolution was left to the regular Magistrates courts.

The third phase of reform faces many new issues.[22] Tenancy legislation has generally allowed the parties to choose the term of the tenancy. Tenants have commonly been offered fixed term agreements for one year or six months or periodic agreements for a month or a week. These terms offer little security of tenure but impose significant liability upon a tenant to pay rent for the remainder of the term even if a tenant chooses to move because of workplace opportunities or the availability of government housing or similar causes. At the same time, landlords have had to follow a detailed process for the recovery of possession. Self-help recovery of possession has throughout been banned and subject to some of the harshest penalties of the legislation. The process for recovery of possession involves a period of default prior to notice, notice offering the opportunity to make good and then a hearing. Whilst allowance must be made for financial difficulty, the process can be exploited. The delay may lead to significant rent loss and in extreme cases property losses from damage to the property going beyond mere neglect. The legislation has concentrated on protection of possession rather than the quality of enjoyment, and problems have arisen with respect to matters such as energy standards and disturbance of neighbours.

This chapter evaluates the significance today of the *Poverty Report* by concentrating on recent reform of the legislation in South Australia (which had

---

[21] Adrian J Bradbrook, 'Residential Tenancy Law — The Second Stage of Reform' (1998) 20 *Sydney Law Review* 402.

[22] See New South Wales Community Law Reform Committee, *Summary of Recommendations* (24 September 2007).

been the pioneering state in 1978). In February 2014 extensive amendments to the legislation were brought into operation.[23] In turn, that legislation followed publication of a Review of the *Residential Tenancies Act 1995* ('*SA Review*')[24] undertaken by the Office of Consumer and Business Services of the South Australian government. The *SA Review* provides the most recent formal indication of attitudes towards the residential tenancy legislation and detailed analysis of its provisions. This chapter covers the significant topics of that legislation, the scope of the legislation, dispute resolution processes, documentation, rent and bonds, general obligations, supply of essential services, repairs and maintenance, troublesome tenants and termination of a tenancy.

II Scope of Legislation

The *Poverty Report* argues for a new concept to which the proposed rights and responsibilities should attach. The essence of the application of the legislation is the concept of a residential tenancy agreement. Such an agreement must be for value and confer a right of occupation of residential premises for the purpose of residence. The definition expressly abandons the common law requirement of exclusive possession, at the same time excluding boarders and lodgers from the protection of the legislation. The original paradigm was a person or persons occupying a single residence. That residence could be part of a larger building but the trend to urban consolidation and legal disputes between close neighbours was not then as prominent as it was to become.

Conceptually, reform was seen as a move from the law of leases to that of contract. A residential tenancy agreement is still (probably but not expressly) regarded as conferring upon the tenant a leasehold interest with proprietary characteristics. A leasehold interest arose wherever one party held exclusive possession of a defined area of land for a defined period of time. Land can be divided vertically and horizontally so the defined parcel of land could be a couple of rooms on the third floor of a flat building. The period of time could be as little as one week and could be on a repeating basis so that a weekly term is a sufficient defined period. The significance of the proprietary characteristics of a leasehold interest means that the tenant can

---

23   *Residential Tenancies (Miscellaneous) Amendment Act 2013* (SA).

24   Government of South Australia, *South Australian Review of the Residential Tenancies Act 1995* (2012).

enforce the interest against third parties generally, and can deal with the interest by assignment and otherwise.

The proprietary classification had many harsh consequences for the tenant. As a tenant is classified as having an estate in land rather than a right to enjoy residential premises, the courts have struggled to apply some contractual doctrines to the relationship. Lord Denning has stated:

> A lease is a demise. It conveys an interest in land. It does not come to an end like an ordinary contract on repudiation and acceptance.[25]

Where the premises have been destroyed or damaged, and the tenant still has the estate in land despite an inability to exercise any right of occupation, the courts have doubted the application of the doctrine of frustration.[26] There is no implied obligation with respect to the state of the premises: there is no law against letting a tumble-down house.[27] Where the landlord has fundamentally failed to fulfil an obligation, the lack of any mutuality of obligation has led to a conclusion that rent remains payable.[28] If the premises are surrendered to the landlord, the lack of any duty to mitigate loss denies any obligation to attempt to re-let and rent remains due.[29] These consequences have all been expressly overturned by the Common Legislation but continuing proprietary status for a tenant has not been expressed. Without a proprietary status, residential tenants would not be protected against a later buyer who becomes the registered proprietor. A tenant with proprietary status does prevail against subsequent buyers because of the Torrens system protection for tenants in possession for a term varying from unlimited in Victoria, to the common three years, to one year in South Australia.[30]

---

[25] *Total Oil Great Britain Ltd v Thompson Garages (Biggin Hill) Ltd* [1972] 1 QB 318, 324; similar concerns as the difficulties of applying contractual doctrines to a lease have been expressed by the Victorian Court of Appeal in *Apriaden Investments Pty Ltd v Seacrest Pty Ltd* (2006) 12 VR 319.

[26] Ibid.

[27] *Hart v Windsor* (1843) 12 M&W 68; *Cavalier v Pope* [1906] AC 428.

[28] *Davis Contractors Ltd v Fareham Urban DC* [1956] AC 686; now overturned, see *National Carriers Ltd v Panalpina (Northern) Ltd* [1981] AC 675.

[29] *Maridakis v Kouvaris* (1975) 5 ALT 197.

[30] *Real Property Act 1886* (SA) s 69(h); the position of tenants as against subsequent owners is analysed in Adrian J Bradbrook et al, *Australian Real Property Law* (Thomson Reuters, 5th ed, 2011) 239-40.

The practical scope of the Common Legislation flows from its definitions.[31] The application of the residential tenancies legislation depends on a detailed definition of a basic concept of residential tenancy agreement with a series of additions and exclusions. The basic concept is consciously adopted in all jurisdictions in preference to that of residential lease, although in Victoria the definition of residential agreement includes a requirement of a lease. This choice, in all jurisdictions except Victoria, to avoid the requirement appears to have been made because of a history of avoidance by the courts of the application of earlier similar English legislation. In England the courts held that one of the elements of a lease is that of an intention to create a lease, and this intention was normally inferred rather than express.[32] To a critical observer the courts seemed to make the inference when they wished the legislation to apply and to find an intention lacking when they wished to avoid the legislation. More fairly, intention was absent more in cases where residence was provided as part of an employment-based or other type of relationship. Furthermore, the courts firmly rejected the view that parties could avoid the application of the legislation either by declaring that there was no intention to create a lease or by describing their agreement as something other than a lease.

Generally the English approach gained little support in Australia. In 1959, the High Court affirmed the position that if the parties entered an agreement whereby exclusive possession of a defined area was granted for a defined period of time, then the parties intended something that was in substance a lease.[33]

Statutory residential tenancy agreements are not explicitly required to be for a defined duration except in Victoria where the 'lease' element seems to import a fixed duration requirement. In particular, parties may prefer to relate duration to the rules as to length of notice for termination; they may wish to specify that their agreement is to last until proper notice to terminate has been given. The Common Legislation sets out a number of rules whereby a landlord or tenant may give notice to terminate.

---

[31] *Residential Tenancies Act 1997* (ACT) ss 5,6; *Residential Tenancies Act 2010* (NSW) ss 5,6; *Residential Tenancies Act 1999* (NT) s 4; *Residential Tenancies Act 1994* (Qld) ss 21-25; *Residential Tenancies Act 1995* (SA) s 5; *Residential Tenancy Act 1997* (Tas) s 6; *Residential Tenancies Act 1997* (Vic) ss 6-14; *Residential Tenancies Act 1987* (WA) ss 5, 6.

[32] *Holiday Flat Co v Kuczera* [1978] SLT 47; *Wilkes v Goodwin* [1923] 2 KB 86 (CA); *Cobb v Lane* [1952] 1 All ER 1199 (CA); *Errington v Errington* [1952] 1 KB 290 (CA); *Somma v Hazelhurst* [1978] 2 All ER 1011 (CA); these cases were substantially repudiated in *Street v Mountford* [1985] AC 809.

[33] *Radaich v Smith* (1959) 101 CLR 209.

These rules provide different periods of notice according to the grounds of the notice, and the periods are different according to whether notice is given by the landlord or the tenant (reflecting the different interests of the party receiving the notice). These rules are intended for leases where no definite duration is intended. They make the period of a periodic tenancy, other than a yearly tenancy, of little meaning as the period does not involve any commitment beyond the term of the notice to terminate except in the case of the yearly tenancy where the parties are usually committing to that one year. Since a monthly or weekly period has little substantive meaning, the parties may more realistically opt not to apply a period to their agreement.

One significant deviation from the common law property classification might appear to be the abandonment of the requirement of exclusive possession. However, that abandonment may be regarded as only nominal. Whilst the statutory definitions describe a residential tenancy agreement as one conferring a right of occupation which need not be exclusive, in substance the element of exclusive possession is revived by the exemption of boarders and lodgers from the scope of the legislation.

Boarders and lodgers constitute the majority of people falling within the common law classification of licensees. The common law authorities on the meaning of 'boarder' and 'lodger' suggest that the terms are sufficiently wide to include all categories of occupant of residential premises who are not classed by the common law as tenants. A boarder is a person who is provided with services, such as meals, that are more than insignificant. Medical treatment or grounds maintenance would appear also as services, which would mean that a resident is a boarder. Lodgers are residents who do not have control over any space (seemingly at least a room).

Consequently, there is little or no scope for the argument that an intermediate category of occupant exists who, although a licensee at common law, is included within the scope of the Common Legislation on the ground that the person has a greater interest in the premises than a 'boarder' or 'lodger'. Under the Common Legislation the position is that either an occupant is a tenant, in which case the occupant is within the scope of the Act, or else the occupant is a boarder or lodger, and thereby is expressly excluded from the legislation.

Beyond the categories of boarders and lodgers, the list of exemptions in the Common Legislation is considerable. The exemptions fall into two categories: one is based on the nature of the premises, the other on the purpose of the agreement. Generally the legislation does not exempt an agreement simply because residence is granted in conjunction with employment. Consequently, termination of employment does not automatically lead to termination of residence. It is not clear that a term of an agreement could provide for termination of the residence agreement upon termination of an employment agreement. There are situations, however, where employment and residence are so entwined, such as the case of a caretaker, that an application for termination of the residence agreement upon termination of the employment agreement might be justified on special grounds such as undue hardship.

Difficulties have also arisen because of the exemption for grants of residence in connection with a contract of sale. With respect to a contract of sale and purchase, the transfer of possession need not coincide with the transfer of title and the exemption seems to be aimed at purchasers taking early possession and vendors staying late. However, the vendor or purchaser may be given a right to possession for a significant period of time and it may become difficult to assess whether that party's right to possession stems from the sale transaction or a separate agreement. Once a sale is complete, a vendor remaining in possession is more likely to depend on an independent arrangement even if packaged in the one document.

The greatest change to the scope of the residential tenancies legislation has been the extension to rooming house and caravan park residents. Because the original legislation excluded persons who were boarders or lodgers, persons who shared premises generally fell outside the legislation. There is now legislative protection for rooming house residents in Victoria, Queensland, South Australia and Tasmania flowing from special provisions in the residential tenancy legislation.[34] A rooming house is generally defined as a premises where a number of persons (in some jurisdictions a minimum number is specified) share the premises subject to supervision; it is a building in which there is one or more rooms available for occupancy on payment of rent. A person who occupies a room in a rooming house as that person's only or main place of residence is a rooming house resident. There are still some residential occupants who fall outside the extended legislation. A student, for example, who occupies a room in a private dwelling, falls outside the tenancy legislation as boarder or lodger and does not reside in a rooming house.

---

[34] *Residential Tenancies Act 1995* (Vic) ss 100-27; *Residential Tenancies and Rooming House Accommodation Act 2008* (Qld) ch 4; *Residential Tenancies Act 1995* (SA) part VII; *Residential Tenancy Act 1997* (Tas) ss 48A-48H; see Adrian J Bradbrook et al, *Australian Real Property Law* (Thomson Reuters, 5th ed, 2011) 755-7.

In all jurisdictions except Tasmania and the two territories, a caravan park resident is also given rights similar to those given to a residential tenant.[35] A caravan park resident has the right to reside on the resident's site and to occupy the caravan on that site. A resident and the park owner may enter into a written agreement specifying the terms and conditions of the resident's use of the caravan park or the caravan. Any term of an agreement that is inconsistent with the Act, or attempts to restrict or modify the resident's rights under the Act, is void.

The extension to rooming houses and caravan parks is a further application of the original concepts of the *Poverty Report*. It applies the principles of the *Poverty Report* to what have later been seen as situations deserving similar legislative control.

The *SA Review* recommends further strengthening of the provisions for rooming house and caravan park residents but otherwise makes few alterations to the original scope of the legislation other than the application of the principles of the *Poverty Report* regarding rooming houses and caravan parks.[36] In the amending legislation,[37] a new Part VII is introduced; it sets out at length the rights and obligations of rooming house owners and residents. Previously these rights and obligations had been expressed by way of codes of conduct set out in regulations. The new provisions set out standard rooming house agreements: house rules; requirements for rent and bonds; rules for the enjoyment, security and cleanliness of rooms and premises; and procedures for termination of an agreement. All of these topics are in line with the rights and obligations of residential tenancy agreements.

Apart from the extensions of the scope of the legislation, little concern has been expressed as to the fundamental definitions despite their unprecedented nature. The *SA Review* concerns itself with matters of detail. It recommends the extension of the legislation to Lifestyle Villages where residents live in self-contained rental units in a retirement environment but are not protected by the *Retirement Villages Act 1987* (SA) because they are not charged a premium;[38] the amendments include

---

[35] *Residential Parks Act 2004* (NSW) ss 30, 69, 80, 81; *Residential Tenancies Act 1994* (Qld) ss 103-7; *Residential Parks Act 2007* (SA) ss 50, 66; *Residential Tenancies Act 1995* (Vic) ss 146-8; *Residential Parks (Long-Stay Tenants) Act 2006* (WA); see Adrian J Bradbrook et al, *Australian Real Property Law* (Thomson Reuters, 5th ed, 2011) 757-9.

[36] Government of South Australia, above n 24, recommendations 49-68.

[37] *Residential Tenancies Act 1995* (SA) part VII is inserted by *Residential Tenancies (Miscellaneous) Amendment Act 2013* (SA) s 69.

[38] Government of South Australia, above n 24, recommendation 1.

such parties as residential tenants.[39] The *SA Review* recommends that definitions in relation to student accommodation and vendors remaining in residence are to be clarified to cover residents of apartment style accommodation not operated by exempt educational institutions and vendors with a right to stay beyond 28 days.[40] The amendments limit the relevant exemption from the legislation to students at exempt educational institutions.[41] The recommendations and consequential amendments are most marginal and the key concept of a residential tenancy agreement is not challenged.

III   DISPUTE RESOLUTION

Before 1974, reliance on the courts for dispute resolution had been rarely questioned. The establishment of a specialist residential tenancy tribunal was argued by the *Poverty Report* as an essential part of the reforms, and was adopted in the original South Australian and Victorian legislation. In the *Poverty Report* the view was strongly advanced that a tribunal solely for residential tenancy disputes was essential if the legislation was to operate fairly. Access to the regular courts was seen to disadvantage tenants because of the role of lawyers in the presentation of cases, the aura of formality and technical rules of evidence and the risk of cost awards against losing parties. These concerns may be viewed as common to a range of consumer disputes and the *Poverty Report* pre-dated procedural reform for consumer matters generally. Residential tenancy disputes have a special concentration on matters of building structure and standards of residential use. However, the *Poverty Report* did not emphasise these building factors as a basis for jurisdiction combining residential tenancy matters with areas such as strata and community title disputes. These disputes have had extensively used specialist dispute resolution systems in New South Wales, Queensland and Western Australia.

Since the time of the *Poverty Report*, jurisdictional consideration has centred on the procedural position common to many consumer claims rather than the housing identity of residential tenancy disputes. In its purest form a residential

---

[39]   *Residential Tenancies Act 1995* (SA) s 5(1)(a)(ii) is inserted by *Residential Tenancies (Miscellaneous) Amendment Act 2013* (SA) s 5.

[40]   Government of South Australia, above n 24, recommendations 2-3.

[41]   *Residential Tenancies Act 1995* (SA) s 5(1)(c) is inserted by *Residential Tenancies (Miscellaneous) Amendment Act 2013* (SA) s 5.

tenancy tribunal remains only in South Australia. In recent years, a model of a single tribunal to hear all minor civil matters and the review of administrative decisions has gained favour. Residential tenancy disputes are now heard by such a tribunal in the Australian Capital Territory, New South Wales and Victoria.

In the remaining jurisdictions, residential tenancy disputes have remained part of the traditional civil court processes but with some modifications. In the Northern Territory and Tasmania, some powers are given to a Tenancies Commissioner.[42] In the Northern Territory, Queensland, Tasmania and Western Australia, dispute resolution is entrusted with all minor civil matters to the Small Claims Tribunal or magistrates.[43]

In all jurisdictions, the courts, tribunals and commissioners are given extensive powers, including the power to make monetary compensation orders (up to a specified limit), orders for possession, orders requiring either party to undertake designated work or to refrain from specified conduct, or to fix rent levels.[44] The disbursement of security bonds is commonly an administrative function of a government official subject to review.[45]

The *SA Review* does not question the continuing role of the Residential Tenancies Tribunal but recommends that its jurisdiction be extended to amounts not exceeding $40 000.[46] The increase in jurisdictional amount has been fixed.[47] The current and proposed jurisdiction does include rooming house, caravan park and retirement village residents as well as residential landlords and tenants. The jurisdiction does not extend to disputes between tenants or involving agents in their individual capacity and similarly does not extend to disputes between community title residents or between such residents and title managers.

---

[42]   *Residential Tenancies Act 1999* (NT) s 124; *Residential Tenancy Act 1997* (Tas) s 7.

[43]   *Residential Tenancies Act 1999* (NT) s 124; *Residential Tenancies Act 1994* (Qld) ch 5; *Residential Tenancy Act 1997* (Tas) s 7; *Residential Tenancies Act 1987* (WA) s 12.

[44]   *Residential Tenancies Act 1997* (ACT) s 115; *Residential Tenancies Act 2010* (NSW) ss 80-5; *Residential Tenancies Act 1999* (NT) s 124; *Residential Tenancies Act 1995* (SA) s 110; *Residential Tenancy Act 1997* (Tas) s 8; *Residential Tenancies Act 1997* (Vic) s 446.

[45]   *Residential Tenancies Act 1997* (ACT) s 32; *Landlord and Tenant (Rental Bonds) Act 1977* (NSW) s 8; *Residential Tenancies Act 1994* (Qld) s 59; *Residential Tenancies Act 1995* (SA) s 63; *Residential Tenancies Act 1997* (Vic) s 407; *Residential Tenancies Act 1987* (WA) s 29.

[46]   Government of South Australia, above n 24, recommendations 18-24.

[47]   *Residential Tenancies Act 1995* (SA) s 24 has been amended by *Residential Tenancies (Miscellaneous) Amendment Act 2013* (SA) s 9.

The *Poverty Report* recommendation for a specialist tribunal has experienced a mixed fortune. The combination of tenancy disputes with similar consumer matters involves an appraisal of the similarity of the range of disputes; the combination of residential tenancy disputes with other [different] consumer matters does involve movement away from reliance on the traditional courts. At the same time, the reliance on magistrates courts, despite procedural reforms, is a rejection of the need for a specialist tribunal.

Procedure rather than jurisdiction has become a greater focus of reform consideration. Emphasis is placed on mediation, especially in Queensland, where a claim may be taken to the Small Claims Tribunal only where mediation fails to resolve a matter, or breach of a mediated agreement is alleged, or the matter is one of urgency.[48] The South Australian amendments place conciliation at the centre of dispute resolution.[49] Parties may apply to the Commissioner of Consumer Affairs for conciliation of a dispute.[50] The Tribunal may refer any application to it to a conciliation conference and it has a duty to use its best endeavours to bring about a settlement acceptable to the parties.[51] A settlement agreed at a conciliation conference is binding on the parties.[52] Reliance on conciliation is a major change for residential tenancy disputes in South Australia but reflects a more general approach to civil litigation; what it shares with the original *Poverty Report* is a concern with costs of litigation and the disadvantage of tenants in terms of litigation resources.

Government agencies to assist consumers were an emerging concept in 1974. The *Poverty Report* stressed the role of the consumer protection agencies in enforcing the legislation and providing assistance to landlords and tenants. Since that time, much of Australia's consumer law has become national as a result of the *Australian Consumer Law* enacted as schedule 2 under the *Competition and Consumer Act 2010* (Cth) and the *National Credit Code* enacted as schedule 1 under the *National Consumer Credit Protection Act 2009* (Cth). Administration of these pieces of legislation is entrusted to the Australian Competition and Consumer Commission and the Australian Securities

---

[48] *Residential Tenancies Act 1994* (Qld) ss 231-2.

[49] *Residential Tenancies Act 1995* (SA) part 8 is inserted by *Residential Tenancies (Miscellaneous) Amendment Act 2013* (SA) s 70.

[50] *Residential Tenancies Act 1995* (SA) s 107.

[51] *Residential Tenancies Act 1995* (SA) s 108.

[52] *Residential Tenancies Act 1995* (SA) s 108B.

and Investments Commission. State and territory agencies are left in a supportive role, although residential tenancies remain a state and territory concern and probably the major consumer responsibility of those agencies. The *SA Review* retains the role of the Commissioner for Consumer Affairs and that role has been strengthened by the conciliation reforms. However, resources for many state and territory government agencies have declined and weakened agencies have less ability to undertake research and initiate means of consumer assistance.

IV DOCUMENTATION

In relation to documentation to be provided by the parties, the *Poverty Report* concentrated on a statement of legislative rights and completion of a condition report. The Common Legislation was generally reluctant to require any formalities for the conclusion of a binding contract. Rather, legislative requirements relate to supplementary aspects of the arrangement. In particular, the parties are required to detail the condition of the premises in accordance with a prescribed format. Furthermore, information must be provided to the tenant as to the rights and obligations under the legislation. The reluctance to insist upon a written agreement seems to reflect an unwillingness to disturb widespread community practice for short-term agreements and particularly periodic agreements to be simply by word of mouth and a handshake.

The current rules as to the content of a written residential tenancy agreement, condition reports, and provision of information as to a tenant's rights and obligations reflect a strong trend to stricter requirements. The current position can be summarised as below:

1. Australian Capital Territory: any written document is to be consistent with prescribed terms. The landlord must give the tenant a copy of the agreement and a copy of the standard residential tenancy terms if they are not already included in the agreement; a condition report is to be provided.[53]

2. New South Wales: a landlord must provide a written agreement and a standard form of agreement is prescribed. The written agreement must follow the standard form. The standard form includes a condition report;

---

[53] *Residential Tenancies Act 1997* (ACT) ss 8, 9, 10.

if a document is given to the landlord and rent paid, the agreement is enforceable. The landlord must give the tenant a copy of the agreement.[54]

3. Northern Territory: any written agreement is to state the parties, the premises, the rent and the term. The landlord is to provide a copy of the written agreement to the tenant; any condition report is to be given to the tenant no later than three days after entry into possession.[55]

4. Queensland: details of any written agreement, a statement of rights and obligations, and any condition report are prescribed. The landlord is to provide a copy of a written agreement and a statement of beneficial information to the tenant. A condition report is evidence as to the condition of the premises.[56]

5. South Australia: if there is a written agreement, the landlord is to provide a copy to the tenant. The landlord is to provide to the tenant details of the landlord's name and address. A condition report must be completed.[57]

6. Tasmania: contents of a written agreement and statement of rights and obligations are prescribed. If there is a bond, a condition report must be completed.[58]

7. Victoria: if an agreement is in writing, it must follow the standard form. Details of a condition report and a statement of rights and obligations are prescribed.[59]

8. Western Australia: if there is a written agreement, a copy must be provided to the tenant. There is no requirement for a condition report.[60]

The need to set out the terms in writing can be seen as a change of approach. The change reflects a need both to inform a tenant as to the obligations and particularly to clarify the term of the agreement. The advantages of an agreement by handshake are outweighed by the lack of clarity as to the terms and are to an extent at odds with

---

[54] *Residential Tenancies Act 2010* (NSW) ss 8, 9, 13, 17.

[55] *Residential Tenancies Act 1999* (NT) ss 19, 25.

[56] *Residential Tenancies Act 1994* (Qld) ss 38, 38A, 39.

[57] *Residential Tenancies Act 1995* (SA) ss 48, 49.

[58] *Residential Tenancy Act 1997* (Tas) ss 13, 14, 26.

[59] *Residential Tenancies Act 1997* (Vic) ss 26, 35, 66.

[60] *Residential Tenancies Act 1987* (WA) s 54.

the need for documents including the condition report. Similarly, documents headed as applications can contain terms whereby on acceptance by the landlord a binding agreement is formed.

In line with the trend, the *SA Review* calls for a standard form tenancy agreement and seeks to strengthen information disclosure.[61] The amendments expand on the lists of information to be provided by a landlord to include manuals for appliances provided with the premises, and any written agreement must follow the standard form.[62]

V RENTS AND BONDS

Interaction of legal controls and the market place is an issue underlying many of the arguments as to the scope of residential tenancy law. It is most obvious in relation to the issue of possible regulation of rent and bonds. Long-term attitudes to residential tenancy regulation were soured by the experience of controls in the Second World War, which fixed rent levels and protected existing tenants' right to possession.[63] The protections endured in some cases for decades after the war. The *Poverty Report* firmly rejected this precedent in favour of a market-based system.

Bonds probably produced the greatest area of self-help prior to the *Poverty Report*. As part of the scepticism about legal redress, tenants did not have faith in the return of bond money and took defensive action such as withholding an equivalent amount of rent. At common law there was no maximum limit on the amount of a security bond which could be demanded; no processes existed to control what could be done with the money during the tenancy; and available procedures meant that getting back a bond on termination could impose expense and time losses disproportionate to the amount involved.

In all jurisdictions the Common Legislation regulates the maximum amount of any bond.[64] In Queensland, a tenant is given the option in lieu of a security deposit

---

[61]   Government of South Australia, above n 24, recommendation 4.

[62]   *Residential Tenancies Act 1995* (SA) ss 48, 49 are inserted by *Residential Tenancies (Miscellaneous) Amendment Act 2013* (SA) ss 22, 23.

[63]   Adrian J Bradbrook, Susan V MacCallum and Anthony P Moore, *Residential Tenancy Law and Practice: Victoria and South Australia* (Law Book, 1983) 315-22.

[64]   *Residential Tenancies Act 1997* (ACT) s 20; *Landlord and Tenant (Rental Bonds) Act 1977* (NSW) s 9; *Residential Tenancies Act 1999* (NT) s 29; *Residential Tenancies Act 1994* (Qld) s 77; *Residential Tenancies*

to provide a guarantee or undertaking from a financial institution of an amount in respect of a contract of insurance relating to the performance of the tenant's obligations.[65] To ensure an even-handed approach to the return of the bond, in all jurisdictions except the Northern Territory and Tasmania, the bond must be deposited with a government agency.[66] In the Northern Territory and Tasmania a receipt must be given for a bond, but the holding of the money is unregulated.[67] The advantage of an independent body to hold a security bond is that disputes must be resolved by an independent body and thus the previous widespread resort to self-help is avoided.

The *SA Review* supports the current system but recommends minor refinements.[68] The amending provisions allow for an extra week's bond where an animal is allowed on the premises and authorise repayment of a bond as claimed if the claim is not disputed within ten days.[69]

With respect to rent, one of the controversial features of the *Poverty Report* was a proposal whereby a tenant could challenge the amount of any rent increase. As well as a challenge to unfair rent increases, the *Poverty Report* made recommendations as details of the rules for payment of rent. Under the Common Legislation, rent increases must follow notice, are limited in frequency and subject to challenge. The form of notice of any rent increase is prescribed. A landlord may only increase the rent if authorised to do so by the agreement and the legislation requires a minimum notice (commonly 60 days) in writing prior to the increase.[70] The frequency of increases is

---

Act 1995 (SA) s 61; *Residential Tenancy Act 1997* (Tas) s 25; *Residential Tenancies Act 1997* (Vic) s 31; *Residential Tenancies Act 1987* (WA) s 29(1).

[65]   *Residential Tenancies Act 1994* (Qld) s 60.

[66]   *Residential Tenancies Act 1997* (ACT) ss 23-4; *Landlord and Tenant (Rental Bonds) Act 1977* (NSW) s 8; *Residential Tenancies Act 1994* (Qld) s 59; *Residential Tenancies Act 1995* (SA) s 62; *Residential Tenancies Act 1997* (Vic) s 406; *Residential Tenancies Act 1987* (WA) s 29(4), sch 1.

[67]   *Residential Tenancies Act 1997* (ACT) s 65; *Residential Tenancies Act 1987* (NSW) s 45; *Residential Tenancies Act 1999* (NT) s 41; *Residential Tenancies Act 1994* (Qld) s 53; *Residential Tenancies Act 1995* (SA) s 55; *Residential Tenancy Act 1997* (Tas) s 20; *Residential Tenancies Act 1997* (Vic) s 44; *Residential Tenancies Act 1987* (WA) s 30.

[68]   Government of South Australia, above n 24, recommendation 7.

[69]   *Residential Tenancies Act 1995* (SA) ss 61(3) and 63(5) are amended by *Residential Tenancies (Miscellaneous) Amendment Act 2013* (SA) ss 35, 37.

[70]   *Residential Tenancies Act 1997* (ACT) s 65; *Residential Tenancies Act 2010* (NSW) s 45; *Residential Tenancies Act 1999* (NT) s 41; *Residential Tenancies Act 1994* (Qld) s 53; *Residential Tenancies Act 1995* (SA) s 55; *Residential Tenancy Act 1997* (Tas) s 20; *Residential Tenancies Act 1997* (Vic) s 44; *Residential Tenancies Act 1987* (WA) s 30.

commonly controlled by the legislation to an interval of six months from the previous increase.[71] Except in Queensland, the amount of any increase may be challenged. A tenant may apply for an order declaring that the proposed rent is excessive. If the relevant decision-making body finds that the rent is excessive, it may determine the maximum amount of rent payable in respect of the premises.[72] A number of factors are listed to be taken into account in determining whether or not the rent is excessive. In South Australia, even the original rent level may be challenged.[73]

In practice, the power to challenge unfair rent increases has proved to have little impact. The reason for the insignificance in practice of what appeared to be an extreme power is probably that the list of factors relies heavily on a comparison with market rents so that a significant difference from a market rent would suggest an unconscionable term. Unconscionability review is a similarly broad power recommended by the *Poverty Report* and included in the Common Legislation,[74] but it has also been of limited application. Presumably because of the limited impact of the power to challenge unfairness of rent increases, the *SA Review* does not touch on the power and its recommendations are concerned with details such as the place of payment and rent records; the amendments specify such matters as the permissible use of electronic forms of payment.[75]

VI   General Rights and Obligations

The *Poverty Report* recommended that the significant rights and obligations of the parties be mandatory; they were to be set out in legislation and unable to be varied

---

[71]   *Residential Tenancies Act 1997* (ACT) s 70; *Residential Tenancies Act 2010* (NSW) s 45; *Residential Tenancies Act 1999* (NT) s 41(3); *Residential Tenancies Act 1994* (Qld) s 53; *Residential Tenancies Act 1995* (SA) s 55(2)(c); *Residential Tenancy Act 1997* (Tas) s 20(3)(c); *Residential Tenancies Act 1987* (WA) s 30(1)(b).

[72]   *Residential Tenancies Act 1997* (ACT) s 71; *Residential Tenancies Act 2010* (NSW) ss 46-7; *Residential Tenancies Act 1999* (NT) s 42; *Residential Tenancies Act 1995* (SA) s 56; *Residential Tenancy Act 1997* (Tas) s 23; *Residential Tenancies Act 1997* (Vic) ss 45, 46; *Residential Tenancies Act 1987* (WA) s 32.

[73]   *Residential Tenancies Act 1995* (SA) s 56(1).

[74]   The scope of the principle in the tenancy context is discussed in Adrian J Bradbrook, Susan V MacCallum and Anthony P Moore, *Residential Tenancy Law and Practice: Victoria and South Australia* (Law Book, 1983) 124.

[75]   Government of South Australia, above n 24, recommendations 4-7; *Residential Tenancies Act 1995* (SA) ss 53-56, 56A, 57, 58, 58A are inserted or amended by *Residential Tenancies (Miscellaneous) Amendment Act 2013* (SA) ss 27-33.

by the parties. However, the major obligations of the legislation reflect the scope of traditional common law terms. Under those terms, the tenant is guaranteed quiet enjoyment of the premises and adequate security, and rights of entry by the landlord are regulated. The Common Legislation sets out as a statutory obligation upon the landlord the entitlement of the tenant to quiet enjoyment of the premises.[76] The tenant is entitled to possession and to be undisturbed in that possession. The landlord is under an obligation to ensure that the tenant has adequate security against intrusion. Generally, neither party may change any lock without the permission of the other. The landlord's entry on to the premises is limited by the Common Legislation to specified purposes including rent collection, the conduct of an examination of the premises after appropriate notice, the carrying out of repairs or maintenance, and showing through prospective tenants or purchasers.[77] In relation to general landlord and tenant obligations, more recent cases have incorporated the quality of enjoyment into a tenant's entitlement.[78] On this approach, a landlord could be required to disclose known pending road works or prior use, such as that of a brothel, where future nuisance could be expected.

Despite their breadth, little argument has arisen over the list of rights and obligations. In part this acceptance is testimony to the flexibility of the common law terms. A similar position occurred in relation to the sale of goods where concepts such as merchantable quality and fitness for purpose were carried into legislation including the *Trade Practices Act 1974* (Cth) but finally revised in the *Australian Consumer Law*. The terms of the Common Legislation do heavily reflect their real property origins, particularly the emphasis on possession rather than quality of enjoyment.

The *SA Review* is not a place where reconsideration of long-accepted terms would take place. In common with much of the review, it concentrates on disclosure of a known sale at the commencement of the tenancy and of any future sale. It

---

[76] *Residential Tenancies Act 1997* (ACT) sch 1; *Residential Tenancies Act 2010* (NSW) s 22; *Residential Tenancies Act 1999* (NT) s 66; *Residential Tenancies Act 1994* (Qld) s 101; *Residential Tenancies Act 1995* (SA) s 65; *Residential Tenancy Act 1997* (Tas) s 55; *Residential Tenancies Act 1997* (Vic) s 67; *Residential Tenancies Act 1987* (WA) s 44.

[77] *Residential Tenancies Act 1997* (ACT) sch 1 cl 82; *Residential Tenancies Act 2010* (NSW) ss 24, 22; *Residential Tenancies Act 1999* (NT) s 686; *Residential Tenancies Act 1994* (Qld) s 109; *Residential Tenancies Act 1995* (SA) 7265; *Residential Tenancy Act 1997* (Tas) s 55; *Residential Tenancies Act 1997* (Vic) s 60; *Residential Tenancies Act 1987* (WA) s 46.

[78] In particular, see *Aussie Traveller Pty Ltd v Marklea Pty Ltd* [1998] Qd R 1.

proposes that entry for rent collection be restricted to situations where alternative collection methods are not agreed, and proposes greater specification in relation to entry for inspections and gardening and open inspections; it does not otherwise attempt any restatement of the terms.[79]

In view of the contractual emphasis, the obligations under the Common Legislation are unsurprisingly expressed as terms of a contract. Consequently, the obligations are between the landlord and the tenant (as defined in the agreement). Persons residing on the premises who are not parties to the agreement cannot claim the benefit of the obligations. Thus, family members other than the tenant cannot, in particular, claim the benefit of any obligation to repair. This inability has led to one of the most disturbing failures of tenant protection in its broadest sense. In *Northern Sandblasting Pty Ltd v Harris* (1997) 188 CLR 313, the earth wire from a stove was not isolated from the active wire carrying the current to the hotplate. The earth wire was connected to water pipes. The tenants' daughter was severely injured by contact with the water pipe whilst the hotplate was in use. Although able to recover on other grounds, the daughter was held to be unable to recover for breach of the landlord's statutory duty. Similarly, a visitor whose car is damaged by a collapsing carport would have no claim under the residential tenancies legislation even if the landlord had been informed of the defect. Surprisingly little attention has been given to this issue.

In addition, the jurisdiction of dispute resolution bodies under the Common Legislation (despite differences as to the composition of such bodies) is limited to disputes between landlords and tenants. Consequently disputes between tenants cannot be heard and dispute resolution bodies may not even be able to apportion liability between tenants where a claim is brought against some or all of them and equitable responsibility for loss is not evenly shared. Furthermore, agents are predominantly involved only as representatives and are not subject to independent duties. Any review of their responsibilities is left to the separate licensing regimes. These problems are not addressed by the *SA Review*.

---

[79] Government of South Australia, above n 24, recommendations 13-17, 28-31; disclosure of sales is required by *Residential Tenancies Act 1995* (SA) 47A and 71A as inserted by *Residential Tenancies (Miscellaneous) Amendment Act 2013* (SA) ss 21 and 43 and rules as to the landlord's entry onto the premises are set out in *Residential Tenancies Act 1995* (SA) s72 as amended by *Residential Tenancies (Miscellaneous) Amendment Act 2013* (SA) s 69.

VII   REPAIRS AND MAINTENANCE

Reversal of the common law immunity of landlords for the condition of the premises is a feature of the *Poverty Report*. The common law did not impose any obligation with respect to the condition of the premises except in the case of furnished premises and then the obligation was limited to their condition at the commencement of the lease. In the extreme, tenants had no recovery where a disconnected gas plug meant that they did not awaken from their sleep. The Common Legislation does make the landlord responsible for the structural condition of the premises.[80] However, it adds an important rider that the tenant must report any defect to the landlord.[81]

Responsibility for repairs and maintenance of the rented premises involves definition of the scope of the responsibility and the means available to enforce any obligation. The situations in which the obligation is applicable can vary from minor problems such as a leaking tap to matters of structural integrity such as a roof beam that cannot carry its load. The consequences can be immediate and physical such as escaping gas or long-term and financial such as an electrical fuse which does not shut off.

Although the primary duty to repair is vested by the tenancies legislation in the landlord, the tenant is required, as soon as practicable, to notify the landlord of any damage to the residential premises of which the tenant becomes aware. At common law the landlord's responsibility for repairs has been held to be dependent upon receipt of notice of lack of repair. This qualification goes beyond cases of breach of the tenant's duty to notify damage; it applies to defects existing at the commencement of the tenancy and those reasonably discoverable by a landlord exercising the right to inspect; it is of no account that the tenant could not reasonably have discovered the defect. It has been held that the common law rule on this matter continues to operate. The continued application of the common law rule has been heavily influenced by

---

[80]   *Residential Tenancies Act 1997* (ACT) sch cl 54; *Residential Tenancies Act 2010* (NSW) s 63; *Residential Tenancies Act 1999* (NT) ss 47, 57; *Residential Tenancies Act 1994* (Qld) s 215; *Residential Tenancies Act 1995* (SA) s 68(1)(a); *Residential Tenancy Act 1997* (Tas) s 32; *Residential Tenancies Act 1997* (Vic) s 65; *Residential Tenancies Act 1987* (WA) s 42(1)(b).

[81]   *Residential Tenancies Act 1997* (ACT) sch cl 63; *Residential Tenancies Act 2010* (NSW) has no express duty to give notice; *Residential Tenancies Act 1999* (NT) s 58; *Residential Tenancies Act 1994* (Qld) s 217; *Residential Tenancies Act 1995* (SA) s 68(1)(b); *Residential Tenancy Act 1997* (Tas) s 32; *Residential Tenancies Act 1997* (Vic) s 61; *Residential Tenancies Act 1987* (WA) s 38(1)(b).

Adrian Bradbrook's own writing; his argument is that nothing has been expressed to overturn the common law and he has not commented on the apparent unfairness of the result at least in relation to latent defects reasonably discoverable by the landlord.[82]

This rule is that the landlord is not under a duty to repair pursuant to an express covenant unless he or she is given notice of the lack of repair. This qualification extends beyond the tenant's duty to report defects, as it applies to latent defects of which the tenant could not be aware. In *Northern Sandblasting Pty Ltd v Harris*,[83] as detailed above, the tenants' daughter was severely injured by contact with the water pipe. She was held not to have any right of recovery under the Queensland residential tenancies legislation, not only because she was not a party to the agreement but also because the landlord was unaware of the defect. Similarly, in *Casey v Aldous* a tenant complained of excessive energy bills because of a defective stove installation, but was denied relief because of lack of notice to the landlord.[84] The courts have, however, accepted that the defence is one of lack of notice and that notice may come from a third party and is not limited to the tenant's performance of the duty to report.

Probably because the issue is seen as one of legal technicality, it is not referred to in the *SA Review*. It is difficult to envision any justification to the absolute defence; clearly a tenant suffers injury for which the tenant has no responsibility; a landlord seems to be rewarded for a lack of involvement with the premises.

VIII   Supply of Essential Services

Climate change impacts on residential occupation as well as most other aspects of current life. At the time of the *Poverty Report*, fitness for habitation was seen as concerned with structural soundness, cleanliness and security of occupation. Government agencies supplied most essential services. Today, water and energy conservation are concerns of any residential occupant. Such occupants are also expected to bargain for the best deal for the supply of essential services. For a tenant, control over the means of conservation depends on structural matters whose responsibility and therefore cost burden falls on the landlord. The landlord may not see long-term benefit in the installation of water- and energy-saving devices. A lack of insulation may, for example,

---

[82]   Bradbrook, MacCallum and Moore, above n 9, 369.

[83]   (1998) 188 CLR 313; the case has already been discussed in relation to the inability to claim as a non-party.

[84]   (1994) 63 SASR 347.

lead to greater use of a bar radiator. This choice is not only costly for the tenant but places a burden on society through increased energy use. Even government assistance policies discriminate against tenants; many concessions for energy improvements have been confined to owner-occupiers presumably on the basis that landlords would reap a financial benefit from increased rents, but the effect is to deny tenants equal access to subsidised energy upgrades.

National building codes set out a system whereby building approval depends on meeting a star rating for energy efficiency. As well as building energy standards, guidance for consumers with respect to energy standards of appliances is also provided by a star energy rating. Leased premises and supplied appliances would in many cases have preceded these rating systems. Importantly, nothing in the Common Legislation requires landlords to disclose whether buildings and appliances have energy ratings or the level of such ratings. Disclosure requirements on the sale of residential premises have been increasing and their scope has been broadening from issues affecting title to those affecting structural quality — and in the Australian Capital Territory, for example, include an asbestos report and an energy efficiency rating.[85] The Council of Australian Governments has been considering a proposal that disclosure of an energy rating be required on any sale or lease of a housing unit.

Amendments to the South Australian Act tackle only peripheral matters; in the absence of agreement, if there are no separate water meter rates, charges for water supply are to be borne by the landlord;[86] and although use manuals for appliances must be provided,[87] information as to energy efficiency is not included.

IX TROUBLESOME TENANTS

The *Poverty Report* recommends that tenants owe a duty not to disturb their neighbours. But in line with the attention to individual dwellings, the Report focuses on nuisance obligations and repeats standard common law obligations. The Common Legislation states that it is a term of every residential tenancy agreement that the tenant shall not

---

[85] The legislation in the Australian Capital Territory is *Civil Law (Sale of Residential Property) Act 2003* (ACT) s 10; see generally Bradbrook et al, *Australian Real Property Law*, above n 3, 468.

[86] *Residential Tenancies Act 1995* (SA) s 73 is substituted by *Residential Tenancies (Miscellaneous) Amendment Act 2013* (SA) s 46.

[87] *Residential Tenancies Act 1995* (SA) s 48 is substituted by *Residential Tenancies (Miscellaneous) Amendment Act 2013* (SA) s 22.

commit any illegal activity on the premises and shall not cause or permit a nuisance.[88] Illegal use of premises and creation of a nuisance have become connected by the use for drug growing and disturbance caused by consumption of those drugs.

Landlords are concerned with property damage and the impact on other tenants of the landlord. Landlords may not even live in the neighbourhood of the rented premises. More recently much greater focus has been given to the extent of the impact of troublesome tenants. Such tenants are seen as detracting from the habitability of the neighbourhood at large. The problem of troublesome tenants is therefore a concern not only for landlords but for neighbours and public authorities. New South Wales has introduced special agreements relating to anti-social behaviour by public housing tenants and the Northern Territory and South Australia allow actions against tenants creating a disturbance by persons affected. Such persons can obtain orders for possession even against the wishes of the landlord.[89]

Whilst troublemakers can be portrayed as bikies and similar irresponsible characters whose anti-social behaviour is deliberate, disturbances can equally result from those with some mental illness who are dwelling within the community as a result of removing such persons from institutions. Society has failed to come to terms with the consequences of removing many mentally ill persons from institutions and in particular has failed to provide support for such persons. Tribunal procedure, which relies primarily on adjudication following personal presentation of factual material by each side, may not be well suited to an investigation of behavioural problems.

The greater concerns about troublesome tenants may be seen as part of the consequences of urban consolidation. The amendments to the South Australian Act add an affected stratum or community corporation, a police officer and an authorised officer within the meaning of the *Fair Trading Act 1987* (SA) as interested persons who can make application for termination of a tenancy. These changes strengthen the community character of coping with troublesome tenants.

---

[88] *Residential Tenancies Act 1997* (ACT) sch cl 70; *Residential Tenancies Act 2010* (NSW) s 23; *Residential Tenancies Act 1999* (NT) s 67; *Residential Tenancies Act 1994* (Qld) s 182; *Residential Tenancies Act 1995* (SA) s 71; *Residential Tenancy Act 1997* (Tas) s 52; *Residential Tenancies Act 1997* (Vic) s 60; *Residential Tenancies Act 1987* (WA) s 39.

[89] *Residential Tenancies Act 2010* (NSW) s 35A; *Residential Tenancies Act 1999* (NT) s 100; *Residential Tenancies Act 1995* (SA) s 90.

X TERMINATION

Termination of a tenancy and recovery of possession for non-payment of rent are subject to statutory procedures. There are two key features of the *Poverty Report*: rules as to when an agreement may be terminated for breach are specified and vary according to the ground for termination; and a tenant has rights to terminate for failure by the landlord to fulfil the landlord's obligations.

Termination is thus almost universally regulated. One of the reasons stated in the *Poverty Report* for the establishment of specialist tribunals was to enable the speedy processing of orders for possession. The provision of a process for recovery of possession cannot be instigated merely because a tenant is late with a rent payment; a specified period of default is the starting point. Under the Common Legislation a landlord is required to provide notice of default and an opportunity to make good the default.[90] Recovery of possession without the tenant's consent is prohibited and the decision-making body has discretion as to whether or not termination and recovery of possession are justified.[91]

Non-payment of rent is not the only breach by a tenant justifying termination. Causing damage to premises and keeping a pet without permission are the other most common grounds for bringing a tenancy to an end; any breach by a tenant can lead to an application to the tribunal but the breach must be shown to justify termination. Notices and processes are established by the Common Legislation for these matters.[92] Cases of an exceptional nature, such as commission of acts of violence by a tenant against a landlord or neighbour, are subject to expedited termination.

---

[90] *Residential Tenancies Act 1997* (ACT) s 49; *Residential Tenancies Act 2010* (NSW) s 57; *Residential Tenancies Act 1999* (NT) s 87; *Residential Tenancies Act 1994* (Qld) s 53; *Residential Tenancies Act 1995* (SA) s 80; *Residential Tenancy Act 1997* (Tas) s 42; *Residential Tenancies Act 1997* (Vic) s 246; *Residential Tenancies Act 1987* (WA) s 62.

[91] *Residential Tenancies Act 1997* (ACT) s 39; *Residential Tenancies Act 1987* (NSW) s 69; *Residential Tenancies Act 1999* (NT) s 104; *Residential Tenancies Act 1994* (Qld) s 151; *Residential Tenancies Act 1995* (SA) s 93; *Residential Tenancy Act 1997* (Tas) s 45; *Residential Tenancies Act 1997* (Vic) s 322; *Residential Tenancies Act 1987* (WA) s 74.

[92] *Residential Tenancies Act 1997* (ACT) s 51; *Residential Tenancies Act 1987* (NSW) s 57; *Residential Tenancies Act 1999* (NT) s 88; *Residential Tenancies Act 1994* (Qld) s 151; *Residential Tenancies Act 1995* (SA) s 80; *Residential Tenancy Act 1997* (Tas) s 42; *Residential Tenancies Act 1997* (Vic) ss 243, 250; *Residential Tenancies Act 1987* (WA) s 62.

The legislation does not protect tenants from eviction without cause, if the term of a tenancy has expired. The tenant's only long-term protection for possession is by the term of the tenancy, and a fixed term tenancy expires at the expiration of the term without any notice by either party. The *Poverty Report* was concerned at the possibility of exploitation of this entitlement through the creation of very short fixed terms and sought to place restrictions on such tenancies. In Australia, there is not a culture of long-term private tenancies, and fixed term residential tenancies are usually only for six months or one year. Even fixed terms can be reduced in extreme circumstances. Periodic tenancies are common, particularly after an initial fixed term. In the case of periodic tenancies, the Common Legislation sets out periods of notice before the tenancy can be terminated. These periods vary between landlord and tenant. Generally, longer periods of notice are required from a landlord, but the period may also vary according to whether or not there is a cause, other than breach by the tenant, for termination.

By contrast, some security of tenure is provided for retail tenants in some jurisdictions by a right of pre-emption; if premises are to be leased at the expiration of a fixed term, a right of first refusal must be given to any existing tenant.[93] Similar rights for residential tenants do not seem to have been considered.

The *SA Review* largely endorses the current termination procedures and seeks to simplify the notice times.[94] The amendments allow shorter notice periods in the case of continued tenant rent default; application to the tribunal can be made without notice if the tenant has failed to pay rent as due and has twice in the previous twelve months been given notice because of rent default.[95] This change is made to address persistent default and particularly to counter what is seen as tenant exploitation of the notice system. At the same time, where the term of a fixed term tenancy is to expire, a landlord must give at least 28 days notice of termination.[96] This reform means that a tenant will be aware of what is likely to happen before the expiration of the term but gives no entitlement beyond the term.

---

[93] Adrian J Bradbrook et al, *Australian Real Property Law* (Thomson Reuters, 5th ed, 2011) pp 740-1.

[94] Government of South Australia, above n 24, recommendations 31-4; 49-68.

[95] *Residential Tenancies Act 1995* (SA) s 87 is amended by *Residential Tenancies (Miscellaneous) Amendment Act 2013* (SA) s 58.

[96] *Residential Tenancies Act 1995* (SA) s 86A is inserted by *Residential Tenancies (Miscellaneous) Amendment Act 2013* (SA) s 57.

XI What does the Legacy Amount to?

At the beginning of this chapter, the comment was made that despite the word 'poverty' in the title of the *Poverty Report*, problems of the homeless are not addressed at any length. In part this omission reflected confidence that the problem would be overcome by the action of state and territory housing authorities whose agreements would be subject to the legislation.[97] But at the time of the original report, the law and economics movement had made little impact in Australia. The *Poverty Report* contained little analysis of the impact of reform on the housing market; it was a law reform project and homelessness was seen as a matter outside legal regulation. The reforms aimed to achieve what in the eyes of an observer was fair as between landlord and tenant. The report did reject the wartime and English approach of allowing sitting tenants to remain. Even though residential tenancies are no longer perceived as confined to those who are less well-off or in a time of transition from parents' home and home ownership, Australian tenancies remain short-term. This feature is particularly troublesome for families with the threatened insecurity of neighbourhood relations and schooling. Whether law reform can affect that balance is a matter that has received little attention.

The most important point that must be made in relation to the *Poverty Report* is that it has been adopted in all Australian jurisdictions and remains the basis of legislation. This chapter has identified issues relating to the scope of the legislation, the required documentation, the limit of obligations to the contracting parties, the qualification to the duty to repair and the lack of provision for energy use and protection for neighbours. In all these instances the criticism relates to the desirability to go beyond both the common law and the Common Legislation.

Further changes to the current position may be properly regarded as steps for a later time without threatening the basis of the Common Legislation. The extension to rooming houses and caravan park residents has essentially applied the original legislation to similar areas and can be seen as an endorsement of the principles of the original legislation. The need for greater documentation and obligations beyond the contracting parties are instances where the contractual focus may have been too limiting. Energy use and troublesome tenants reflect issues of a different era. The

---

[97] Perversely the original South Australian legislation did not apply to South Australian Housing Trust tenants and some lack of application remains: *Residential Tenancies Act 1995* (SA) s 5(3).

SA Review has not seen the present as an opportune time for a fundamental rethinking of the ideas that have flowed from the *Poverty Report*; its proposals concentrate simply on keeping an existing system in working order.

The absence of strident opposition to the continuation of the legislation probably reflects the market base of the *Poverty Report* and the Common Legislation. Little credit seems to have been given for a probable impact of an enforceable right to repairs on maintenance of overall building standards; it has been tenant behaviour not building standards that have caused some outcry. Alternatives to action before the court to enforce rights (including the landlord's ability to recover possession) have led to different tribunals and procedures and a continuing role for state and territory consumer agencies. It is to the credit of Bradbrook's work on the *Poverty Report* that few reformers can boast such ongoing nation-wide acceptance of a range of concepts and details.

8

SUSTAINABLE TRANSPORT: TRENDS, ISSUES AND PERSPECTIVES FOR INTERNATIONAL CO-OPERATION IN THE IMPLEMENTATION OF RIO+20 DECISIONS

Ralph Wahnschafft

I Introduction

Transport and mobility are essential preconditions for economic growth, social development and global trade. However, they are also often associated with significant environmental impacts, including local air pollution and pollution of the atmosphere, and they thus pose major challenges for the achievement of sustainable development. Transport policies as they relate to sustainable development have periodically been discussed at the United Nations. Transport is dealt with in Chapter 7, 'Promoting sustainable human settlements development', and Chapter 9, 'Protection of the atmosphere', of Agenda 21 adopted at the Earth Summit in 2012,[1] and in Chapter 3, 'Changing unsustainable patterns of consumption and production' of the Johannesburg Plan of Implementation ('JPoI').[2] Sustainable development requires

---

[1]   *Report of the United Nations Conference on Environment and Development (Rio de Janeiro, 3-14 June 1992)*, UN Doc A/CONF.151/26 (Vol. 1) (12 August 1992) res I, annex II.

[2]   *Plan of Implementation of the World Summit on Sustainable Development*, UN Doc A/CONF.199/20 (4 September 2002).

a comprehensive and integrated approach to policy- and decision-making with a view to developing adequate and efficient, economically viable, socially acceptable and environmentally sound transport systems, as envisaged in decision 9/3 adopted by the Commission on Sustainable Development at its ninth session in 2001[3] and reiterated by the World Summit on Sustainable Development ('WSSD') in 2002.

The Commission on Sustainable Development more intensively discussed transport policies and sustainable development at its more recent eighteenth and nineteenth sessions held at UN Headquarters in New York in May 2010[4] and May 2011.[5] The high-level United Nations Conference on Sustainable Development ('UNCSD 2012'), also known as Rio+20, held in Rio de Janeiro, Brazil, in 20-22 June 2012, also re-emphasised the need for action at local, national, regional and global levels to make transport systems more sustainable.

This chapter provides an overview of the intergovernmental debate on transport policies during recent years. It highlights some major trends and points out important policy issues that need to be addressed. It concludes by identifying important areas for further international policy dialogue and technical and financial co-operation in the future.

Over the past 15 years, Professor Adrian Bradbrook, Bonython Professor of Law at the University of Adelaide, Australia, has actively participated in several expert-level and intergovernmental meetings organised by the United Nations Secretariat as a part of the related preparatory process for the intergovernmental debate. Participating experts and delegations have greatly appreciated his expert advice, his suggestions on possible regulatory measures and his technical background information papers, which were made available to delegations at the meetings of the United Nations Commission on Sustainable Development ('UNCSD'), in particular during the second and during the fourth cycle of consultations ('CSD 14/15' in 2002/07 and 'CSD 18/19' in 2010/11).

---

[3] Commission on Sustainable Development, *Report on the Ninth Session (5 May 2000 and 16-27 April 2001)*, UN Docs E/2001/29 and E/CN.17/2001/19 (2001) 19-24.

[4] Commission on Sustainable Development, *Report on the Eighteenth Session (15 May 2009 and 3-14 May 2010)*, UN Docs E/2011/29 and E/CN.17/2010/15 (2010).

[5] Commission on Sustainable Development, *Report on the Nineteenth Session (14 May 2010 and 2-13 May 2011)*, UN Docs E/2011/29 and E/CN.17/2011/20 (2011).

II   Salient Trends and Issues in (Un)sustainable Transport[6]

Economic activity, globalisation, national and international trade and transport are closely interlinked. Since 1971, global transport energy use rose steadily at 2.0-2.5 per cent per annum, closely reflecting global economic growth. Road transport used the most energy and experienced the highest growth in absolute terms. Aviation was the second largest user of energy, and increased the most in relative terms.

Different countries and regions show very diverse patterns of transport activity with large disparities in national and per capita transport energy use, depending on the amount of travel undertaken, as well as the modes of transport and types of fuels used. Whilst in North America energy consumption in transport exceeded 2000 kgoe[7] per person in 2007, consumption in some of the developing countries — for example, in Africa — averaged less than 100 kgoe per person per year. According to the International Energy Agency ('IEA') data, transport energy use in industrialised countries grew by an annual average of 1.2 per cent between 2000 and 2006, whereas in developing countries it increased by an annual average of 4.3 per cent during the same period.

Transport relies on oil and oil products for more than 95 per cent of its energy needs. Gasoline and diesel are very effective transport fuels, providing high energy density and relatively easy handling characteristics. Over the past twenty years, oil prices have on average been low when compared to available alternatives, contributing to a growing oil dependence on the part of the entire transport economy. From 1990 to 2005, the global stock of motor vehicles grew by about 60 per cent, or about 3 per cent per year, dominated in most countries by gasoline-fuelled vehicles. The total worldwide stock of private light-duty vehicles is estimated at the time of writing as 800 to 900 million, and is projected to continue to increase to between 1.8 and 2.5 billion by 2030.[8] Private motor vehicle ownership and motorised mobility are strongly related to disposable personal income. In almost all developing countries,

---

[6]   The trend analysis in this chapter summarises the main findings presented to the United Nations Commission on Sustainable Development in the Report of the Secretary-General: *Review of progress achieved in implementation of Agenda 21 and the Johannesburg Plan of Implementation: transport*, UN ESCOR, 18th sess, Agenda Item 3, UN Doc E/CN.17/2010/4 (18 February 2010).

[7]   kilogram of oil equivalent ('kgoe').

[8]   Daniel Sperling and Deborah Gordon, *Two Billion Cars: Driving towards Sustainability* (Oxford University Press, 2009).

private motor vehicle ownership is still very low, and the types of vehicle used are mostly of a smaller size and engine capacity.

In spite of the rapid growth of investments in transport infrastructure, World Bank and other land transport indicators suggest that not only the rail but also road infrastructure, including bridges and tunnels, are still very inadequate in many developing countries, where often less than 50 per cent of roads are paved. In many of the low- and middle-income developing countries, road networks are increasing in length, on average, by about 2 per cent per year. In India and China, the length of roads grew by some 4 and 6 per cent per annum, respectively, during the past decade. While road infrastructure remains inadequate, vehicle ownership and registration has been increasing rapidly. From 2008 to 2012, the motor vehicle population in India grew by about 12 per cent per year and in China by about 20 per cent per year.[9] Most additional vehicles are used in large cities, further aggravating the already serious problems of traffic congestion, inefficient fuel use and high accident rates, as well as air and noise pollution.

Railways are an energy efficient and climate-friendly but capital-intensive means of land transport. Whereas most industrialised countries have an extensive railway infrastructure, often with double tracks and electrification, most developing countries have only a limited length of often single tracks. Most developing countries face great challenges, including financial constraints, which often delay the necessary modernisation and expansion of the mostly publicly owned railways.

Over the past three decades, air transport has grown faster than any other transport mode. Commercial air travel volumes increased by an average of 5 per cent per year during the 1990s. In addition to business travel, domestic and international tourism has grown into a global service industry, with many long-distance trips undertaken by air.

Shipping capacities and activities nearly doubled between 1985 and 2007. In 2005 alone, the world merchant fleet expanded by 7.2 per cent. The International Maritime Organisation ('IMO') estimates that 90 per cent of global trade is conducted by sea. As of March 2008, the global merchant fleet comprised almost 62 000 registered large ships of more than 400 Gross tonnage ('GT') capacity each with a total dead-weight tonnage of 1.1 billion tons. Oil tankers and dry bulk carriers

---

[9]   World Bank, *The World Bank Group's Transport Business Strategy for 2008-2012* (2008) 3, 48-50 <http://go.worldbank.org/RSESS3TIJ0>.

still continue to dominate the world fleet, whilst containerised trade grew eight-fold between 1985 and 2007.

Geographical conditions can pose particular disadvantages for transport infrastructure development. Some mountainous and landlocked countries face particular challenges in the development of transport infrastructure and in participation in international trade and travel. For many landlocked least-developed countries ('LDC's) in sub-Saharan Africa, economic development prospects are constrained by high transport costs. Similarly, many of the small island developing States ('SIDS') are also often experiencing transport and trading cost disadvantages as the volumes of their maritime and other transport services are often comparatively small.

A   Rural Transport Infrastructure and Lack of Access to Transport Services in Developing Countries

Inadequate transport infrastructure and inadequate access to affordable transport services are often cited as perpetuating poverty and posing major obstacles to the achievement of the Millennium Development Goals ('MDG's), in particular in rural areas. Rural roads are characterised by traffic of less than 50 vehicles per day and include engineered roads and bridges that link towns and villages as well as trafficable tracks and trails. The main purpose of trips in rural areas is to buy provisions, sell crops/products, pursue education, process agricultural products, fetch water, collect fuel wood, access medical care, visit family and friends, commute to places of work and obtain official documentation. The most used transport modes remain motorbikes, bicycles, barrows, carts, small boats or walking, often with back/head loading. Due to low population densities in remote rural areas, adequate public transport services are rarely available.

The World Bank Rural Access Index measures the number of rural people who live beyond 2 kilometres (equivalent to a 20-25 minute walk) from the nearest all-weather road as a proportion of the total rural population, and indicates that over 1 billion of the world's rural inhabitants do not have access to adequate transport, 98 per cent of whom are in developing countries. Physical isolation is a strong contributor to poverty and the marginalisation of rural communities. Women and children are particularly affected. Various studies indicate that the extent of poverty is not just dependent on family income but also on the availability of infrastructure and services, such as education, safe drinking water, basic sanitation, clean and affordable modern energy services and medical care. A disproportionate burden is placed on rural women, especially in regions of sub-Saharan Africa, who spend a major part of the day on travel and transport just to meet household subsistence needs.

Basic rural transport infrastructure and services contribute directly and indirectly to local income generation through the use of appropriate technologies, local contractors, local workers and local materials. Disaster relief and food-for-work types of transport infrastructure project can also contribute to rural poverty reduction.

B Urban Transport

Urban transport poses great challenges in many of the rapidly growing metropolitan and other urban areas of developing countries where lack of adequate planning and public transport services causes economic losses. These losses are due to high consumption of fuels, congestion and air pollution, through sulphur dioxide ('SOx'), oxides of nitrogen ('NOx'), volatile organic compounds ('VOC's) and particulates, with the associated impact on public health. According to projections of UN-Habitat, by 2050, two-thirds of humanity will live in towns and cities. Hence cities in developing countries urgently need affordable high-quality public urban transport systems.

Urban planners face the challenge of balancing an appropriate separation and mix of residential, industrial, commercial and recreation zones so that jobs, markets and residences are not separated by long distances. The bicycle is by far the most affordable mode of transport for the urban poor. Adequate provision of safe cycle routes and parking facilities can enhance sustainability in urban transport systems. Similarly, policies to support walking as a prime mode of transport through the provision and maintenance of walkways can also be effective in urban areas. Many European cities and towns have successfully restricted motor vehicle use in commercial centres by introducing pedestrian-only shopping zones.

Subway and light-rail systems form the basis for rapid, cost-effective and environmentally benign urban passenger transport. Located mostly in the industrialised countries, 116 cities operate their own metro systems, which are used by an estimated 155 million passengers each day. In addition, there are about 400 light-rail systems worldwide, while over 200 new systems are planned. However, the construction of subways in existing cities poses major challenges and is often very costly, and thus not easily affordable for developing countries, even though tunnel construction technologies are now very advanced.

A growing number of developing countries have embarked on, or are considering, the introduction of bus rapid transit ('BRT') systems, which are characterised by mostly larger buses that run on segregated lanes parallel to the local traffic. In comparison with light-rail transit or subway systems, BRT systems are much less costly whilst still achieving comparable high transport efficiency. Enhanced BRT systems offer climate-controlled buses with platform-level entry, pre- or post-fare payment and global positioning systems to inform customers of expected waiting times and transfer connections. Modern BRT systems can move up to 45 000 passengers per hour along a single route direction compared to less than 10 000 passengers for mixed traffic on the same corridor. Although the costs of individual buses and BRT systems are moderate, many such systems are urgently needed to enable developing countries to tackle growing urban transport problems. For many developing countries, BRT systems would be affordable only with significant international technical and financial support.

Area licensing, road pricing and parking charge schemes, such as those applied in Singapore, London and Paris, have proven effective in terms of reduction of urban vehicular traffic. Some cities, in particular those where air pollution poses a major threat to human health, have implemented temporary restrictions on the use of cars, for example by day of week, number plate or minimum occupancy. Public information and public health campaigns advocating car-free days or temporary road closures for biking, walking or street markets have also become increasingly popular.

In a growing number of cities, new urban planning and innovative business concepts, including car-free housing,[10] car sharing and short-term car rentals and 'dial a ride' services, as well as company bicycles and urban bicycle rental schemes, are offering new low-carbon transport options. In many European capitals and most of the larger cities, bicycles are now easily available for rent at major train or subway stations.

---

[10] *Improving Global Road Safety*, GA Res 62/244, UN GAOR, 62nd sess, 87th plen mtg, Agenda Item 46, Supp No 49, UN Doc A/RES/62/244 (25 April 2008).

Since the adoption of the *Convention on the Rights of Persons with Disabilities*,[11] transport planners in many countries have initiated additional projects and programs to provide persons with disabilities with better, equal and affordable transport access and personal mobility, in particular in the urban public transport systems.

C   Integrated Planning of Regional, Inter-urban and Cross-border Transport Systems

Many transport experts recommend a three-pronged approach to make transport systems more sustainable. The first prong is to avoid unnecessary transport through better spatial planning and other measures. In the Netherlands, for example, a new multi-stakeholder partnership involving a group of large corporations set an example to reduce traffic congestion and the associated waste of time and energy by staggering work hours for employees and by introducing telecommuting and video-conferencing. As a result, traffic volume and congestion were reduced in several cities, in particular during rush hour.

The second prong relates to the promotion of modal shifts, favouring transport modes with high transport and fuel efficiency, for example high-speed passenger trains or rail and barge freight on inland waterways. In Europe and Japan, the average energy consumption per passenger-kilometre for high speed rail is generally one-third to one-fifth lower than that for aeroplane or car use. Whilst freight transported by truck is more versatile and flexible and, therefore, the preferred mode of transport for many types of goods and in many countries, shifting freight from road to rail, where possible, may increasingly be in the public interest considering the environmental advantages.

The third prong is to improve efficiency for all modes that contribute significantly to reductions in emissions and air pollution while saving energy. Various regulatory and fiscal policy tools are available to promote modal shifts, increase fuel economy and efficiency, and enhance the internalisation of negative environmental effects.

Globalisation and economic specialisation require increased mobility between urban centres, for which adequate public transport systems are needed. Experience has shown that suitable and affordable inter-city rail services can compete with air

---

[11]   *International Covenant on the Rights of Persons with Disabilities*, opened for signature 13 December 2006, 2515 UNTS 3 (entered into force 3 May 2008).

traffic. In particular in developing countries, buses play an important role in inter-city passenger travel.

D   Transport Safety

Worldwide, an estimated 1.2 million people are killed in road accidents each year and as many as 50 million are injured with about 90 per cent of such accidents occurring in low- and middle-income countries. The World Health Organisation ('WHO') conducts comprehensive periodical assessments of the global status of road safety.[12] Separating different modes of transport through appropriate infrastructure and, where possible, through crossing-free intersections can greatly reduce accidents. Road safety concerns need to be fully integrated into transport planning. Permanent, seasonal or other temporary speed limits, driver safety and eco-training programs, mandatory seat belt or cycling helmet requirements and public awareness campaigns are all proven tools for preventing accidents and serious injuries.

In its resolution 62/244, the General Assembly welcomed the offer of the Government of the Russian Federation to host the First Global Ministerial Conference on Road Safety, held in Moscow on 19 and 20 November 2009.[13] In its declaration the Conference called upon the General Assembly to declare 2011-2020 as the 'Decade of Action for Road Safety'. Many countries have endorsed the United Nations Road Safety Initiative and have launched local, regional and national programmes aimed at reducing personal injuries and casualties from road accidents.

E   Transport and Climate Change

The transport sector is responsible for almost a quarter of greenhouse gas ('GHG') emission from fossil fuel sources and is the fastest growing sector with respect to GHG emissions, yet it has received little attention from international climate initiatives and support programs. Whereas GHG emissions in some other economic sectors decreased slightly between 1990 and 2007, emissions from transport in the industrialised countries listed as Annex-1 Parties to the United Nations Framework Convention on Climate Change ('UNFCCC') have increased significantly, on average

---

[12]   World Health Organisation, *Global Status Report on Road Safety: Time for Action* (2009) <http://www.who.int/violence_injury_prevention/road_safety_status/2009/en/>.

[13]   *Improving Global Road Safety*, GA Res 62/244, UN GAOR, 62nd sess, 87th plen mtg, Agenda Item 46, Supp No 49, UN Doc A/RES/62/244 (25 April 2008).

by 17 per cent. Hence, as a group, Annex-1 Country Parties to the Convention are not likely to achieve the emission reduction targets agreed under the *Kyoto Protocol*. In 2007, per capita GHG emissions from transport in the industrialised world ranged from 603 kg to 16 716 kg equivalent carbon dioxide ('CO_2eq'), whilst in the developing world per capita emissions invariably remained very low.[14]

In 2006, aggregate global CO_2 emissions from the transport sector were 6.452 Gigatons ('Gt') CO_2. Road transport accounted for 73 per cent of these emissions, aviation for 11 per cent, international shipping for 9 per cent, inland navigation for 2 per cent, rail for 2 per cent and other traffic for the remaining 3 per cent. Transport also accounts for a large share in black carbon particulate emissions, which can also contribute significantly to climate change.

Motor vehicle fuel economy and emission standards offer important policy options for mitigating climate change. Existing regulatory approaches differ considerably among countries, depending on technical definitions of standards, vehicle categories and weight classes, as well as test driving cycles. Several countries have introduced mandatory standards, whilst others still rely on voluntary approaches and industry self-regulation. Motor vehicle standards in Japan, the Republic of Korea, the European Union and China require higher fuel economy (or lower emissions) relative to the standards applied in Australia, Canada and the USA. In many countries, the average fuel economy has gradually improved since standards were first introduced in the mid-1970s. However, significant further review of these regulations will be required if the projected increase in global CO_2 emission is to be curbed. The United States has recently increased the Corporate Average Fuel Economy ('CAFE') standards with a view to improving vehicle fuel economy to 35.5 miles per gallon in 2016 (equivalent to 6.6 l/100 km).[15]

Several initiatives and international partnerships have been formed to support multi-stakeholder collaboration on fuel economy, including the Low Carbon Vehicle Partnership ('Low CVP') based in the UK, and the Global Fuel Economy Initiative ('GFEI') of the United Nations Environment Programme ('UNEP'), the International Energy Agency ('IEA'), the International Transport Forum ('ITF') and the Foundation of the International Automobile Federation ('FIA Foundation').

---

[14] Based on data reported to the UNFCCC.

[15] United States Government, Department of Transportation, *Average Fuel Economy Standards Passenger Cars and Light Trucks Model Year 2011*.

Retail prices for motor fuels differ considerably from country to country, even up to a factor of eight, for various reasons, including different types and levels of taxation.[16] Agricultural vehicles and machinery, as well as most trucks, buses and commercial vehicles, commonly use diesel fuel, which is often taxed and priced lower than gasoline. Fuel price subsidies have the disadvantage that they cannot be clearly targeted, and other users and affluent constituencies can equally benefit. One of the challenges faced by fiscal policy-makers is the design and implementation of fuel and motor vehicle taxes and subsidies in a manner such that negative external effects, including emissions and their impacts, can be internalised and reduced. Countries that continue to subsidise motor fuels may consider alternative options in order to more directly support eligible industries or the poor. Higher fuel taxes can discourage wasteful use of energy, contribute to lower levels of emissions and generate revenues to finance public transport projects.

Whereas fuel efficiency is important for the operation of commercial vehicles such as trucks and taxis, passenger cars are frequently seen as representing social status. Modern designs, larger engine power, increased seating capacities and additional features tend to attract more consumer interest than fuel efficiency. As long as the majority of affluent consumers associate big cars and high resource use with high social status, the marketing of small fuel-efficient vehicles will face formidable challenges.[17] A number of countries have mandated consumer information and fuel economy labels for cars to create greater consumer preference for fuel economy.

F   Transport Technologies: Developments and Prospects

Considerable potential exists for increasing fuel economy and reducing CO_2 emissions with existing motor vehicle technologies by reducing vehicle size and weight, and rolling and air resistance as well as accessory loads. The GFEI Partnership estimated that vehicle fuel efficiency of approximately 4 litres per 100 kilometres is achievable with existing technologies. Greater use of advanced direct injection engines as well as hybrid drive-trains and turbochargers can raise fuel efficiency. Several studies suggest that fuel-efficient tyres can also help to save up to 5 per cent or more fuel.

---

[16]   German Technical Co-operation Agency ('GTZ'), *International Fuel Prices 2007* (German Technical Co-operation Agency, 5th ed, 2007).

[17]   Wolfgang Sachs, *For Love of the Automobile: Looking Back Into the History of Our Desires* (Don Reneau, University of California Press, 1992).

High emissions from older vehicles are largely due to poor maintenance. Mandatory periodical technical inspections can significantly contribute to road safety and reduce noise and air pollution. Effective enforcement of existing regulations and adoption of adequate air quality and emission control standards can offer low-cost options for enhancing sustainability of transport.

Several countries have launched economic stimulus programmes in 2009 with a focus on the car industry. Some of these programmes aim to accelerate the scrapping of older cars and increase the rate of change in the vehicle fleet towards more fuel-efficient models. Some countries have also passed legislation including obligations for car manufacturers to increase the rate of recycling of motor vehicle parts and materials. Many of these initiatives have made important contributions to the 'greening' of economic growth, safeguarding existing and creating new jobs and simultaneously reducing the environmental footprint of transport in the future.

Many second-hand vehicles are exported from industrialised countries to developing countries. Developing countries' restrictions on such imports are important to prevent high-emitting, unsafe or unsuitable older cars from being imported. Kenya now restricts used vehicles to a maximum of eight years old. Other developing countries implementing import restrictions on used vehicles include, among others, Bolivia, Mexico, Pakistan, the Philippines, Thailand and Uzbekistan. South Africa has banned the importation of used motor vehicles altogether.

Poor-quality fuels can also contribute to poor performance and negative environmental impacts. Adding lead to fuel was banned in most countries after it was found to have serious implications for human health. The presence of lead in gasoline also greatly impedes catalytic exhaust treatment. The Partnership for Clean Fuels and Vehicles ('PCFV') lead by UNEP has successfully assisted many developing countries in reducing vehicular air pollution through the promotion of lead-free, low-sulphur fuels and cleaner vehicle standards and technologies. PCFV has achieved an almost complete global phase-out of leaded gasoline.[18]

Another pollutant commonly found in fuel is sulphur, which is present in varying quantities in different crude petroleum stocks. Refining processes can remove sulphur from fuel but doing so raises production costs. Heavy fuel oil used in shipping often contains high levels of sulphur. In order to reduce air and maritime pollution

---

[18] See United Nations Environment Programme, *Partnership for Clean Fuels and Vehicles* <http://www. unep.org/pcfv>.

in coastal areas, a growing number of countries are implementing regulations to progressively limit the sulphur content in shipping fuel.

Electric vehicle propulsion technologies are widely expected to play a greater role in the future. A growing number of vehicle manufacturers have announced plans or started production of electric vehicles, primarily for use in urban areas. In several countries, including China, electric bicycles have become very popular. In Israel and in several other countries, including France and the United Kingdom, pilot projects aim to introduce electric vehicles in larger numbers, together with networks of service stations for rapid on-site battery exchange and battery charging.[19]

Significant increases in public and private funding will be needed to enhance the development, testing, demonstration, commercialisation and dissemination of new sustainable low-carbon transport technologies, transport fuels and fuel storage systems, including durable high-capacity and high-efficiency electric vehicle batteries. Attractive incentives can also play an important role in motivating sustainable transport inventions. Larger-scale production of affordable electric vehicles will require a number of alternative materials, notably lithium, for which new industries and sustainable mining and processing technologies will need to be developed. New information technologies, such as global positioning and intelligent transportation systems (for example, 'smart highway' systems), provide various opportunities to facilitate traffics flows, reduce pollution levels and increase transport safety.

III OUTCOME OF THE POLICY DEBATE ON TRANSPORT AT THE NINETEENTH SESSION OF THE UNITED NATIONS COMMISSION FOR SUSTAINABLE DEVELOPMENT

The nineteenth session of the Commission for Sustainable Development was held in New York from 2-13 May 2011. The Commission deliberated over transport, chemical, waste management, mining, and a 10-year framework of programs on sustainable consumption and production. Whereas the Commission was unable to find consensus on some other issues, participating delegations agreed *ad referendum* on a proposed package of recommended policies and measures to enhance sustainability of transport. Whilst these recommendations do not formally constitute a decision of the Commission, which would have required unanimous agreement of all participants

---

[19] See <http://www.stromtankstellen.eu/better_place.html>.

on all issues under discussion, they nevertheless provide a useful and informative indication of the recommended action. The recommendations agreed *ad referendum* are contained in the Summary of the Chairman of Commission,[20] as follows:

1. Sustainable transport is a central component of sustainable development and economic growth. Addressing the growing transport challenges is increasingly urgent. Access to mobility is essential to achieve the MDGs. But the growing use of motorized transport can have negative impacts on environment and human health. Transport infrastructure development often requires long lead times, visionary decision-making and thorough and integrated planning, as well as significant investment. At the same time, transport infrastructure is very durable and can provide services and benefits for decades or even generations. Appropriate and effective policies and measures can facilitate and enhance safe, efficient, secure, affordable and environmentally sustainable transport (and) enhance transport and mobility for poverty eradication. (agreed ad ref)

2. Sustainable transport and mobility are as much about the sustainability of the automotive and transport sectors, not only from a business and economic perspective, but also to meet environmental and social needs. (agreed ad ref)

3. Integrated urban and rural transport planning that takes into account the circumstances of location and community, as well as supportive fiscal and regulatory policies, voluntary programs and partnerships combined with the development of new technologies, strategies and greater international cooperation, are key factors for achieving a more sustainable transport sector. Coordinating sustainable transportation planning, such as planning for housing and economic development, can significantly improve access to jobs, markets and social services. (agreed ad ref)

4. In order to achieve the internationally agreed development goals and eradicate poverty, it is necessary to sustainably optimize the development of the current transport infrastructure and transport services as well as their expansion and connectivity in developing countries, in particular in rural areas, optimizing modal choices for both people and goods. (agreed ad ref)

---

[20] Commission on Sustainable Development, *Report on the Nineteenth Session (14 May 2010 and 2-13 May 2011)*, UN Docs E/2011/29 and E/CN.17/2011/20 (2011). The following is a direct quote from the Report.

5. Countries should develop measures, as appropriate, to allow economic growth without the negative impacts on the environment and human health caused by traffic. (agreed ad ref)

6. We recognize constraints and structural impediments faced by the least-developed countries, the special needs of and challenges faced by the land-locked developing countries, especially in accessing international routes and port infrastructures, the unique and particular vulnerabilities of small island developing States, and the resulting difficulties due to, inter alia, distance, isolation and difficulties in reaching economies of scale, that more attention should be given to African countries with regard to transport and safety, health and environment friendly infrastructure. Special attention should be given for actions that are aligned and adapted to national and local conditions, through coordinated efforts by key stakeholders, particularly national Governments, civil society and the private sector. (agreed ad ref)

7. Increasing urbanization and private motorization have resulted in unprecedented congestion, wasteful energy use, increased motor vehicle emissions and noise pollution, with serious negative impacts on urban air quality, quality of life, efficient use of energy and public health. (agreed ad ref)

8. Policies, programs, technologies and partnerships can achieve an affordable, less polluting, more energy efficient and sustainable transport system, while contributing to important co-benefits including reduced greenhouse gas emissions, noise and air pollution and enhanced energy efficiency. (agreed ad ref)

9. Transport systems may be managed across multiple levels of government and this may determine the choice and appropriate mix of policy tools. These tools featuring appropriate combinations of measures, effective communications and information technologies and partnerships can enhance sustainability and promote transport technology and systems innovation. Development of these policies should involve stakeholder participation, be transparent and practically and predictably enforceable. (agreed ad ref)

10. Sustainable transport solutions are directly linked to the objective of promoting sustainable consumption and productions patterns. (agreed ad ref)

Policy options / actions needed

11. Take actions at different levels of governments to enhance access to sustainable transport, in particular in rural areas of developing countries and to promote improved transport linkages between urban, suburban and rural communities. (agreed ad ref)

12. It is important to employ integrated transportation, housing, and economic development planning that takes into account the circumstances of the location and community and decision making for sustainability in all communities, seeking to reduce vehicle miles travelled by coordinating investments in development in transportation infrastructure while providing transportation choices that improve access to better jobs, educational facilities, health care, and markets. Involve citizens and consider strengthening stakeholders' participation in planning to ensure practical design of systems that work on the ground, (agreed ad ref)

     (a) Encourage the provision of basic rural infrastructure and services, with a view to further improving the quality of rural public transport services to make villages and rural settlements accessible year round wherever feasible. (agreed ad ref)

     (b) Promote integrated rural development programmes, including through wider use of integrated rural transport, accessibility, and land use planning, investing in rural roads, implementing new road networks and enhancing existing ones, to enhance poverty eradication and the achievement of the MDGs. (agreed ad ref)

     (c) Develop policies and strategies to take steps to ensure persons with disabilities access, based on reasonable accommodation and on equal basis with others to transportation infrastructure and services. (agreed ad ref)

     (d) Highlight the opportunity for developing countries to nominate sustainable transport as a priority in requests for development assistance of financial institutions to assist in this endeavor. (agreed ad ref)

13. Improve public transport systems to more sustainable urban as well as suburban and rural development. Each State should take appropriate actions, which may include: (agreed ad ref)

(a) Improve public transportation systems and transportation choices through, inter alia, integrated land use planning, in ways that link communities and facilitate access to jobs, markets and social services; (agreed ad ref)

(b) Encourage local authorities in their efforts to plan and implement sustainable transport policies and programmes, and promote improved coordination within and between levels of government; (agreed ad ref)

(c) Promote public transport systems that are affordable, less polluting, more energy efficient and sustainable, and address the specific needs of women, youth, the elderly and persons with disabilities; (agreed ad ref)

(d) Consider enhancing bus rapid transit, metro and light rails systems, taking into account successful experiences; (agreed ad ref)

(e) Promote public-private partnerships as appropriate to contribute to the construction and operation of transport systems; (agreed ad ref)

(f) Encourage improvements in the management of vehicle fleets, including vehicle maintenance and inspection, operational practices and logistics and the replacement of old vehicles by more efficient newer ones and/or the upgrading of old vehicles with the use of advanced technologies, recognizing that the achievement of this goal may require the transfer of such technologies to developing countries on mutually agreed terms; (agreed ad ref)

(g) Encourage non-motorized transport such as bicycling and walking, and improve dedicated infrastructure for safe walking and non-motorized transport in conjunction with public transport initiatives, in particular in urban centers and suburban communities; (agreed ad ref)

(h) Encourage the improvement of safety of motor vehicle transportation; (agreed ad ref)

(i) Consider measures to reduce the use of private cars in urban areas, where possible, in order to improve the living conditions in urban areas. (agreed ad ref)

14. Enhance modal shifts, where possible, towards less energy intensive modes of transport for people and goods. (agreed ad ref)

    (a) Enhance and strengthen coordination of multi-modal transport systems and services through integration of multi-modal mobility planning, goods, movement systems and easy and fast inter-modal transfer options including promoting greater inland and coastal shipping and navigation; (agreed ad ref)

    (b) Promote greater use of railways and inland waterways, in particular for high-volume passenger and freight transport over long distances and between cities and commercial centers as well as the modernization of railways and the integration of ports and airports with the hinterland, including through the promotion of technological improvements; (agreed ad ref)

    (c) Promote innovative goods movement systems, taking advantage of approaches to increase fuel efficiency, and encourage the integration of technological awareness across the supply chain for enhance sustainability. (agreed ad ref)

15. Further develop and improve transport technologies and operational procedures. Each State should take appropriate action, and ensure that they are consistent with their international obligations to: (agreed ad ref)

    (a) Reduce air pollution from the transport sector by improving fuel quality, developing cleaner fuels, and promoting vehicle fuel economy and emission standards, noting the need for greater international cooperation in this field, (agreed ad ref)

    (b) Emphasize that the transport industry has an important role to play in ensuring, independently and in partnership, more responsible product creation, in more sustainable facilities and for more efficient, eco-friendly and innovative public transport options for an expanding global population, (agreed ad ref)

    (c) Improve the phasing out of lead in gasoline and the continued further reduction of the sulphur content in motor fuels, as appropriate, including through partnerships such as the Partnership for Clean Fuel and Vehicles, (agreed ad ref)

    (d) Support the phasing out of lead in gasoline and the continued further reduction of the sulphur content in motor fuels, as appropriate, including through partnerships such as the Partnership for Clean Fuels and Vehicles, (agreed ad ref)

(e) Recognize the importance of investment in innovation, research and deployment of advanced motor vehicle and transport technologies, including the investment in technologies for cleaner vehicles and fuels and improved fuel use and engine efficiency, (agreed ad ref)

(f) Support through international cooperation efforts and the promotion of public and private investment, the production of environmentally sound public transport and the improvement of transport infrastructure, including though strategies and technologies that address particular challenges faced by developing countries, especially LDCs, LLDCs, SIDS and Africa, (agreed ad ref)

(g) Encourage the use of renewable energy and energy efficiency and advanced energy technologies, including advanced and cleaner fossil fuel technologies, in order to achieve a sustainable transport system, (agreed ad ref)

(h) Promote the scientific research and development of renewable energies, including biofuels, in order to enhance, with a view to achieve their sustainability, (agreed ad ref)

(i) Promote efforts for manufacturing lighter, less polluting and less fuel consuming vehicles, (agreed ad ref)

(j) Encourage improvement in motor vehicle registration, inspections and motor vehicles emission and safety regulations, in accordance with national priorities and policies, (agreed ad ref)

(k) Considering the likelihood of the continued need for developing countries to purchase second-hand vehicles due to their limited financial resources, efforts should be made to reduce the resale and use of inefficient or unsafe motor vehicles through national environmental, fuel efficiency and safety regulation of motor vehicles. (agreed ad ref)

16. Create an enabling environment for sustainable transport (agreed ad ref)

(a) Recognize the importance and as appropriate strengthen the capacity of the public sector in the provision of affordable transport infrastructure and services, (agreed ad ref)

(b) Promote sound planning of roads and transport to reduce impacts on biodiversity and land degradation; ensure regular public and other stakeholder participation in decision-making on transport, (agreed ad ref)

(c) Strengthen sustainable transport infrastructure and services by enhancing transport data collection and analysis, development of tools and indicators, and use of modern information technologies, (agreed ad ref)

(d) Encourage information and data accessibility to transport users, to inform choices about sustainable transport options, (agreed ad ref)

(e) Encourage, where feasible, improved transport management methods and share best practices in the use of these methods, (agreed ad ref)

(f) Provide adequate consideration for public and non-motorized transport in transportation programmes, including in budgets and other policy measures; (agreed ad ref)

(g) Optimize the use of renewable energy in SIDS' and other countries' transportation plans, (agreed ad ref)

(h) Make efforts that financial austerity programmes do not result in a reduction of public transport services, (agreed ad ref)

(i) Factor the impacts of climate change into transport infrastructure planning to ensure resilience while addressing the associated costs, (agreed ad ref)

(j) Encourage voluntary initiatives, programmes and partnerships to reduce the negative environmental impacts from transport. (agreed ad ref)

17. Enhance international cooperation in transport (agreed ad ref)

(a) Identify and address opportunities to achieve affordable, economically viable, socially acceptable, safe and environmentally sound transportation systems including infrastructure, technologies and institutional capacities in developing countries, via collaborative actions such as public-private and other relevant partnerships, by inviting international financial institutions to consider ways to facilitate greater access and taking advantage of and supporting partnerships that create an environment under which technologies and investments in clean transportation can succeed reflecting international agreements related to sustainable development, national circumstances and priorities as appropriate. (agreed ad ref)

(b) Highlight the role of regional and international financial institutions in providing financial support to developing countries in their national policies and projects of rural-urban transport infrastructure development and in facilitating sustainable transport planning, including resilience to natural disasters. (agreed ad ref)

(c) Encourage cooperation on transport technologies with a view to improve the transportation systems, in particular In developing countries, including through renewable energy and energy efficiency and advanced energy technologies, including advanced and cleaner fossil fuel technologies. (agreed ad ref)

(d) Support the sharing of knowledge through partnerships in international sharing of experiences in the sustainable production and use of energy sources. (agreed ad ref)

(e) Promote international sharing of experiences in renewable energies through South-South, North-South and triangular cooperation considering the benefits and sustainability of all options and taking into account the ongoing multilateral dialogue on the challenges and opportunities posed by biofuels, in view of the world's food security, energy and sustainable development needs, and noting ongoing efforts in this regard at the international, regional and national levels. (agreed ad ref)

(f) Foster regional transport integration and corridor development efforts as appropriate to use full potential of multi-country infrastructure and facilitate market access for landlocked countries. (agreed ad ref)

(g) Enhance transport and road safety through active participation and contribution to the United Nations Decade of Action for Road Safety (2011-2020). (agreed ad ref)

(h) Promote training and research development on transportation systems through strengthening education and research institutions, particularly in developing countries. (agreed ad ref).

IV   DECISIONS OF THE RIO+20 CONFERENCE ON SUSTAINABLE DEVELOPMENT

On the occasion of the twentieth anniversary of the United Nations Conference on Environment and Development, also known as the Earth Summit — first held in Rio de Janeiro, Brazil, in 1992 — the Government of Brazil hosted the United Nations Conference on Sustainable Development (UNCSD on 13-22 June 2012 in the same location). This high-level segment of the 'Rio+20' Conference was attended by more than a hundred Heads of State and Government. Representatives of all nine major groups, including representatives of business and industry, women, youth, farmers, local authorities, indigenous people, non-governmental organisations, scientists and academia, also participated in the Conference and its many side events in large numbers.[21] The Rio+20 Conference adopted a consensus decision on 'The Future We Want', which was subsequently endorsed by the United Nations General Assembly.[22] The Rio+20 outcome document includes the following summary statement on transport in its paragraphs 132 and 133:

132.   We note that transportation and mobility are central to sustainable development. Sustainable transportation can enhance economic growth and improve accessibility. Sustainable transport achieves better integration of the economy while respecting the environment. We recognize the importance of the efficient movement of people and goods, and access to environmentally sound, safe and affordable transportation as a means to improve social equity, health, resilience of cities, urban-rural linkages and productivity of rural areas. In this regard, we take into account road safety as part of our efforts to achieve sustainable development.

133.   We support the development of sustainable transport systems, including energy efficient multi-modal transport systems, notably public mass transportation systems, clean fuels and vehicles, as well as improved transportation systems in rural areas. We recognize the need to promote an integrated approach to policymaking at the national, regional and local levels for transport services and systems to promote sustainable development. We also recognize that the special development needs of landlocked and transit

---

[21]   For information on the participation of major groups in the consultative process on sustainable development at the United Nations see also <http://sustainabledevelopment.un.org/majorgroups.html>.

[22]   *The Future We Want*, GA Res 66/288, UN GAOR, 66th sess, 123rd plen mtg, Agenda Item 19, Supp No 49, UN Doc A/RES/66/288 (11 September 2012).

developing countries need to be taken into account while establishing sustainable transit transport systems. We acknowledge the need for international support to developing countries in this regard.

V   Main Areas for International Co-operation in the Implementation of Rio+20 Decisions[23]

A   Expanding Access to Sustainable Transport in Rural Areas of Developing Countries

As suggested by many delegations at the Rio+20 Conference, greater investments in integrated rural development programmes are urgently needed, including programmes that provide adequate access to all-weather roads. Such programmes can contribute to poverty reduction and enhance the achievement of the MDGs. As appropriate, national sustainable development strategies and plans should include construction and improvement of rural roads to be designed and constructed with the active participation and involvement of the communities concerned. In this endeavour, the local communities should be supported with capacity building and technical support, as well as with financial assistance from both domestic and international sources. The particular needs of the landlocked LDCs, especially in sub-Saharan Africa, as well as of SIDS, require urgent attention.

B   Promoting Urban Public Transport for Sustainable Development

Sustainable transport policies will need to comprise a combination of measures, including:

a.   improvement and expansion of urban public transport systems which are more affordable, safe, clean, reliable, time-saving and environmentally sound;

b.   facilitation and encouragement of non-motorised transport modes in urban centres, including greater use of walking and cycling for short-distance trips in good weather;

---

[23]   Most of the policy recommendations in this section were also presented to the United Nations Commission on Sustainable Development in the Report of the Secretary-General: *Policy options for implementation of Agenda 21 and the Johannesburg Plan of Implementation: transport*, UN ESCOR, 19th sess, Agenda Item 3, UN Doc E/CN.17/2011/4 (17 December 2010).

   c.   coherent regulatory measures to regulate the use of private motor vehicles as well as commercial urban transport service providers, such as operators of small buses, vans, taxis, three-wheelers or pedicabs; and

   d.   integration of transport considerations in urban development planning in order to ensure more sustainable urban transport systems in the future by reducing the need for travel and the intra-urban travel distance in cities that are yet to be built.

1   *Urban Bus Rapid Transport ('BRT') and other public transport systems*

While the costs of individual buses and BRT systems are moderate, many more of such systems are urgently needed to tackle the growing urban transport problems in developing countries and those cities that do not have such systems in place. For many developing countries, BRT systems would be affordable only with external technical assistance and financial support. International financial institutions could play a greater role in supporting urban BRT systems in developing countries. At the Rio+20 Conference, the participating multi-lateral development banks committed to significantly shift and increase their lending towards urban public transport projects in developing countries. BRT can also offer a low-cost solution to urban traffic congestion in industrialised countries.

Public forms of transport, notably public buses, often remain stigmatised as the 'poor man's car'. It is essential to ensure that urban public transport is safe, clean, fast, environmentally sound and affordable. Ideally, public transport tariffs should be lower than the marginal costs of using private motor vehicles. Only where and when these conditions are met can public transport be expected to become the preferred transport choice for all.

2   *Taxi regulations*

Taxis are the motor vehicles that move around the most in urban areas. Many metropolitan cities have taxi fleets comprising some 50 000 or even more vehicles. In cities where urban air pollution is a serious concern, municipalities may consider reviewing van and taxi fleet licensing and management with a view to improving services, encouraging the modernisation of vehicles and fleets, ensuring the most economical use of fuels, monitoring transport tariffs, controlling vehicle emissions and ensuring adequate but not excessive competition, particularly between public and private services.[24]

3 Non-motorised transport and urban planning

Encouraging walking and cycling within inner city centres and in urban areas requires adequate provision of segregated bicycle lanes, without which cycling may be unsafe. This should be supported by provision of sufficient bicycle parking facilities, and regulations are also essential.

4 The role of city administration and local authorities in sustainable urban transport

Decisions on transport policies, infrastructure and services largely fall under the authority of city administrations, municipalities and other local authorities. Since 1990, the International Council for Local Environmental Initiatives ('ICLEI') facilitates the exchange of experiences among city administration and other local authorities, including in the area of sustainable transport. The C40 Cities Initiative, supported by the Clinton Climate Initiative, also recognises the important role of cities in designing sustainable transport projects and in mitigating climate change. International exchange of experiences among city administrations and among the public and private stakeholders concerned can greatly facilitate the replication and development of policies, projects and models which have proved successful elsewhere.

C Improving Transport Technologies and Systems: Cleaner Motor Fuels, Enhanced Fuel Efficiency and Electric Mobility

Most countries that manufacture motor vehicles also regulate fuel quality, fuel economy and vehicle emissions. Whereas standards, regulations and test protocols differ among countries, the aims are common and include:

a.   curbing the growing motor fuel consumption,

b.   reducing energy import dependence, and

c.   protecting urban air quality.

---

[24]   Policy options and practical experience in advancing sustainability in urban transport by modernising and 'greening' vans and taxi fleets was the focus of a regional expert group meeting co-organised by the Transport Engineering Programme of the Alberto Luiz Coimbra Institute ('COPPE') and the United Nations Department for Economic and Social Affairs ('DESA') and held in Rio de Janeiro in April 2011.

Experience has shown that mandatory fuel economy standards as well as mandatory periodic motor vehicle inspections and emission testing can offer useful and effective tools for curbing growing fuel use and for improving urban air quality, provided that the applicable regulations are effectively implemented and enforced.

1   *Motor vehicle fuel efficiency regulations and consumer information*

In May 2009, the United States President Barack Obama endorsed a new national policy aimed at both increasing fuel economy and reducing GHG emissions for all new cars and trucks sold in the US. The new standards, covering model years 2012-16, and ultimately requiring an average fuel economy standard of 35.5 mpg in 2016, are projected to save 1.8 billion barrels of oil over the life of the programme with a fuel economy gain averaging more than 5 per cent per year and a reduction of approximately 900 million metric tons of GHG emissions.[25]

The UNECE and its Inland Transport Committee have established the World Forum for Harmonisation of Vehicle Regulations (Working Party 29) which administers three important international agreements, adopted in 1958, 1997 and 1998, pertaining to uniform prescriptions for wheeled vehicles, equipment and parts, periodical technical inspections, and global technical regulations for wheeled vehicles. The World Forum and its six subsidiary Working Parties on Pollution and Energy, General Safety Provisions, Brakes and Running Gear, Light and Light-Signalling, Noise and Passive Safety are presently accelerating work to develop common global methodologies, test cycles and measurement methods for light vehicles, including CO_2 emissions.[26] Most countries manufacturing motor vehicles, including such developing countries as Brazil, China, India, Malaysia, Mexico, South Africa and Thailand, actively participate in meetings of the Forum, which has a significant potential to contribute to a 'greening of the transport sector'. Countries that have not as yet regulated fuel efficiency measurement and labelling of motor vehicles for purposes of consumer information may consider doing so, taking into account national and international experiences in this regard.

---

[25]   The White House, Office of the Press Secretary, 'President Obama Announces National Fuel Efficiency Policy' (19 May 2009) <http://www.whitehouse.gov/the-press-office/president-obama-announces-national-fuel-efficiency-policy>.

[26]   Economic Commission for Europe, Inland Transport Committee, *UNECE activities on the reduction of emissions of gaseous pollutants and greenhouse gases in the transport sector*, UN ESCOR, 151st sess, Agenda Item 8.5, UN Doc ECE/TRANS/WP.29/2010/84 (9 April 2010).

2 Improvement in fuel quality

The Partnership for Clean Fuels and Vehicles of UNEP has successfully assisted many developing countries in reducing vehicular air pollution through the promotion of lead-free, low-sulphur fuels and cleaner vehicles standards and technologies. Enforcement of fuel quality standards and improvements can significantly reduce urban air pollution. In many developing countries and their cities, urban air quality is still frequently below standards recommended by the WHO.

3 Natural gas vehicles

Compressed natural gas ('CNG') offers a preferable alternative to diesel engines in urban traffic. CNG produces comparatively low emissions, including nitrogen oxide. Moreover, the natural gas engine is also appreciably quieter. Other factors in favour of commercial vehicles equipped with natural gas engines are the 25 per cent lower well-to-wheel CO_2 emissions and the relative abundance of the natural gas reserves. The comparatively low price of natural gas also reduces operating costs. In many countries, CNG is used in public buses, taxis and other commercial vehicles servicing urban areas.

4 Electric mobility

In recent years, a growing number of motor vehicle manufacturers have announced plans or started production and sales of hybrid and plug-in electric vehicles, primarily for use in urban areas. In China, and in a growing number of other countries, electric bicycles and scooters have become popular. Electric vehicles are quiet and produce no emissions at the point of use. The potentials for greater use of electric mobility was discussed at a 'Global Forum on Electric Mobility' also held in Rio de Janeiro, Brazil, in conjunction with the Rio+20 Conference.[27]

Several motor vehicle manufacturers have also successfully tested and demonstrated hydrogen-based emission-free fuel-cell technologies. New information technologies, such as global positioning and intelligent transportation systems, including 'smart highway' systems, provide many opportunities to facilitate traffic flows, reduce pollution levels and increase transport safety. More incentives should be provided to stimulate indigenous innovations in developing countries.

---

[27] Ralph D Wahnschafft, *Global Forum on Electric Mobility: Greening Transport for Sustainable Development* (2012) <http://sustainabledevelopment.un.org/content/documents/summary.pdf>.

5   International trade in used vehicles

Some developing countries import many used motor vehicles, sometimes even old ones, which can be unsafe and inefficient. Regulating the trade in second-hand vehicles is an important policy option, in particular for developing countries.

6   Transfer of technologies to developing countries

Clean fuel, alternative vehicle and advanced information technologies are available mostly in industrialised countries. In most developing countries, no or only limited capital is available to finance the necessary research and technology development. Much greater sharing and transfer of cleaner transport technologies to developing countries will be needed if sustainable transport systems for all are to be realised.

D   Enhancing Investment in Transport Infrastructure and Services

Conventional lending and project financing by the World Bank Group and the Regional Development Banks has traditionally emphasised road transport infrastructure, which typically accounted for some 75 per cent or more of all transport project financing. In the fiscal year 2010, World Bank transport sector lending amounted to US$9.4 billion, representing a 43 per cent increase over 2009. The World Bank Group has recently adopted a new transport financing strategy in which transport safety, urban transport systems and environmental and social concerns are projected to play a greater role. At present, the World Bank supports more than 200 transport projects in developing countries with a total net commitment of over US$34 billion, representing 21 per cent of the Bank's project portfolio.

Carbon finance support for the transport sector is generally limited in scale. There are considerable methodological difficulties in determining and measuring the mitigation potential of specific transport policies and projects. Furthermore, there is often a lack of the data required for measuring, reporting and verifying mitigation actions. Hence, only very limited carbon finance support has become available so far for sustainable transport, in spite of the fact that transport is the fastest growing source of GHG emissions. Also, availability of financing from the Global Environment Facility for transportation projects is very limited. Greater financial support is urgently needed to invest in sustainable low carbon transport in developing countries.

Planning sustainable transport systems, including long-distance cross-border transport corridors, requires well-co-ordinated multi-modal integration. The construction or expansion of new ports or airports needs to be accompanied by the appropriate upgrading of transport infrastructure and services in the associated hinterland.

Travel for domestic and international tourism is a rapidly growing service industry creating employment and income opportunities. However, tourism is often associated with high energy consumption. With growing environmental awareness, eco-friendly forms of travel and leisure, including hiking, biking and boating, are becoming increasingly popular in a growing number of countries. This is particularly true in Europe, where public investment in the required infrastructure, including short- and long-distance hiking trails, bicycle paths and other recreational facilities, is relatively advanced. Agro- and eco-tourism can significantly contribute to the economic revitalisation of rural and peripheral areas, and thus contribute to sustainable development.

E   *Enhancing Policy Coherence, Integration and Stakeholder Participation*

Decision-making on transport sector investments is often decentralised, with local, regional and national public sector and parastatal institutions taking charge of different elements of the transport system. Inter-institutional collaboration is essential to ensure cost-effective planning and rational investments, in particular in situations in which the institutional mandates, objectives and agenda vary.

Many fiscal policy tools, including taxation and subsidies, can significantly influence costs and prices of fuels, transportation tariffs and vehicles and should, therefore, be applied in a very consistent, coherent and market-conforming manner. It is essential to avoid situations in which the effects of one policy measure counteract the intended effects of another.

There is a perception that investments in, and the maintenance of, public transport, including urban public transport, require high subsidies, some of which may not always be justified. The public policy debate often disregards the fact that there are many large hidden subsidies benefiting private car users in urban areas.[28]

---

[28]   See ICLEI — Local Governments for Sustainability, *Hidden Subsidies for Urban Car Transportation, Public Funds for Private Transport* (2005) <http://www.increase-public-transport.net/fileadmin/user_upload/Procurement/SIPTRAM/Hidden_subsidies_final.pdf>.

F   Facilitating International Trade and Transport Co-operation

Given the inherent geographical difficulties that deprive them of direct access to seaborne trade, the landlocked developing countries ('LLDC's) find themselves on a disadvantaged development path, compounded by long distances from major international markets, cumbersome transit procedures, inadequate transport infrastructure and dependence on infrastructure and institutional quality of coastal transit countries. These challenges not only affect economic development and growth but have major ramifications for the social and environmental aspects of development, including the achievement of the MDGs.

SIDS and their prospects for sustainable development are also often negatively affected by diseconomies of scale in trade and transport, leading to higher per unit transport costs, which in turn lead to low trade volumes. Low trade volumes often do not justify investment in technologies and transport infrastructure. In order to address these interrelated challenges, SIDS require immediate and substantial international support, including through retaining market access preferences for their exports, grants or concessionary financing for transport, information technologies and communication equipment, as well as assistance in accelerating the use of renewable energy, making tourism sustainable and better tapping the potential of island cultures.

G   Promoting Employment, Sustained Economic Recovery and 'Green Jobs'

Some economists suggest that further economic stimulus packages may be necessary to support a global economic recovery process. For the enhancement of overall sustainable development, many experts consider it essential that a growing portion of stimulus funding be directed towards the development and deployment of public transport and 'greener' transport technologies, in lieu of only funding 'shovel-ready' conventional transport infrastructure. Economic stimulus programmes should provide opportunities for creating new 'green jobs' in the transport sector.

H   Mainstreaming Climate Change Considerations in Transport Policy Formulation

Voluntary programmes and measures to offset the carbon generated from transport activities by purchasing Certified Emission Reduction Units ('CER's) could effectively complement the avoid-shift-improve strategy towards sustainable transport. Some 30 airline companies, many tour operators and some hotel chains already offer carbon-neutral travel services. Efforts to promote sustainable tourism should in future also routinely offer tourists options to offset their carbon emissions.

VI OUTLOOK

United Nations Secretary General Ban Ki-Moon announced in January 2012 that, as part of his Action Agenda for his second five-year term, he would like to forge consensus around a post-2015 sustainable development framework and to mobilise the UN system to support global, regional and national strategies to address the building blocks of sustainable development. Sustainable Transport was identified as one of the six key building blocks. The Secretary-General called for the UN to

> convene aviation, marine, ferry, rail, road and urban public transport providers, along with Governments and investors, to develop and take action on recommendations for more sustainable transport systems that can address rising congestion and pollution worldwide, particularly in urban areas.[29]

The UN Secretariat will continue to provide relevant fora for international debate and consultations on sustainable development, including transport for sustainable development. However, the key to successful and comprehensive implementation of the recommendations and decisions rests with member states, the private sectors and all the other stakeholders concerned.

---

[29] See Ban Ki-Moon, 'Sustainable Development' on *The Secretary General's Five-Year Action Agenda* (25 January 2012) <http://www.un.org/sg/priorities/sustainable_development.shtml>.

9

ADRIAN J BRADBROOK'S CONTRIBUTIONS TO THE LAWS GOVERNING ENERGY, CLIMATE CHANGE AND POVERTY ALLEVIATION

RICHARD L OTTINGER

Adrian J Bradbrook is internationally renowned for his scholarship on the environment as a human right. Many of the energy and climate solutions he has proposed have been the foundation of innovations that nations and municipalities around the world have adopted and in the formulation of international law. Bradbook has made very significant contributions to teaching and scholarship in the field of property law, but I write here in the area of our collaboration, in which he has been a prominent international and national leader in formulating energy and climate change laws and their role in overcoming poverty (though I do include a summary of his co-authored book on the nexus between energy and poverty law). He is internationally renowned for his scholarship on the environment as a human right. Many of the energy and climate solutions he has proposed have been the foundation of innovations that have been adopted in nations and municipalities around the world and in the formulation of international law.

An important distinguishing feature of Bradbrook's energy and climate change scholarship is that in every case he not only details the environmental, developmental and social challenges about which he writes, but he invariably recommends and details possible solutions to those challenges, often even drafting model codes that could be adopted to address these challenges. This feature makes his writings particularly useful for influencing outcomes.

In this chapter, I can only engage with a few of Bradbrook's contributions to the law of sustainable energy and climate change which I view as principally significant. He is the author or co-author of 26 books and over 100 book chapters and articles.

I THE LAW OF ENERGY FOR SUSTAINABLE DEVELOPMENT[1]

Perhaps the best place to start in reviewing Bradbrook's many important contributions to the energy and climate change law fields is with our first scholarly collaboration, organising the inaugural international colloquium of the IUCN Academy of Environmental Law, on *The Law of Energy for Sustainable Development*, held at Shanghai Jaio Tong University ('SJTU') in 2004. The colloquium presentations by many of the leading authorities in the field were published in a book by the same name published in English by Cambridge University Press, which we jointly edited with Professor (and now also Vice President of SJTU) Wang Xi and Professor Rosemary Lyster of Sydney University Law School. The book was translated and published in Chinese by Professor Wang Xi.

In his article in that publication, entitled 'International Law and Global Sustainable Energy Production and Consumption',[2] he proposes a Statement of Principles to guide future international enactments to achieve sustainable energy production and consumption (though these principles would be equally useful in guiding national legislation). After reciting the difficulties experienced in advancing action to address climate change and sustainable energy through the United Nations Framework Convention on Climate Change / Intergovernmental Panel on Climate Change ('UNFCCC'/'IPCC') and other international organisation processes, he points out that no comprehensive policy guidelines in this field have yet been established. He points to the *Universal Declaration of Human Rights* as perhaps 'the

---

[1] Adrian Bradbrook, Rosemary Lyster and Richard Ottinger (eds), *The Law of Energy for Sustainable Development* (Cambridge University Press, 2005). Cambridge also published a simultaneous companion volume, *Compendium of Sustainable Energy Laws*, presenting the text of the laws referred to in the initial volume.

[2] Adrian Bradbrook and Ralph D Wahnschafft, 'International Law and Global Sustainable Energy Production and Consumption', in Bradbrook, Lyster, and Ottinger (eds), above n 1, 181. Wahnschafft is at the time of writing Economic Affairs Officer with the UN Department of Economic and Social Affairs.

best known and most frequently cited soft law document' as an example of the utility of establishing such guidance principles.[3]

The article summarises the principles he recommends as follows:

- the need for universal access to clean and affordable energy;

- the essentiality of sustainable energy regimes to achieve sustainable development;

- the need to take account of the needs of future generations in determining energy policies;

- the adverse environmental, social, public health, security, gender burdens, and economic consequences of current heavy reliance on fossil fuels;

- the need to reduce wastage of fossil fuels, promoting energy efficiency measures in buildings, transportation, appliances, and all industrial processes;

- the importance of renewable energy resources and research and development on all efficiency and renewable energy measures;

- the importance of consideration of external environmental costs in evaluation of energy alternatives;

- phasing out of subsidies to fossil fuels;

- the importance of forest preservation;

- the requirement of Environmental Impact Statements to be performed for all energy projects, with their attendant public education and participation;

- the obligation of nations in adopting energy measures not to cause harm to the health and environment of other States; and

- the need to continue to recognize the need for common but differentiated responsibility in addressing sustainable energy in light of the lesser capability of developing countries to finance and administer measures to achieve sustainable energy, including the need for developed countries to assist with the financing, personnel training and technology transfer to developing countries expressing need for such assistance.[4]

These principles are by no means new, though they have not all been articulated before in an internationally agreed comprehensive statement of principles.

---

[3] GA Res 217A (III), UN GAOR, 3rd sess, 183rd plen mtg, UN Doc A/810 (10 December 1948).

[4] Bradbrook and Wahnschafft, above n 2.

They express the essential elements of what is necessary for a sustainable energy programme meeting the economic, environmental and climate change requirements of all countries, municipalities and populations. As Bradbrook observes, the closest international agreement to address such principles is the Johannesburg World Summit on Sustainable Development ('WSSD') Plan of Implementation,[5] which for the first time addressed many of these sustainable energy considerations. But, as he points out, the WSSD plan is necessarily vague and general compared to the concrete actions proposed in the principles he enunciates in this article. There is a large gap between agreement on principles and commitments to take action to effectuate the principles, but the possible formal adoption of principles might well facilitate agreement on action to make them obligatory.

Bradbrook goes on to detail principles that would apply to energy efficiency in supply and consumption areas, addressing both command and control measures, market-based incentives (principally 'Cap and Trade') including pricing (and externality costs so often ignored) and labelling, and the necessity of regulations, including efficiency standards and renewable energy portfolio standards, to protect public health and the environment in dealing with privatised energy supply, giving examples of various measures that have been adopted. He points to the essentiality of considering full life cycle costs, including transmission losses that often are ignored. He similarly discusses the renewable energy options, their costs and benefits, for promoting sustainability and various innovative means of implementing and financing them.

Bradbrook notes the diverse opinions and policies relating to nuclear energy, observing the positives of the absence of release of carbon dioxide in the operation of nuclear plants (though not in the mining and processing of uranium) versus the grave risks of catastrophic damages from nuclear plant failures as in Chernobyl and Fukushima, of the possible radioactive releases from terrorist attacks on nuclear power plants, of the risk of conversion of peaceful uses of nuclear materials to construct nuclear weapons, and of the failure to provide for safe long-term storage of nuclear wastes. His principles are designed to achieve a compromise by making nuclear power expansion conditional on a satisfactory resolution of nuclear waste disposal and release of radiation.

---

[5] United Nations, *Plan of Implementation of the World Summit on Sustainable Development* (2002) <http://www.un.org/esa/sustdev/documents/WSSD_POI_PD/English/WSSD_PlanImpl.pdf>.

He concludes that the principles he proposes might be considered too weak to be effective and that he 'would consequently prefer the negotiation of a new Convention on Energy or a new Energy Protocol to the United Nations Framework Convention on Climate Change' but that 'such a binding treaty would as a practical matter be impossible to achieve in the short to medium term'.[6] Certainly the principles presented in the paper would be a significant help to the eventual negotiation of a binding treaty.

Perhaps the most important part of this paper, and the greatest contribution to any future treaty, is the Annex to his paper, which presents a detailed proposed draft document setting forth in statutory form the principles he discussed. The Annex provides to all jurisdictions a statutory model they can emulate.

II THE DEVELOPMENT OF RENEWABLE ENERGY TECHNOLOGIES AND ENERGY EFFICIENCY MEASURES THROUGH PUBLIC INTERNATIONAL LAW

In his 2008 article, 'The Development of Renewable Energy Technologies and Energy Efficiency Measures through Public International Law',[7] Bradford goes further, urging consideration of:

1. a UN General Assembly declaration, with binding targets for renewable energy for electricity and reduced energy intensity for all sectors of the economy;

2. a new protocol specific to energy efficiency and renewable energy;[8]

3. creation of a specialized agency under the United Nations for Renewable Energy and Efficiency modelled on the International Atomic Energy Agency;[9]

4. achieving a more active role by international non-governmental agencies, particularly the International Union for the Conservation of Nature[10] and

---

[6] Bradbrook and Wahnschafft, above n 2.

[7] Adrian J Bradbrook, 'The Development of Renewable Energy Technologies and Energy Efficiency Measures Through Public International Law' in Donald N Zillman et al (eds), *Beyond the Carbon Economy: Energy Law in Transition* (Oxford University Press, 2008) 109.

[8] As presaged in Adrian Bradbrook, 'The Development of a Protocol on Energy Efficiency and Renewable Energy to the United Nations Framework Convention on Climate Change' [2001] (5) *New Zealand Journal of Environmental Law* 55.

[9] See *International Atomic Energy Agency* (2013) <http://www.iaea.org>, as was considered as part of the agenda of the Rio+20 Convention in June 2013.

[10] See *International Union for Conservation of Nature* (22 November 2013) <http://www.iucn.org>.

the World Wildlife Fund,[11] both of which, as he points out, have placed their major emphases elsewhere, and the specialised NGOs such as the World Energy Council, World Wind Energy Association, International Solar Energy Society, World Council for Renewable Energies, and the International Network for Sustainable Energy, which require much greater resources;

5. a greater focus on sustainable energy from the international finance agencies charged with environmentally related functions such as the World Bank and UN regional development banks; and

6. a much greater sustainability focus by the United Nations Environmental Programme, and the United Nations Development Programme — or, as recommended for consideration above, the concentration of these functions in a single new international energy agency.

He concludes that ultimately action on such measures depends on public pressure deriving from concern about pollution, climate change, peaking of oil resources, population growth and economic welfare, sufficiently strong to overcome political and diplomatic inertia and pressure from vested interests determined to preserve the status quo.

III   PROPERTY AND THE LAW IN ENERGY AND NATURAL RESOURCES

In a fascinating, ground-breaking book that combines his expertise in property and energy law, *Property and the Law in Energy and Natural Resources*,[12] Bradbrook and his collaborators point to the adverse effects to public health and the environment from privatisation of electricity and other energy resources, often resulting in rejection of regulatory protections on grounds of violation of the supposed property rights created.

The authors point out that these issues arise in the control of and access to fossil fuels, mineral reserves and clean drinking water; failure to regulate the risks of pollution, including greenhouse gases and toxic chemical emissions, and to protect individual property rights, for instance the protection of forests, the displacement of agricultural lands for food, and the claims of access to lands for cultural and

---

[11]   See *World Wildlife Fund* (2013) <http://www.worldwildlife.org>.

[12]   Aileen McHarg et al (eds), *Property and the Law in Energy and Natural Resources* (Oxford University Press, 2010).

ethnic groups. They point out that also affected are land use planning to minimise transportation and fuel requirement, building of roads through sensitive areas, disruption of wildlife and biodiversity through fracturing of lands and allowing off-street vehicles to disrupt the tranquillity and wildlife protection in parklands.

They point out that as fossil fuels become rarer, less priority is given to protection of natural resources. They also observe that the new technologies to produce oil and gas through deep water drilling, particularly in environmentally sensitive waters — hydraulic fracturing technology to vastly increase resources of petroleum and natural gas resulting in contamination of air and water, endangering the lives of people affected and disrupting communities — present very great environmental risks.

They thus state:

> Moreover, as fossil fuel reserves become more valuable, and by contrast, water and unpolluted air become increasingly scarce, control and access issues become ever more important … Long-term sustainability of energy and resources and the role that property and law might play in achieving such goals become the most fraught questions of all.[13]

They also address the problems regarding claims of expropriation deriving from regulatory health, safety and environmental limits on use of private property in the increasingly privatised energy sector. And Bradbrook explicitly deals with how adjustments to the ancient property laws of easements (for example, by protecting solar and wind access) might advance protection for solar and wind energy projects, as well as how energy efficiency requirements for buildings can increase their property values.

The authors deal with the influence of neo-economic theories, advocating reliance on markets rather than public ownership and regulation, on protecting social and environmental values — for example, the relatively ineffective prevalence of Cap and Trade schemes as opposed to regulatory requirements or carbon taxes, to deal with greenhouse gas emissions and climate change.

The book concludes that there are many complex relationships between property law and laws to promote sustainable energy, many of which require further investigation, but that the relationships are important both for property and energy law.

---

[13]   Ibid 3-4.

IV 'CREATING LAW FOR NEXT GENERATION ENERGY TECHNOLOGIES'[14]

Bradbrook's remarkable 2011 article, 'Creating Law for Next Generation Energy Technologies' analyses many of the ad hoc international, national and municipal approaches for promoting next generation technologies needed to cope with the environmental challenges of the global future. It emphasises the overwhelmingly important challenges of dealing with global climate change, and recommends a co-ordinated approach for planning a comprehensive legal management regime consistent with sustainable energy development for promoting such new technologies on all of these levels.

Bradbrook documents the dominance of the burning of fossil fuels for energy as a cause of climate change, accounting for 83 per cent of the carbon dioxide emissions in developed countries, and the significant contribution of fossil fuel dependence to pollution, damaging human health and environment, particularly to women and children; its contribution to poverty and as an impediment to development; and its threat to both energy security and to world conflict. This leads him to argue that these consequences mandate the formulation of new co-ordinated legal regimes to replace fossil fuels with non-polluting, sustainable energy resources.

Bradbrook states well the rationale for the need for co-ordinated legal regimes:

> First, investment will not occur without adequate legal protection for consumers and investors. The transition from a fossil-fuel dominant energy sector to clean energy solutions will require massive investment, and interested parties will need assurance that their legal position is protected. Investment is always risky, and investors will factor sovereign risk and the likelihood of financial returns into their decisions. Therefore, governments seeking to encourage investment in the energy sector must establish a fair and reasonable legal management regime that protects the interests of consumers and investors and provides adequate forms of legal recourse.
>
> Second, history shows that energy development requires a legal management regime. No jurisdiction in the world has achieved a prominent energy sector without a comprehensive legal regime, except where the energy sector is nationalized …

---

[14] Adrian Bradbrook, 'Creating Law for Next Generation Energy Technologies' [2011] 2 *Journal of Energy & Environmental Law* 17.

Third, the need for adequate legal protection for investors is not altered merely because many next generation energy technologies are less centralized than traditional fossil fuel industries and may be implemented at local and regional levels. For example, individuals will be hesitant to invest in solar energy appliances, such as solar water heaters or solar photovoltaic cells for electricity generation, if their investment might be rendered ineffective by a large building or tree on a neighboring property shading their solar collector panels. For this reason, investment in this field necessitates an adequate law of solar access protection. Failure to adopt even simple laws of this nature can hinder the development of solar energy by individuals and businesses.

Fourth, the flexibility of legal responses is often underestimated or misunderstood by non-lawyers. A legal management regime need not consist solely of traditional regulation, but may include financial incentives to investors. It may also act as a form of education to consumers and society generally. ... [such as energy labelling laws]

Finally, the credibility of next generation energy technologies requires governments to enact a legal management regime. In light of the comprehensive legal regimes enacted in respect of fossil fuel industries, the absence of such a regime would indicate to investors in particular, and society in general, that clean energy solutions are regarded by the government as peripheral or second-best. [Citations omitted][15]

The legal regime Bradbrook contemplates emphasises energy efficiency and renewable energy, citing the following United Nations Development Programme ('UNDP') conclusions:

The UNDP advises that renewable energy resources and energy efficiency measures will play a key role in reducing poverty. Solar and wind energy are seen as particularly important because they are capable of fueling stand-alone energy systems. These systems will continue to be indispensable in rural areas of less developed nations, where electrification programs are unlikely to extend beyond major cities and towns.[16]

He states that it is essential for new sustainable energy technologies to conform to the Brundtland Commission definition of sustainable development. This is, in

---

[15]   Ibid 19-20.

[16]   Ibid 18 (citations omitted).

Bradbrook's paraphrasing, 'development that meets the needs of the present without compromising the ability of future generations to meet their own needs'.[17]

Bradbrook then refers to the indicators for achieving these objectives from the International Energy Agency's ('IEA') report, *Energy Indicators for Sustainable Development: Guidelines and Methodologies*,[18] of which he states the most important indicators are those prescribed (a bit oddly by the Atomic Energy Commission), that:

energy production must

(1)   be universally accessible;

(2)   be affordable;

(3)   satisfy health and safety requirements;

(4)   assure efficiency of energy conversion and distribution;

(5)   promote energy efficiency in all sectors of the economy;

(6)   maintain diversification of energy supplies;

(7)   maximize energy security;

(8)   preserve soil and water quality; and

(9)   avoid excessive deforestation.[19]

In this article, Bradbrook reviews comprehensively the international and national enactments seeking to promote sustainable energy programs to illustrate the need for a comprehensive approach. He places great belief that international law, including soft (non-binding) treaties, can help influence nations to adopt such programs. There follows a summary of these enactments and his evaluation of them.

A   *The* United Nations Framework Convention on Climate Change *and the* Kyoto Protocol

Bradbrook first examines all the surprisingly many international efforts to tackle these challenges, starting with the 1992 United Nations Conference on Environment and Development ('UNCED'),[20] the main energy contribution of which was

---

[17]   Ibid.

[18]   International Atomic Energy Agency, *Energy Indicators for Sustainable Development: Guidelines and Methodologies* (2005) 11-15 <http://www-pub.iaea.org/MTCD/publications/PDF/Pub1222_web.pdf>.

[19]   Bradbrook, above n 14, 19.

[20]   United Nations Conference on Environment and Development, Rio de Janeiro, Brazil, June 3-14, 1992.

the establishment of the United Nations Framework Treaty on Climate Change ('UNFCCC')[21] which, without much specificity, obliges signatories to enact legislation to reduce their greenhouse gas emissions, applying the precautionary principle. It purports to require all developed nation signatories to formulate, implement, publish and update national and regional programs to mitigate climate change and to take climate change into account when undertaking environmental impact assessments. Its Agenda 21 provided that UNCED signatories should promote energy efficiency, including efficiency labelling of products, and renewable energy.[22]

The paper examines the provisions of the UNFCCC and the later *Kyoto Protocol*,[23] the only binding international climate change treaty dealing with energy. The Protocol sets forth mandatory reductions in carbon dioxide emissions for each developed country, but only voluntary commitments for developing countries (defined as including China, now the greatest emitter of greenhouse gases, and India and Brazil, which have the fastest growing level of emissions). Parties to the Protocol must formulate cost-effective national and regional programs to mitigate climate change from the energy, transportation, industry, agricultural and other sectors. They must submit information on these programs to the Conference of the Parties. The Protocol specifies that each party should implement measures for the enhancement of energy efficiency; conduct research on renewable energy and environmentally sound technologies; facilitate reduction of market imperfections; encourage reforms in relevant sectors to reduce greenhouse gases; and reduce methane in waste management.[24]

But, as Bradbrook observes, most developed country signatories have not fulfilled their specified commitments under the Protocol and in fact world greenhouse gas emissions have increased considerably. The paper analyses both the strengths and weaknesses of these treaties. The strengths principally are that they

---

[21] *United Nations Framework Convention on Climate Change*, opened for signature 9 May 1992, 1771 UNTS 107 (entered into force 21 March 1994) ('UNFCCC').

[22] *Report of the United Nations Conference on Environment and Development (Rio de Janeiro, 3-14 June 1992): Agenda 21*, UN GAOR, UN Doc A/CONF151/26/Rev. 1 (12 August 1992).

[23] *Kyoto Protocol to the United Nations Framework Convention on Climate Change*, opened for signature 11 December 1997, 2303 UNTS 148 (entered into force 16 February 2005). The United States is a party to the UNFCCC. President Clinton signed the *Kyoto Protocol*, but President George W Bush rejected it and refused to submit it to the Senate for ratification, so the United States is not a party to it.

[24] Ibid art 10.

recognise the seriousness of the climate change threats and declare a determination to address them — and the *Kyoto Protocol* contains greenhouse gas emission reduction commitments from developed countries. The weaknesses principally are that there are no commitments from the US, then the top-emitter, nor from Australia and Canada (which are now heavily emitting, too). Nor are there commitments from developing countries, including the BASIC countries such as China (the leading world emitter at the time of writing), and other countries which are projected to have the largest increase in emissions in future decades.

A renewal of the *Kyoto Protocol* was achieved at the recent Warsaw COP 19 negotiations, and voluntary commitment promises were pledged by the US and BASIC countries (Brazil, South Africa, India and China), but many important issues remain to be resolved and a new stumbling block was added with a demand by the developing countries that the developed countries pay them reparations from 'loss and damages' caused by their historic contributions of greenhouse gas emissions, a demand that the developed countries, excepting Norway, firmly rejected. Lengthy and difficult negotiations also have been under way to find alternative means of addressing climate challenges and to assist developing countries in mitigation efforts and efforts to adapt to the threats of climate change that have already occurred.

Bradbrook goes on to review the various non-binding treaties that have sought to address the energy-related climate change challenges.

B   *The* Energy Charter Treaty[25] *and its Associated Protocol on Energy Efficiency and Related Environmental Aspects*[26]

This 1988 treaty, while only ratified by 51 countries, directly addresses a requirement for promotion of energy efficiency and renewable energy policies and other technologies nationally and internationally consistent with sustainable development. It calls for 'a fuller reflection of environmental costs and benefits', thus for the first time advocating for consideration of environmental externalities and reflecting the 'polluter pays' principle (though the use of the word 'fuller' is ambiguous). The list of activities for which energy efficiency measures are to be applied is comprehensive.

---

[25]   *European Energy Charter Conference: Final Act, Energy Charter Treaty, Decisions and Energy Charter Protocol on Energy Efficiency and Related Environmental Aspects*, opened for signature 17 December 1994, 34 ILM 360 (entered into force April 1998).

[26]   Ibid 446.

C The Johannesburg Plan of Implementation

This plan emanated from the 2002 World Summit on Sustainable Development ('WSSD').[27] While non-binding, it contains the most extensive and specific energy requisites of any international agreement to date. The UN Secretary General established the Working Group on Energy, which published a report entitled *A Framework For Action on Energy* that set forth in detail the requisites for a program of sustainable energy, emphasising the need for aggressive programs in all countries for energy efficiency and renewable energy.

The report recommends, as Bradbrook describes it, 'specific energy efficiency measures, including "energy efficiency standards, appliance and product labeling, demand side management ... building and construction standards," and the development of regional partnerships to set norms and institutional frameworks for energy efficiency'. It identifies renewable energy technologies as 'particularly well suited for rural energy development and an environmentally sound alternative to grid extension. These technologies were declared to be "particularly promising for technology transfer to developing countries"'.

Bradbrook sets forth with approval the many other useful recommendations of the Plan of Implementation, including integrating energy considerations into socio-economic programs; development and dissemination of alternative energy technologies with a greater share of renewable energies into the energy mix of countries; developing and utilisation of indigenous energy resources; community participation in energy policy-making; having international finance agencies promote sustainable energy programs in developing countries and promote research and development and transfer of clean technologies; and development of policies to reduce market distortions through the use of improved market signals, restructured taxation, phasing out of harmful subsidies, and assuring that the prices of energy systems reflect their environmental impacts.

Bradbrook notes that the Plan of Implementation calls for nations to increase their investment in renewable energies without specifying any numerical requirements or targets, but observes that those who describe the Plan of Implementation's omission in this regard as a failure are misguided, since the Plan is so much more detailed

---

[27] *Plan of Implementation of the World Summit on Sustainable Development*, UN Doc A/CONF.199/20 (4 September 2002).

and far-reaching than previous efforts. He predicts that the Plan's strong stance on renewables will promote more far-reaching future measures and greater investment in renewables — an observation that has subsequently come to pass.

D   The Group of Eight ('G8') Gleneagles 2005 Plan of Action

In Bradbrook's words:

> In its 2005 Gleneagles Plan of Action, *Climate Change, Clean Energy and Sustainable Development* ('Gleneagles Plan of Action'), the G8 sought to take action in a number of key areas, including '[t]ransforming the way we use energy[,]' '[p]owering a cleaner future[,]' '[p]romoting energy research and development[,]' and 'financing the transition to cleaner energy[.]'[28]

Bradbrook opines that the support by the major economies of the G8, in very specific terms, of measures to support energy efficiency and renewable energy and assist developing countries with adoption of these measures was a major step forward toward international promotion of these objectives. The Plan also proposed launching a Global Bioenergy Partnership to support wider, cost-effective biomass and biofuels deployment, measures now being strongly questioned by the international environmental community. Finally, it advocated for a menu of financing for the measures proposed, both nationally and by the international finance institutions. Bradbrook and Lyster describe the Gleneagles Plan of Action as 'the most comprehensive and supportive international instrument to date in relation to sustainable energy issues and the promotion of energy efficiency and renewable energy'.[29]

E   Beijing Declaration on Renewable Energy for Sustainable Development[30]

The Beijing Declaration represents the then latest international foray to promote a regime of sustainable energy for development as of 2005. It reiterates the commitment of the international community to support clean energy initiatives and to assist with their financing in the developing countries.

---

[28]   Bradbrook, 'Creating Law', above n 14, 25 (citations omitted).

[29]   Rosemary Lyster and Adrian Bradbrook, *Energy Law and the Environment* (Cambridge University Press, 2006), 76.

[30]   *Beijing Declaration on Renewable Energy for Sustainable Development*, Beijing International Renewable Energy Conference 2005 ('BIREC') (9 November 2005) <http://www.un.org/esa/sustdev/whats_new/beijingDecl_RenewableEnergy.pdf>.

F   The Role of International Institutions

The paper outlines the activities of international institutions such as the IEA, UNEP, UNDP, WHO, the CSD and FAO, and regional organisations such as the Latin American OLADE, in promoting sustainable energy, but observes that none of them have a prime focus on the subject. It also notes that the international finance agencies such as the World Bank, the regional banks and particularly the GEF have funded sustainable energy projects in developing countries, but again without a principal focus on these issues. The failure of major economies such as the United States, China, India and Brazil to fully participate in many of these international efforts is a matter of major concern. But Bradbrook expresses the hope that the need for an agency that would focus on promotion and financing of renewable energy may be fulfilled by the new International Renewable Energy Agency in Abu Dhabi. He also finds that '[e]ncouragement can be drawn from the fact that many nations that were initially wary of or hostile to international instruments promoting renewable energy and energy efficiency have been willing to sign declarations and non-binding commitments in this field'.[31]

The paper's near-term prescription is that:

> In the short term, the goal should be to achieve a comprehensive soft law instrument, preferably in the form of a United Nations General Assembly declaration, promoting renewable energy and energy efficiency technologies. This could contain binding targets for the adoption of renewable energy in electricity generation and a reduction in energy intensity in all the sectors of the economy (industry, buildings, appliances, and transportation).[32]

In the longer term, Professor Bradford recommends the drafting of a new international convention or protocol to an existing convention such as the UNFCCC, specifically focusing on and promoting renewable energy and energy efficiency

---

[31]   Bradbrook, above n 14, 27.

[32]   Ibid. A draft of a possible non-binding declaration, entitled *Draft Non-Legally Binding Statement of Principles for a Global Consensus on Sustainable Energy Production and Consumption,* has been prepared by Professor Bradbrook, published in the excellent article, Adrian J Bradbrook and Ralph D Wahnschafft, 'A Statement of Principles for a Global Consensus on Sustainable Energy Production and Consumption' (2001) 19(2) *Journal of Energy & Natural Resources Law* 143, 158-63, which unfortunately I am unable to review in this article. For each nation, this draft proposes comprehensive objectives, common principles, measures for improving efficiency in energy supply systems and consumption, appropriate energy pricing measures, the mitigation of environmental impacts, actions to promote consumer information and environmental education, and international co-operation.

technologies, with binding commitments by contracting parties on specified timetables. Again, in the article cited above, he and Wahnschafft have proposed specific language that could be used in such a convention. But the enormous difficulties that have been encountered in extending the *Kyoto Protocol* or other climate change measures for mitigation and adaptation under the UNFCC treaty demonstrate the difficulties in achieving this fine objective, particularly in these times of severe economic stringency. These difficulties may not have been so apparent at the time of the writing of the article.

Bradford then goes on to suggest that separate provision will have to be made for the different sustainable energy technologies, depending on the suitability of them for different climates and societal organisations and the affordability of the various technologies. He proceeds to go into considerable details about the presently known advanced technologies and the provisions necessary to promote each technology. For example, under energy efficiency for transportation, he considers the use of ethanol from a variety of sources, natural gas, and hydrogen fuel cells; planning and zoning laws to minimise automobile necessities; tax, registration fees, standards, labelling and other incentives to promote efficient vehicles and public transportation, and so on; and the same kinds of specificities for efficiency in industrial processes, consumer products, and buildings. He then proceeds to renewable energy technologies, including solar pholtovoltaics, solar thermal, onshore and offshore wind and geothermal energy; and carbon capture and storage.

He gives many examples of legislation for each technology, and recites both the advantages and economic and environmental problems with each. Many of his proposed enactments are innovative. Examples include permitting vehicles to pick up passengers at designated areas; implementing a 'feebate' system — that is, imposing higher sales/goods and services taxes for inefficient vehicles with tax rebates for relatively efficient vehicles; requiring the establishment of energy officers by industries, whose task would be to monitor energy consumption and to suggest various means of reducing consumption; adopting New York's *Solar Energy Products Warranty Act*,[33] which requires express warranties to purchasers of all solar energy products in the state; developing a course of education for renewable energy installers and implementing a system of trade accreditation; adoption of a mandatory system

---

[33]   12 NY Energy Law § 106 (McKinney 2004).

of assigning energy and resource option points to buildings; a mandatory system requiring the building's vendor to disclose the insulation installed in the building in the contract of sale; and many others, besides a description of the many widely used standards and incentives currently in use.

In terms of obstacles to the measures Bradbrook proposes, the top of his list is population growth, particularly in the developing countries, which may mandate increased use of fossil fuels despite any available new technologies or measures to promote them. The growth of energy demand from economic growth in emerging countries, particularly China, India and Brazil, also may engulf efforts to reduce use of fossil fuel resources.

Bradbrook cites lack of capacity, trained personnel and financial resources in the less developed countries as major obstacles. He also cites the difficulties of obtaining international co-operation to enable achievement of his objectives, as best illustrated by the UNFCC negotiation difficulties between North and South countries, rich and poor countries, and between oil-producing and oil-consuming countries. Last, he points to the lack of a focal point for energy within the United Nations for promotion of new clean energy technologies, with UNDP, UNEP, UN DESA and six regional commissions all playing largely uncoordinated roles — though, as he observes, the Secretary General has made recent efforts through establishment of a UN Energy Committee to better co-ordinate their efforts.

In conclusion, Bradbrook finds that a co-ordinated approach is necessary to support and promote next generation energy technologies, with separate legal management regimes at both international and domestic levels.

V 'PLACING ACCESS TO ENERGY SERVICES WITHIN A HUMAN RIGHTS FRAMEWORK'[34]

The last publication I will review is an article on one of the subjects for which Bradbrook is best known: energy services as a human right. The article, co-written with Judith G Gardam, emphasises the vital importance of energy services to enable poor countries' economic development, and to relieve poverty by providing universal

---

[34] Adrian J Bradbrook and Judith G Gardam, 'Placing Access to Energy Services within a Human Rights Framework' [2006] 28 *Human Rights Quarterly* 389.

access to sustainable energy. In order to achieve these goals, the authors advocate for inclusion of access to modern energy services as an internationally recognised human right.

The authors cite the fact that access to modern energy service was a key factor in achieving economic development in the developed countries and that denial of that access is a continued obstacle to economic progress in developing countries. As they observe, the fact that there are almost 2 billion people worldwide without access to modern energy services and an even larger number without adequate access, dooms them and their countries to abject poverty and severe health and environmental risks. Indeed, achievement of the United Nations' Millennium Development Goals is virtually impossible without access to modern energy services.

As the authors point out, by now it is widely recognised that the lack of modern energy condemns women and children to spend much of their time gathering wood to make fires for cooking and home heating, and that this wood burning fills their small residences with asphyxiating smoke; and that lack of access to modern energy services prevents adequate educational opportunities because of the inability of students to study in the dark, thus virtually requiring child labour for collection of wood. Energy services also are essential for pumping clean water, for agricultural irrigation, and for sterilising water and providing refrigeration for vaccines and medicines and to store agricultural crops. It has also been found that lack of access to energy services contributes to population growth because of the need to have children to provide for their households. In addition, lack of energy services contributes to the vast migration of people to cities that have energy services, condemning thousands to live in squalid urban slums.[35] The majority of the population of developing countries do not have electric lighting, clean cooking facilities, modern, efficient and non-polluting fuel supplies, or clean water and sanitation services, all of which are dependent on access to energy services.

The importance of energy services to poverty alleviation has long been recognised. Bradbrook and Gardam cite the recognition of this reality in the Brundtland Report as early as 1987. The Report stated:

> Energy services are a crucial input to the primary development challenge of providing adequate food, shelter, clothing, water, sanitation, medical care,

---

[35] José Goldemberg and Thomas B Johansson (eds), *World Energy Assessment: Overview 2004 Update* (United Nations Development Programme, 2004).

218

schooling, and access to information. Thus energy is one dimension or determinant of poverty and development, but it is vital. Energy supports the provision of basic needs such as cooked food, a comfortable living temperature, lighting, the use of appliances, piped water or sewerage, essential health care (refrigerated vaccines, emergency and intensive care), education aids, communication and transport. Energy also fuels productive activities, including agriculture, commerce, manufacture, industry, and mining. Conversely, lack of access to energy contributes to poverty and deprivation and can contribute to economic decline.[36]

This report dedicated a separate chapter to energy (Chapter 7) and stated that energy should be at the cutting edge of national policies for sustainable development.[37]

Bradbrook and Gardam observe that the amount of energy required to lift developing country families out of poverty is very small, citing the United Nations' World Energy Assessment of 2004 estimating that each person in a rural community needs only the energy equivalent of 100 watts of electricity to meet his or her basic energy needs. And for the largely rural poor population of the world, it is unlikely that electricity grids will reach them, so they will have to rely on stand-alone generation such as can be provided most efficiently and cheaply by locally available renewable energy resources.[38]

Despite the overwhelming evidence that energy services are essential to economic development, human health and the environment, the authors observe that '[t]o date there are no international treaties that specifically refer to access to energy as a right'.[39] They indicate that the two international treaties addressing human rights, the 1966 International Covenant on Civil and Political Rights ('ICCPR')[40] and the 1966 International Covenant on Economic, Social and Cultural Rights ('ICESCR')[41], do not specifically include energy services, and at any rate have not been universally

---

[36] World Commission on Environment and Development, *Our Common Future* (Oxford University Press, 1987) as cited in Goldemberg and Johansson (eds), above n 35.

[37] Ibid.

[38] Goldemberg and Johansson (eds), above n 35, 36.

[39] Bradbrook and Gardam, above n 34, 405.

[40] *International Covenant on Civil and Political Rights*, opened for signature 19 December 1966, 999 UNTS 171 (entered into force 23 March 1976) ('ICCPR').

[41] *International Covenant on Economic, Social and Cultural Rights*, opened for signature 19 December 1966, 993 UNTS 3 (entered into force 3 January 1976) ('ICESCRI').

adopted, therefore raising questions about their applicability to non-signatories, and requiring resort to customary norms.

However, the authors opine that whatever international action may be taken to promote energy services as a human right will have to rely on the general treaty obligations pertaining to socio-economic rights. They conclude:

> It is increasingly apparent that the socioeconomic goals contained in the ICESCR cannot be achieved without access to such services. So, in effect, the argument can be made that the right to access to modern energy services is already implicit in a range of existing human rights obligations.[42]

Bradbrook and Gardam observe that the provisions of the ICESCR proclaiming a right to an adequate standard of living, continuous improvement of living conditions, and to food, physical and mental health conditions, housing, clothing, work and working conditions, implicitly require access to the energy services necessary to provide these treaty-required conditions. They also point to other international agreements that similarly implicitly require a right to access to energy services, such as The Convention on the Elimination of Discrimination against Women, which requires states to eliminate discrimination, particularly in rural areas, to ensure that they 'enjoy adequate living conditions, particularly in relation to housing, sanitation, electricity and water supply, transport and communication'.[43] They also reference the Additional Protocol to the American Convention on Human Rights in the Area of Economic, Social and Cultural Rights providing that everyone 'shall have the right to live in a healthy environment and to have access to basic public services'.[44] As they observe, these rights would traditionally include supply of transport, health, and clean water — which resources are not available without access to energy.

Bradbrook and Gardam also refer to other soft law documents that imply the necessity for access to energy. A particularly interesting example is the African Charter on Human and Peoples' Rights 'to enjoy the best attainable state of physical and mental health'.[45] The African Commission on Human and Peoples' Rights found

---

[42] Bradbrook and Gardam, above n 34, 405.

[43] See *Convention on the Elimination of all Forms of Discrimination against Women*, opened for signature 18 December 1979, 19 ILM 33 (entered into force 3 September 1981) art 14(2)(h).

[44] *Organization of American States: Additional Protocol to the American Convention on Human Rights in the Area of Economic, Social and Cultural Rights*, opened for signature 14 November 1988, 28 ILM 156.

[45] *African Charter on Human and Peoples' Rights*, opened for signature 27 June 1981, 21 ILM 58 (entered into force 21 October 1986).

that the failure of the Zaire government to provide safe drinking water and electricity was a violation of the Charter.[46] They also cite a number of other examples of a right to access to energy implied from related enactments.

A   Recommendations for a Human Rights Regime to Address Energy Access

As is the strength of virtually all of Bradford's scholarship, here he and Gardam conclude with specific recommendations as to what a human right to access to energy should contain. They prescribe that '[t]he basic right would be designed to ensure access on the basis of equality and nondiscrimination to a sufficient, regular, reliable, efficient, safe, and affordable supply of (ideally clean and sustainable) energy'.[47]

A summary of their requirements for the human right is that it must be clearly realistic and achievable, matching the needs of the community to be served, safe, reliable, affordable (which may require temporary subsidies for the poorest households), clean (from non-polluting sources, not from traditional sources of wood or dung) and sustainable. The right must include application that is non-discriminatory and provides for equality of application to all sectors of society. It must be particularly accommodating of the needs of women.

The implementation of the right should require the supply of sufficient energy to meet the pressing needs of cooking, lighting and refrigeration. It should facilitate provision of clean water, safe sewage disposal, agricultural production for adequate food supplies, health care facilities and education. To achieve these goals, a constant and reliable energy supply system is essential. Adequate safety measures are needed to avoid pollution and exposure to toxic substances. The balancing of energy supply with sustainable development is another requisite. Any decentralisation of energy supply must be accompanied by regulations, fully enforced, which take account of environmental and social welfare needs, particularly of women. The system should prioritise the public provision of food, water, sanitation, health and energy, the key sectors in which women often provide unpaid labour.

To provide progressively for provision of sustainable energy services to total populations, including the very poor, on the basis of non-discrimination and equality,

---

[46]   African Commission on Human and Peoples' Rights, Communication Nos 25/89, 47/90, 56/91, 100/93, 47.

[47]   Bradbrook and Gardam, above n 34, 409.

Bradbrook and Gardam cite the examples of providing energy services on such a basis to large populations such as the energy programs for very poor favelas in Brazil and poor communities in South Africa.[48] The right must be adequately regulated and enforced. Despite the difficulties of enforcement of socio-economic requirements, the authors assert that the establishment of a legal framework of norms would create community pressure for compliance. They suggest that implementation of a human rights approach might be undertaken through the ICESCR and its established reporting requirements as an enforcement mechanism.

An advantage to taking the human rights approach is that it would introduce energy access into the entire United Nations human rights framework. This should compel the various UN human rights agencies to include energy accessibility within their agenda. This approach might also facilitate a more co-ordinated approach to energy issues among the many disparate UN agencies presently dealing with these issues.

VI CONCLUSION

While energy bodies throughout the world continue to make extensive efforts to secure the benefits of access to energy to the some 2 billion people presently lacking it, and to relieve the poverty that results from deficient energy access, the authors conclude that little progress has been made in alleviating these deficiences. Moreover, the issues themselves fail to receive adequate attention. A legal human rights approach might assist in treating these energy access challenges through focusing on the dire consequence of this failure and the need to take remedial action. It would put energy access into the compelling sphere of providing human rights to redress the environmental, health and economic consequences of our failure to address energy access. For this reason alone, Adrian Bradbrook's publications break new ground by influencing our thinking on access to energy services and climate change.

---

[48] See Walt Patterson et al, 'Towards Sustainable Electricity Policy' in Thomas B Johansson and José Goldemberg (eds), *Energy for Sustainable Development: A Policy Agenda* (United Nations Development Programme, 2002) 77.

10

INTERNATIONAL ENERGY LAW: AN EMERGING ACADEMIC DISCIPLINE

ALEXANDRA WAWRYK[1]

I   INTRODUCTION

Adrian Bradbrook has been a leading international academic in the field of energy law for many years, in particular in the fields of renewable energy and energy conservation. Not only did he write pioneering legal works in this area, but he instituted the key law course on Mining and Energy Law at the University of Adelaide at a time when most other Australian universities did not teach energy or resources law as a mainstream legal subject.[2]

In 1996, Bradbrook wrote a seminal paper on teaching Energy Law as an academic discipline.[3] While 'Energy Law' as conceived of in his paper largely focused

[1]   I would like to thank Ms Katelijn Ven Hende, course co-ordinator and lecturer, Energy and Resources Law, and International Policy and Geopolitics of Energy and Resources, University College of London (Adelaide), and Professor Kim Talus, director of the LLM diploma programme on International and European Energy Law and Policy, University of Eastern Finland, for their helpful comments on this chapter.

[2]   In 1996, some years after Bradbrook instituted the Mining and Energy Law course at the University of Adelaide, out of the 26 Australian law schools, the subject of Mining and Energy law was only taught at the University of Adelaide and the University of Wollongong. Adrian Bradbrook, 'Energy Law as an Academic Discipline' (1996) 14 *Journal of Energy & Natural Resources Law*, 193.

[3]   Ibid.

on Australian national and state issues, he identified the fact that energy law is increasingly acquiring an international law dimension as one of the most significant developments of the time. This 'international law dimension' of energy law includes both the increasing internationalisation and standardisation of national laws, where, for example, 'traditionally national subjects such as taxation laws now have an international dimension',[4] and the growth and influence of public international law in the context of energy, an area which, he argued, had 'evolved and continues to evolve very rapidly and … represents the real cutting edge of energy law at the present time'.[5]

The increasing recognition of the 'international law dimension' of energy law among legal scholars, legal practitioners and those working in any role with energy markets has led to the growing recognition and development of 'international energy law' as a separate academic discipline. Although certain 'sub-disciplines' of laws within 'international energy law', such as oil and gas law, are well developed fields of practice, research and study in their own right, the study and teaching of international energy law in its own right is still very new.

Journals that address energy law have been in existence for a number of years. For example, the *Journal of Energy & Natural Resources Law* of the International Bar Association — which covers many issues of international energy law — has existed as a premier journal for many years, although it was not self-styled as addressing 'international energy law'. The *International Energy Law and Taxation Review*, established in 1982, was renamed the *International Energy Law Review* in 2009. However, new academic journals devoted specifically to international energy law have been created comparatively recently, reflecting the increasing recognition that international energy law forms its own field of learning. These include OGEL, the Oil, Gas and Energy Law Intelligence online service,[6] which contains a database of laws and articles for scholars and practitioners, in 2003, and the *Journal of World Energy Law and Business* in 2008.

Similarly, while many universities have taught the sub-disciplines within international energy law such as oil and gas law for some time, the teaching of

---

[4] Ibid 212.

[5] Ibid 203.

[6] See <http://www.ogel.org>.

international energy law as a distinct branch of learning is a new development, with, for example, the University of Adelaide and the University College of London (Adelaide Campus) introducing specific courses in their Masters degrees since 2010, and the University of Eastern Finland doing so from 2013.

This chapter builds on Bradbrook's ground-breaking work in energy law to provide an overview of international energy law as a coherent academic legal discipline. As far as 'coherence' is concerned, this is much more difficult than it may sound to those unfamiliar with the field. To the uninitiated, the phrase 'international energy law' may seem to presuppose the existence of uniform international rules or laws applying to one 'global' energy sector. The reality is extremely different. There is no single, easily identifiable global energy market or industry and it is difficult to identify precisely the parameters of the energy markets or industries which can be seen as the subjects of international energy laws; nor is there one easily identifiable 'source' of energy law. The 'fragmented' or 'specialised' state of international energy law is a reflection of the historical development of energy resources and markets. The content and parameters of international energy law as a discipline is something that is understood by scholars and practitioners though experience and accumulated knowledge, rather than something that has been defined or articulated to date.

In this chapter I present international energy law as a holistic discipline first, by identifying certain key themes that underlie the whole of international energy law. These include the 'internationalisation' of principles of national energy law, the importance of 'soft law', and the fundamental importance of understanding non-legal factors (such as geopolitics and concerns over energy security), and their influence on the development of international energy law. I will then identify various subsets or 'sub-disciplines' of international energy law according to different types of energy resource. As with any exercise of this nature, there may well be varying opinions on the boundaries of the discipline, and the relative weight or importance of each topic within it. In this chapter, I distinguish oil and gas law, nuclear energy law, renewable energy law, and electricity and gas markets law as fundamental sub-disciplines. I will then discuss briefly the energy law of the European Union, which is universally acknowledged to be a crucial part of international energy law, as well as a separate legal specialty. I finish by discussing some cross-cutting issues, such as energy and the environment, energy and trade, and dispute resolution.

II Definitions and Sources of Law

A preliminary issue this chapter addresses is the meaning of 'energy sources'. Energy sources may be renewable (an energy source that can be easily replenished) or non-renewable (an energy source that is used up and cannot be recreated).[7] Non-renewable energy sources include the fossil fuels — oil, natural gas, and coal — and uranium (used to make nuclear energy). Well-known renewable energy sources include hydro-electric power,[8] wave, tide, ocean, wind, solar and geothermal energy.[9] Secondary energy sources, such as electricity and hydrogen, are energy carriers, because they move energy in a useable form from one place to another.[10] Energy conservation, which encompasses measures to reduce consumer demand for energy, including through improved energy efficiency, may also be seen as an energy resource because of its potential role in satisfying society's demand for energy.[11]

Energy law identifies and analyses the legal issues associated with the exploitation of all the primary and secondary sources of energy, where 'exploitation' refers to any stage of the process which involves finding a resource and bringing it to commercial use.[12] It regulates 'the allocation of rights and duties concerning the exploitation of all energy resources between individuals, between individuals and the government, between governments and between states'.[13]

---

[7] US Energy Information Administration, *What is Energy?* <http://www.eia.gov/energyexplained/index.cfm?page=about_home>.

[8] Small or micro-hydro-electric power plants may be distinguished from large-scale hydro-electric power plants. In many legislative systems that seek to mandate the use of renewable energy in electricity, large hydro-electric power systems are excluded from the definition of renewable energy. This is because of the potentially huge environmental, social and cultural impacts of large hydro-electric schemes that require large dams.

[9] Other renewable energy sources are hot dry rock, energy crops, wood waste, agricultural waste, waste from processing of agricultural products, food waste, food processing waste, bagasse, black liquor, biomass-based components of municipal solid waste, landfill gas, sewage gas and biomass-based components of sewage.

[10] Electricity and hydrogen are obtained from the conversion of primary sources of energy, such as coal, nuclear, or solar energy. Hydrogen is a non-renewable energy source, made by separating atoms from water, biomass, or natural gas molecules. US Energy Information Administration, *What are Secondary Energy Sources?* <http://www.eia.gov/energyexplained/index.cfm?page=secondary_home>.

[11] Bradbrook, above n 2, 195.

[12] Ibid 197.

[13] Ibid 194.

Energy law at an *international* level is best understood with reference to the *sources* of law that regulate the allocation of rights and duties concerning the exploitation of all energy resources between individuals, between individuals and the government, between governments, and between states. In this respect, it is crucial to understand that no single international governing body exists to set down a uniform set of energy laws that apply in all countries and cover all aspects of energy production, trade, transport and consumption. There is no single international energy 'law'. Rather, international energy 'law' stems from three broad sources.

First, 'law' refers to the principles enumerated in traditional sources of international law, such as treaties and customary international law. Various treaties on nuclear energy, such as the Convention on Nuclear Safety,[14] are a clear example of this source of law. Although to date few, if any, principles of customary international law of specific relevance to energy have been identified, it has been argued there is a nascent *Lex Petrolea*, or a set of rules of customary international law valid for the international oil industry.[15]

Secondly, 'law' here refers to the internationalisation or global spread of national laws and regulatory principles relevant to energy law, so that we can see common principles of energy law applied across countries, even though there is no treaty binding the Parties to apply these principles of law. An example is the global spread of principles of national laws for deregulating national electricity and gas industries.

Thirdly, 'law' here refers to principles of 'soft law', such as treaties expressed in non-mandatory language, and also the non-binding codes, guidelines, resolutions, directives, standards or model codes of international bodies, including intergovernmental organisations such as the International Atomic Energy Agency. While such guidelines and standards are not 'hard' or binding law per se, their importance in regulating behaviour in the energy industries/markets cannot be underestimated.

---

[14] *Convention on Nuclear Safety*, opened for signature 20 September 1994, 1963 UNTS 293 (entered into force 24 October 1996).

[15] R Doak Bishop, 'International Arbitration of Petroleum Disputes: The Development of a Lex Petrolea' (1998) 1 XXIII *Yearbook Commercial Arbitration* 1131; Thomas CC Childs, 'Update on *Lex Petrolea*: The Continuing Development of Customary Law Relating to Oil and Gas Exploration and Production' (2011) 4(3) *Journal of World Energy Law and Business* 214; Kim Talus, Scott Looper and Steven Otillar, '*Lex Petrolea* and the Internationalization of Petroleum Agreements: Focus on Host Government Contracts' (2012) 5 *Journal of World Energy Law and Business* 181-93.

International energy law is thus a conglomeration of rules of custom, treaties, national and regional laws, and principles of intergovernmental and non-governmental international institutions, which together regulate the various facets of energy production, supply, consumption and trade. The exploitation of each different energy resource will involve a different interface with the law. Energy law covers a multitude of legal issues, which will differ between resources but may include laws relating to research and development, exploration, production/generation, transportation, investment and financing, business and contractual arrangements, market access, subsidies and taxation, trade, dispute resolution, and environmental and safety issues, to name but a few. Energy law transcends legal boundaries, encompassing, for example, aspects of contracts, torts, property, constitutional law, administrative law, taxation law, environmental law and competition law.[16]

III   Underlying Themes of International Energy Law

The internationalisation of energy law and the importance of soft law, are two fundamental features of the discipline of international energy law, and form two of the crucial 'underlying themes' of international energy law. It is simply not possible to appreciate the complexity of regulation of energy markets and industries, nor the scope of international energy law, without an understanding of these features.

A   *The Internationalisation of Energy Law*

Historically, energy supply and consumption, with the possible exception of oil exploitation, were seen by nations to be matters solely of domestic concern. Energy markets started as small localised markets, eventually developing into nationally segregated electricity, coal and nuclear industries, with the supply and regulation of electricity provided by large, vertically-integrated, state-owned enterprises. The lack of international trade in energy prior to the 1970s, and the lack of understanding about the transboundary environmental impacts of energy use prior to the 1960s, meant that resource exploitation and environmental protection were largely seen as matters for internal control by nation-states, and therefore not a matter for international regulation. As a result, prior to the 1970s, there were few treaties or rules of custom

---

[16]   Bradbrook, above n 2, 211.

which dealt with energy markets.[17] Because, under traditional analyses of international law, only treaties and customary international law and the other forms of law set out in Article 38 of the Statute of the International Court of Justice could be seen as sources of international law,[18] there was no 'international energy law'.

This situation has changed markedly since the 1970s. First, the changing structure of energy markets has led to an increase in the number of treaties concerning energy, particularly in the European Union, and upon matters of key importance to international energy markets, including free trade[19] and the environment.[20] Second, there has been increasing internationalisation of principles of energy law which were previously confined in application to national markets. These emerging common global principles of law are an integral part of international energy law, even though they are not necessarily mandated as binding principles of international law through a treaty. They may come to be included in a treaty or, over time, may become part of custom; but in general this type of internationalisation of energy law refers to the increasing spread and application across the globe of common national laws and practices in energy, in the absence of a treaty.

There are many examples of the internationalisation of energy law. One example is the increasing global application of principles of law relevant to the privatisation of electricity and gas corporations, and the restructuring of electricity and gas markets as competitive markets. The restructuring of the European Union internal electricity and gas markets has been underpinned largely by the European Union's Directives and Regulations, given the emergence of cross-border trading in energy between its members. However, the spread of the principles to other countries, such as those in South America, has taken place through a different process, in particular through tying the funding of World Bank and international multilateral financial institutions to the privatisation of national electricity markets.

---

[17]   There were some rules of customary international law which affected investment, these being property protection rules, and some environmental treaties, such as those concerning marine pollution, relevant to the transport of oil, and nuclear liability.

[18]   Statute of the International Court of Justice, 3 Bevans 1179; 59 Stat 1055; TS No. 993; [1945] ATS 1.

[19]   For example, the GATT/WTO rules: see below nn 100-8, and accompanying text.

[20]   For example, the *United Nations Framework Convention on Climate Change*, opened for signature 14 June 1992, 1771 UNTS 107 (entered into force 21 March 1994) and the *Kyoto Protocol to the United Nations Framework Convention on Climate Change*, opened for signature 11 December 1997, 2303 UNTS 148 (entered into force 16 February 2005).

Another example is provided by the renewable energy industry, where countries are increasingly adopting national laws to put in place common mechanisms for supporting the development of renewable energy — for example, feed-in tariffs[21] and renewable portfolio standards[22] in the electricity industries. There are no universal treaties regarding renewable energy law, although the European Union has a Directive (a secondary source of law) on renewable energy,[23] which is binding on the EU's member countries.

Oil and gas law provides one of the most well-known examples of international energy law arising from the internationalisation of domestic laws. There is no treaty which regulates the exploration and production of oil, as this is achieved through the domestic laws of each country. These generally include a Petroleum Law, Regulations and, in many countries, a separate contract — called a Host Government contract — between the government (in many cases, represented by the national oil company) and the international oil company undertaking exploration and production activities. Although upstream activities are subject to domestic regulation, there are many legal principles common to petroleum arrangements around the world, reflecting the international nature of world oil markets.

First, the international oil industry is characterised by the use of numerous standardised model contracts and practices which govern the commercial relations between oil companies worldwide. These contain similar types of clauses and structures. The early discovery of oil in the US in the nineteenth century spawned a body of contract law which developed to foster oil exploration and production on lands belonging to private landowners. When the US oil companies extended their activities across the globe over the course of the twentieth century, they carried with them their customary forms of contracts, business organisation and jurisprudential

---

[21]   A feed-in tariff is a type of price support for renewable energy technologies, guaranteeing that electricity generated from renewable technologies will sell for a certain minimum price in electricity markets.

[22]   A renewable portfolio standard is a legal mechanism whereby an electricity provider, usually the wholesaler, is legally obliged to source a certain percentage of their electricity from different renewable energy sources.

[23]   *Directive 2009/28/EC of the European Parliament and of the Council of 23 April 2009 on the Promotion of the Use of Energy from Renewable Sources and Amending and Subsequently Repealing Directives 2001/77/EC and 2003/30/EC* [2009] OJ L 140/16.

concepts.[24] There has been continuing development, widespread acceptance and use of model petroleum contracts drafted by national and international organisations such as the Association of International Petroleum Negotiators. These contracts span a whole range of commercial issues including (to name but a few) model Farmout Agreements, Unitisation Agreements and Confidentiality Agreements. This has contributed to a global standardisation of upstream petroleum contracts.[25]

Second, the internationalisation and standardisation of principles of oil and gas law has occurred through the internationalisation and standardisation of governments' petroleum legislation and Host Government Contracts between national governments and international oil companies. For example, the legal principles of the concession contract, which has its basis in the contracts developed in the US oil industry in the nineteenth century, spread globally as the major oil companies of the US and Europe explored and produced in the Middle East, Africa and Asia in the twentieth century. Other more recent types of petroleum agreements, such as the production sharing contract, most famously used by Indonesia in the mid-late twentieth century, have also spread internationally. Although there are no generally accepted model Host Government contracts, as these tend to be drafted to meet the specific ends and goals of each country involved, the contracts contain similar clauses and similar structures worldwide.[26] Their use has become increasingly globalised through their application by actors such as the World Bank and private lawyers advising host governments internationally; by the desire of governments to learn from previous experience; and by growing international education and awareness in this area.[27]

Furthermore, international dispute resolution under commercial arbitration treaties, investment treaties, and arbitration under the *Energy Charter Treaty*[28] has given rise to standard principles of international, rather than purely national, application. As many disputes have gone to international commercial arbitration in tribunals such

---

[24] Claude Duval et al, *International Petroleum Exploration and Exploitation Agreements: Legal, Economic and Policy Aspects* (Barrows, 2nd ed, 2009).

[25] A Timothy Martin and J Jay Park, 'Global Petroleum Industry Model Contracts Revisited: Higher, Faster, Stronger' (2010) 3(1) *Journal of World Energy Law and Business* 7; Talus, Looper and Otillar, above n 15, 185.

[26] Ibid 181.

[27] Ibid 181, 193.

[28] *Energy Charter Treaty*, opened for signature 17 December 1994, 34 ILM 360 (entered into force 16 April 1998).

as the International Centre for Settlement of Investment Disputes ('ICSID'), a major source of case law has arisen, which has given rise to standardised principles of law applicable at an international level to the global petroleum industry. This has given rise, as mentioned above, to an argument that there is in existence at least a nascent *Lex Petrolea* — a specific legal regime, or 'body of international norms' — which instructs or regulates the international petroleum industry.[29] This concept first arose in *Kuwait v AMINOIL*,[30] and, although not accepted by the Arbitral Tribunal in that case, appears to have become legitimised to a certain extent by subsequent academic research and writing on the topic.[31]

Whether or not there is an international law of specific application to the international oil industry, model contracts are evidence of international best practices being applied globally regardless of the location of the commercial transaction, while the existence of similar clauses in Host Government contracts are evidence of the internationalisation of initially domestic principles of oil and gas law.

B   *The Importance of Soft Law*

The norms, principles or standards contained in the guidelines, declarations of principles and codes of practice of non-governmental organisations ('NGO's), intergovernmental organisations ('IGO's) and other international institutions, known as 'soft law', are a key part of international energy law. A norm is soft either when it is not part of a binding regime or when it is contained in a binding instrument but is not stated in obligatory terms. There are many actors and institutions which draft principles, norms and standards relevant to international energy law, including IGOs, NGOs and international lending institutions.

IGOs relevant to energy law include the International Energy Agency ('IEA'); the Energy Charter Conference and Secretariat; the International Atomic Energy Agency ('IAEA'); the United Nations Development Programme ('UNDP'); the

---

[29]   Bishop, above n 15; Childs, above n 15.

[30]   *Kuwait v American Independent Oil Co (AMINOIL) (Award)* (1982) 21 *International Legal Materials* 976.

[31]   Bishop, above n 15; Childs, above n 15; Talus, Looper and Otillar, above n 15; A Timothy Martin, '*Lex Petrolea* in the International Oil and Gas Industry' in R King (ed), *Dispute Resolution in the Energy Sector: A Practitioner's Handbook* (Globe Law and Business, London, 2012); Alfredo de Jesús O, 'The Prodigious Story of the Lex Petrolea and the Rhinoceros: Philosophical Aspects of the Transnational Legal Order of the Petroleum Society', *TPLI Series on Transnational Petroleum Law*, Vol. 1, No 1 (2012).

United Nations Environment Programme ('UNEP'); the OECD Nuclear Energy Agency; and the International Renewable Energy Agency ('IRENA'). The primary and traditional role of IGOs, especially international energy institutions, is to provide secretariat services for conferences out of which energy regulatory instruments such as treaties emerge. They claim a 'service' role to governments, with whom rest formal decision powers, treaty-making powers and making or subsidiary law under treaties. However, IGOs can also influence the negotiation of, or create, technical standards, usually in collaboration with experts in government, industry associations and companies.[32]

NGOs relevant to international energy law, such as Greenpeace, Oxfam, WWF and Friends of the Earth, postulate the emergence/existence of new principles (for example, the human rights liability of transnational oil corporations), influence the negotiation of treaties, influence the negotiation of, or create, non-binding guidelines, principles and codes of conduct, and participate in international dispute settlement. Industry associations, such as the International Association of Oil and Gas Producers, the American Petroleum Institute and the World Nuclear Association, also influence the negotiation of treaties, influence the negotiation of, or create, non-binding technical standards, guidelines, principles and codes of conduct and participate in international dispute settlement.[33]

Finally, international financial institutions, such as the World Bank, the IMF and the Asian Development Bank, have a key role in the formulation of energy law and policy by lending money, particularly to emerging economies/developing countries, on the basis of certain conditions. Privatisation of electricity in Latin American countries, a very controversial issue in many of those countries, came about at least in part because of World Bank conditions attached to loans. In the environmental sphere, the requirement of prior environmental impact assessment has become a standard requirement of World Bank projects.[34]

---

[32] Thomas Wälde, 'The Role of Selected International Agencies in the Formation of International Energy Law and Policy Towards Sustainable Development' in Adrian J Bradbrook and Richard L Ottinger (eds), *Energy Law and Sustainable Development* (IUCN, 2003) 171, 173.

[33] Thomas Wälde, *International Energy Law: An Introduction to Modern Concepts, Context, Policy and Players*, unpublished draft manuscript, November 2001 (on file with author).

[34] See Alexandra S Wawryk, 'Adoption of International Environmental Standards by Transnational Oil Companies: Reducing the Impact of Oil Operations in Emerging Economies' (2002) 20 *Journal of Energy & Natural Resources Law* 402.

Whether so-called 'soft law' can truly be seen as a source of international law remains a controversial question to international legal scholars.[35] However, a failure to appreciate the source and extent of this type of 'regulation' will lead to a failure to truly understand the complexity of the way in which energy markets are regulated. It is also critical to understand that the continuing development and use of standards and guidelines has legal implications beyond the formal status of these documents as 'non-binding' guidelines. In both the international and national sphere, these non-legally-binding guidelines have the potential to 'harden' into binding law.[36]

First, soft law may contribute to the formation of binding international law, either through the incorporation of initially non binding norms into a treaty, or, when these guidelines, codes or principles are viewed as legally authoritative by a sufficient number of countries over a sufficient length of time, through the creation of customary law.

Nationally, industry statements of best practice may come to be binding through their application by national courts or arbitral bodies, as evidence of industry 'best practice' in litigation or arbitration, when interpreting petroleum contracts that require the use of best practice, or to interpret legislative provisions that require the use of good international practice. National courts may also invoke international guidelines in prosecutions for environmental offences, where international technical standards may become the legal standard of due care in negligence cases concerning the environment. Alternatively, implementation of these standards may provide the basis for a 'due diligence' defence in cases of prosecution for environmental offences, reduce the risk of regulators implementing a prosecution, or, if a prosecution is mounted, may mitigate the penalty imposed by the court.[37]

---

[35] For a discussion of soft law see Christine Chinkin, 'The Challenge of Soft Law and Change in International Law' (1989) 38 *International and Comparative Law Quarterly* 850; Pierre-Marie Dupuy, 'Soft Law and the International Law of the Environment' (1990-91) 12 *Michigan Journal of International Law* 420; Hartmut Hillgenberg, 'A Fresh Look at Soft Law' (1999) 10(3) *European Journal of International Law* 499; Sir Geoffrey Palmer, 'New Ways to Make International Environmental Law' (1992) 86 *American Journal of International Law* 259; Paul C Szasz, 'International Norm-Making' in Edith Brown Weiss, *Environmental Change and International Law: New Challenges and Dimensions* (United Nations University Press, 1992) 69-72.

[36] See Wawryk, above n 34.

[37] See, eg, *EPA v Great Southern Energy* [1999] NSWLEC 192; *EPA v The Shell Company of Australia Ltd* [1999] NSWLEC 16.

International guidelines also raise the standard expected of oil companies in ways other than their application by the courts. For example, governments themselves may require implementation of good environmental practices as a condition for granting development approval, even where these practices are not required by legislation. The practices voluntarily adopted by one company may become a model for national oil and gas legislation, thereby raising the standard expected of other companies seeking to operate in that country in the future.[38]

C   International Energy Law as a Multidisciplinary Subject: the Importance of Political, Social, Economic and Environmental Factors

In 2008, Thomas Wälde wrote that 'leading practitioners and scholars have always been able to sharpen their analysis and application of law and contractual commercial transactions by a more than superficial understanding of the forces which underlie and determine the law'.[39] A true understanding of the development, current state and possible or likely future trends in international energy law, and a critical perspective on the law, requires a knowledge and understanding of non-legal factors that drive the law. While it is not possible in this chapter to identify and discuss all of these, some crucial examples can be given.

Understanding international oil and gas law requires an understanding of the changing market structure over the past century, from an industry in the early- to mid-twentieth century dominated by the former 'Seven Sisters', to one where the majority of production and reserves are in the oil-producing nations, under the control of state oil and gas companies, who are now themselves becoming international operators. Understanding the development and structure of the international oil industry provides a better understanding of the types of international petroleum contracts, their advantages or disadvantages for host countries/oil companies, and the types of clauses that are commonly included in these contracts. Geopolitics, issues of sovereign risk, and oil pricing are also key drivers in international oil and gas law.

In the electricity industry, changing economic views about the most efficient ownership structures of electricity enterprises led to restructuring and privatisation of

---

[38]   *The Oil Industry: Operating in Sensitive Environments*, 'Texaco Exploration in North East Bangkok' (IPIECA/E&P Forum, Report No. 2.73/255, London, May 1997). At the time of the report, the Thai government was intending to use Texaco's procedures for closure of the site as the case study for future reference for other concessionaire operations onshore in Thailand.

[39]   Thomas Wälde, 'Editor's Note' (2008) 1(1) *Journal of World Energy Law and Business* 1, 1.

the large, integrated, state-owned electricity companies in many countries, achieved only through legislative amendment.

More generally, concerns over energy security remain strong and persistent since the oil crises of the 1970s, particularly in Western countries, thus shaping the directions of trade between countries, and the desire to diversify energy sources. Concerns over energy security and climate change in Western countries have prompted movements towards energy efficiency and conservation as well as renewable energy, through a range of legal mechanisms, including emissions trading schemes. Access to energy remains a key and crucial concern in many developing countries, heavily influencing negotiations and the structure of international law on climate change. Climate change concerns may well see a renaissance in nuclear energy, notwithstanding the 2011 incident at Fukushima, and this will continue to raise the issue of the adequacy of laws to ensure the safety and security of nuclear energy installations and the transport of nuclear material. Understanding these, and other non-legal drivers behind the law, is arguably necessary for a deeper understanding of international energy law as an academic discipline.

IV Law by Energy Source

The laws governing various stages of development of the major sources of energy — such as oil and gas, nuclear power and renewable energy — form their own discrete body, as well as comprising a 'sub-discipline' or area of specialisation of international energy law. One part of the approach to teaching or researching international energy law is to study some of the most important laws and issues relevant to the exploitation of each energy source. Thus, for example, the various treaties relevant to the use of nuclear power can be examined to obtain an understanding of how the risks of nuclear power are regulated by the international community, and this is a worthy stand-alone topic. However, the laws regarding particular energy sources can also be researched or taught to demonstrate the themes that underlie international energy law, such as the theme of internationalisation of energy law.

A Oil and Gas Law

The regulation of the international oil industry is a mix of treaty law and internationalised principles of law and uniform practice. I have discussed the internationalisation of principles of oil and gas law above. The history, principles and structures of petroleum agreements between companies, and between companies and host governments, are a key part of international oil and gas law as a sub-discipline of international energy law. Dispute resolution in the international oil industry, in particular international commercial arbitration, is a growing area of practical and academic focus.

One aspect of the international oil industry that is heavily regulated by treaty is the international legal regime for the protection of the marine environment, in particular from pollution caused by the maritime transport of oil.[40] Accidents involving oil tankers such as the Exxon Valdez and Torrey Canyon focused world attention on the grave environmental consequences of oil spills on the marine environment. Other types of actions that may also have a negative impact on the marine environment are the routine operational discharge of oil from tankers into the ocean; the deliberate dumping of wastes at sea, including the decommissioning and disposal of offshore oil platforms at sea; and the discharge of oil and wastes from land-based installations. The general obligations of states to protect the marine environment are set out in treaties such as the United Nations Convention on the Law of the Sea,[41] and specific obligations concerning these matters are set out in other multilateral and regional agreements and protocols.[42] However, the regulation of offshore oil exploration and production on the continental shelf (as well as onshore exploration and production) is still primarily a matter of domestic concern, and there is no global regime that

---

[40] For example, the *International Convention for the Prevention of Pollution from Ships* (MARPOL) 1973, absorbed by the *Protocol relating to the Prevention of Pollution from Ships*, 17 ILM (1978), 546 (in force 2 October 1983); *International Convention for the Safety of Life at Sea*, 1184 UNTS 2, UKTS 46 (1980) Cmnd 7874, TIAS 9700 (entered into force 25 May 1980); *International Convention on Oil Pollution Preparedness, Response and Cooperation* (London) 30 ILM (1991), 735 (entered into force 13 May 1995); *International Convention Relating to Intervention on the High Seas in Cases of Oil Pollution Damage* (Brussels), UKTS 77 (1971), Cmnd. 6056, 9 ILM (1970), 25 (entered into force 6 May 1975); and various treaties on liability and compensation.

[41] *United Nations Convention on the Law of the Sea* (Montego Bay), Misc. 11(1983), Cmnd. 8941; 21 ILM (1982), 1261 (entered into force 16 November 1994).

[42] For example, *Convention on the Prevention of Marine Pollution by Dumping of Wastes and Other Matter* (London), 26 UST 2403, TIAS 8165, UKTS 43 (1976), CMND. 6486, 11 ILM (1972), 1294 (entered into force 30 August 1975); *Convention for the Prevention of Marine Pollution by Dumping from Ships and Aircraft* (Oslo), 932 UNTS 3, UKTS 119 (1975), Cmnd. 5551, 11 ILM 262 (1972) (entered into force 7 April 1974); *Convention for the Protection of the Marine Environment of the North-East Atlantic* (Paris) 32 ILM (1993), 1072 (entered into force 25 March 1998); *Convention on the Protection of the Mediterranean Sea Against Pollution* (Barcelona), 15 ILM (1976), 290 (in force 12 February 1978).

establishes norms or principles governing the issue of authorisations in offshore areas, environment and safety standards, and compensation and liability for oil pollution from incidents such as well blowouts.[43]

It is no coincidence that marine pollution caused by the maritime transport of oil is regulated by treaties, as the environmental impacts are often transboundary and require international co-operation for effective regulation. However, pollution of the marine environment is not the only area of international concern for the environment, with a growing focus on the link between oil exploitation and the abuse of human rights, the rights of indigenous peoples and onshore environmental degradation, and the means by which international and national laws, and industry standards and codes of conduct, can protect and preserve the environment, culture and human rights of the citizens of host countries.

B *Nuclear Energy*

Nuclear energy is a major fuel for generating electricity, accounting for some 13.4 per cent of the world's electricity generation in 2009,[44] and 19 per cent of the OECD's electricity production from January to May 2012.[45] Because of the many risks associated with the use of nuclear power, a relatively large body of international law has developed to regulate nuclear activities. It is an area of international law where there are many conventions, technical standards and Codes of Conduct. The major agreements and standards have been promulgated under the auspices of the IAEA

---

[43] However, there is some regionalisation of these issues: for example, the European Union has issued a number of Directives to member states, including Directive 94/22/EC of the European Parliament and of the Council of 30 May 1994 on the conditions for granting and using authorisations for the prospection, exploration and production of hydrocarbons, OJ L 164/3, 30 June 1994; Directive 2004/35/EC of the European Parliament and of the Council of 21 April 2004 on environmental liability with regard to the prevention and remedying of environmental damage, OJ L 143/56, 30 April 2004; and Directive 2013/30/EU of the European Parliament and of the Council of 12 June 2013 on safety of offshore oil and gas operations and amending Directive 2004/35/EC, OJ L 178/66, 28 June 2006. See also the *Protocol for the Protection of the Mediterranean Sea against Pollution Resulting from Exploration and Exploitation of the Continental Shelf and the Seabed and its Subsoil*, adopted 14 October 1994 (entered into force 24 March 2011).

[44] International Energy Agency, *Key World Energy Statistics 2011* <http://www.iea.org/publications/freepublications/publication/key_world_energy_stats-1.pdf>.

[45] International Energy Agency, *Monthly Electricity Statistics: May 2012* <http://www.iea.org/stats/surveys/mes.pdf> 1.

and the OECD Nuclear Energy Agency, while the *Euratom Treaty* is the key treaty by which the member of the EU aims to ensure the safe and sustainable use of nuclear energy.[46]

There are two broad headings under which the current numerous international instruments can be categorised: first, ensuring the safety of nuclear power; and second, putting in place effective safeguards against weapons proliferation and terrorism. Nuclear power safety issues that are addressed by law include the health and safety of workers in the nuclear energy industry, in particular protection from radiation; the prevention of nuclear accidents; the transport of nuclear materials; the transport and disposal of radioactive waste; the duty to notify other states in case of a radiological emergency or nuclear accident, and the right to seek assistance; liability for harm from nuclear accidents; and the decommissioning of nuclear power plants.[47]

C   Renewable Energy and Energy Conservation

As with oil and gas laws, the internationalisation of renewable energy laws stems from the increasingly global application of national legal principles and measures to foster the use of renewable energy. A key problem with the large-scale development and deployment of renewable energy is its cost. Historically (and at the time of writing), many sources are not cost-competitive with traditional energy sources such as coal and oil, and the technologies are not sufficiently developed to provide reliable and cost-competitive power for electricity markets, or to power consumer cars on a large scale. As a result, legal initiatives to promote renewable energy are concerned with

---

[46]   *Treaty establishing the European Atomic Energy Community*, opened for signature 25 March 1957, 298 UNTS 167 (entered into force 25 March 1957).

[47]   Some of the major IAEA Conventions in these areas are as follows: *Statute of the International Atomic Energy Agency*, opened for signature 23 October 1956, 276 UNTS 3 (entered into force 29 July 1957); *Convention on Nuclear Safety*, opened for signature 20 September 1994, [1997] ATS 5 (entered into force 24 October 1996); *Joint Convention on the Safety of Spent Fuel Management and on the Safety of Radioactive Waste Management*, opened for signature 5 September 1997, [2003] ATS 21 (entered into force 18 June 2001); *Convention on Early Notification of a Nuclear Accident*, opened for signature 26 September 1986, [1987] ATS 14 (entered into force 27 October 1986); *Convention on Assistance in the Case of a Nuclear Accident or Radiological Emergency*, opened for signature 26 September 1986, [1987] ATS 15 (entered into force 26 February 1987); *Convention on the Physical Protection of Nuclear Material*, opened for signature 3 March 1980, [1987] ATS 16 (entered into force 8 February 1987); *Treaty on the Non-Proliferation of Nuclear Weapons*, opened for signature 1 July 1968, 729 UNTS 161 (entered into force 5 March 1970); *Convention on Civil Liability for Nuclear Damage*, opened for signature 21 May 1963, 2 ILM 727 (entered into force 12 November 1977).

providing financial incentives for renewable energy development, or for reducing the gap in cost-competitiveness by, for example, the provision of subsidies to the renewable energy industry or by price support schemes; or by mandating the use of renewable energy in the supply of electricity. Other concerns relate to electricity market reform; grid integration; the removal of national legal barriers to renewable energy; and, at the international level, trade barriers.

Although there are some international agencies concerned with fostering renewable energy, these are not charged with legislative mandates, and no single international agency is charged with drafting and administering treaties. While many bodies, including IGOs and industry and community NGOs, undertake activities concerning renewable energy, the list of actors is extensive and changes constantly, with little systematic pooling of information, analysis and co-ordination at the international level. The main focus of the International Renewable Energy Agency ('IRENA'), created in Bonn on 26 January 2009, is to bring all stakeholders in renewable energy together at the global level.[48] Although IRENA's member states pledge to advance renewables in their own national policies and programs, and to promote, both domestically and through international co-operation, the transition to a sustainable and secure energy supply, IRENA itself does not have a mandate to undertake any law reform or to draft and supervise any international law in the form of treaties pertaining to renewable energy.

There is no body of treaties that deals specifically with renewable energy.[49] The same is true of energy conservation measures. While there are well-known legislative mechanisms for encouraging energy conservation — for example, vehicle fuel efficiency standards, energy efficiency standards for electrical goods and buildings, and educational and informational measures such as energy efficiency labelling of cars, electrical goods and buildings — these have very much stemmed from national measures which have spread to different countries, and are not the subject of treaties.

---

[48]   As of 11 July 2012, the European Union and 100 States were Members of the Agency, and 58 States were IRENA Signatories/applicants for membership: *IRENA: List of Members, signatories and applicants for membership as of 11.07.2012* <http://www.irena.org/DocumentDownloads/Signatory/IRENA_List_of_Members.pdf>.

[49]   As noted above, the European Union has issued a Directive on Renewable Energy, which is not a treaty but is binding on member states: *Directive 2009/28/EC of the European Parliament and of the Council of 23 April 2009 on the Promotion of the Use of Energy from Renewable Sources and Amending and Subsequently Repealing Directives 2001/77/EC and 2003/30/EC (Text with EEA relevance)* [2009] OJ L 140/16.

Again, an exception may be the very few European Union Directives regarding energy efficiency, which, although secondary sources of law, and not treaties, are binding on its member states.[50]

D   *Secondary Energy — Electricity and Gas Markets — Access to Markets, Competition Laws*

Another subset of international energy law is the set of rules concerning the functioning of electricity and gas markets. Since the 1970s, common principles of law have spread across the globe regarding the operation of electricity and gas markets, particularly with respect to the dismantling of large, integrated electricity companies into generation, transmission and distribution companies, the privatisation of electricity and gas markets, and the emergence of cross-border trading between members of the European Union and in North America. The laws cover a wide range of issues, including electricity and gas generation and distribution/transport, market arrangements (that is, rules governing buying and selling in the marketplace, including retail sales), and competition issues such as pricing and access to electricity grids and gas pipelines. These emerging common principles of law are part of international energy law, and many are expressed in what is known as European Union energy law.

V   EUROPEAN UNION ENERGY LAW

European Union energy law is an integral part or subset of 'international' energy law[51] and conversely, energy law itself has played a fundamental role in the formation of the European Union, with two of the three founding treaties focusing on energy. The initial aim of European Union energy law was to restructure the institutional and legal foundation of its members' national energy industries to develop a European Union-wide energy industry. Key issues concerned the liberalisation of national energy industries, especially the dismantling of national energy trade monopolies, and ensuring that the owners of natural monopolies (transport, storage and distribution)

---

[50]   See below n 67.

[51]   Wälde, above n 32, 192. There are many references on European Union energy law. For a recent description of the development of European Union energy law, see Ludwig Gramlich, 'Regulating Energy Supranationally: EU Energy Policy' (2012) 3 *European Yearbook of International Economic Law* 371.

provide non-discriminatory access as reasonable conditions to competitors.[52] The objectives and principles of competition law are thus an integral part of EU energy law.[53]

The main law in this respect is the *EU Treaty*,[54] with its key general provisions for freedom of movement and control of anti-competitive conduct; a series of specific Directives concerning electricity and gas markets, which began with the Electricity Market Directive of 1996[55] and the Gas Market Directive of 1998,[56] and which were later superseded by new Directives in 2003[57] and 2009[58] by the second and the third legislative packages for an internal EU gas and electricity market respectively;[59] various Regulations addressing access to gas and electricity networks,[60] and a number

---

[52]   Wälde, above n 32, 193.

[53]   On this topic, see Peter Cameron, *Competition in Energy Markets. Law and Regulation in the European Union* (Oxford University Press, 2nd ed, 2007).

[54]   *Treaty on European Union*, opened for signature 7 February 1992, [1992] OJ C 191/1 (entered into force 1 November 1993) ('*EU*'). The *Treaty of Lisbon Amending the Treaty on European Union and the Treaty Establishing the European Community*, opened for signature 13 December 2007, [2007] OJ C 306/1 (entered into force 1 December 2009). The *Treaty Establishing the European Community* has been renamed the *Treaty on the Functioning of the European Union* ('*FEU*'). For a consolidated version of the *EU* and *FEU*, see European Union Consolidated Versions of the *Treaty on European Union and of the Treaty Establishing the European Community*, OJ C 306, 17 December 2007 <http://europa.eu/lisbon_treaty/full_text/index_en.htm>.

[55]   *Directive 96/92/EC of the European Parliament and of the Council of 19 December 1996 Concerning Common Rules for the Internal Market in Electricity* [1997] OJ L 27/20.

[56]   *Directive 98/30/EC of the European Parliament and of the Council of 22 June 1998 Concerning Common Rules for the Internal Market in Natural Gas* [1998] OJ L 204/1.

[57]   *Directive 2003/54/EC of the European Parliament and of the Council of 26 June 2003 Concerning Common Rules for the Internal Market in Electricity and Repealing Directive 96/92/EC* [2003] OJ L 176/37; *Directive 2003/55/EC of the European Parliament and of the Council of 26 June 2003 Concerning Common Rules for the Internal Market in Gas and Repealing Directive 98/30/EC* [2003] OJ L 176/57.

[58]   *Directive 2009/72/EC of the European Parliament and of the Council of 13 July 2009 Concerning Common Rules for the Internal Market in Electricity and Repealing Directive 2003/54/EC (Text with EEA relevance)* [2009] OJ L 211/55; *Directive 2009/73/EC of the European Parliament and of the Council of 13 July 2009 Concerning Common Rules for the Internal Market in Natural Gas and Repealing Directive 2003/55/EC* [2009] OJ L 211/94.

[59]   The latest Electricity and Gas Directives are those under the Third Package: see <http://ec.europa.eu/energy/gas_electricity/legislation/legislation_en.htm>.

[60]   For example, *Regulation (EC) No 714/2009 of the the European Parliament and of the Council of 13 July 2009 on Conditions for Access to the Network for Cross-Border Exchanges in Electricity and Repealing Regulation (EC) No 1228/3003* [2009] OJ L 211/15; *Regulation (EC) No 715/2009 of the European Parliament and of the Council of 13 July 2009 on Conditions for Access to the Natural Gas Transmission*

of Directives and Regulations directed to other issues, such as security of supply.[61] More recently, the EU has introduced a range of measures to reduce greenhouse gas ('GHG') emissions and meet its obligations under the *Kyoto Protocol*,[62] including the EU emissions trading scheme,[63] and measures to encourage renewable energy,[64] carbon capture and storage[65] and energy efficiency.[66]

EU energy law has influence beyond those countries that are its member states. As well as the laws and Directives being binding upon its 27 member states,[67] the countries of the European Economic Area[68] apply most of the EU's energy law. The EU exports its energy laws and policies both formally and informally. The *Energy*

Networks and Repealing Regulation (EC) No 1775/2005 (Text with EEA relevance) [2009] OJ L 211/36.

[61] Kim Talus, 'OGEL Ten Years Special Issue: Internationalisation of Energy Law', Editorial (2002) 10(3) *Oil, Gas and Energy Law* <www.ogel.org>. As examples of other Directives and Regulations see also *Directive 2003/96/EC of 27 October 2003 Restructuring the Community Framework for the Taxation of Energy Products and Electricity* [2003] OJ L 283/51, and amending Directives; and *Regulation (EC) No 713/2009 of the European Parliament and of the Council of 13 July 2009 Establishing an Agency for the Cooperation of Energy Regulators (Text with EEA relevance)* [2009] OJ L 211/1.

[62] Talus, above n 62. For an overview of the EU's Climate and Energy package, see <http://ec.europa. eu/clima/policies/package/index_en.htm>. Energy efficiency is addressed separately under the EU's Action Plan for Energy Efficiency 2007-2012 and Energy Efficiency Plan 2011: see <http://ec.europa. eu/energy/efficiency/action_plan/action_plan_en.htm> and <http://europa.eu/legislation_summaries/ energy/energy_efficiency/l27064_en.htm>.

[63] *Directive 2003/87/EC of the European Parliament and of the Council of 13 October 2003 Establishing a Scheme for Greenhouse Gas Emission Allowance Trading within the Community* [2003] OJ L 275/32, plus various amending Directives, Regulations and Decisions.

[64] *Directive 2009/28/EC of the European Parliament and of the Council of 23 April 2009 on the Promotion of the Use of Energy from Renewable Sources and Amending and Subsequently Repealing Directives 2001/77/ EC and 2003/30/EC (Text with EEA relevance)* [2009] OJ L 140/16.

[65] *Directive 2009/31/EC of the European Parliament and of the Council of 23 April 2009 on the Geological Storage of Carbon Dioxide and Amending Council Directive 85/337/EEC, European Parliament and Council Directives 2000/60/EC, 2001/80/EC, 2004/35/EC, 2006/12/EC, 2008/1/EC and Regulation (EC) No 1013/2006 (Text with EEA relevance)* [2009] OJ L 140/114.

[66] See *Directive 2012/31/EC of the European Parliament and of the Council of 19 May 2010 on the Energy Performance of Buildings* [2012] OJ L 153/13; *Directive 2012/27/EU on Energy Efficiency, Amending Directives 2009/125/EC and 2010/30/EU and Repealing Directives 2004/8/EC and 2006/32/EC (Text with EEA relevance)* [2012] OJ L 315.

[67] Austria, Belgium, Bulgaria, Cyprus, the Czech Republic, Denmark, Estonia, Finland, France, Germany, Greece, Hungary, Ireland, Italy, Latvia, Lithuania, Luxembourg, Malta, the Netherlands, Poland, Portugal, Romania, Slovakia, Slovenia, Spain, Sweden and the United Kingdom.

[68] The members of the EEA are the EU and its 27 member states, plus Iceland, Liechtenstein and Norway.

Charter Treaty of 1994,[69] for example, commits its Parties to certain principles that in many ways reflect the early days of EU energy law.[70] The fundamental aim of the *Energy Charter Treaty* is to 'strengthen the rule of law on energy issues, by creating a level playing field of rules to be observed by all participating governments, thereby mitigating risks associated with energy-related investment and trade'.[71] Its key provisions concern the protection of investment, trade in energy materials and products, transit and dispute settlement. Those states that have signed the Treaty, such as Australia, are members of the Energy Charter Conference, the IGO established by the Treaty to be the governing and decision-making body for the Energy Charter process. To date, the Treaty has been signed or acceded to by 51 states, the European Community and Euratom.[72]

More recently, the *Energy Community Treaty*[73] of 2006 creates an internal market for electricity and natural gas between the 27 member states of the EU and seven European states and territories in the Balkans, who comprise the 'Energy Community'.[74] One of the crucial obligations of Contracting Parties to the Treaty is to implement part of EU legislation, the relevant '*acquis communautaire*', on energy, environment, competition and renewable energies, as well as to ensure compliance

---

[69] *Energy Charter Treaty*, opened for signature 17 December 1994, 34 ILM 360 (entered into force 16 April 1998).

[70] Talus, above n 62. The aim of the Treaty is to establish a legal framework to promote long-term co-operation in the energy sector based on the principles enshrined in the *European Energy Charter* of 1991. The *European Energy Charter* is a political declaration of the principles underpinning international energy co-operation, based on a shared interest in secure energy supply and sustainable economic development. The Energy Charter has been signed by 58 countries, including the US and Canada, as well as the European Communities. All Charter signatories are observers to the Charter process, and signing is a first and necessary step towards accession to the 1994 Energy Charter Treaty: Home Page Energy Charter <http://www.encharter.org/index.php?id=1&L=0>.

[71] Energy Charter Secretariat, *About the Charter* <http://www.encharter.org/index.php?id=7&L=0>.

[72] Ibid.

[73] *Treaty Establishing the Energy Community*, opened for signature 25 October 2005, [2006] OJ L 198/18 (entered into force 1 July 2006); see also *Council Decision 2006/500/EC of 29 May 2006 on the Conclusion by the European Community of the Energy Community Treaty* [2006] OJ L 198/15.

[74] The Parties to the Treaty are the European Union, Albania, Bosnia and Herzegovina, Croatia, the former Yugoslav Republic of Macedonia, Moldova, Montenegro, Serbia, Ukraine and the United Nations Interim Administration Mission in Kosovo. Armenia, Georgia, Norway and Turkey take part as observers. For a good article on this, see Heiko Prange-Gstöhl, 'Enlarging the EU's Internal Energy Market: Why Would Third Countries Accept EU Rule Export?' (2009) 37 *Energy Policy* 5296.

with certain general Community standards relating to technical systems[75] and to develop an adequate regulatory framework and liberalise their energy markets in line with the *acquis* under the Treaty.

Informally, the provision of technical assistance to countries through various development assistance programs, such as the Tacis (former USSR), Phare (Eastern Europe) and Synergie programs, has enabled the EU to influence energy policies in those countries.[76] It has also been seen as a pilot for integrating energy markets in other regions, with Thomas Wälde stating that 'the importance of the EU as the global economy's laboratory for modern, post-privatisation energy law as an instrument of economic and environmental regulation in emerging integrated energy markets cannot be over-estimated'.[77]

VI OTHER THEMES AND CROSS-CUTTING ISSUES

As well as identifying legal issues particular to the regulation of the markets for each energy source, various topics can be identified that cut across the whole of the international energy sector. These are all areas of specialisation in their own right. I will raise these only briefly here, in order to provide an overview of some cross-cutting topics of the practical and topical importance.

A *Energy and Environment*

The exploitation of energy is inextricably entwined with issues of environmental protection, with numerous issues of planning and environment protection and conservation law relevant to the industry. For example, the nuclear power industry has enormous potential environmental impacts, in terms of the storage and disposal

---

[75] *Treaty Establishing the Energy Community*, art 3. Title II of the Treaty, which deals with the 'Extension of the Acquis Communautaire', is organised as follows: arts 10 and 11 are directed to the Acquis on Energy, arts 12-17 to the Acquis on Environment, arts 18-19 to the Acquis on Competition, art 20 the Acquis on Renewables, arts 21-3 on Compliance with Generally Applicable Standards of the European Community, and art 21 on the Adaption and Evolution of the Acquis. *The Energy Community Treaty* (20 November 2007) Europa: Summaries of EU Legislation <http://europa.eu/legislation_summaries/energy/external_dimension_enlargement/l27074_en.htm>; see also *About Us* (30 August 2013) Energy Community, <http://www.energy-community.org/portal/page/portal/ENC_HOME/ENERGY_COMMUNITY>.

[76] Talus, above n 62; Wälde, above n 32, 196.

[77] Wälde, above n 32, 193.

of radioactive wastes, and the impacts of nuclear accidents. The onshore and offshore exploration and production of oil, the maritime transport of oil, and transport of oil by pipelines, require regulation to control the potentially negative environmental impacts of this industry, while the burning of coal in electricity has led to problems of acid rain and air pollution over large cities. Large hydro-electric plants can have massive environmental consequences because of the damming of rivers, while wind farms can affect birds and bats, create noise and interfere with landscape and amenity.

The energy industry is also inextricably entwined with the climate industry.[78] With energy use emissions from stationery energy use and from transport accounting for some 80 per cent of world greenhouse gas emissions,[79] the mechanisms for reducing greenhouse gas emissions and moving the world towards a 'low carbon economy' have a fundamental impact on the producers and users of energy.[80] Just a few of these mechanisms include carbon taxes; emissions trading schemes;[81] mechanisms such as feed-in tariffs and renewable portfolio standards which mandate the use of renewable energy in electricity; measures to improve energy efficiency standards in buildings, cars and white goods; and the support of carbon capture and storage technologies.

---

[78] The Montreal Protocol to the United Nations Convention on Substances that Deplete the Ozone Layer is also relevant to preventing climate change, as it controls emissions of chlorofluorocarbons (CFCs), which are greenhouse gases. *Vienna Convention for the Protection of the Ozone Layer*, opened for signature 22 March 1985, 1513 UNTS 293 (entered into force 22 September 1988); *Montreal Protocol on Substances that Deplete the Ozone Layer*, opened for signature 16 September 1987, 1522 UNTS 3 (entered into force 1 January 1989).

[79] Elizabeth Bossley and Andy Kerr, *Climate Change and Emissions Trading: What Every Business Needs to Know* (CEAG Ltd, 3rd ed, 2009) 37.

[80] The two major international legal instruments which comprise the response of the international community to climate change are the *United Nations Framework Convention on Climate Change*, opened for signature 14 June 1992, 1771 UNTS 107 (entered into force 21 March 1994), and the *Kyoto Protocol to the United Nations Framework Convention on Climate Change*, opened for signature 11 December 1997, 2303 UNTS 148 (entered into force 16 February 2005).

[81] While there is as yet at time of writing no single, global, international emissions trading scheme in existence, there are a number of national and regional schemes either in place or proposed. The European Emissions Trading Scheme, a regional scheme, has been in existence for some time, and forms the backbone of the billion-dollar global carbon market. Other non-European jurisdictions that have introduced an emissions trading scheme include New Zealand, Australia (currently the carbon pricing mechanism, destined to become a fully flexible ETS by 2014, unless repealed by the new Coalition government which took office in September 2013), and the US State of California, while China introduced a pilot emissions trading scheme in 2013.

The numerous environmental impacts of energy exploitation are addressed through treaties and/or domestic laws, and/or by the numerous instruments of 'soft' law which are relevant to each energy industry.

B   *Energy and Indigenous Peoples*

Issues of 'good governance' and the 'licence to operate' of corporations, which include a consideration of the social and cultural impacts of energy projects as well as the environmental impacts, is a major theme in international energy law. Particular issues include reducing the negative impacts on indigenous peoples, and the provision of social services to local communities. Again, this is an issue that cuts across energy sources. Construction of dams for large hydro-electricity projects can have devastating impacts on indigenous peoples, who may need to be relocated away from their traditional lands. The exploitation of oil and gas has had a long and often shameful history regarding local and indigenous communities. In some cases, the degradation caused by oil and gas exploration and production to the physical environment and to the health, cultural, religious and traditional economic activities of local and indigenous communities has been so devastating that a breach of human rights has occurred.[82]

Because of this, the development of various treaties and declarations,[83] and domestic laws, which pertain to the protection of human rights in general, and indigenous peoples in particular, have a cross-cutting impact on the development of energy. Again, and as a constant theme in international energy law, simply considering the formal or binding sources of law does not provide an adequate understanding of the entirety of the way in which corporate behaviour is modified or regulated. The

---

[82]   Inter-American Commission on Human Rights, *Report on the Situation of Human Rights in Ecuador*, OAS Doc OEA/Serv.L/V.II.96, doc 10, rev 1, 24 April 1997, Inter-American Commission on Human Rights <http://www.cidh.oas.org/country.htm>.

[83]   For example, the *United Nations Declaration on the Rights of Indigenous Peoples*, United Nations General Assembly, A/RES/61/295, adopted 13 September 2007; *ILO Convention (No. 169) Concerning Indigenous and Tribal Populations in Independent Countries*, 72 ILO Off Bull 59; 28 ILM 1382 (1989) (entered into force 5 September 1991); *Convention on the Elimination of All Forms of Racial Discrimination*, 660 UNTS 195; [1975] ATS 40 (entered into force 4 January 1969); *International Covenant on Civil and Political Rights*, 999 UNTS 171; [1980] ATS 23; 6 ILM 368 (1967) (entered into force 23 March 1976); *African Charter on Human and Peoples' Rights*, OAU doc CAB/LEG/67/3/Rev.5 (1981); 21 ILM 58 (1982) (entered into force 18 July 1978); and the *American Convention on Human Rights*, OAS TS No. 36 at 1; OAS Off Rec OEA/Ser.L/V/II.23, doc 21, rev 6; 9 ILM 99 (1970) (entered into force 18 July 1978).

development of an idea of 'corporate social responsibility' has been reinforced through the internal codes of conduct of transnational corporations, through the codes and guidelines of particular industry bodies (for example, the International Association of Oil and Gas Producers) and general business organisations (for example, the World Council on Sustainable Development), of multilateral lending institutions such as the World Bank, and the codes and guidelines of various NGOs.

C   Energy and Human Rights: Universal Access to Energy

Providing access to modern energy is a key policy objective in many developing countries where large parts of the population, particularly in rural areas, live without electricity for cooking, heating and light. In recent years, there has been increasing international awareness of the fundamental importance of access to energy services in eradicating poverty and achieving many of the recognised economic and social and cultural human rights.[84] Although there are no binding international commitments in public international law in relation to universal access to energy services,[85] and access to modern energy services is not recognised as an express human right in any international human rights instrument, it has been argued that

> access to energy services should be an implied human right given that many
> express rights (such as the right to education and the right to an adequate
> standard of living, to name but a few) cannot be achieved without access to
> energy services.[86]

---

[84]   See, eg, the UN Secretary-General's Advisory Group on Energy and Climate Change, *Energy for a Sustainable Future: Summary Report and Recommendations* (2010) <http://www.un.org/wcm/webdav/site/climatechange/shared/Documents/AGECC%20summary%20report[1].pdf>; United Nations General Assembly, *Resolution Adopted by the General Assembly 65/151, International Year for Sustainable Energy for All*, UN Doc A/65/436, 6 December 2010, 28-9; The UN Secretary-General's High-Level Group on Sustainable Energy for All, *Sustainable Energy for All: A Framework for Action* (January 2012) <http://www.un.org/wcm/webdav/site/sustainableenergyforall/shared/Documents/SE%20for%20All%20-%20Framework%20for%20Action%20FINAL.pdf>.

[85]   A key issue in this regard concerns the perceived tensions between achieving universal access to energy where that is sourced from traditional fossil fuels, with the need to stabilise greenhouse gas emissions to avoid climate change.

[86]   Adrian Bradbrook and Judith Gardam, 'Placing Access to Energy Services within a Human Rights Framework' (2006) 28 *Human Rights Quarterly* 389, 405. See also Adrian Bradbrook, Judith Gardam and Monique Cormier, 'A Human Dimension to the Energy Debate: Access to Modern Energy Services' (2008) 26 (4) *Journal of Energy &Natural Resources Law* 526; Stephen Tully, '*The Contribution of Human Rights to Universal Energy Access*' (2006) 4 *Northwestern Journal of International Human Rights* 518; United Nations Office of the High Commissioner for Human Rights, *Claiming the Millennium*

This issue of universal access to energy services will continue to receive growing legal attention through the possible development of a framework for access to energy services as a human right; increasing national and international action to expand access to energy, promote energy efficiency and invest in renewable energy in developing countries, which must be underpinned by law; and by a myriad of issues related to the provision of baseload power and transmission of electricity.

D   Protection of Investment

The protection of foreign investors through international investment treaties is a major topic which transcends the laws pertaining to each different source of energy. The major concern has been to achieve stability by a reduction of political and regulatory risk associated with energy production in order, thereby, to protect investment and facilitate investment flows and trade.[87] The need for legal and political stability is 'particularly acute' in the energy sector, where projects are usually long-term and highly capital-intensive.[88] The reduction of political and regulatory risk encompasses a range of issues designed to ensure a level playing field for investors and government/ state 'good governance', in contrast to corruption and cronyism, and disrespect for property and the law.

There is no agreed definition of 'international energy investment', which can be defined to include investment in the exploitation of raw materials, energy production and generation, and the transportation and distribution of energy.[89] Historically, the focus of analysis has been on oil and gas production, where the investor oil companies and host companies have had both an 'antagonistic and interdependent' relationship. Indeed, international energy law and international investment law have shared a common history with some of the first cases adjudicated by international arbitral tribunals in the twentieth century concerning the expropriation of international oil companies' property interests by host governments.[90] While disputes between

---

Development Goals: A Human Rights Approach (2008) 1 <http://www2.ohchr.org/SPdocs/Claiming_ MDGs_en.pdf?bcsi_scan_FFD951F933E7491A=0&bcsi_scan_filename=Claiming_MDGs_en.pdf>.

[87]   Thomas Wälde, 'International Energy Investment' (1996) 17 *Energy Law Journal* 191.

[88]   Yulia Selinova, 'The Energy Charter and the International Energy Governance' (2012) 3 *European Yearbook of International Economic Law* 307, 315.

[89]   Markus Krajewski, 'The Impact of International Investment Agreements on Energy Regulation' (2012) 3 *European Yearbook of International Economic Law* 343, 348-9.

[90]   Ibid 343-4.

investors in the international oil industry and host governments continue to form a key part of the case load of international dispute settlement bodies, in recent times disputes have arisen regarding the protection of investment in other energy sectors, including coal mining, coal-based power generation including coal supply, the generation and distribution of electricity, the construction of transmission lines and carbon-related energy investments.[91]

As with the entirety of international energy law, international energy investment law is not a distinct and coherent body of public international law. It arises from 'a variety of different legal sources which contain some core principles despite their heterogeneity', including bilateral investment treaties, regional free trade agreements with an investment chapter such as the *Energy Charter Treaty*; and in a broader sense, the internationalisation of principles stemming from the body of state-investor contracts signed between the foreign investor and the host government.[92] Some common principles or provisions in investment treaties and investor-government contracts include the protection against the expropriation of assets without the payment of compensation; the requirement to afford the investor fair and equitable treatment; and umbrella clauses, which require the host state to fulfil 'any other obligations' it may have entered into with regard to investments protected by a treaty.[93]

E   *Dispute Resolution*

Dispute resolution in energy industries cuts across the different energy sources, and has many different facets of interest. I will raise only a few here in the context of the international oil industry to give an idea of the range of issues of interest.

The use of international commercial arbitration in energy-related disputes has become of increasing importance since the 1970s. Of application initially in the context of disputes between international oil companies and host states in the mid-twentieth century, the use and implications of international commercial arbitration in this industry have received much attention.[94] Crucially, as discussed above, the

---

[91]   Ibid.

[92]   Ibid 353-4.

[93]   Ibid 360-1.

[94]   For an early article on this topic, see Thomas Wälde, 'The Role of Arbitration in the Globalisation of Energy Markets' (2000) 6 *The Centre for Energy, Petroleum and Mineral Law and Policy Journal* (online)

findings and decisions of international arbitral bodies, particularly in relation to disputes over oil and gas investments in the upstream sector, have contributed to an internationalisation of principles of law and led to the assertion that there is a *lex petrolea* regulating international oil and gas exploration and production. More recently, the use of arbitration has spread beyond the oil sector to encompass a range of disputes between states and investors over energy-related investments.

Other important issues of dispute resolution concern the extraterritorial application of laws, and access to the court system of the country of incorporation of large transnational corporations for environmental and/or human class actions, undertaken by people, often local or indigenous peoples, where resource exploitation (in particular oil) has occurred. Examples include legal actions undertaken by people of Ecuador against Chevron in the US;[95] by people of Nigeria against Chevron in the US[96] and Shell in the UK;[97] and people of Columbia against BP in the UK.[98]

There are many other aspects of energy-related disputes which may be resolved in international courts and tribunals — for example, maritime boundary delimitation in the International Court of Justice, which is highly relevant to determining which

---

<http://www.dundee.ac.uk/cepmlp/journal/html/vol6/article6-18.html>.

[95] *Aguinda v Chevron Texaco*; a bitter, long running and continuing court case that has moved between the US and Ecuador and also involved international commercial arbitration between Chevron and the Ecuadorean government.

[96] *Bowoto v Chevron Texaco Corp*, 312 F Supp 2d 1229 (ND Cal, 2004) was a class action lawsuit charging Chevron/Texaco Corporation with gross violations of human rights including extrajudicial killing, crimes against humanity, and cruel, inhuman or degrading treatment against villagers in the Niger Delta region who were engaging in environmental protest against Chevron. It was filed in both the US District Court for the Northern District of California and the Superior Court of California. The suit was dismissed on December 1, 2008, with the jury unanimously finding Chevron not guilty. Centre for Constitutional Rights <http://ccrjustice.org/ourcases/current-cases/bowoto-v.-chevron>.

[97] In March 2012, a unit of Royal Dutch Shell Plc (RDSA) was sued in Britain by 11 000 Nigerians seeking compensation for two massive oil spills in the Niger River delta in 2008. Erik Larson, 'Shell Sued in U.K. Over "Massive" 2008 Nigerian Oil Spills', *Bloomberg News*, 23 March 2012 <http://www.businessweek.com/news/2012-03-23/shell-sued-in-u-dot-k-dot-over-massive-oil-spills-in-nigeria-in-2008>.

[98] In 2005, more than 1000 Colombian farmers instructed British lawyers to bring a human rights challenge against BP in the High Court in London to support a claim for compensation of £15 million, arguing BP benefited from harassment and intimidation meted out by Colombian paramilitaries employed by the government to guard an oil pipeline. In 2006, the BP Exploration Company (Colombia) agreed to set up a trust fund to pay compensation in settlement of the dispute. Robert Verkaik, 'BP pays out millions to Colombian farmers', *The Independent*, 22 July 2006 <http://www.independent.co.uk/news/world/americas/bp-pays-out-millions-to-colombian-farmers-408816.html>.

state has the right to regulate offshore oil installations and levy taxes/royalties on the oil produced from them.

F Energy and Trade Law

Ensuring the free trade in energy materials and products is a major, integral sub-topic on international energy law. As Mireille Cossy has stated so succinctly, the World Trade Organisation and energy has become 'a fashionable topic'.[99] The sources of law most relevant to energy and free trade are those established by treaties, in particular the rules of the multilateral trading system established by the *General Agreement on Tariffs and Trade* ('GATT') and other WTO Agreements,[100] but also the *Energy Charter Treaty* and the *North American Free Trade Agreement* ('NAFTA').[101]

Neither the GATT nor the WTO have dealt with energy as a distinct sector (the rules of the GATT developed prior to 1947 when there was little trade in energy products and resources), nor has a special agreement on trade in energy been concluded. However, because the WTO rules are applicable to all forms of trade, they apply to trade in energy products or services, and can be enforced through the WTO dispute settlement procedures.[102] Some of the most important rules are:[103] the

---

[99] Mireille Cossy, 'Energy Trade and WTO Rules: Reflexions on Sovereignty over Natural Resources, Export Restrictions and Freedom of Transit' (2012) 3 *European Yearbook of International Economic Law* 281, 281.

[100] *General Agreement on Tariffs and Trade*, opened for signature 30 October 1947, 55 UNTS 194 (entered into force 1 January 1948); *Marrakesh Agreement Establishing the World Trade Organization*, opened for signature 15 April 1994, 1867 UNTS 3 (entered into force 1 January 1995); *Marrakesh Agreement Establishing the World Trade Organization*, opened for signature 15 April 1994, 1867 UNTS 187 (entered into force 1 January 1995) annex 1A ('*General Agreement on Tariffs and Trade 1994*'); *Marrakesh Agreement Establishing the World Trade Organization*, opened for signature 15 April 1994, 1869 UNTS 299 (entered into force 1 January 1995) annex 1C ('*Agreement on Trade-Related Aspects of Intellectual Property Rights*'); *Marrakesh Agreement Establishing the World Trade Organization*, opened for signature 15 April 1994, 1869 UNTS 401 (entered into force 1 January 1995) annex 2 ('*Understanding on Rules and Procedures Governing the Settlement of Disputes*'). Trade in services, which is an important part of energy trade, has been covered since 1995 by the *General Agreement on Trade in Services* ('*GATS*'). *Marrakesh Agreement Establishing the World Trade Organization*, opened for signature 15 April 1994, 1869 UNTS 183 (entered into force 1 January 995) annex 1B ('*General Agreement on Trade in Services*').

[101] *North American Free Trade Agreement*, Canada-Mexico-US, opened for signature 17 December 1992, 32 ILM 289 (entered into force 1 January 1994).

[102] Ludwig Gramlich, 'Regulating Energy Supranationally: EU Energy Policy' (2012) 3 *European Yearbook of International Economic Law* 371.

[103] See Gabrielle Marceau, 'The WTO in the Emerging Energy Governance Debate' (2010) 5 *Global Trade and Customs Journal* 83.

national treatment obligation, which prohibits discrimination in taxes or regulation between imported and domestic products; the most-favoured nation obligation, by which energy goods and materials cannot be discriminated against on the basis of their origin or destination; the prohibition on quantitative restrictions on import and exports; and the principle of freedom of transit.[104] Important exceptions of application to energy include arts XX and (b) and (g) which permit members to take measures 'necessary to protect human, animal and plant life and health' and measures 'relating to protection of exhaustible natural resources'. Members can also take certain measures relating to fissionable material (art XXI).[105]

Most recently, the increasing demand for renewable energy technologies within the last 2-5 years has led to fierce competition between the major producers and exporters of these technologies, in order to gain market share.[106] The existence of national laws to encourage renewable energy technology, including grants or subsidies to the manufacturers of renewable energy products, and local procurement laws, have become the subject of WTO complaints, and the degree to which countries can help support their burgeoning renewable energy sectors is now coming under scrutiny from the WTO. For example, Japan and the EU have brought two separate complaints against Canada over local content requirements in the province of Ontario's feed-in tariff scheme, with the parties disputing as to whether the scheme is a legitimate government procurement or an illegal subsidy, providing less favourable treatment to imported equipment than that accorded to like products originating in Ontario.[107]

---

[104] Cossy, above n 92, 282.

[105] Ibid 282.

[106] Ibid 281.

[107] Dispute Settlement: Dispute DS412, *Canada — Certain Measures Affecting the Renewable Energy Generation Sector* <http://www.wto.org/english/tratop_e/dispu_e/cases_e/ds412_e.htm>; Dispute Settlement: Dispute DS426, *Canada — Certain Measures Affecting the Renewable Energy Generation Sector* <http://www.wto.org/english/tratop_e/dispu_e/cases_e/ds426_e.htm>. On 22 December 2010, the United States requested consultations with China concerning certain measures providing grants, funds or awards to enterprises manufacturing wind power equipment (including the overall unit, and parts thereof) in China. See Dispute Settlement: Dispute DS419, *China — Measures Concerning Wind Power Equipment* <http://www.wto.org/english/tratop_e/dispu_e/cases_e/ds419_e.htm>. On 25 May 2012, China requested consultations with the United States concerning the imposition of countervailing duty measures by the United States. Dispute Settlement: Dispute DS437, *United States — Countervailing Duty Measures on Certain Products from China* <http://www.wto.org/english/tratop_e/dispu_e/cases_e/ds437_e.htm>

The *Energy Charter Treaty* also sets out terms under which energy can be traded and transported. It covers a wide range of energy materials and products including coal, natural gas, oil, petroleum and petroleum products, electricity, charcoal and nuclear energy.[108] Its trade framework is based on the rules established by the GATT and other WTO Agreements, and non-derogation from WTO rules is the cornerstone of the trade regime.[109] The *Energy Charter Treaty* applies the WTO rules to the trade of Contracting Parties that are not members of the WTO, whether that trade is with WTO members, or with one another. While this has historically been an important tool to extend the rules of the WTO to non-WTO members, the more recent accession of states to the WTO, particularly Eastern European states and other key energy-exporting and transit countries, will reduce the significance of this effect.[110]

G   *Financing, Taxation, Subsidies, Royalties*

Finally, and extremely briefly, there are many laws and issues concerning different aspects of financing (for example, access to finance for renewables), taxation and subsidies (issues of free trade, creating a level playing field, implicit subsidies in relation to fossil fuels and nuclear energy, encouraging investment in renewable and energy conservation) and royalties (particularly in relation to oil and gas).

VI   CONCLUSION

The supply and consumption of energy, and the legal issues associated with that supply and demand, will continue to become internationalised. There are numerous legal issues that will continue to be the focus of global developments. Of major importance will be the ongoing internationalisation and standardisation of principles of oil law, stemming from the use of common or model forms of contracts and the resolution of disputes regarding petroleum arrangements; and international developments as countries respond to the Deepwater Horizon incident off the coast of the US, in particular developments regarding the regulation of the safety of offshore oil installations, and the possible development of a regime (or regimes) for civil liability for offshore incidents by the International Maritime Organisation.

---

[108]   Annex EM I.

[109]   Selinova, above n 88, 311.

[110]   Wälde, above n 32, 184.

Other developments to monitor include the possibility of new treaties or other forms of international agreements on the security of energy supply; further developments in the intersection between resource exploitation, the environment and human and indigenous rights law; the issue of universal access to energy; and developments in climate change law, including developments in (global) carbon markets. There is likely to be a continuing internationalisation and standardisation of principles of renewable energy law and energy conservation, in particular in relation to mechanisms to encourage renewable energy sources in electricity generation and to conserve energy, and WTO decisions regarding renewable energy and trade. As these and other developments continue, International Energy Law will come into its own as a legal academic discipline.

11

PROPERTY LAW AND ENERGY LAW: ONE ACADEMIC'S PERSPECTIVE

ADRIAN J BRADBROOK

I   INTRODUCTION

My academic career has spanned over 41 years, spread over eight countries.[1] The areas that have most dominated my teaching and writing have been property law and energy law. In my opinion, these areas complement each other very effectively.

Property law is of ancient origin and is, of course, one of the mainstream common law subjects. It covers a broad range of topics, from ancient ones, such as the law of perpetuities and future interests, to modern ones, such as the law of restrictive covenants and residential leases. In nearly all common law jurisdictions its evolution over the centuries has been slow and ponderous, and has been beset by the continued application of ancient principles. These made sense at the time of their initial development and operation, but in the modern era they have operated unjustly and inappropriately because of changing societal values. I will develop and illustrate this theme later.

Energy law is a much more recent development. Unlike property law, its content is not consistent between common law jurisdictions, but tends to vary

---

[1]   The United Kingdom, Australia, Canada, the United States, France, Switzerland, Germany and Hong Kong (China).

according to the energy mix of each jurisdiction. Energy law courses originated in specific courses on oil and gas law, which developed in the late 1960s and 1970s. The courses later expanded to include additional topics due to the increased use of other energy technologies (such as nuclear energy, renewable energies and energy efficiency), and the recognition of the impact of energy production and consumption on the environment. The advent of international environmental law, which has its origins in the Stockholm Declaration on the Environment in 1972,[2] and the recognition that energy production can lead to transboundary pollution, has led to the further expansion of energy law in the past twenty years to include international as well as national laws. A classic illustration of the recognition of the relevance of international law to energy was the Chernobyl nuclear accident in the Soviet Union in 1986, which led to two new energy-related international environmental conventions: the *Convention on Early Notification of a Nuclear Accident*[3] and the *Convention on Assistance in the Case of a Nuclear Accident or Radiological Emergency*.[4]

During my career I have had the opportunity to witness and conduct legal research into many interesting aspects of, and developments in, property law and energy law. I believe that I am in a good position to offer insights into why the law has developed in the way it has and, more importantly, to suggest likely avenues of development and reform for these two legal areas. This is the purpose of this chapter.

II   PROPERTY LAW

At the start of my academic career at Dalhousie University Law School (Nova Scotia, Canada) in 1970, property law was a very unpopular course both from the perspective of students, many of who declared it to be 'boring and difficult', and from staff, who tended to shy away from the subject for reasons that they never really articulated. Like many new academics I was drafted into teaching the course by the Dean, who was unable to interest any of the more senior staff in teaching it. While I was initially depressed and anxious about teaching the course, and was reassured by other staff that I could change courses if I wished after a couple of years, I actually enjoyed teaching the subject more than my favourite course at the time — family law. In fact, I enjoyed

---

[2]   *Declaration of the United Nations Conference on the Human Environment*, 21ˢᵗ plen mtg, UN Doc A/CONF.48/14/Rev.1 (16 June 1972).

[3]   Opened for signature 26 September 1986, 25 ILM 1370 (entered into force 27 October 1986).

[4]   Opened for signature 26 September 1986, 25 ILM 1377 (entered into force 26 February 1987).

it so much that I declined all later offers to change courses and continued to teach the course in Canada, and later at the Universities of Melbourne and Adelaide, until I finally retired in 2011.

After my initial unease, I soon became aware how much the course needed reform, and how it would remain boring and difficult without a fundamental revision of its content. I should add, at the outset, that I inherited a course that was well overdue for change. One of the topics I had to learn myself, before I could teach the course, was the law of dower and curtesy, which at that time still existed in many Canadian provinces. The course paid considerable attention to the law of future interests, and to the law of perpetuities. To my mind these topics should have little (if any) attention given to them in modern property law courses. While their origin is of some historical interest, and while a handful of the ancient cases are mildly amusing (if only because of the outrageously unjust results that the application of the antiquated laws produced),[5] the course as taught in the 1960s and 1970s in most common law jurisdictions seemed to regard these topics as interesting mind games and intellectual challenges. I do not believe that this is sufficient justification for their teaching. The reality is that problems involving future interests and perpetuities rarely occur in practice, and the worst excesses of the law (such as *Shelley's case*)[6] have been modified by legislative amendment.

In contrast, the law of leases, which generates more reported court decisions than any other aspect of property law, was often given short shrift by property teachers. Other property law principles of pressing modern relevance, such as easements and restrictive covenants, also did not receive the attention in the classroom that they merited. Whilst academic challenges must be addressed, any course must bear in mind the relevance of each topic to modern practice and give the issue the appropriate weight in the course that this dictates. This point, which to me seems self-evident, is not always respected by legal academics, even today.

Arriving at the Melbourne Law School in August 1972, I discovered that property law in Australia was somewhat more progressive than in Canada, especially as the Torrens system of land registration had long since substantially replaced the system

---

5   See, eg, *Ward v Van der Loeff* [1924] AC 653; *Re Fawaz* [1958] VR 426; *Re Atkins' Will Trusts* [1974] 1 WLR 761; *Re Frost* (1889) 43 Ch D 246; *Re Wood* [1894] 2 Ch 310 (first instance); [1894] 3 Ch 381 (Court of Appeal).

6   (1581) 1 Co Rep 93b; 76 ER 206.

of deeds registration still in existence in many Canadian provinces. Nevertheless, Australian law was still rife with many legal anomalies and inconsistencies, and obscure principles of property law still seemed to dominate classroom discussion. There was still the problem of inappropriate weighting given in the classroom to the various property principles. It is still the case that the topic given the longest and most detailed attention in Australian property law courses is the Torrens system of land titles registration. To be fair, it must be accepted that as the Torrens system was a fundamental improvement to the common law system of deeds registration and that, as it was first developed in Australia[7] and later spread to many other common law jurisdictions, it is a legal development of which Australia can be justifiably proud. The topic thus merits considerable attention.

But does it really justify the overwhelming attention that it commonly receives in Australian property law courses, to the detriment of other topics? In my opinion, the answer is 'no'. It must be remembered that the Torrens system concerned the acquisition of title and, with few exceptions, did not disturb the application of common law property law principles.[8] Further, while some very significant cases on the interpretation of the Torrens legislation have been considered over the decades by the High Court, there is very little litigation generated by the law. The Torrens system had the advantage of simplifying and clarifying the law to such an extent that, in many jurisdictions, the vast majority of property transfers are now undertaken by conveyancers rather than by lawyers. For every one case involving the Torrens legislation which reaches the state Supreme Courts or the High Court, there are hundreds of cases on leases, easements and restrictive covenants. This in itself suggests that the relative weighting of topics in many current property law courses is wrong.

One topic that seems to warrant little attention is the reason (or reasons) behind why property law, unlike contracts or torts, has proved so resistant to reform. To my mind, this is a more important issue than the application of obscure principles. As far as I am aware, this topic has not been specifically examined, and is still a matter of speculation. There are a number of explanations. One factor is the lack of interest in, and (in many cases) the lack of understanding of, property law principles.

---

[7] It is arguable that the system of land titles registration was first introduced in the Hanseatic Ports of Germany and later adopted in Australia: see Antonio Esposito, 'Ulrich Hubbe's Role in the Creation of the Torrens System of Land Registration in South Australia' (2003) 24 *Adelaide Law Review* 263.

[8] See Adrian J Bradbrook et al, *Australian Real Property Law* (Thomson Lawbook, 5th ed, 2011) ch 4.

This follows from the assertion that the subject is boring, as discussed earlier. Lack of interest usually leads to minimalist study (sufficient only to pass exams), and a corresponding failure to fully comprehend the details. A further factor is the lack of available parliamentary time to consider reforms, and the competition for such time from other more easily understood subjects, such as consumer law, contracts, family law and the like. Finally, there is the fact that no electoral votes turn on the reform of obscure principles of property law, and thus there is little incentive for politicians of either political persuasion to pursue such issues.

I believe that the emphasis in property courses should be on the need for, and the process of, law reform. In the process, the rationale for the various obscure historical property law principles can be explained and made sense of, rather than treated as anomalous. The message to impart to the students here is that all property principles made logical sense at the time they were originally introduced, and it is only changes in society that have made them look absurd in modern times.

There are some fascinating matters to discuss here which, if properly explained, should dispel the unfair notion that property law is 'boring'. Let me explain this by reference to the law of leases as an illustration. It is not commonly realised, even by property law teachers, that the common law development of this subject was influenced by the fact that during the thirteenth and fourteenth centuries leases were commonly used by unscrupulous moneylenders to circumvent the church's prohibition of usury.[9] Instead of lending money to borrowers for cash interest, moneylenders demanded a lease over borrowers' lands and proceeded to lay waste to the property during the term of the lease. In this situation, where all the bargaining power was with the moneylender, it was not surprising to find the courts developing principles favouring borrowers (that is, landlords) rather than lenders (that is, tenants). From the perspective of justice, this made perfect sense. Problems arose because of the unwillingness, or seeming inability, of the common law to keep pace with the times. After the fifteenth century, the laws against usury were modified in such a way that moneylenders no longer took leases over borrowers' lands, and leases were used exclusively in the modern context — that is, possession of property for residential, commercial or agricultural purposes in return for the payment of rent to

---

9   I explored this in my PhD thesis at The University of Melbourne: *The Law Relating to the Rights and Duties of Landlords and Tenants Concerning Residential Premises: A Re-Assessment* (PhD Thesis, The University of Melbourne, 1975); see also John Forrester Hicks, 'The Contractual Nature of Real Property Leases' (1972) 24 *Baylor Law Review* 443, 448.

the landowner. During this era land ownership signified wealth and influence, and for this reason the bargaining power in relation to negotiating the terms of a lease almost inevitably favoured landlords. Despite this development, the common law continued to pursue the old principles favouring landlords. Thus, what was a fair law in earlier times became unreasonable through the later inertia of the legal profession. Especially in the residential context,[10] the common law proved so unreasonable that legislatures throughout Australia and most other jurisdictions have enacted residential tenancies legislation to replace common law principles by a more evenly balanced statutory regime.[11]

The effect is that the inaction and conservatism of the common law courts in property matters are leading to the demise of common law as a result of new legislation. The common law of leases has only very limited scope of application today. Inroads into common law principles have been made elsewhere in property law; one could cite the modern perpetuities legislation, the laws relating to adverse possession and prescription, and mortgages. Indeed, one could provocatively, but legitimately, ask whether modern property law is in reality still a common law course.

The areas of property law where there has been little legislative intervention have been easements and restrictive covenants. These areas are still governed almost exclusively by common law principles. Here again, however, anomalies and absurdities caused by the lack of change to the common law has led to a situation where the areas are ripe for the repeal of the common law and for its replacement by a legislative regime. One such illustration arises in the context of easements of light: how should a court assess the quantum of light that the beneficiary of such an easement is entitled by law to expect; and how much interference with such light can occur before the beneficiary can succeed in an action for nuisance?[12] It appears that the common law 'grumble point' method of assessment still prevails. This was defined by Eve J

---

[10] But also in the context of small retail premises leases: see *Retail Leases Act 1994* (NSW); *Retail Leases Act 2003* (Vic); *Retail Shop Leases Act 1994* (Qld); *Retail and Commercial Leases Act 1995* (SA); *Commercial Tenancy (Retail Shops) Agreements Act 1985* (WA); *Leases (Commercial and Retail) Act 2001* (ACT); *Business Tenancies Fair Dealings Act* (NT).

[11] *Residential Tenancies Act 2010* (NSW); *Residential Tenancies Act 1997* (Vic); *Residential Tenancies and Rooming Accommodation Act 2008* (Qld); *Residential Tenancies Act 1995* (SA); *Residential Tenancies Act 1987* (WA); *Residential Tenancy Act 1997* (Tas); *Residential Tenancies Act 1997* (ACT); *Residential Tenancies Act* (NT).

[12] On this point, see Adrian Bradbrook and Susan MacCallum, *Bradbrook and Neave's Easements and Restrictive Covenants* (LexisNexis, 3rd ed, 2011) 233-4 [8.21].

in *Charles Semon & Co Ltd v Bradford Corporation*[13] as 'the point whereat ordinary common sense people would begin to grumble at the quantum of light'. In light of scientific developments over the past century it is absurd to pretend that such a test is appropriate in the modern era. The common law is in danger of making a laughing stock of itself.

Still in the context of easements, other anachronisms and injustices are perpetuated by the interpretation given to the doctrine of prescription,[14] the application of s 36 of the *Law of Property Act 1936* (SA) (and its equivalent in other Australian jurisdictions),[15] and the frustrating lack of clarity in the application of the common law of easements to Torrens land.[16] As with leases, such anachronisms and absurdities are leading to calls for law reform in this area, as witnessed by the recent report on easements and restrictive covenants by the Law Reform Commission of Victoria.[17] Once again, it seems that common law's rigidity will lead to its own demise as new legislation codifying the law is enacted. Perhaps there is a loose analogy here with the rise of equity, and the courts of equity, at the expense of the common law and the King's Courts in England due to the perceived injustices caused by the common law judges' refusal to modernise the law. It is interesting to speculate.

Developments have occurred differently in the United States. In comparison with their Anglo-Australian counterparts, US judges have shown themselves far less conservative in respecting precedent in property law, and far more willing to overturn existing principles where the justice of the case demands.[18] Leases again provide a fascinating example. In the US, rather than take no action and wait for the state legislatures to intervene, the judiciary sought to counter the unfairness caused to tenants by the application of the *caveat emptor* principle by developing new, and extending existing, contractual common law principles and doctrines for application in the law of leases: for example, constructive eviction,[19] interdependence

---

[13]   [1922] 2 Ch 737, 747. See also *Fishenden v Higgs and Hill* (1935) 153 LT 128, 137.

[14]   See Bradbrook et al, above n 8, ch 5.

[15]   *Conveyancing Act 1919* (NSW) s 67; *Property Law Act 1958* (Vic) s 62; *Property Law Act 1974* (Qld) s 239; *Property Law Act 1969* (WA) s 41; *Conveyancing and Law of Property Act 1884* (Tas) s 6.

[16]   See Bradbrook and MacCallum, above n 12, ch 11.

[17]   Victorian Law Reform Commission, *Easements and Restrictive Covenants*, Report No 22 (2011).

[18]   I discussed this issue in Adrian J Bradbrook, 'The Role of the Judiciary in Reforming Landlord and Tenant Law' (1976) 10 *Melbourne University Law Review* 459.

[19]   See, eg, *Reste Realty Corp v Cooper*, 251 A 2d 268 (NJ, 1968).

of covenants,[20] and mitigation of damages.[21] As a result, in many states in the US the common law of leases continues to apply as the legislatures saw no reason to intervene by enacting new legislation.

How could property law possibly be regarded as 'boring' with such issues to discuss in the classroom? The fault surely lies with the teachers rather than the subject matter.

III   ENERGY LAW

My interest in energy law is of more recent origin. The subject did not exist in the typical law school curriculum at the start of my academic career in 1970. Modern interest in the subject has its origin in the oil shocks of the 1970s and 1980s, as a result of the creation of the Organisation of Petroleum Exporting Countries ('OPEC') and the Arab embargo against some Western nations. This in turn led Western, oil-importing nations to establish the International Energy Agency ('IEA'), which was designed to ensure that no effective oil embargos could occur in the future. It was in the 1980s that some law schools in Australia, and other countries with significant oil supplies, commenced courses in oil and gas law, but other aspects of energy were largely ignored. It was not until the mid-1990s that courses on energy law were commonly found in law school curricula. There were a number of reasons for this development:

1.   This was the era of privatisation of the electricity and gas industries in most Western countries. Previously the industries had operated as government monopolies under their own legislation. The effect of this was that pricing and other major decisions affecting consumers were totally at the discretion of the government of the day. The only effective remedy for disgruntled consumers was political rather than legal, and energy-related decisions by governments were largely dictated by electoral factors rather than the prudent development of the industries. The effect of privatisation was to create law, and legal remedies, where none had existed before.

---

[20]   *Pines v Perssion*, 111 NW 2d 409 (Wis, 1961); *Marini v Ireland*, 265 A 2d 526 (NJ, 1970); *Javins v First National Realty Corp*, 428 F 2d 1071 (DC Cir, 1970).

[21]   See, eg, *Roberts v Watson*, 195 NW 211 (Iowa, 1923); *Vawter v McKissick*, 159 NW 2d 538 (Iowa, 1968).

2. The effect of climate change and other environmental concerns (such as acid rain, ozone depletion, and air pollution in major cities) has led society to seek out alternative sources of energy in place of traditional fossil fuels. One of these is nuclear energy, which is favoured by some developed countries (particularly France and Belgium) but outlawed in some others (such as Australia and New Zealand).[22] In countries using nuclear energy there is now comprehensive national legislation covering its production, its environmental effects and its safety aspects. This has again created work for the legal profession.

    Other sources of energy which have rapidly developed in recent years include energy efficiency and renewable energy resources. In most countries, energy efficiency is being promoted in all sectors of the economy: transport, industry, buildings and consumer goods. Energy efficiency is sometimes referred to as a 'Cinderella issue', as it has attracted only limited government subsidies and comparatively little discussion in legal circles. Recent research by the IEA shows, however, that energy efficiency can potentially make a greater contribution to stabilising carbon dioxide emissions than all other energy sources (including nuclear energy).[23] Energy efficiency is perhaps discounted because it does not generate new energy, but instead simply reduces the rate of consumption of existing energy. However, this is a misleading characterisation. As Amory Lovins once noted,[24] a unit of energy saved is equivalent to a unit of energy generated. He coined the phrase 'negawatt' (a negative watt) to make this point. 'Renewable energy resources' includes a multitude of different technologies: solar energy, wind energy (both onshore and offshore), geothermal energy, hydro-electric power, biomass, and ocean energy (tidal, wave and ocean thermal energy conversion). In the long-term there is a possibility for a major energy-generating contribution from hydrogen and (conceivably) nuclear fusion. These new technologies have produced, and continue to produce new, complex legislation in most developed countries.

---

[22] See, eg, *Nuclear Activities (Prohibition) Act 1983* (Vic).

[23] International Energy Agency, *World Energy Outlook 2006* (International Energy Agency, 2006) 192.

[24] Amory B Lovins, *Soft Energy Paths: Toward a Durable Peace* (Penguin Books, 1977); Amory B Lovins, 'Negawatts: Twelve Transitions, Eight Improvements and One Distraction' (1996) 24 *Energy Policy* 331.

3. Another aspect of energy which has interested me has been the expansion of the subject from a purely national one to one that is in part international. All the time that energy resources consisted solely of fossil fuels, energy policy and law was almost exclusively national. The advent of other energy sources (particularly nuclear), together with the recognition that energy production and consumption can have transboundary environmental consequences, has resulted in energy law becoming significantly internationalised. In this context it is worth remembering that energy production and consumption is responsible for up to 95 per cent of all atmospheric carbon dioxide emissions,[25] and that therefore the problem of climate change cannot be effectively tackled without addressing energy from a global perspective. The trend towards internationalisation in this field has been strengthened by the rapid increase of international trade in energy resources, which has led to a number of international conventions.[26] The trend has also been boosted by advances in technology. For example, wind farms are no longer limited to onshore facilities regulated by national law but have been constructed at sea, and now fall under the international law of the sea. As a result of this trend, there are now several courses offered in law schools on international energy law.

4. The advent of sustainable development, based on the Brundtland Report in 1986,[27] as a cornerstone of international environmental law has opened up a new field of research in energy law. As stated in the Report, renewable energy and energy efficiency are at the cutting edge of sustainable development.[28] Such development will not occur unless, and until, the energy sector adopts sustainable development principles. The

---

[25] According to the Global Carbon Project, in 2011, coal burning (43 per cent), oil (34 per cent), and gas (18 per cent) accounted for 95 per cent of CO_2 emissions into the atmosphere: Global Carbon Project, *Global Carbon Budget: Highlights* (2012) <http://www.globalcarbonproject.org/carbonbudget/12/hl-full.htm>.

[26] See, eg, *Energy Charter Treaty*, opened for signature 17 December 1994, 34 ILM 360 (entered into force 16 April 1998).

[27] World Commission on Environment and Development, *Our Common Future* (Oxford University Press, 1987).

[28] Ibid 240.

law has a major role to play in this context, as such a move requires the creation of laws and policies consistent with this goal.[29]

My interest in energy law and policy began around 1979, and occurred almost accidentally. At that time I was preparing the first edition of my book (with Marcia Neave) entitled *Easements and Restrictive Covenants*, which was published by Butterworths Pty Ltd in 1980. While researching the different types of easements recognised historically by the common law, I came across articles written in US law journals on the possibility of an easement of solar access.[30] This was argued to be either an extension of the traditional easement of light, or a novel easement that fitted within the recognised common law parameters of easements. Further research showed that at that time there was no effective protection against the shading of solar collectors by tall buildings erected on neighbouring land, or the growth of large trees on such land. This struck me as important from an environmental perspective, as why would anyone invest several thousand dollars in erecting a solar device on his or her roof if a neighbour could block solar access, and thereby render the device ineffective with impunity? Having finished my book on easements and restrictive covenants, I pursued the issue of the legal protection of solar access from an Australian perspective and published my first energy law article on this issue in the *University of New South Wales Law Journal* in 1982.[31]

The US perspective on this subject, and the promotion of solar energy generally, was extensively considered and researched during the Presidency of Jimmy Carter from 1976 to 1980; he established and generously funded the Solar Energy Research Center in Golden, Colorado. This institution contained a substantial legal section,

---

[29]   I have conducted extensive research on this topic: see Adrian J Bradbrook, Judith G Gardam and Monique Cormier, 'A Human Dimension to the Energy Debate: Access to Modern Energy Services' (2008) 26 *Journal of Energy & Natural Resources Law* 526; Adrian J Bradbrook and Judith G Gardam, 'Energy and Poverty: A Proposal to Harness International Law to Advance Universal Access to Modern Energy Services' (2010) 57 *Netherlands International Law Review* 1.

[30]   See, eg, Russel J Adams, 'An Analysis of Solar Legislation — Taxes and Easements' (1979) 14 *Land and Water Law Review* 393; Ralph E Becker, Jr, 'Common Law Sun Rights: An Obstacle to Solar Heating and Cooling?' (1976) 3 *Journal of Contemporary Law* 19; W Wade Berryhill and William H Parcell III, 'Guaranteeing Solar Access in Virginia' (1979) 13 *University of Richmond Law Review* 423; Melvin M Eisenstadt and Albert E Utton, 'Solar Rights and Their Effect on Solar Heating and Cooling' (1976) 16 *Natural Resources Journal* 363.

[31]   Adrian J Bradbrook, 'The Development of an Easement of Solar Access' (1982) 5 *University of New South Wales Law Journal* 229.

which even produced a law journal dedicated to the subject — the *Solar Law Reporter*. Sadly, this era came to a rapid end with the election in 1980 of President Ronald Reagan, who in his first year of office reduced funding for solar energy research in the US by 90 per cent, and abolished the Solar Energy Research Center. The last edition of the *Solar Law Reporter* was published in early 1982. While this funding-cut did not affect legal research in American law schools, the growing body of legal articles on solar energy dried up very rapidly and little (if any) research on renewable energy laws was done during the remainder of the decade. At one stage I wondered if I was the only legal academic continuing to research this area of energy law in the world! Interest in this area did not return until the mid-1990s, largely driven by the climate change debate. I am delighted that there is now a substantial body of legal scholars, both in Australia and elsewhere, who are continuing legal research where I left off.

During the 1980s I was fortunate to receive a substantial research grant from the National Energy Research Development and Demonstration Council ('NERDDC'), as it was then called, to conduct further legal research designed to promote solar energy and wind energy. Thus, my interest in solar energy expanded to include wind energy, which in turn further expanded to geothermal energy when I received a further grant from NERDDC to investigate the promotion of this energy source in Australia. My interest in renewable energy resources led naturally to a consideration of the law relating to energy efficiency, which I discovered to be a vast, legally unexplored area, as different laws had to be developed to foster efficiency in each sector of the economy. This research was in turn fostered by several grants received from the Australian Research Council ('ARC').

Of course, property law and energy law share more in common than easements of solar access. Besides easements, my research over the years has considered the application to energy law of the law of leases, proprietary licences, *profits à prendre* and restrictive covenants. It has also investigated the ownership of airspace and the subsoil, and the creation of new property rights.[32] In truth, I like the contrast between property law, with its fascinating history dating back almost a millennium and its ancient common law principles, and energy law, with its very limited history and its train of rapid development. There is also a contrast between my research collaborators. Property law research is regarded as 'lawyer's law', and is limited to

---

[32]   Adrian J Bradbrook, 'The Relevance of the *Cujus Est Solum* Doctrine to the Surface Landowner's Claims to Natural Resources Located Above and Beneath the Land' (1988) 11 *Adelaide Law Review* 462.

the legal profession and legal academics; energy law requires an engagement with a wide variety of non-legal professionals working on energy-related matters, such as architects, engineers and town planners. Over my academic life, I have alternated my research activities between these two areas of law, and have found that the contrasts have continually rejuvenated my research.

IV FUTURE DEVELOPMENTS: PROPERTY LAW

Where is property law heading in the foreseeable future? Gazing into a crystal ball and making an educated guess, I suggest as follows:

1 *The first and most obvious change is the abolition of the law of perpetuities and all existing anomalies relating to future interests*

This change has been recommended by various academics for years.[33] This abolition has already occurred in South Australia,[34] and the adoption of this legislation has generated little controversy.

2 *The abolition of adverse possession and prescriptive rights*

Both principles are based on the notion that unless landowners actively protect their legal rights in respect of land, such rights may be lost (adverse possession) or made subject to rights acquired by others (prescription). While it is reasonable to expect landowners to enforce their rights if threatened by persons illegally entering their land over sustained periods of time, the common law in relation to adverse possession is unnecessarily complex and, over the centuries, has produced some bizarre decisions.[35] In relation to prescription, the continued application in some states of the obscure provisions of the *Prescription Act 1832* (UK) seems anachronistic.[36] All Australian jurisdictions apply the fiction of the lost modern grant, whereby the rights of illegal entrants onto other persons' land is legally justified by the common law fiction that

---

[33] See, eg, W Barton Leach, 'Perpetuities Reform: London Proposes, Perth Disposes' (1964) 6 *University of Western Australia Law Review* 11.

[34] *Law of Property Act 1936* (SA) s 61 (added in 1996). The operation of this law is explained in Bradbrook et al, above n 8, 531 [11.115].

[35] See Bradbrook et al, above n 8, ch 3.

[36] The UK legislation still applies in South Australia and Western Australia: see Bradbrook and MacCallum, above n 12, 152 [5.41]ff.

they did so pursuant to a grant by the landowner which has been lost.[37] Such fictions and principles are simply inappropriate in the modern era, and are inconsistent with the concepts justifying the Torrens system of title registration.

3   *The abolition of all remaining land titles subject to the deeds registration system*

For many decades the Torrens legislation in each jurisdiction has contained provisions allowing for existing common law titles to be converted to the Torrens system. Despite this, there are still significant parcels of land outside the Torrens system in some states (Victoria and New South Wales), particularly in inner city areas where development occurred early after first settlement, and there is no sign that this will change in the foreseeable future. Land transfers of such parcels are rendered more expensive and the title more uncertain. The work of the legal profession is rendered more complex than necessary. It is time to introduce legislation requiring all remaining common law titles to be converted to the Torrens system, and for the existing deeds registration legislation to be repealed.

4   *The existing Torrens legislation in all States and Territories should be harmonised in order to promote simplicity in the law and to render interstate land dealings less complex legally, and less expensive*

The first jurisdiction to introduce Torrens legislation was South Australia in 1858.[38] While other jurisdictions were undoubtedly influenced by the terms of this legislation, the details of the legislation, which was highly controversial at the time, were argued separately and strenuously in the legislatures and different outcomes were produced. In earlier times, when there was comparatively little interstate emigration, there was little problem, but the existence in Australia of eight different versions of the Torrens legislation (one for each state and territory) makes little sense and is inefficient. There is no intrinsic reason why the details and application of this law should vary across the country.

5   *The existing common law relating to easements and restrictive covenants should be rationalised by legislation*

There is an overlap between the two areas as in some (but not all) cases the same goal could be achieved by using either easements or restrictive covenants. For example,

---

[37]   See *Bryant v Foot* (1867) LR 2 QB 161 and the discussion in Bradbrook and MacCallum, above n 12, 132-3 [5.7]ff.

[38]   *Real Property Act 1858* (SA).

if landowners wish to ensure that they have a sufficient right of support for any building proposed to be erected on their land, they could achieve this aim either by negotiating an easement of support or by negotiating a restrictive covenant, whereby the neighbour would agree not to build or excavate his or her land within a specified distance of the land boundary. Research on the protection of solar access, discussed above,[39] shows that such access could be achieved by either easements *or* restrictive covenants.[40] Conceptually, there is a world of difference between easements and restrictive covenants: easements are protected by the law of nuisance whereas restrictive covenants are protected by a modified extension of the law of contracts into the realm of property. The law of easements is of ancient origin, dating back to Roman law,[41] whereas the law of restrictive covenants is more modern, having only been developed by the English courts during the nineteenth century in the well-known case of *Tulk v Moxhay*.[42] The Law Reform Commission of England and Wales produced a Working Paper — as long ago as 1971 — on statutory reforms required in this area, and, in particular, considering whether easements and restrictive covenants should be replaced by a single statutory land obligation.[43] Such a change would be equally appropriate in Australia, and would simplify and clarify the law.

6   *The common law applying to commercial leases should be codified*

As a result of legislation passed in recent times to codify the law relating to residential tenancies and retail tenancies in all jurisdictions, there are now effectively three separate bodies of law relating to leases: the common law, the law of residential tenancies and the law of retail tenancies. While the scope of the retail tenancies legislation varies between the jurisdictions, in general terms the common law of leases is now restricted in its application to industrial leases and leases of large commercial premises. The rationale for these exemptions is presumably that in these situations there is an approximate equality of bargaining power between landlords and tenants, and that such tenants do not need the statutory forms of protections contained in the residential and retail tenancies legislation. While this may be the case, such tenants

---

[39]   Above nn 30-1 and accompanying text.

[40]   Adrian J Bradbrook, 'The Role of Restrictive Covenants in Furthering the Application of Solar Technology' (1983) 8 *Adelaide Law Review* 286.

[41]   Bradbrook and MacCallum, above n 12, 1 [1.1].

[42]   (1848) 2 Ph 774; 41 ER 1143.

[43]   Law Reform Commission of England and Wales, *Transfer of Land: Appurtenant Rights*, Working Paper No 36 (1971).

are still disadvantaged by the application of the *caveat emptor* principle. There are some very interesting decisions of the High Court of Australia debating the extent to which contractual rules should apply to the proprietary concept of leases,[44] but such conceptual niceties could be avoided, and the law made more certain, by statutory intervention. In addition, there are some very quaint common law rules relating to leases which have no relevance to the modern era of business transactions: for example, the law of waste, the obligations of the respective parties to repair the premises, the implied condition of fitness of habitation by the landlord, and the rules relating to covenants 'touching and concerning' the land.[45] Simplicity requires that there should be one law of leases. There is sufficient similarity of content between the residential tenancies and retail legislation that they could be merged into one enactment, and there seems to be no reason why this could not extend to all leases.

7   It is important that the law moves with the times, and that new and novel rights should be recognised as proprietary

This could be achieved either as part of the common law process, or by legislation. It is unfortunate that the Anglo-Australian courts have been reluctant to extend the existing range of recognised proprietary rights. A good example is *Victoria Park Racing and Recreation Grounds Co Ltd v Taylor*,[46] where the High Court refused to recognise the right to broadcast a spectacle as a property right. It is only in exceptional cases, such as *Mabo v Queensland [No 2]*[47] where the rights to indigenous lands were recognised as proprietary, that new proprietary rights have been recognised. Indeed, there are dicta by some well-known and well-respected members of the judiciary to the effect that the common law should act very cautiously in creating new property rights; even a jurist as far-sighted as Lord Denning stated in *Phipps v Pears* that courts should be very chary of creating any new negative easements.[48] As discussed earlier in a different context,[49] US judges have adopted a far less conservative approach. A good

---

[44]   *Shevill v Builders' Licensing Board* (1982) 149 CLR 620; *Progressive Mailing House Pty Ltd v Tabali Pty Ltd* (1985) 157 CLR 17; *Laurinda Pty Ltd v Capalaba Park Shopping Centre Pty Ltd* (1989) 166 CLR 623.

[45]   See Bradbrook et al, above n 8, ch 14.

[46]   (1937) 58 CLR 479.

[47]   (1992) 175 CLR 1. See also *Wik Peoples v Queensland* (1996) 187 CLR 1.

[48]   [1965] 1 QB 76, 82-3.

[49]   Above nn 18-21 and accompanying text.

illustration is *Prah v Maretti*,[50] where the Wisconsin Supreme Court held that a right of solar access to solar collectors on a householder's roof could exist at common law. American state legislatures also seem less conservative in this respect. For example, in some states the right to solar access is now declared to be a property right.[51]

V   Future Developments: Energy Law

A   At the National Level

Where is the law relating to sustainable energy heading in the foreseeable future? This is by no means an easy question to answer, as energy planning has been notoriously unsuccessful in the past. In fact, it has been so unsuccessful that energy policy advisers now prefer to prepare energy scenarios, rather than energy plans, in light of the prevailing uncertainty.

The first task in formulating a response to this question is to determine which energy sources we should be encouraging in order to foster a viable sustainable energy future. The most obvious contributor to sustainable energy is energy efficiency. This needs to be promoted in all sectors of the economy. Recent research by the International Energy Agency shows that energy efficiency can potentially make a greater contribution to stabilising carbon dioxide emissions than all the other energy sources (including nuclear energy).[52]

Many industrialised countries have already legislated to promote energy efficiency. Such legislation tends to be piecemeal, in the form of amendments to specific legislation and building codes rather than in the form of comprehensive new legislation. This amended legislation tends to be patchy in its scope. For example, some countries have legislated to promote energy efficiency in certain types of domestic goods but not others. Some countries have limited their measures to strict regulations, without adopting financially stimulating measures (such as tax incentives) or educational measures (such as energy consumption labelling on domestic appliances). This suggests that legislators in some countries do not recognise the full potential scope of the role of the law in achieving a new sustainable energy future.

[50]   321 NW 2d 182 (Wis, 1981).

[51]   Illustrations are cited in Adrian J Bradbrook, 'Australian and American Perspectives on the Protection of Solar and Wind Access' (1988) 28 *Natural Resources Journal* 229, 240.

[52]   International Energy Agency, above n 23, 192.

In developed nations we should expect to see, in the foreseeable future, a more comprehensive approach to legislating for energy efficiency at the national level. There is little justification for inaction as there is no environmental downside to energy efficiency, and many existing precedents for legislators to follow. However, the situation in developing nations is far less clear. In countries where a large percentage of the population lacks access to modern energy services,[53] the notion of energy efficiency is regarded as totally irrelevant. Yet if efficiency is ignored in the drive towards developing new energy generation capacity, there will be profligate squandering of the remaining fossil-fuel resources, and unnecessary aggravation of atmospheric carbon dioxide emissions and other environmental issues. For developing nations, the best that can be hoped for is that while achieving access to modern energy services and economic development, energy efficiency measures are included as an adjunct to all new legislation. This will only occur, however, if the significance of energy efficiency is continually brought to the attention of national leaders and legislators.

In relation to renewable energy resources, the basic starting premise should be that the development of all commercially exploitable renewable energy resources should be encouraged by national governments, including by new legislation where appropriate. However, it would be a mistake to assume that all renewable energy resources are environmentally benign. Wind energy development onshore is often controversial due to a variety of alleged environmental problems: aesthetic injury, bird kills, television and radio reception interference as well as health issues arising from the noise of the rotating turbines.[54] Hydro-electricity development can cause the displacement of indigenous populations and the drowning of agricultural land. Biomass can be problematic due to the displacement of food crops in favour of energy crops. Geothermal energy can cause pollution to waterways and extreme noise problems.[55] Even solar energy is not free from environmental controversy, as noted elsewhere.[56]

---

[53] This issue is discussed in detail above: see above nn 30-1 and accompanying text.

[54] Adrian J Bradbrook, 'Nuisance and the Right of Solar Access' (1983) 15 *University of Western Australia Law Review* 148; republished as Adrian J Bradbrook, 'Nuisance and the Right of Solar Access' (Occasional Paper No 6, University of Colorado Natural Resources Law Center, 1984).

[55] See Adrian J Bradbrook, 'Environmental Controls Over Geothermal Energy Exploitation' (1987) 4 *Environmental and Planning Law Journal* 5.

[56] See Adrian J Bradbrook, 'The Tortious Liability of the User of a Solar Energy System' (1983) 14 *Melbourne University Law Review* 151.

It is necessary to strike a balance between the environmental issues associated with renewable energy and the need to promote a clean energy future. The solution is obviously subjective. I suggest, however, that the way forward is for national governments to adopt the following forms of legislative control:

1. Wind planning guidelines should be included in local planning controls, so as to ensure that development does not unduly disrupt the life of nearby residents.[57] Where practicable, offshore wind farms should be preferred.

2. Geothermal legislation regulating the exploitation of the resource should be adopted in all jurisdictions where the resource exists in exploitable quantities.

3. Small-scale 'run of the river' hydro-electric schemes (less than 10 MW) should be favoured over large-scale hydro-electric schemes. Small-scale schemes do not involve damming rivers and flooding agricultural land, and appear to have no adverse environmental consequences.

What is the position regarding nuclear energy? The issue is highly controversial and there is little consensus worldwide. The advent of concern over climate change over the past 20 years has given a boost to the resource as (apart from the process of plant construction) nuclear energy emits only very small quantities of carbon dioxide emissions. Climate change concerns led to a short-term renaissance of nuclear energy in the first decade of this century, and helped to erase memories of the Chernobyl disaster in 1986. Sadly for the nuclear industry, however, the fears that a nuclear accident can result in extreme environmental and health consequences were resurrected as a result of the Fukushima disaster in March 2011, and some countries are now curtailing or abandoning future use of this energy source.

Regardless of the differing views of the environmental safety of nuclear energy, it appears that this energy source is not the panacea for the world's future energy needs, as suggested by some industry representatives. The reality is far different from that mooted in the 1950s, when the International Atomic Energy Authority was established by the United Nations to promote the resource worldwide,[58] and nuclear

---

[57] See, eg, Department of Planning and Community Development (Vic), 'Planning and Policy Guidelines for Development of Wind Energy Facilities in Victoria' (Guidelines, July 2012) amendments VC 82, VC 91.

[58] *Statute of the International Atomic Energy Agency*, opened for signature 23 October 1956, 276 UNTS 3 (entered into force 29 July 1957).

energy was touted as potentially too cheap to meter. In fact, nuclear energy has proved to be significantly more expensive to produce than traditional fossil fuel-fired energy sources. In addition, nuclear energy can only be profitably used in countries or areas where there is a large and dense population due to the need for economies of scale. Further, the problems of the disposal of nuclear waste, which it was confidently assumed would be shortly resolved, have proved to be intractable and no satisfactory scientific solution appears to be in sight, despite decades of intense research. In countries where the electricity industry is privatised, insurance has also proven to be impossible to obtain as the consequences of a nuclear accident are potentially so devastating that nuclear energy is considered an uninsurable risk. This has meant that governments have been forced to legislate to limit the financial liability of nuclear companies in the case of accidents. Finally, it should be noted that research by the IEA shows that nuclear energy is likely to make only a minor contribution to sustainable energy future. The agency has predicted that the contribution of nuclear energy to achieving global, sustainable atmospheric carbon dioxide emissions by 2030 is only approximately 10 per cent.[59]

In my opinion, for all the above reasons, nuclear energy will not play a part in sustainable energy solutions for the long-term. It goes without saying, however, that those countries that continue to use this resource must adopt, at the national level, all the necessary controls developed by international conventions, including procedures for safety, the disposal of nuclear waste, the notification of nuclear accidents, the reprocessing of nuclear waste, the transport of nuclear waste and the recruitment of international assistance in a nuclear emergency.[60] In addition, national laws requiring greater oversight of the operations of nuclear companies would appear to be necessary following the revelations of the failures and negligence of the Tokyo Electric Power Company ('TEPCO'), the operator of the Fukushima plant, in Japan. National laws will also be required in respect of storage facilities for nuclear wastes, and the long-term liability for such storage facilities will need to be established by legislation.

---

[59] International Energy Agency, above n 23, 192.

[60] See, eg, *Convention on Nuclear Safety*, opened for signature 17 June 1994, 1963 UNTS 293 (entered into force 24 October 1996); *Convention on Early Notification of a Nuclear Accident*, opened for signature 26 September 1986, 25 ILM 1370 (entered into force 27 October 1986); *Convention on Assistance in the Case of a Nuclear Accident or Radiological Emergency*, opened for signature 26 September 1986, 25 ILM 1377 (entered into force 26 February 1987).

B   At the International Level

Although detailed energy policies will in most cases be legislated by national governments, international developments have the capacity to shape the direction of such policies.

Significant change is necessary in respect of international institutions. The United Nations has devoted considerable attention over the past decade to the promotion of sustainable energy, but its efforts have often been uncoordinated. Research and policy development has been undertaken within the United Nations by the United Nations Development Programme ('UNDP'), the United Nations Environment Program ('UNEP'), the Department of Economic and Social Affairs ('UN DESA') and most of the six regional economic commissions. While there is an overarching program called UN-Energy, this is merely an information exchange rather than a policy development facility.

The basic need is for a United Nations agency focused on sustainable energy development. The agency could be modelled on the existing International Atomic Energy Agency ('IAEA'). This institution was established in 1957 with the function of promoting the worldwide development of nuclear energy. Its focus has since expanded to tackle the wide range of environmental and safety concerns associated with such development. While there is a considerable cost associated with the creation of a new agency, which nations may not be willing to bear, it will be possible either to expand the role of the IAEA (and rename it) so as to include all aspects of sustainable energy development or, in light of the limited future potential of nuclear energy, to focus exclusively on sustainable development.

Significantly, in response to the frustration felt by many nations about the lack of international action supporting sustainable development, the German government has recently taken the initiative by taking the lead role in the creation of the International Renewable Energy Agency ('IRENA').[61] A Statute was created for IRENA, which has now entered into in effect, having acquired the requisite number of state parties.[62] This agency has already commenced policy and scientific research, but lacks the imprimatur of the United Nations. A simple and cost-effective option

---

[61]   See International Renewable Energy Agency <www.irena.org>.

[62]   As at January 2013 there are 104 state parties to the Statute, as well as the European Union. Additionally, there are 55 state signatories to the Statute.

would be for the United Nations to adopt this agency, while (preferably) expanding its role beyond that of renewable energy to include other aspects of sustainable energy, particularly energy efficiency.

A further necessary development in the coming decades is for non-governmental organisations ('NGO's) to become more actively involved in energy issues and policy development. In light of the large number of environmentally focused and effective NGOs, it is perhaps surprising that this has not occurred already. The reasons for this are unclear, and have been considered elsewhere.[63] Historically, it appears that the major and most respected environmental NGOs, such as the International Union for the Conservation of Nature ('IUCN') and the World Wildlife Fund ('WWF'), have focused on the physical environment and, while accepting that energy is important from an environmental perspective, have felt more uncomfortable and less willing to focus their attention on this area. These attitudes are slowly changing as the role of energy in the climate change debate is being progressively highlighted, but much remains to be done.

Turning to international instruments, there is considerable scope for further action on a number of energy-related matters.

One important development would be the adoption by the United Nations General Assembly of a declaration either supporting sustainable energy generally, or supporting renewable energy and energy efficiency specifically. Such a declaration in other areas in the past has had a powerful influence in focusing world attention on necessary reforms. The best illustration of this is the United Nations' *Universal Declaration of Human Rights*,[64] which has taken this issue from relative obscurity to centre stage in world politics. A parallel declaration on sustainable energy could similarly advance the cause of sustainable energy worldwide.

In addition to a sustainable energy declaration, we need either a new international convention supporting sustainable energy, or a new protocol to an existing convention on sustainable energy. If the latter approach is adopted, a new protocol on sustainable energy could be added to the *United Nations Framework Convention on Climate Change* ('UNFCCC') or the *Energy Charter Treaty* ('ECT'). The UNFCCC is perhaps the most appropriate vehicle in light of the large number of

---

[63] See Adrian J Bradbrook, 'Energy Law: The Neglected Aspect of Environmental Law' (1993) 19 *Melbourne University Law Review* 1.

[64] GA Res 217A (III), UN GAOR, 3rd sess, 183rd plen mtg, UN Doc A/810 (10 December 1948).

ratifications to the convention and the close link between energy and climate change. While the ECT is an energy-focused convention, its application is limited by the fact that it has only 52 state parties, and does not cover many major energy consuming and producing nations (the US, Canada, Brazil, India, China and South Africa).

What provision should the new convention or protocol contained? I suggest clauses relating to the following issues:

1. Establishing domestic programs for energy efficiency and conservation;

2. Creating binding, differentiated targets for nations to increase their electricity supply from renewable energy resources;

3. In the case of developed countries, creating binding, differentiated targets for nations to reduce energy intensities, and by so doing improve energy efficiency;[65]

4. Integrating energy considerations, including energy efficiency, affordability and accessibility, into socio-economic programs;

5. Developing and utilising indigenous energy sources and infrastructures for various local uses;

6. Promoting increased research and development in the fields of renewable energy, energy efficiency, and advanced and cleaner fossil fuel technologies;

7. Adopting the principle of externalities costings when examining competing energy sources, so that the price of each source reflects its environmental impacts;[66]

8. Providing for the transfer on concessional terms to developing nations of advanced, cleaner, more efficient, affordable, and cost-effective energy technologies;

9. Requiring nations to develop policies promoting sustainable energy by reducing market distortions and phasing out subsidies to fossil fuel industries.

From the standpoint of developing nations, perhaps the most important energy issue to be addressed is the need to provide universal access to modern energy

---

[65]   This issue is explored in Adrian J Bradbrook, 'The Development of a Protocol on Energy Efficiency and Renewable Energy to the United Nations Framework Convention on Climate Change' (2002) 5 *New Zealand Journal of Environmental Law* 5.

[66]   See Richard L Ottinger et al, *Environmental Costs of Electricity* (Oceana Publications, 1990).

services.[67] The United Nations has recently been focusing its attention on this area and declared 2012 to be the Year of Sustainable Energy for All.[68] The concern of the UN is based on the fact that reports undertaken by various UN agencies have shown that in many developing nations less than 10 per cent of the population have access to electricity and modern cooking facilities. Worldwide, over 1.6 billion people lack such access, the majority being located in Sub-Saharan Africa and South Asia.[69] The reports have shown that the lack of access to modern energy services entrenches poverty, causes respiratory diseases (due to indoor air pollution resulting from the burning of wood and animal dung for cooking), makes medical care difficult (due to the lack of refrigeration) and renders schooling difficult (due to the lack of electric light).[70] While energy was not mentioned in the Millennium Development Goals ('MDG's) declared by the UN General Assembly in its Millennium Declaration 2000,[71] none of the nine declared goals can be achieved without access to modern energy services.

What role could international law play in achieving access to modern energy services? One option would be for an additional protocol focused on the issue, which would require international co-operation and support to achieve the desired goal. Another option with potential would be to work towards the recognition that access to modern energy services is essential to the achievement of the vast bulk of economic, social and cultural human rights, and so to invoke the existing human rights network of obligations and protections. While it is unrealistic to imagine that individuals could achieve access to energy services by litigating against their national government, the recognition of energy access as a human right would bring significant pressure to

---

[67] For a detailed discussion of this issue, see above nn 30-1 and accompanying text.

[68] See *International Year of Sustainable Energy for All*, GA Res 65/151, UN GAOR, 65th sess, 69th plen mtg, Agenda Item 20, UN Doc A/RES/65/151 (16 February 2011).

[69] International Energy Agency, above n 23, 157. Generally speaking, the problem of access to modern energy services in most developed countries was overcome early in the 20th century, in many cases by the introduction of national legislation: see, eg, *Rural Electrification Act*, 7 USC §§ 901-950b (1936).

[70] The first major investigation in this area (and still the most influential) is UN Department of Economic and Social Affairs, UN Development Programme and World Energy Council, *World Energy Assessment: Energy and the Challenge of Sustainable Development* (2000). See also: UN Department of Economic and Social Affairs, UN Development Programme and World Energy Council, *World Energy Assessment: Overview 2004 Update* (2004).

[71] *United Nations Millennium Declaration*, GA Res 55/2, UN GAOR, 55th sess, 2nd mtg, Agenda Item 60b, UN Doc A/Res/55/2 (18 September 2000).

bear on national governments to take action. Any international instrument in this field would need to include measures for technology transfer and new, additional funding for developing countries, as otherwise the costs would be prohibitive.

It is important to be realistic as to what is likely to be achieved. While all of the possible future actions discussed above could be adopted at both the national and international levels, it would be naïve to assume that this will occur. In all likelihood, only a limited number will come into effect. There are a range of factors that make significant progress in sustainable energy difficult, which include: the vested interests of fossil fuel industry leaders, who are reluctant to reduce their operations and influence; the large costs of developing and adopting new technologies; the lack of political influence of leaders in the sustainable energy industries, relative to their competitors; the lack of foresight and knowledge of politicians about energy-related issues; and the inability of political leaders to see beyond the next election.

VI CONCLUSION

My 41-year academic career represents only a very short period in the history of the common law, which extends back nearly a millennium. Yet despite my complaints in this chapter relating to the antiquity and anachronism of certain laws, it must be recognised that during my career law reform and modernisation has proceeded apace. Ground-breaking changes have included the *Family Law Act 1975* (Cth) and the *Trade Practices Act 1974* (Cth), now renamed the *Competition and Consumer Act 2010* (Cth). Instead of courses on Roman Law I and Roman Law II, which I studied at Cambridge University in the late 1960s, we now find in modern law school curricula courses on superannuation law, consumer law, sports law and the like. Outside the fields of property law and energy law even the courts have created some new remedies, especially in the field of equitable doctrine and remedies.

But is it enough? The fundamental issue of the day, in my opinion, is whether common law is capable of keeping pace with the times — consistently, and in all areas of law. The common law developed several centuries ago during an era where societal changes proceeded very slowly, if at all. As discussed above in the context of property law, on many occasions where common law has failed to change, the legislature has intervened to amend and codify the law. The effect of this has been to slowly erode the areas of law where the common law continues to operate. Looking at the common law more broadly, while torts law continues to operate largely unaffected by statutory intervention,[72] nearly all of the common law of contracts appears to be subject to statutory control, and large swathes of property law have seen legislative intervention. In the context of new areas of development, such as energy law, the contribution of the common law has been minimal and almost all new laws have been created by legislation.

By adopting a conservative approach to the development of the common law, the courts appear to be unwittingly destroying the common law, as disgruntled litigants take their complaints to the state legislatures. As noted above, common law lost jurisdiction to the equity courts in the sixteenth century as a result of its refusal to abandon its conservative approach to change. Are we now repeating history? By the end of the current young academics' careers in approximately 40 years' time, will the role of the courts simply be that of interpreting legislation?

---

[72] Although even here there has been some legislative intervention: for example, in the field of occupiers' liability law: see, eg, *Occupiers' Liability Act 1985* (WA); *Civil Liability Act 1936* (SA) pt 4.

Adrian J Bradbrook — A Selected Bibliography

Arranged alphabetically under each category.
Republished works listed as separate entries.

A   Books

1.   *A Manual of the Victorian Residential Tenancies Act* (Lawbook, 1982) (with JG Gardam and SV MacCallum)

2.   *Australian Property Law: Cases and Materials* (LBC Methuen, 1st ed, 1996) (with SV MacCallum and AP Moore)

3.   *Australian Property Law: Cases and Materials* (Thomson Lawbook, 2nd ed, 2003) (with SV MacCallum and AP Moore)

4.   *Australian Property Law: Cases and Materials* (Thomson Lawbook, 3rd ed, 2006) (with SV MacCallum and AP Moore)

5.   *Australian Property Law: Cases and Materials* (Thomson Lawbook, 4th ed, 2011) (with SV MacCallum, AP Moore, S Grattan and L Griggs)

6.   *Australian Real Property Law* (Butterworths, 1st ed, 1991) (with SV MacCallum and AP Moore)

7.   *Australian Real Property Law* (Thomson Lawbook, 2nd ed, 1997) (with SV MacCallum and AP Moore)

8.   *Australian Real Property Law* (Thomson Lawbook, 3rd ed, 2001) (with SV MacCallum and AP Moore)

9.   *Australian Real Property Law* (Thomson Lawbook, 4th ed, 2008) (with SV MacCallum and AP Moore)

10. *Australian Real Property Law* (Thomson Lawbook, 5th ed, 2011) (with SV MacCallum, AP Moore and S Grattan)

11. *Bradbrook and Neave's Easements and Restrictive Covenants* (Butterworths, 3rd ed, 2011)

12. *Commercial Tenancy Law* (Butterworths, 1st ed, 1990) (with CE Croft)

13. *Commercial Tenancy Law* (Butterworths, 2nd ed, 1997) (with CE Croft)

14. *Commercial Tenancy Law* (LexisNexis Butterworths, 3rd ed, 2009) (with CE Croft and R Hay)

15. *Easements and Restrictive Covenants in Australia* (Butterworths, 1st ed, 1981) (with MA Neave)

16. *Easements and Restrictive Covenants in Australia* (Butterworths, 2nd ed, 2000) (with MA Neave)

17. *Energy Conservation Legislation for Building Construction and Design* (Canadian Institute of Resources Law, 1992)

18. *Energy Law and the Environment* (Cambridge University Press, 2007) (with R Lyster)

19. *Family Law: Cases and Commentary* (Butterworths, 1st ed, 1986) (with HA Finlay and RJ Bailey-Harris)

20. *Family Law: Cases, Materials and Commentary* (Butterworths, 2nd ed, 1993) (with HA Finlay and RJ Bailey-Harris)

21. *Poverty and the Residential Landlord-Tenant Relationship* (Australian Government Publishing Service, 1975)

22. *Residential Tenancy Law and Practice* (Lawbook, 1983) (with SV MacCallum and AP Moore)

23. *Revenue Law: Cases and Materials* (Butterworths, 1990) (with Y Grbich and K Pose)

24. *Solar Energy and the Law* (Lawbook, 1984)

B   Edited Books

25. (ed), *Energy Law and Sustainable Development* (IUCN Publications, 2003) (with R Ottinger)

26. (ed), *Property and the Law in Energy and Natural Resources* (Oxford University Press, 2010) (with A McHarg, B Barton and L Godden)

27. (ed), *The Emergence of Australian Law* (Butterworths, 1989) (with MP Ellinghaus and AJ Duggan)

28. (ed), *The Law of Energy for Sustainable Development* (Cambridge University Press, 2005) (with R Lyster, R Ottinger and Wang Xi)

C   Articles

29. 'Sustainable Energy Law: the Past and the Future' (2012) 30(4) *Journal of Energy & Natural Resources Law* 511

30. 'A Human Dimension to the Energy Debate: Access to Modern Energy Services' (2008) 26 *Journal of Energy & Natural Resources Law* 526 (with JG Gardam and M Cornier)

31. 'A Reassessment of the Laws Relating to the Determination of Tenancies' (1976) 5 *Adelaide Law Review* 357

32. 'A Reassessment of the Scope of the Gift *Mortis Causa*' (1971) 17 *McGill Law Journal* 567

33. 'A Statement of Principles for a Global Consensus on Sustainable Energy Production and Consumption (2001) 19 *Journal of Energy & Natural Resources Law* 143

34. 'Access to Landlocked Land: A Comparative Study of Legal Solutions' (1983) 10 *Sydney Law Review* 39

35. 'Advising a Purchaser of Land on Easements and Freehold Covenants' (1984) 58 *Law Institute Journal* 651

36. 'Australian and American Perspectives on the Protection of Solar and Wind Access' (1988) 28 *Natural Resources Journal* 229

37. 'An Empirical Study of the Attitudes of the Judges of the Supreme Court of Ontario Regarding the Workings of the Present Child Custody Adjudication Laws' (1971) 49 *Canadian Bar Review* 557

38. 'An Empirical Study of the Need for Reform of the Victorian Rent Control Legislation' (1975) 2 *Monash University Law Review* 82

39. 'Australian Initiatives Promoting Renewable Energy Resources in Electricity Generation' (2005) 23 *Journal of Energy & Natural Resources Law* 188 (with AS Wawryk)

40. 'Constitutional Implications of the Restructuring of the Electricity Industry' (1996) 3 *Australasian Journal of Natural Resources Law and Policy* 239

41. 'Creating Law for Next Generation Energy Technologies' (2011) 2 *George Washington Journal of Energy and Environment Law* 2

42. 'Creeping Reforms to Landlord and Tenant Law: The Case of Boarders and Lodgers' (2004) 10 *Australian Property Law Journal* 157

43. 'Discrimination Against Families in the Provision of Rented Accommodation' (1978) 6 *Adelaide Law Review* 439 (with SV MacCallum)

44. 'Eco-labelling: Lessons from the Energy Sector' (1996) 18 *Adelaide Law Review* 35

45. 'Electric Power Interconnection in North-East Asia: Towards a North-East Asian Energy Charter?' (2002) 20 *Journal of Energy & Natural Resources Law* 135

46.   'Energy and Poverty: A Proposal to Harness International Law to Advance Universal Access to Modern Energy Services' (2010) 57 *Netherlands International Law Review* 1 (with JG Gardam)

47.   'Energy Conservation Legislation for Industry' (1992) 10 *Journal of Energy & Natural Resources Law* 145

48.   'Energy Efficiency and the Energy Charter Treaty' (1997) 14 *Environmental and Planning Law Journal* 327

49.   'Energy Efficiency in Road Transport after the WSSD: An Evolving Area of Environmental Law' (2003) 20 *Environmental and Planning Law Journal* 16

50.   'Energy Law as an Academic Discipline' (1996) 14 *Journal of Energy & Natural Resources Law* 193

51.   'Energy Law: The Neglected Aspect of Environmental Law' (1993) 19 *Melbourne University Law Review* 1

52.   'Energy Use and Atmospheric Protection' (1996) 3 *Australasian Journal of Natural Resources Law and Policy* 25

53.   'Energy, Sustainable Development and Motor Fuels: Legal Barriers to the Use of Ethanol' (1999) 16 *Environmental and Planning Law Journal* 196 (with AS Wawryk)

54.   'Environmental Aspects of Energy Law — New Means of Achieving Reform' (1993) 10 *Environmental and Planning Law Journal* 185

55.   'Environmental Aspects of Energy Law: The Role of the Law' (1994) 5 *International Journal of Renewable Energy* 1278

56.   'Environmental Controls Over Geothermal Energy Exploitation' (1987) 4 *Environmental and Planning Law Journal* 5

57.   'Fencing Easements in Australia' (1979) 53 *Australian Law Journal* 306

58.   'Future Directions in Solar Access Protection' (1988) 19 *Environmental Law* 167

59.   'Government Initiatives Promoting Renewable Energy for Electricity Generation in Australia' (2002) 25 *University of New South Wales Law Journal* 124 (with AS Wawryk)

60.   'Green Power Schemes: The Need for a Legislative Base' (2002) 26 *Melbourne University Law Review* 15

61.   'Le Développement du Droit sur les Énergies Renouvelables et les Économies d'Énergie' (1995) 47 *Revue Internationale de Droit Comparé* 527

62. 'Legal Aspects of Promoting Energy Cogeneration' (1989) 6 *Environmental and Planning Law Journal* 332

63. 'Legal Issues for Lay Commercial Arbitrators' (1998) 20 *Adelaide Law Review* 265

64. 'Legislative Implementation of Financial Mechanisms to Improve Motor Vehicle Fuel Efficiency' (1998) 22 *Melbourne University Law Review* 537 (with AS Wawryk)

65. 'Liability in Nuisance for the Operation of Wind Generators' (1984) 1 *Environmental and Planning Law Journal* 128

66. 'Loss of Services: An Anachronistic Alternative to the Child Custody Laws' (1977) 4 *Monash University Law Review* 71 (with RRS Tracey)

67. 'Methods of Improving the Effectiveness of Substandard Housing Control Legislation in Australia' (1976) 5 *University of Tasmania Law Review* 166

68. 'Motor Vehicle Registration Charges as a Means for Improving Fuel Efficiency' (1998) 15 *Environmental and Planning Law Journal* 33

69. 'Nuisance and the Right of Solar Access' (1983) 15 *University of Western Australia Law Review* 148

70. 'Placing Access to Energy Services within a Human Rights Framework' (2006) 28 *Human Rights Quarterly* 389 (with JG Gardam)

71. 'Recent Developments in Partnership Taxation' (1988) 1 *Corporate and Business Law Journal* 12

72. 'Regulating for Fuel Efficiency in the Transport Sector' (1994) 1 *Australasian Journal of Natural Resources Law and Policy* 1

73. 'Rented Housing Law: Past, Present and Future' (2003) 7 *Flinders Journal of Law Reform* 1

74. 'Residential Landlord-Tenant Law Reform in Tasmania' (1978) 6 *University of Tasmania Law Review* 83

75. 'Residential Tenancies Law — Lessons from France' (1997) 5 *Australian Property Law Journal* 107

76. 'Residential Tenancies Law — The Second Stage of Reforms' (1998) 20 *Sydney Law Review* 402

77. 'Section 27 of the Uniform Commercial Arbitration Acts: A New Proposal for Reform' (1990) 18 *Australian Business Law Review* 214

78. 'Section 27 of the Uniform Commercial Arbitration Acts: A New Proposal for Reform' (1990) 9 *The Arbitrator* 107

79. 'Solar Access Law: 30 Years On' (2010) 27 *Environmental and Planning Law Journal* 5

80. 'Solar Access Legislation' (1984) 58 *Law Institute Journal* 1054

81. 'Teaching Arbitration to Non-Lawyers' (1998) 17 *The Arbitrator* 173

82. 'The Access of Wind to Wind Generators' (1986) 20 *South Wind* 7

83. 'The Access of Wind to Wind Generators' [1984] *Australian Mining and Petroleum Law Association Yearbook* 433

84. 'The Actions for Double Rent and Double Value Against Overholding Tenants' (1978) 13 *University of Western Australia Law Review* 420

85. 'The Application of the Principle of Mitigation of Damages to Landlord-Tenant Law' (1977) 8 *Sydney Law Review* 15

86. 'The Contents of New Geothermal Legislation' (1987) 5 *Journal of Energy & Natural Resources Law* 81

87. 'The Delivery of Deeds in Victoria' (1981) 55 *Australian Law Journal* 267

88. 'The Development of a Protocol on Energy Efficiency and Renewable Energy to the United Nations Framework Convention on Climate Change' (2001) 5 *New Zealand Journal of Environmental Law* 55

89. 'A Legislative Framework for Renewable Energy and Energy Conservation' (1997) 15 *Journal of Energy & Natural Resources Law* 313

90. 'The Development of a Regulatory Framework on Consumer Protection and Consumer Information for Sustainable Energy Use' (2000) 5 *Asia Pacific Journal of Environmental Law* 239

91. 'The Development of an Easement of Solar Access' (1982) 5 *University of New South Wales Law Journal* 229

92. 'The Development of Energy Conservation Legislation for Private Rental Housing' (1991) 8 *Environmental and Planning Law Journal* 91

93. 'The Development of Energy Efficiency Laws for Domestic Appliances' (1990) 12 *Adelaide Law Review* 306

94. 'The Discretionary Powers of the Hong Kong Housing Authority' (1977) 7 *Hong Kong Law Journal* 209

95. 'The Scope of Protection for Leases Under the Victorian Transfer of Land Act' (1988) 16 *Melbourne University Law Review* 837

96. 'The Future of Domestic Rent Control in Hong Kong' (1978) 7 *Hong Kong Law Journal* 321

97. 'The International Legal Development of Energy Conservation and

Renewable Energy Technologies' (1992) 9 *Environmental and Planning Law Journal* 31

98. 'The Law Relating to the Residential Landlord-Tenant Relationship: An Initial Study of the Need for Reform' (1974) 9 *Melbourne University Law Review* 589

99. 'The Legal Regime Governing the Exploitation of Offshore Wind Energy in Australia' (2001) 18 *Environmental and Planning Law Journal* 30 (with AS Wawryk)

100. 'The Legal Right to Solar Access' (2011) 68 *Environment Design Guide* 1

101. 'The Legal Right to Solar Access' [1996] (February) *Environment Design Guide* 1

102. 'The Liability of the User of a Wind Generator in Tort for Personal Injuries' (1985) 15 *Melbourne University Law Review* 249

103. 'The New Era of Tenancy Protection' (1987) 61 *Australian Law Journal* 593

104. 'The Ownership of Geothermal Resources' [1987] *Australian Mining and Petroleum Law Association Yearbook* 353

105. 'The Protection of Solar Access' (1985) 59 *Law Institute Journal* 1326

106. 'The Relevance of Psychological and Psychiatric Studies to the Future Development of the Law Governing the Settlement of Inter-Parental Child Custody Disputes' (1972) 11 *Journal of Family Law* 557

107. 'The Relevance of the *Cujus Est Solum* Doctrine to the Surface Landowner's Claims to Natural Resources Located Above and Beneath the Land' (1988) 11 *Adelaide Law Review* 462

108. 'The Repair Obligations of Landlords and Tenants: A Plea for Reform' (1976) 12 *University of Western Australia Law Review* 437

109. 'The Retail Tenancies Legislation: Stage Two in the Landlord-Tenant Law Reform Saga' (1989) 15 *Monash University Law Review* 2

110. 'The Right of a Mother to Change her Child's Surname Unilaterally' [1977] *Australian Current Law Digest* 111

111. 'The Rights and Duties of Landlords and Tenants Under the Victorian Residential Tenancies Act' (1981) 13 *Melbourne University Law Review* 159

112. 'The Role of Judicial Discretion in Child Custody Adjudication in Ontario' (1971) 21 *University of Toronto Law Journal* 402

113. 'The Role of Restrictive Covenants in Furthering the Application of Solar Energy Technology' (1983) 8 *Adelaide Law Review* 286

D   Book Chapters

129. 'International Institutional Arrangements in Support of Renewable Energy' in D Assmann (ed), *Renewable Energy: A Global Review of Technologies, Policies and Markets* (Earthscan Publication, 2007) 152 (with A Steiner, T Waelde and F Schutyser)

130. 'Legal Issues relating to Electricity Production by Offshore Wind Turbines' in P Catania, B Golchert and C Zhou (eds), *Energy 2000: The Beginning of a New Millennium* (Technomic Publishing and Balaban International Science Publishers, 2000) 1105

131. 'Mining and the Environment: The Legal Perspective' in K Anderson (ed), *Finding Common Ground: Mining, the Environment, and Indigenous Australians* (Centre for International Economic Studies, 1996) 1

132. 'Promotion of National Legislation for Energy Conservation: Advocacy for Market Transparency and Sustainable Development' in *Guidebook on Promotion of Sustainable Energy Consumption* (United Nations, 2002) 50

133. 'Property and the Law in Energy and Natural Resources' in A McHarg et al (eds), *Property and the Law in Energy and Natural Resources* (Oxford University Press, 2010) 1 (with A McHarg, B Barton and L Godden)

134. 'Regulatory Framework for the Promotion of Energy Conservation and Energy Efficiency in Australia' in *Compendium of Energy Efficiency Legislation in Countries of the Asia and Pacific Region: Volume One* (United Nations, 1999) 113

135. 'Resource Use Conflicts: The Role of the Common Law' in M Ross and J O Saunders (eds), *Resource Use Conflicts* (Canadian Institute of Resources Law, 1993) 344

136. 'Solar Access and the Law of Restrictive Covenants' in SV Szokolay (ed), *Solar World Congress: Proceedings of the Eighth Biennial Congress of the International Solar Energy Society, Perth, 14-19 August, 1983* (Pergamon Press, 1984) vol 4, 2625

137. 'Study Methods and Sitting Law Exams' in J Corkery (ed), *A Career in Law* (Federation Press, 2nd ed, 1989) 140

138. 'Study Methods and Sitting Law Exams' in J Corkery (ed), *The Study of Law* (Adelaide Law Review Association, 1988) 110

139. 'Study Methods and Sitting Law Exams' in R Krever (ed), *Mastering Law Studies and Law Exam Techniques* (Butterworths, 2nd ed, 1989) 58

140. 'Study Methods and Sitting Law Exams' in R Krever (ed), *Mastering Law*

Studies and Law Exam Techniques (Butterworths, 3rd ed, 1995) 59

141. 'The Australian Torrens System: A Reappraisal' in D Meurer and H Leser (eds), *Aktuelle Entwicklungen des Rechts aus Deutscher und Franzosischer Sicht* (Institute fur Rechtsvergleichung, 2001) 87

142. 'The Commercial Arbitration Legislation' in Vicki Waye (ed), *A Guide to Arbitration Practice in Australia* (Institute of Arbitrators and Mediators Australia, 2001) 55

143. 'The Development of Renewable Energy Technologies and Energy Efficiency Measures through Public International Law' in D Zillman et al (eds), *Beyond the Carbon Economy: Energy Law in Transition* (Oxford University Press, 2008) 109

144. 'The Evolution of Australian Landlord and Tenant Law' in MP Ellinghaus, AJ Bradbrook and AJ Duggan (eds), *The Emergence of Australian Law* (Butterworths, 1989) 104

145. 'The Rights and Duties of Landlords and Tenants Under the Victorian Residential Tenancies Act' in Leo Cussen Institute for Continuing Legal Education, *The New Residential Tenancies Act: Papers Delivered at a Seminar Held at the Leo Cussen Institute on 14th and 25th February 1981* (1981) 72

146. 'The Role of the Common Law in Promoting Sustainable Energy Development in the Property Sector' in A McHarg, B Barton, A Bradbrook and L Godden (eds), *Property and Law in Energy and Natural Resources* (Oxford University Press, 2010) 391

147. 'The Rule Against Perpetuities' in *Halsbury's Laws of Australia* (Law Book Co, 2000) ch 28.6

148. 'The Taxation of Partnerships' in R Krever (ed), *Australian Taxation: Principles and Practice* (Longman Professional, 1987) 212

E   *Theses*

149. *The Inter-Parental Conflict Over Ownership of Children: Judicial Discretion versus Behavioral Science* (LLM Thesis, Osgoode Hall, York University, 1970)

150. *The Law Relating to the Rights and Duties of Landlords and Tenants Concerning Residential Premises: A Re-Assessment* (PhD Thesis, The University of Melbourne, 1975)

151. *Renewable Energy Resources in Australia: Legal Planning for the Year 2000* (LLD Thesis, The University of Melbourne, 1987)

F *Other*

152. 'Liability in Nuisance for the Operation of Wind Generators' (Occasional Paper No 5, University of Colorado Natural Resources Law Center, 1984)
153. 'Nuisance and the Right of Solar Access' (Occasional Paper No 6, University of Colorado Natural Resources Law Center, 1984)
154. 'The Access of Wind to Wind Generators' (Occasional Paper No 7, University of Colorado Natural Resources Law Center, 1985)

TABLE OF CASES AND LEGISLATION

I   AUSTRALIA

A   *Legislation*

Aboriginal Heritage Act 2006 (Vic)

Agricultural Reserves Act 1859 (Qld)

Building Energy Efficiency Disclosure Act 2010 (Cth)

Business Tenancies Fair Dealings Act (NT)

Civil Law (Sale of Residential Property) Act 2003 (ACT)

Civil Liability Act 1936 (SA)

Clean Energy Act 2008 (Qld)

Commercial Tenancy (Retail Shops) Agreements Act 1985 (WA)

Competition and Consumer Act 2010 (Cth)

Conservation, Forests and Lands Act 1987 (Vic)

Conveyancing Act 1919 (NSW)

Conveyancing and Law of Property Act 1884 (Tas)

Crown Land (Reserves) Act 1978 (Vic)

Development (Regulated Trees) Amendment Act 2009 (SA)

Development (Significant Trees) Amendment Act 2000 (SA)

Development Act 1993 (SA)

Development Regulations 2008 (SA)

Electricity (Feed-In Scheme — Solar Systems) Amendment Act 2008 (SA)

Electricity Supply Act 1995 (NSW)

Electricity Supply General Regulation 2001 (NSW)

Energy Legislation Act 2000 (Vic)

Environment Effects Act 1978 (Vic)

Environmental Protection and Biodiversity Conservation Act 1999 (Cth)

Fair Trading Act 1987 (SA)

Family Law Act 1975 (Cth)

Flora and Fauna Guarantee Act 1988 (Vic)

Forests Act 1958 (Vic)

Heritage Places Act 1993 (SA)

Land Act 1958 (Vic)

Landlord and Tenant (Rental Bonds) Act 1977 (NSW)

Law of Property Act 1936 (SA)

Leases (Commercial and Retail) Act 2001 (ACT)

National Consumer Credit Protection Act 2009 (Cth)

Native Title Act 1993 (Cth)

Native Vegetation Act 1991 (SA)

Natural Resources Management Act 2004 (SA)

Nuclear Activities (Prohibition) Act 1983 (Vic)

Occupiers' Liability Act 1985 (WA)

Planning and Environment Act 1987 (Vic)

Property Law Act 1958 (Vic)

Property Law Act 1969 (WA)

Property Law Act 1974 (Qld)

Real Property Act 1858 (SA)

Renewable Energy (Electricity) Act 2000 (Cth)

Residential Parks Act 2004 (NSW)

Residential Tenancies (Miscellaneous) Amendment Act 2013 (SA)

Residential Tenancies Act (NT)

Residential Tenancies Act 1987 (WA)

Residential Tenancies Act 1995 (SA)

Residential Tenancies Act 1997 (ACT)

Residential Tenancies Act 1997 (Vic)

Residential Tenancies Act 2010 (NSW)

Residential Tenancies and Rooming Accommodation Act 2008 (Qld)

Residential Tenancy Act 1997 (Tas)

Retail and Commercial Leases Act 1995 (SA)

Retail Leases Act 1994 (NSW)

Retail Leases Act 2003 (Vic)

Retail Shop Leases Act 1994 (Qld)

Sustainable Planning Act 2009 (Qld)

Town and Country Planning Act 1944 (Vic)

Trade Practices Act 1974 (Cth)

Traditional Owners Settlement Act 2010 (Vic)

B Cases

Apriaden Investments Pty Ltd v Seacrest Pty Ltd (2006)12 VR 319

BP Refinery (Westernport) Pty Ltd v Shire of Hastings (1977) 180 CLR 266

Casey v Aldous (1994) 63 SASR 347

EPA v Great Southern Energy [1999] NSWLEC 192

EPA v The Shell Company of Australia Ltd [1999] NSWLEC 16

Fejo v Northern Territory (1998) 195 CLR 96

Hislop & Ors v Glenelg SC , (Unreported, Victorian Civil and Administrative Tribunal, Tribunal Application No. 1997/88762)

Laurinda Pty Ltd v Capalaba Park Shopping Centre Pty Ltd (1989) 166 CLR 623

Mabo v Queensland [No 2] (1992) 175 CLR 1

Maridakis v Kouvaris (1975) 5 ALT 197

Members of the Yorta Yorta Aboriginal Community v Victoria (2002) 214 CLR 422

Northern Sandblasting Pty Ltd v Harris (1997) 188 CLR 313

Perry v Hepburn Shire Council (2007) 154 LGERA 182

Progressive Mailing House Pty Ltd v Tabali Pty Ltd (1985) 157 CLR 17

Radaich v Smith (1959) 101 CLR 209

Shevill v Builders' Licensing Board (1982) 149 CLR 620

Taralga Landscape Guardians Inc v Minister for Planning and RES Southern Cross Pty Ltd (2007) 161 LGERA 1

Thackeray v Shire of South Gippsland [2001] VCAT 739

Victoria Park Racing and Recreation Grounds Co Ltd v Taylor (1937) 58 CLR 479

Western Australia v Ward (2002) 191 ALR 1

Wik Peoples v Queensland (1996) 187 CLR 1

II NEW ZEALAND

A Legislation

Bill of Rights Act 1990 (NZ)

Building Act 2004 (NZ)

Consumer Guarantees Act 1993 (NZ)

Education Act 1989 (NZ)

Energy Efficiency and Conservation Act 2000 (NZ)

Fair Trading Act 1986 (NZ)

Health Act 1956 (NZ)

Housing Corporation Act 1974 (NZ)

Housing Improvement Regulations 1947 (NZ)

Real Estate Agents Act 2008 (NZ)

Real Estate Agents Act (Professional Conduct and Client Care) Rules 2009 (NZ)

Residential Tenancies Act 1986 (NZ)

Urban Renewal and Housing Improvement Amendment Act 1969 (NZ)

B   Cases

Balcairn Guest House Ltd v Weir [1963] NZLR 301

Felton v Brightwell [1967] NZLR 276

Gabolinscy v Hamilton City Corp [1975] 1 NZLR 150

Garden City Developments Ltd v Christchurch City Council (Unreported, HC Christchurch, AP168/92, 29 July 1992)

Hiatt v Christchurch City Council (Unreported, HC Christchurch, A179/77, 7 October 1980)

Housing NZ Corp v Ladbrook [2010] DCR 102

Jackson v McClintock (1998) 8 TCLR 161

Lawson v Housing New Zealand [1997] 2 NZLR 474

Small v Lawry [2011] NZTT Hamilton 11/01447/HN (26 September 2011)

III   United Kingdom

A   Legislation

Energy Act 2011 (UK)

Energy Performance of Buildings (Certificates and Inspections) (England and Wales) Regulations 2007 (UK)

Prescription Act 1832 (UK)

Waste Lands Act 1842 (Imp)

B   Cases

Aussie Traveller Pty Ltd v Marklea Pty Ltd [1998] Qd R 1

Bryant v Foot (1867) LR 2 QB 161

Cavalier v Pope [1906] AC 428

IV   UNITED STATES OF AMERICA

A   *Legislation*

B   *Cases*

EME Homer City Generation LP v EPA, 696 F 3d 7 (DC Cir, 2012)

Javins v First National Realty Corp, 428 F 2d 1071 (DC Cir, 1970)

Marini v Ireland, 265 A 2d 526 (NJ, 1970)

Pierson v Post, 3 Cai R 175 (NY Sup Ct, 1805)

Pines v Perssion, 111 NW 2d 409 (Wis, 1961)

Prah v Maretti, 321 NW 2d 182 (Wis, 1981)

Reste Realty Corp v Cooper, 251 A 2d 268 (NJ, 1968)

Roberts v Watson, 195 NW 211 (Iowa, 1923)

Vawter v McKissick, 159 NW 2d 538 (Iowa, 1968)

V INTERNATIONAL

A *Treaties*

African Charter on Human and Peoples' Rights, OAU doc CAB/LEG/67/3/Rev.5 (1981); 21 ILM 58 (1982) (entered into force 18 July 1978)

American Convention on Human Rights, OAS TS No 36 at 1; OAS Off Rec OEA/Ser.L/V/II.23, doc 21, rev 6; 9 ILM 99 (1970) (entered into force 18 July 1978)

Convention on Assistance in the Case of a Nuclear Accident or Radiological Emergency, opened for signature 26 September 1986, [1987] ATS 15 (entered into force 26 February 1987)

Convention on Civil Liability for Nuclear Damage, opened for signature 21 May 1963, 2 ILM 727 (entered into force 12 November 1977)

Convention on Early Notification of a Nuclear Accident, opened for signature 26 September 1986, [1987] ATS 14 (entered into force 27 October 1986)

Convention on Nuclear Safety, opened for signature 20 September 1994, 1963 UNTS 293 (entered into force 24 October 1996)

Convention on the Elimination of all Forms of Discrimination against Women, opened for signature 18 December 1979, 1249 UNTS 13 (entered into force 3 September 1981)

Convention on the Elimination of All Forms of Racial Discrimination, 660 UNTS 195; [1975] ATS 40 (entered into force 4 January 1969)

Convention on the Physical Protection of Nuclear Material, opened for signature 3 March 1980, [1987] ATS 16 (entered into force 8 February 1987)

Energy Charter Treaty, opened for signature 17 December 1994, 34 ILM 360
(entered into force 16 April 1998)

*European Energy Charter Treaty and Energy Charter Protocol on Energy Efficiency and
Related Environmental Aspects*, opened for signature 17 December 1994, 34
ILM 360 (entered into force 16 April 1998)

General Agreement on Tariffs and Trade, opened for signature 30 October 1947, 55
UNTS 194 (entered into force 1 January 1948)

International Covenant on Civil and Political Rights, opened for signature 19
December 1966, 999 UNTS 171 (entered into force 23 March 1976)

International Covenant on Economic, Social and Cultural Rights, opened for signature
19 December 1966, 993 UNTS 3 (entered into force 3 January 1976)

International Covenant on the Rights of Persons with Disabilities, opened for signature
13 December 2006, 2515 UNTS 3 (entered into force 3 May 2008)

*Joint Convention on the Safety of Spent Fuel Management and on the Safety of
Radioactive Waste Management*, opened for signature 5 September 1997,
[2003] ATS 21 (entered into force 18 June 2001)

Kyoto Protocol to the United Nations Framework Convention on Climate Change,
opened for signature 11 December 1997, 2303 UNTS 148 (entered into
force 16 February 2005)

Marrakesh Agreement Establishing the World Trade Organization, opened for signature
15 April 1994, 1867 UNTS 3 (entered into force 1 January 1995)

Montreal Protocol on Substances that Deplete the Ozone Layer, opened for signature
16 September 1987, 1522 UNTS 3 (entered into force 1 January 1989)

North American Free Trade Agreement, Canada-Mexico-US, opened for signature 17
December 1992, 32 ILM 289 (entered into force 1 January 1994)

Statute of the International Atomic Energy Agency, opened for signature 23 October
1956, 276 UNTS 3 (entered into force 29 July 1957)

Treaty Establishing the Energy Community, opened for signature 25 October 2005,
[2006] OJ L 198/18 (entered into force 1 July 2006)

Treaty Establishing the European Atomic Energy Community, opened for signature 25
March 1957, 298 UNTS 167 (entered into force 25 March 1957)

*Treaty of Lisbon Amending the Treaty on European Union and the Treaty Establishing
the European Community*, opened for signature 13 December 2007, [2007]
OJ C 306/1 (entered into force 1 December 2009)

Treaty on European Union, opened for signature 7 February 1992, [1992] OJ C
191/1 (entered into force 1 November 1993)

Treaty on the Non-Proliferation of Nuclear Weapons, opened for signature 1 July
1968, 729 UNTS 161 (entered into force 5 March 1970)

United Nations Framework Convention on Climate Change, opened for signature 14
June 1992, 1771 UNTS 107 (entered into force 21 March 1994)

Vienna Convention for the Protection of the Ozone Layer, opened for signature 22
March 1985, 1513 UNTS 293 (entered into force 22 September 1988)

B *Cases*

Kuwait v American Independent Oil Co (AMINOIL) (Award) (1982) 21 ILM 976

Selected Index

This book is available as a free fully-searchable ebook from
www.adelaide.edu.au/press